Social Movements

SOCIAL MOVEMENTS

Identity, Culture, and the State

Edited by David S. Meyer,
Nancy Whittier, & Belinda Robnett

UNIVERSITY PRESS

2002

OXFORD
UNIVERSITY PRESS

Oxford   New York
Auckland   Bangkok   Buenos Aires   Cape Town   Chennai
Dar es Salaam   Delhi   Hong Kong   Istanbul   Karachi   Kolkata
Kuala Lumpur   Madrid   Melbourne   Mexico City   Mumbai   Nairobi
São Paulo   Shanghai   Singapore   Taipei   Tokyo   Toronto

and an associated company in Berlin

Published by Oxford University Press, Inc.
198 Madison Avenue, New York, New York 10016

www.oup.com

Oxford is a registered trademark of Oxford University Press

Library of Congress Cataloging-in-Publication Data

Social movements : identity, culture, and the state / edited by David S. Meyer,
Nancy Whittier, Belinda Robnett.
p.   cm.
Includes bibliographical references and index.
ISBN 0-19-514355-8; ISBN 0-19-514356-6 (pbk.)
1. Social movements. I. Meyer, David S. II. Whittier, Nancy, 1966–
III. Robnett, Belinda, 1956–
HM881 .S63 2001
303.48'4–dc21   2001036973

9 8 7 6 5 4 3 2 1

Printed in the United States of America
on acid-free paper

To Zena,
Jonah,
David and Jonah

Acknowledgments

We are grateful to a number of people and institutions for their help in this project. The workshop that led to this volume was partly supported by a small grant from the American Sociological Association/National Science Foundation Fund for the Advancement of the Discipline and was organized under the auspices of the American Sociological Association Section on Collective Behavior and Social Movements. Manisha Desai, Rob Kleidman, Paul Lichterman, and Jo Reger helped organize that workshop. We appreciate the excellent services provided by Teresa Brown, Coordinator of the UC-Davis Conference and Event Services, without whom the workshop could not have taken place. We had research and clerical assistance from Meg Chilton and Morgan Lynn at Smith College, supported by the Smith College Committee on Faculty Compensation and Development, and from Jeanne Batalova Treigherman and Yuki Kato at the University of California–Irvine. We are also grateful to the Center for the Study of Democracy, at the University of California–Irvine, which provided help when it was most needed. Finally, we appreciate the efforts of the contributors, many of whom not only wrote their own chapters but provided useful comments that helped to shape the book.

Contents

Contributors   xiii

PART I. INTRODUCTION

1. Opportunities and Identities: Bridge-Building in the Study
   of Social Movements   3
   David S. Meyer

PART II. STATES AND POLICIES

Introduction to Part II   25

2. State Repression and Democracy Protest in Three Southeast
   Asian Countries   28
   Vincent Boudreau

3. Mobilization on the South African Gold Mines   47
   T. Dunbar Moodie

4. Multiple Mediations: The State and the Women's Movements
   in India   66
   Manisha Desai

5. The Contradictions of Gay Ethnicity: Forging Identity
   in Vermont   85
   Mary Bernstein

6. Creating Social Change: Lessons from the Civil
   Rights Movement   105
   Kenneth T. Andrews

PART III. ORGANIZATIONS AND STRATEGIES

Introduction to Part III   121

7. The "Meso" in Social Movement Research   124
   Suzanne Staggenborg

8. Strategizing and the Sense of Context: Reflections on the
   First Two Weeks of the Liverpool Docks Lockout,
   September–October 1995   140
   Colin Barker and Michael Lavalette

9. Factions and the Continuity of Political Challengers   157
   Mildred A. Schwartz

10. More Than One Feminism: Organizational Structure and the
    Construction of Collective Identity   171
    Jo Reger

11. The Development of Individual Identity and Consciousness among
    Movements of the Left and Right   185
    Rebecca E. Klatch

PART IV. COLLECTIVE IDENTITIES, DISCOURSE,
AND CULTURE

Introduction to Part IV   205

12. Toward a More Dialogic Analysis of Social
    Movement Culture   208
    Marc W. Steinberg

13. Materialist Feminist Discourse Analysis and Social
    Movement Research: Mapping the Changing Context
    for "Community Control"   226
    Nancy A. Naples

14. From the "Beloved Community" to "Family Values": Religious
    Language, Symbolic Repertoires, and Democratic Culture   247
    Rhys H. Williams

15. External Political Change, Collective Identities, and Participation
    in Social Movement Organizations   266
    Belinda Robnett

PART V. CONCLUSION

16. Meaning and Structure in Social Movements   289
    Nancy Whittier

    References   309

    Index   347

Contributors

KENNETH T. ANDREWS is assistant professor of sociology at Harvard University. His research examines questions about the impacts of social movements. He is completing a book, *"Freedom Is a Constant Struggle": The Dynamics and Consequences of the Mississippi Civil Rights Movement*, that traces the development of the movement and its impact on electoral politics, educational institutions, and social policies. He is beginning a project on contemporary environmental politics in the United States.

COLIN BARKER teaches in the sociology department at Manchester Metropolitan University. An active socialist, he organizes the annual "Alternative Futures & Popular Protest" conference series each Easter and convenes the British Sociological Association Study Group on Protest and Social Movements. Publications include *Festival of the Oppressed: Solidarity, Reform and Revolution in Poland* (1986) and *Revolutionary Rehearsals* (1987).

MARY BERNSTEIN is assistant professor of sociology at the University of Connecticut. Her research, which has appeared in the *American Journal of Sociology* and the *American Sociological Review*, focuses on sexuality, social movements, and the law. Her recently published edited book *Queer Families, Queer Politics, Challenging Culture and the State* (Columbia University Press) connects the microdynamics of gender, sexuality, and the family with the macrodynamics of politics and the law. Currently, she is completing a book on lesbian, gay, bisexual, and transgender political strategies and legal change.

VINCENT BOUDREAU is associate professor of political science at the City College of New York. He is the author of *At the Margins of the Movement: Grassroots and Cadre in a Philippine Socialist Network* and has written more generally about political contention in Southeast Asia, especially in the Philippines. His current research investigates how established patterns of repression and state violence shape political contention, but this project is part of a larger program to broaden and deepen the theoretically informed study of social movements outside of the global north.

MANISHA DESAI is associate professor of sociology and chair of the Department of Anthropology and Sociology at Hobart and William Smith Colleges in Geneva, New York. Her research and teaching have focused primarily on social movements in India, international women's movements, international development, women and globalization, feminist theory, and human rights. She is currently completing an edited book with Nancy Naples, *Women in Globalization from Below: Multiple Sites of Women's Activism* (forthcoming, Routledge), and starting work on an edited book, *Globalization and Human Rights: Women's Interventions in Asia*, to be published by Greenwood.

REBECCA E. KLATCH is professor of sociology at the University of California–San Diego. She is author of *Women of the New Right* (Temple University Press, 1987) and *A Generation Divided: The New Left, The New Right, and the 1960s* (University of California Press, 1999), as well as numerous articles on social movements, gender, and family politics.

MICHAEL LAVALETTE teaches in the sociology, social policy and social work studies department at Liverpool University. He writes on child labor, Marxism and social policy, and collective action. Among his publications on social movements are *Leadership and Social Movements* (edited with Colin Barker and Alan Johnson, forthcoming), *Solidarity on the Waterfront* (1996), and *Class Struggle and Social Welfare* (2000). He is an active member of the Socialist Workers Party in Britain.

DAVID S. MEYER is associate professor of sociology at the University of California, Irvine. In addition to numerous articles on social movements, he is author of *A Winter of Discontent: The Nuclear Freeze and American Politics*, coeditor, with Sidney Tarrow, of *The Social Movement Society*, and coeditor, with Thomas Rochon, of *Coalitions and Political Movements*. He is most interested in the connections among social movements, public policy, and institutional politics.

T. DUNBAR MOODIE is professor of sociology in the Department of Anthropology and Sociology at Hobart and William Smith Colleges. He is the author of *The Rise of Afrikanerdom* and *Going for Gold*, as well as numerous articles. His early work dealt with the origins of the Afrikaner ethnic movement and its impact on the development of apartheid ideology and the attainment of political power. He now writes mostly about black South African gold miners, with special attention to modes of survival and resistance in their everyday lives in the context of wider South African economic, political, and social changes.

NANCY A. NAPLES is associate professor of sociology and women's studies at the University of California–Irvine. She has a Ph.D. in sociology from the Graduate Center and an M.S.W. from Hunter College, City University of New York. Her research emphasizes women's community activism; the intersection between race, class, gender, sexuality, and region; and the contradictory role of the state for women's social and political citizenship. Much of her scholarship focuses on bridging the so-called gap between theory and practice, as well as explicating a feminist epistemology of activist research. She is author of *Grassroots Warriors: Activist Mothering, Community Work, and the War on Poverty* and editor of *Community Activism and Feminist Politics: Organizing across Race, Class, and Gender*, both published by Routledge in 1998. She is coeditor of *Women's Activism and Globalization: Linking Grassroots Movements and Transnational Politics* with Manisha Desai, forthcoming from Routledge, 2001.

JO REGER is an assistant professor at Oakland University whose work examines gender and social movements. Her current research focuses on the U.S. women's movement and the influence of community and identity on organizational continuity.

BELINDA ROBNETT is associate professor of sociology and director of African American studies at the University of California, Irvine. Her work has appeared in the *American Journal of Sociology* and other venues. She is the author of *How Long? How Long? African-American Women in the Struggle for Civil Rights* (Oxford University Press, 1997), which received the American Sociological Association Race, Gender, and Class Section and Sex and Gender Section Honorable Mention Book Award in 2000. She is currently working on a new book manuscript entitled *Our Struggle for Unity: African-Americans in the Age of Identity Politics*.

MILDRED A. SCHWARTZ is a visiting scholar in the Department of Sociology at New York University and Professor Emeritus of sociology and political science at the University of Illinois at Chicago. Her chapter is part of an ongoing examination of political challengers in western Canada and the United States. She has additional research under way on transnational ties that have developed in Canada, the United States, and Mexico as a result of the North American Free Trade Agreement. She is also collaborating with three colleagues in preparing a handbook of political sociology.

SUZANNE STAGGENBORG is professor of sociology at McGill University. Her work includes *The Pro-Choice Movement: Organization and Activism in the Abortion Conflict* (Oxford University Press, 1991), *Gender, Family, and Social Movements* (Pine Forge Press, 1998), and a number of articles about abortion politics and social movements in the United States and Canada.

MARC W. STEINBERG teaches sociology at Smith College. He is the author of *Fighting Words: Working-Class Formation, Collective Action and Discourse in Early Nineteenth-Century England* (Cornell, 1999) and a number of articles on class conflict, social movements, and discourse processes. He is currently working on a project concerning the role of law in labor conflict in Victorian England.

NANCY WHITTIER is associate professor of sociology at Smith College and is author of *Feminist Generations: The Persistence of the Radical Women's Movement* and numerous articles on gender, collective identity, generations, and feminist movements and coeditor (with Verta Taylor and Laurel Richardson) of *Feminist Frontiers*. She is working on a book about activism against child sexual abuse, tentatively titled *The Politics of Trauma: Feminism, Child Sexual Abuse, and Social Change*.

RHYS H. WILLIAMS is associate professor and head of the Department of Sociology at the University of Cincinnati. His research interests focus on the intersection of politics, religion, culture, and social movements in the United States. He is coauthor (with Jay Demerath) of *A Bridging of Faiths: Religion and Politics in a New England City* (Princeton University Press, 1992) and editor of *Cultural Wars in American Politics: Critical Reviews of a Popular Myth* (Aldine de Gruyter, 1997), as well as articles in *American Sociological Review*, *Social Problems*, *Theory and Society*, *Journal for the Scientific Study of Religion*, and *Sociology of Religion*. He is currently chair of the American Sociological Association's Section for the Sociology of Religion.

Part One

INTRODUCTION

Opportunities and Identities: Bridge-Building in the Study of Social Movements

DAVID S. MEYER

Students of social movements fought, and won, a lengthy battle to legitimate academic interest in the field. As the study of social movements is increasingly embraced by the academy, however, practitioners and scholars now face the challenge of using this hard-won legitimacy to afford the time and space to ask and answer important questions about collective action and social movements: How and why do movements emerge? Why do they take the forms they do? When and how do protest movements bring about meaningful social change? Alas, the exigencies of academic study often lead scholars to cultivate niches and burrow more deeply into narrow areas of inquiry, rather than return to the issues that gave rise to the study of social protest in the first place. The essays in this volume represent a concerted effort to build bridges among people researching collective action and social movements and to encourage the construction of comprehensive and synthetic approaches to the study of social movements.

In this introductory essay, I mean to explain the need for bridge-building within this area of study and suggest ways to cross disciplinary and sub-disciplinary boundaries, for none has a monopoly on useful knowledge on movements. The important things that have to happen in the study of social protest involve connecting what distinct groups of scholars do into a larger whole. The puzzles of social protest politics mandate a response from the academy that is inherently collective. Indeed, if substantial progress in the study of social movements is really to occur, it will come from a community of scholars that triangulates (cf. Tarrow 1995a) the problems described here, working on pieces of the problems. Despite the difficulties, the essays in this volume give good reason for optimism on these matters. The chapters all emphasize building bridges and cutting corridors between generally separate paradigms in the study of social protest and advance synthetic understandings of the material at hand. In this case, the material at hand ranges from women working within, and outside, the state in India (Manisha Desai), to weavers in nineteenth-century England (Marc Steinberg) to the American civil rights movement (Kenneth Andrews, Belinda Robnett). They also point the way for subsequent work. I will first describe the challenges that animated this book, then suggest the unity of purpose of collective identity and political process approaches to the study of social movements, with a detour to narrate my own history in coming to this work. I'll conclude with a list of challenges for academic work on the horizon and a call to remain mindful of the inherent professional and political responsibilities of studying social protest.

The Challenge of Bridge-Building

If we mean to define a synthetic and comprehensive approach to the study of social movements, we should first set out the specific challenges delineated in the last few decades of research. A few challenges stand out; the work in this book confronts them head-on.

1. *Levels of Analysis.* We need to bring together the perspectives and insights of people who analyze movements at different levels. From those who look at large-scale patterns of contention across nations and movements (e.g., Tarrow 1989a; Tilly 1995b) to those who study organizational politics and decision making (e.g., Rupp and Taylor 1987; Whittier 1995), to those who look at the biographies of the individuals who animate social protest movements (e.g., Kenniston 1968; Klatch 1999; McAdam 1988b), scholars must begin with the specifics, but they need not end there.

Broadly speaking, students of social movements fit into two rough categories: those who begin from the inside out, starting with activists and their concerns, and those who start from the outside in, looking first at states, political alignments, and policies and then at patterns of collective action. Regardless of the starting point, however, we need to look at both efforts. By this triangulation, collectively if not individually, we can get a deeper understanding of the causes and consequences of social and political protest politics. We must go beyond the "theory-bashing" that often characterizes advancement in any discipline (see Lofland 1993). Rather, we can honestly recognize what cases which theories explain well and commit to work in synthetic paradigms as a part of the regular course of scholarship.

2. *Politics and Identity.* We need to link notions of identity to an analysis of the political process. This need is particularly evident in the apparently dichotomous character of paradigms emphasizing the political process and those emphasizing "collective identity" or "culture" (Jasper and Goodwin 1999; Koopmans 1999; Rochon 1998). Both deductive logic, however, and close examination of cases point to the necessary relationship between identity and state processes (Clemens 1997; Stevens 1999). If we can move beyond the crudest biological determinism, we recognize that the process of turning physical features or social practices into "identities" is forged from the interaction between people and that state. By forcing some people to sit in the back of the bus, wear a yellow star, or hide their sexual orientations, states create the conditions in which particular identities develop. States can create identities by endorsing or prohibiting religious or sexual practices, by regulating access to social goods, and by setting rules of interaction between groups and individuals. Within these parameters, activists choose how to define themselves, by alliances, claims, and tactics, as Mary Bernstein shows in her chapter about gay and lesbian politics in Vermont (also see Bernstein 1997).

3. *Cross-Disciplinary Boundaries.* The study of social protest has succumbed to the same disciplinary turf wars that bedevil the academy generally. Unfortunately, such disputes are particularly problematic in the study of social protest, which historically has been located in several disciplines throughout the social sciences and humanities. Historians have chronicled the tales of movements or particular constituencies; political scientists have looked at the policy process and institutional politics; sociologists and anthropologists have studied the organizations that animate protest movements; and psychologists have studied the people who mount protest movements. (Of course, the actual conduct of individual researchers does not fit so neatly. Innovative researchers have always crossed the borders of disciplines and always risked misunderstanding from professional journals and departments.) Fuller understanding of social movements necessitates breaking out of disciplinary trenches.

4. *Multiple Movements.* Scholars often start by looking at a movement that they have some personal stake in, perhaps as sympathizer, target, or activist—a fine start, but, to understand the larger phenomenon of social protest politics, we need to be wary about generalizing from any single case and to test theories aggressively across alternate cases and contexts.

The community of scholars should study the broad range of social movements, including those most academics might oppose. Indeed, regardless of the partisan balance of the academy, the library of studies of movements tilts fairly heavily to the Left, with the American civil rights and labor movements gaining the lion's share of academic attention, generally from sympathetic, if often critical, scholars. Less-studied movements of the Right, though not completely ignored (e.g., Aho 1990; Blanchard 1994; Blee 1991, 1996; Klatch 1987), are often characterized as "deviance" rather than social movements. By ignoring movements from the other side of the spectrum, we collect less information on political realities, with a sampling of movements whose bias jeopardizes the generalizability of what we have learned. Looking at multiple movements in different contexts, we can discern the factors that matter across cases, as well as case-specific, contingencies.

5. *Policy and Protest.*   We must not lose sight of the policy dimension of political protest. This critical topic has received insufficient attention from scholars of social movements (but see Amenta 1998; Amenta, Dunleavy, and Bernstein 1994; Burstein 1990; Markoff 1997). This is an unfortunate product of the historical development of the study of social protest. Although the political scientists who studied social movements in the 1960s and early 1970s (esp. Lipsky 1970; Piven and Cloward 1971) focused on government action and public policy, particularly policies affecting poor people, sociologists who entered the debate brought somewhat less attention to the material bases driving activist concerns. Important work that brings attention to the affective dimensions of social protest (e.g., Polletta 1997; Taylor 1996) actually calls for more attention to the concrete policies that provoke emotional reactions.

Manisha Desai's chapter on the women's movements' development in contemporary India tells a story in which tactics and concerns constantly shift in response to the actions of a sometimes somewhat sympathetic state—that is, government policy. Similarly, Belinda Robnett's chapter on the Student Non-Violent Coordinating Committee's (SNCC) organizational form focuses on the enactment of the Voting Rights Act in an analysis that shows activists making decisions in response to meaningful changes in public policy. In both chapters, we see public policy reform not only as the result of movement activities but also as the cause of changes in movement strategy, claims, and tactics. In theoretical parlance, changes in policy influence political opportunities, and activists respond accordingly, trying to mobilize, or to affect new policy changes in these new circumstances.

6. *Relevance.*   We must remember the concerns of the social movement and ask relevant questions. Finally, and perhaps most important, in the paradigm battles that animate academic inquiry, it is too easy to stop asking questions whose answer might help make the world better. The people who make social movements, often at great costs and under conditions of threat and danger, do so in the perverse belief that their efforts can make the world better, more just, and indeed, that those actions are necessary to make substantial change.

It is professionally irresponsible to expend efforts on projects that elucidate theories or advance analyses that don't harken back to critical questions about the quality of our lives and of others. Social science could be a powerful tool for social justice, a Promethean notion too readily abandoned.

In short, we need an approach to studying social movements that values what animates social movements. This is, of course, no small order, but we cannot escape the responsibility of building toward that end.

Origins of a Social Movement Analyst

Let me illustrate these points by reviewing my own emerging interest in this area of inquiry. My story is not atypical, and it helps illuminate, I hope, critical issues in the study of social protest.

I was an activist as a college student, engaged in several movement campaigns in the 1970s in western Massachusetts. I did the political work that students in that area did at the time, on behalf of farm workers, against nuclear power, against my college's investments in apartheid South Africa. Living the life of a college student at a private school in the United States, when federal financial aid was relatively lush, I came to none of these concerns from lived experience involving farm work, nuclear power, or racial segregation on the other side of the world. Rather, they came to me because other political activists approached me and asked me to do something for some political goal (see Rosenstone and Hansen 1993 on mobilization). Sometimes there was a "political education" in the form of a fast course on the dangers of nuclear power or horrors of apartheid, but I started learning the issues already knowing the positions I would take. I was briefly engaged in an unsuccessful effort to oppose President Jimmy Carter's reintroduction of registering young men for the draft. Although such registration could have affected me, it did not, and the filling out of a form at the post office proved too distant from the actual conduct of the military to inspire sustained opposition.

Friends asked me, in spring 1979, to get involved with an effort, sponsored by the American Friends Services Committee, to promote a "nuclear freeze" resolution by conducting public education and supporting a ballot initiative. I recall a few arguments pretty clearly, in which I opined at length and with great certainty about the futility of such an effort. First, I argued, most people were uninterested in nuclear weapons issues, as well they might be. There was little the average citizen could do to prevent the use of nuclear weapons. I could point to the weekly vigil on the town common as evidence: every Sunday a handful of pacifists would assemble for an hour to call for world peace, with no discernible impact on the people around them, much less policy makers. Second, and more significantly, I thought at the time that the politics of nuclear weapons did not really affect people's daily lives and the most important work any movement could conduct at this point would be to address economic inequality in the United States.

Within three years, the "nuclear freeze" movement had captured political attention by doing what movements in liberal polities do: conducting educational events, staging civil disobedience actions, organizing conferences and "teach-ins" on American college campuses, preparing high school curricula, sponsoring concerts and fund-raising events, staffing tables at community events across the country, engaging in petition and electoral campaigns, and mounting demonstrations, including the assembly of 1 million people in the streets of New York City on June 12, 1982. Obviously, I was wrong, and one reason I went to graduate school was to figure out why.

The first thing I learned in graduate school was that I had not been completely wrong; rather, circumstances had changed in such a way that my earlier judgment was no longer appropriate. This formulation is not just the style of academic discourse that is part of the socialization process in graduate education. In examining this case, I was pushed to look more closely at the external context, what scholars call the "structure of political opportunity." About the same time the freeze was proposed to activists, U.S. strategic policy, including that regarding nuclear weapons and arms control, was changing. The United States adopted a more aggressive and expensive posture, and political leaders spoke about it with a careless and unprecedented candor (Meyer 1990). In short, the concerns the nuclear freeze meant to address *should* have been more salient.

But changes in political circumstances do not automatically translate into a social protest movement; most people who would participate in the freeze over the ensuing years would have found it difficult to explain policy changes in any detail. Activists framed the freeze proposal as a solution to distinct problems of policy and politics. They designed it as a political strategy even more than as a policy proposal. To understand the reality of that movement, we would have to untangle the processes organizers went through to craft demands, to make claims, and to mobilize activism. The freeze proposal was disseminated among activist networks and ultimately picked up by already existing organizations for their own purposes, sometimes even supporting the political strategy while opposing the policy proposal. There were heated disputes about language, about what the freeze actually meant, and about the issues to which it might be linked effectively (Benford 1993b; Rochon and Meyer 1997). Initial mobilization was primarily *en bloc*, as the freeze message was mediated by other organizations, as new organizations formed, as individuals hooked up with neighbors and colleagues through participation in the freeze. Obviously, to understand this movement—or other social movements—we need to look at organizations and the process of crafting appeals.

We can gain some insight into the interplay of levels of analysis by think-ing about an individual's decision to participate in social movement activ-ism. At once, an individual decides whether to participate in political activism, what issues to engage, with whom to participate, and how. Under "normal" circumstances, people are unlikely to endure the costs of social movement participation for distant political goals. Of course, all activists' decisions are not fully informed in terms of narrow strategic calculations; rather, they develop in the course of collective action and social engagement.

Think about how people might have made choices about whether to come to the Common or to engage in any collective action. Ideology or religious belief can drive some people to take strong stands consistently, regardless of their vision of the likely political outcome (Smith 1996). Such actions can become routinized for the regulars at the Common I described, and individuals and organizations can become habituated to particular actions unusual for others. Sometimes the choice to participate is a reaction to what others do, whether allies or opponents. Astonishingly, most people who participate in a political action like this witness don't offer elaborate theories about how their actions will bring about the political change they seek. Sometimes, like pigeons in a Skinner box, activists repeat activities that they believe once succeeded, without unfolding the causal mechanisms that actually promoted social change. Sensing the need to act, they pick the most promising *and* available activity they can find, even if the connections between the Com-mon and, say, the National Security Council seem attenuated. What seems promising or available depends on one's social location, embedded networks, and ideology.

Yet every weekend in the town common, well before the freeze, and for years after the peak of mobilization, a few people stood for an hour or two, regardless of the weather, to make their claim against the threat of nuclear war. Either these committed people are extraordinarily bad calculators, or the narrowest frame of choice analysis is too restrictive. It is not so much that they think that their witness on the Common will likely bring nuclear disar-mament directly or quickly. Rather, they see a moral responsibility to act against what they view as dangerous and wrong, regardless of the anticipated policy or political consequences. Bearing witness, even if it did not bring about nuclear disarmament, was a concrete step toward becoming the kind of people they wanted to be: moral or righteous or decent, with or without the sanc-tion of an established religion (see Epstein 1991). Fundamentally, in the de-cision to participate one's identity, as defined by self and others, plays a critical role.

But most people are more sporadically active in particular causes. At the height of the nuclear freeze movement, hundreds would assemble on the town common, people who did not previously or subsequently identify themselves primarily as peace activists. After the freeze peaked in the middle 1980s, the turnout at the demonstrations retreated to the prefreeze levels.

Now, given the real inconveniences of turning up on a Sunday afternoon, given the other demands and attractions of a life, it's clear that people need motivation for even this rather modest social movement participation. For the long-term crusaders, standing publicly against nuclear weapons, among people they felt some connection with, was enough. They did not need to believe that their acts would make an immediate difference on policy; they had visions of morality and of themselves that nonetheless required action. But this was not enough for most people. Others, who joined later on, doubtless had other motivations. When the policies of the U.S. government changed, the threat of nuclear war and the conduct of national security provided more of a provocation than before, such that participation became more *urgent*. As more and more people turned out each Sunday, and as mass media paid more attention to both a growing movement and the issues it addressed, the effort might also seem more *promising*. At one level then, people engage in social movement action because they believe their efforts are both necessary and potentially efficacious.

Beyond policy demands and moral action, when hundreds assemble on the town common, you will likely see people you know or meet people you might like to talk with. Perhaps someone there will sing, tell stories, or sell attractive buttons or vegetarian hot dogs. You get the sense that by participating you are part of something larger, engaged in efforts bigger than yourself, defining your own identity by your participation in the construction of a larger community through collective action (Buechler 1990).

As government and other authorities respond to the demands of social movements, they affect the costs and potential benefits of participation, altering the marginal decisions of people on the periphery of a movement, as well as their senses of urgency and possibility. Importantly, these responses can entail real changes in policy or in the treatment of protestors (see McCarthy and McPhail 1998; della Porta and Reiter 1998). They can also include changes in rhetoric and symbolism (Edelman 1971). As more people join or leave a movement, the choices available to those who remain change, as do the political claims, tactics, and the definitions of self. The rhetoric of a movement becomes available to others, including opponents, as Nancy Naples points out here, altering the possibilities for other challengers. Understanding the reality of a social movement necessitates considering the process of collective action and social mobilization from different levels of analysis. The constellation of external political realities, the opportunities for action offered by mainstream political institutions, the resources and commitments of organizations, and affective and intellectual factors that lead individuals to choose whether to participate in a social movement and how.

More Movements

Substantive demands of research make it hard not to specialize in *a* movement at *a* time with *a* method. In doing so, however, we risk not really understanding what's going on, and making generalizations and promoting misunderstandings by abstracting from a particular case. In attending professional conferences, sometimes it is hard not to be reminded of François Truffaut's film of Ray Bradbury's *Fahrenheit 451*. In an age of book burning, the rebels have committed themselves to keeping literature alive by memorizing books, reciting them in the woods. Over there, the new recruit is told, is *Great Expectations*, or *Moby-Dick*, or some other classic. Individuals sacrifice their identity to that of the great work of literature to which they've committed their lives. In a similar way, scholars can become too closely identified with a particular movement.

Although scholars can become identified with a particular movement, activists generally are not. Scholarly definition of a "social movement" lends to an identification with a bounded set of issues, but the careers of activists are rarely so narrowly circumscribed. Protesting and organizing for a variety of related social change goals over several decades is the rule rather than the exception for individual activists, as studies of participants in the civil rights, student, and women's movements show (Carroll and Ratner 1996; Clegg 1996; Fendrich and Lovoy 1988; McAdam 1988b; Whalen and Flacks 1987; Whittier 1995). Activists can shift goals and groups in response to the changing political environment, responding to proximate threats and opportunities, while maintaining an essentially consistent political worldview (Meyer 1993). Among activists, a favorite truism is that the same group of people show up at demonstration after demonstration, even as the issues change. Scholars have been slower to recognize the extent to which related movements share personnel or the broader diversity of issues seemingly narrow movements address.

The pattern of sustained networks working on several issues over time is recurrent in social movements. The range of potential issues a group, network, or individual may address is related to self-identification. The ideological component of collective identity includes a political analysis which identifies a range of social injustices that merit redress and a range of potential activities that a group or individual might undertake. Movement issues may link as the result of ideological, cultural, organizational, or tactical continuity. (Thus, the initial surprise when a group on the Right, for example, Operation Rescue, can adopt political tactics innovated and developed by the Left [Johnson 1999].) Indeed, the cross-fertilization of activists, organizations, and tactics across movements often promotes innovation and revitalization (Voss and Sherman 2001). The characteristics of challengers determine the issues they may take on and how.

For convenience, we identify movements by a particular constituency or cause: *the* women's movement, *the* peace movement, *the* environmental movement. The credulous observer might incorrectly think that these periodic formations are distinct and self-contained, when in fact people and organizations frequently work in a variety of social movements, some not obviously related by ideology or constituency. In fact, specific movement campaigns reflect a larger social movement community (Buechler 1990), comprised broadly of groups and individuals who share more than agreement on particular political issues. A social movement community includes diverse individuals and groups whose primary focus at any one time may vary tremendously, but who are united by a generally shared view of the world and their place in it (see also della Porta and Rucht 1995). Cycles of apparent political engagement and quiescence on a particular issue then (Meyer 1993) reflect less the volatility of mass concerns than the continuous challenges and tactical choices movements make, focusing their efforts in response to changing political circumstances (Morris 1984; Taylor 1989). An activist concerned with peace and social justice may work for a nuclear test ban in 1963, for civil rights in 1965, against the war in Vietnam in 1967, and for women's rights in 1969. Surely, she would recognize the continuity in these efforts, even if scholars have been slower to see connections activists view as obvious.

Collective Identity and Political Opportunity

As noted, of the scholars studying social protest, some look at movements from the outside in, that is, starting with the grievances, resources, and opportunities provided by forces outside the social movement; and some look at movements from the inside out, that is, starting with the self-conscious decisions and values of those within movements and their lives prior to and through social movement participation. A broader perspective will help us understand the process and politics of social protest and will reveal the meaningful realities of social protest. You cannot understand the reality, genesis, and outcome of a movement without a broader picture, and even if the focus is on one level, we need to fill in the background. We need to avoid false dichotomies of culture and structure to see the interaction of factors exogenous to a social movement and the choices made within it.

Activists choose issues, tactics, and allies, but not in the circumstances they please. They can subsequently be trapped in particular positions, wed to odd tactics, or caught in uncomfortable alliances. The issues they express reflect what they think is most promising, important, or urgent—given the constraints of how they see themselves. Unlike the pigeons in Skinner boxes, people who make movements are moral *and* instrumental actors, if not always narrowly "rational" calculators. They do what they think they can do. Claims are defined not only by what activists want but also by what they think is possible. The nature of the state and the content of public policy define both urgency and possibility. In Eastern Europe during the cold war, for example, dissidents agreed to press for democratic rights of political participation as a foundation for making any other claims. This was true even for dissidents who were generally no friends of democracy. Now that the states they face are more open, we find they agree on much less.

Now think about the state and identity. In this case, the state makes "dissidents," creating common cause and thus an identity. To ignore government policy in creating causes and constituencies is to essentialize identity and ignore the importance of possibility and human agency. Only by understanding structure and constraints can we have a meaningful—and ultimately empowering—understanding of agency. In the case of East European dissidents, the state, by limiting democratic means of participation, turns everyone with a grievance into a democracy activist—at least for a time.

Conversely, states can create narrow constituencies and have done so in familiar ways: by pinning yellow stars on some people; excluding some colors of people from full participation in social, political, or economic life, or finding some hue in skin tone that defines rights; by criminalizing some sexual behaviors. In other words, the action of the state creates these collective identities and sets the boundaries of a dissident collective.

Movements are bound neither by narrow issues nor by particular tactics. Although some individuals or groups habitually use the same years to pursue their goals, for example, firebombing, demonstrations, boycotts, or electioneering, most choose strategies they think most likely to be effective, given their perceptions of resources, opportunities, and constraints, including organizational limits and self-imposed moral commitments.

The Women's Pentagon Action provides a clear example of the mix of pragmatic calculations and moral imperatives that shapes collective action. The WPA staged large demonstrations and civil disobedience actions outside the Pentagon in the early 1980s, linking the nuclear arms race to broader social injustices, including violence against women, poverty, and other violations of human rights (Epstein 1991). The Pentagon actions included expressions of mourning for societal injustice, and anger at the perpetrators of injustice and ended with participants symbolically "exorcising" the evil spirits of the Pentagon by weaving a "web of life" around the building, simultaneously trying to shut the building down. These symbols reprised decades-old, self-consciously dramatic tactics. Activists combined direct political action with spiritual rituals they claimed drew on the strength of goddesses and other sources of women's power (Spretnak 1982). We can't begin to understand this, location and frame, without reference to the ideology of the group, the political culture it emerged from, and the political climate of the 1980s, which made the Pentagon a likely site for protest.

As the political landscape changes, activists reconsider their choices of issues and tactics. After the United States and the Soviet Union negotiated the first strategic arms agreement (SALT) and the antiballistic missile treaty in 1972, there was no large and visible peace activism during the following decade (Meyer 1993). Activists, however, continued their efforts, choosing other challenges. Many women shifted their efforts to reproductive rights, either through advocacy or service provision (Staggenborg 1991). Women from the liberal wing of the feminist movement worked through more conventional political institutions, participating in party politics and electoral campaigns, and winning some victories. Finally, women not ostensibly engaged with the feminist movement in the 1970s nonetheless carried its values through what Katzenstein (1998) calls "unobtrusive mobilization" within mainstream institutions and professions. The boundaries between movement activism and more conventional political and social engagement are easily blurred.

It might seem that one movement reemerged just as the other faded. Rather, the interplay between the collective identity asserted by dissident claimants and the authorities they challenge is expressed through claims, conduct, and coalitions. The outside configuration of issues and alliances suggests certain claims and tactics as most promising or urgent to challengers at any given time. As states alter the costs and benefits of collective action and develop new techniques for controlling collective action, they allow, encourage, provoke, or discourage movements' particular changing strategies of influence. A cyclic pattern emerges, as states respond to movement challenges and alter the opportunities available to contemporary and subsequent movements (Tarrow 1989a). The early 1980s, for example, offered a resistant cultural and political climate for women's rights activists (see Faludi 1991) just as dissenting elites encouraged and supported public mobilization on peace issues. No wonder, then, that many women's movement activists chose peace issues as the most promising means of advancing political claims (Meyer and Whittier 1994; Sawyers and Meyer 1999).

The social and political climate affects potential activists' perception of the necessity for and possibilities of protest. Social mobilization itself becomes a factor in the volatile political opportunity structure for incipient movements. Social protest on one set of issues along with what comes along with that (including media attention, political responses, foundation support, constituency interest) provides new opportunities on other issues. For example, marginal Left parties turn up at virtually all moderate-to-Left demonstrations and actions because they can find people available to social protest; such "message events" (see Oliver and Maney 2001) are among the few public occurrences where recruitment is potentially viable. We can understand the process of putting together movements by looking at the coalitions that animate, negotiate, cooperate, and compete within a social movement (McCarthy and Zald 1977; Meyer and Rochon 1997; Staggenborg 1986; Zald and McCarthy 1987).

The socially constructed collective identity of a social movement community and activists' identity within are negotiated by both movement adherents and their opponents. Within a movement, there are ranges of orthodoxy in adherence to shared norms, styles of presentation of self, values, and implicit beliefs about the goals and means of social change. The range of adherence and contestation change in respect to changes in the external world, such that a collective identity of any dissident group is in constant and dynamic interaction and redefinition in relation to mass culture and the state. Understanding of collective identity and social structural opportunities must focus on this dynamic interaction.

There is much work to be done in subsequent studies of social movements; the chapters that follow pursue some of them. In all the following cases, I am arguing for a synthetic approach that uses a variety of disciplinary insights. The book before you offers serious progress on key issues.

What Is to Be Done?

1. *Separating Opportunities, Mobilization, and Influence.* In the past, analysts who studied movements generally studied only movements, so they looked for the visible signs of dissent, then read back expanding opportunities or new tactical choices. This approach risks conflating opportunities with mobilization, a problem of method more than theory. Moreover, opportunities must be perceived in order to be meaningful, and the perceptions of opportunities are culturally constructed (Gamson and Meyer 1996).[1]

There is, of course, another problem implicitly identified here. Opportunity analysts look at opportunities to act collectively (e.g., McAdam 1982; Tilly 1978) and opportunities to act effectively, that is, to influence policy (e.g., Piven and Cloward 1979), although these two are not necessarily related. Indeed, for groups that mobilize in the face of increased exclusion, opportunity to mobilize extra-institutionally should be inversely related to the opportunity to exercise meaningful influence on policy. Too rarely have analysts separated these issues analytically (but see McAdam 1996; Meyer and Minkoff 1997).

Political and policy changes do not automatically translate into predictable social movements. As Rebecca Klatch shows in her chapter on the New Left and the New Right, similar historical conditions can create dramatically different, even, opposing, movements. In the same vein, Rhys Williams shows how the rhetoric of Christianity in America has animated radically different movements, who divide not only on goals but also on organizational styles; at the same time, they share similar language. Individuals and groups actively make sense of the world and their actions based on a constellation of values and beliefs, depending on their social location. Similarly, Marc Steinberg, in his chapter on weavers and spinners in nineteenth-century England, shows how broader political and economic changes in context essentially forced workers to think of themselves differently. Drawing from dominant culture, they found ways to redefine their interests and activities, but they were still constrained by the culture—and economy—in which they lived.

2. *The Good News/Bad News Paradox.* Activists respond to changes in policy and target particular policies and practices, but we know little about how or why. McAdam's (1982) work on the civil rights movement suggests that openings in government, represented by favorable decisions on matters of policy, rhetorical concessions from political leaders, and the increased number of substantial allies in government aid mobilization. In this formulation, good news on matters of policy is also good news for mobilization. Costain (1992) finds a similar pattern for women mobilizing in the second wave of the women's movement. But in my own work on movements against nuclear weapons (1990, 1993), the opposite seems to be the case. Antinuclear movements in the United States have emerged in the face of unfavorable decisions on policy when their established allies were excluded from the inner councils of policy making. When they got favorable changes in rhetoric, policy, and political inclusion, extra-institutional mobilization faded. Smith (1996) identifies a similar pattern for activists against U.S. intervention in Central America. Similarly, in matters of abortion policy in the United States, one side mobilizes in response to envisaged threats from government. Thus, both sides eagerly claim defeat in the wake of ambiguous Supreme Court decisions (Meyer and Staggenborg 1996).

We should certainly be mindful of cases and causes, but we should not hesitate to try to build broader theories and generalizations. We should be working to figure out the circumstances under which different sorts of constituencies mobilize and the issues on which they mobilize. Einwohner (1999a) suggests that animal rights activists achieved radically different outcomes depending on their choice of target. We should be able to identify which movements respond to which opportunities, and specifically, why some claimants protest in response to favorable policy from the state, others to unfavorable policies. In his chapter, Kenneth Andrews shows that at the local level, movements play a role in bringing about the policy changes that undermine their ability to mobilize the same constituencies in the same way. His chapter calls for a fuller consideration of movement outcomes, including paths available for subsequent political efforts.

3. Missed Opportunities. Movements are efforts, not always successful, to take advantage of opportunities, so we should begin identifying elements of favorable opportunity when strong extra-institutional movements do not take place. Periods of apparent quiescence can be as interesting as periods of mobilization (see Gaventa 1980). Understanding the whys and wherefores of such *missed opportunities* may give us analytical insight into the importance of activists' strategic and tactical choices and their differential effects (Sawyers and Meyer 1999). It may also produce an activist social science that could be of use to people who want to make, not just study, social change.

4. Movement-Movement Influences. With a few notable exceptions (e.g., Gamson 1990; Kriesi, Koopmans, Duyvendak, and Giugni 1995; Tarrow 1989b; Tilly 1995b), most studies of movements concern the trajectory (or some smaller piece) of one movement in one country. Moreover, people usually study movements they like—although the study itself may change initial feelings of affection. Thus, certain cases are neglected, and this is problematic for the development of theory and, indeed, for the comprehensiveness of knowledge produced by the academy. Subsequent research that details the web of relationships among movements over time may show that grouping movements in one of these categories is neither so easy nor so useful. We need to know how movements alter the opportunities for both allies (Meyer and Whittier 1994; Minkoff 1997) and for opponents (Meyer and Staggenborg 1996).

5. Political Processes in Different Settings. The separation of First and Third World theories presents an analytical challenge, as most of the theories forged in the context of advanced industrial democracies stay there, and vice versa (but see Almeida and Stearns 1998; Boudreau 1996; Brockett 1995; Hochstetler 1995; Schneider 1995; Schock 1996). We do not really know how applicable these theories are to the rest of the world, so we need to talk across the equator. Comparative work in less developed countries, and work that addresses the effects of other nations and supranational bodies on opportunities for dissent within them, will inform and broaden political process explanations for social protest. Such work will necessarily consider both structural factors (e.g., the multinational economic boycott of apartheid South Africa) and cultural-cognitive factors (e.g., the support and encouragement Vaclav Havel claimed to take from peace campaigners in the United States and Western Europe).

In this volume, Dunbar Moodie approaches the basic premises of political process theory and tries to apply them to the campaigns of South African miners. He finds the theory forged in North America and Western Europe insufficiently nuanced in explaining the contingencies of strategizing in South Africa. He shows that activists made strategic decisions, cognizant of the cultural resonance of particular rhetoric and tactics. Vincent Boudreau, in his chapter on comparative responses to repression, shows that authoritarian state strategies in controlling dissent affected the movements that emerged. He shows how states effectively shape the challengers they encounter.

6. Movement Operations in Different Venues. Within any state, claims making takes place in different venues, and challengers' choices of venues depend on the nature of rules, institutions, norms, procedures, and alliances well below the broad level of the state. We would benefit from work explicitly addressing how states can channel conflict or dissent into particular political institutions and how movement conduct changes over time as a result (Amenta and Young 1999a). In a liberal polity, we would expect courts' openness to challenges on rights, for example, to influence the strategic choices of dissidents concerned with rights, perhaps focusing on the courts to the exclusion of other venues (e.g., Meyer and Staggenborg 1998). We must ask why movements choose to make their demands in particular institutions at particular times and how states condition these choices.

7. Tactical Choice. The issue of tactics at once raises two critical issues: how activists choose tactics and, how tactics produce effects (i.e., when does nonviolent protest, for example, produce the outcomes activists desire?). To understand tactical choice, we need to look at movement activists from both the outside (what tactics are encouraged or discouraged by state policies) and from the inside (what activists consider legitimate or effective). We need to consider not only organized interests and claims but also the perceived moral and political constraints that emerge when one is considering institutional participation or political violence.

In looking at a local labor struggle, Colin Barker and Michael Lavalette in their chapter examine activists' strategy in close detail, showing how tactical choices reflect constant calculation not only about the actions of authorities but also in the likely constellation of supporters particular tactics will engage. By tightly examining a brief period, they provide insight into what makes for a successful campaign. This close attention to the reality of political organizing shows the interplay of tactics, organizational form, ideology, and political leadership.

8. Organizational Forms and Norms. When people launch challenges, they organize themselves, albeit not in circumstances they design. The form of organization, loose, decentralized, and democratic, or tight and hierarchical, reflects the larger political and cultural environment, even as it shapes the longevity and ultimate impact of a movement. Suzanne Staggenborg's chapter shows how focusing on this organizational, or "meso" level, can delineate connections to both individual choices and the larger political and cultural context. Her case of a women's movement community shows how the reality of a social movement is far more than its explicit claims and narrowly political tactics.

Recognizing the diverse aims of people who participate in social movement, Jo Reger shows how structural accommodation allows an organization to survive and thrive. She shows, by studying a large local chapter of the National Organization for Women (NOW), how diversity can strengthen a movement. By making space for women who were more interested in "consciousness-raising" than policy-oriented political activism, New York City NOW was able to serve and contain a larger segment of a feminist constituency and to revivify a women's movement. In effect, factionalism promoted continuity. On a somewhat larger scale, Mildred Schwartz examines how a regional labor alliance became a national political party in Canada and how that party has survived by making space for factional disputes. The key issue in both cases was finding cultural and structural ways to allow for, and manage, divisions.

9. *Public Policy.*   Public policy is both a dependent variable, as a measure of movement success, and a component in political opportunity that movements address. Yet, at least partly because of the odd division of labor between political science and sociology, few scholars of movements explicitly consider changes in policy. The language used by policy analysts (e.g., Baumgartner and Jones 1993; Kingdon 1984) is strikingly similar to that of some social movement analysts, but the literatures generally speak past each other. Changes in policy can be the achievements (e.g. Amenta, Dunleavy, and Bernstein 1994; Burstein, Bricher, and Einwohner 1995; Piven and Cloward 1979) of social movements, as well as the grievances for subsequent movements (e.g., Meyer 1993; Smith 1996). Not only do policies create grievances; they also create constituencies, that is, the people identified by their behavior, interests, beliefs, or some ascriptive characteristic as aggrieved or empowered. In this way, we can understand how the state structures collective identity. We need to develop a better understanding of how. Belinda Robnett's chapter here shows how the passage of the Voting Rights Act effectively split the American civil rights movement, as demonstrated dramatically in SNCC. We would do well to emulate this kind of focused crossing of levels, in which national policy changes are felt through organizations that operate in both national and local venues.

Why We Do It

It is too easy to forget the critical importance of what we study. The people who make social movements are trying to change the world, trying to promote their visions of peace, justice, and social progress—sometimes at great personal risk. This means that we start with subjects invested with emotion, import, conflict, and tension from the outset. I hope that the work of scholars can be more clearly animated by the importance of such commitments, treating the puzzles of collective action with the passion employed by activists about their own efforts. Recent work that places the voices of activists at the center of analysis is particularly admirable (see Naples 1998a; Taylor 1996). Additionally, however, it is critical to ask important questions whose answers could lead to making the world better. Too often, the efforts of scholars draw on the concerns of activists, then translate them into an academic discourse far distanced from the social concerns that spur movements, offering little of use to those who make social movements.

Scholars from completely different disciplines have developed practical knowledge that can address practical problems. The zoologist who visits a zoo can offer practical advice about the care and feeding of particular animals, suggesting habitat and nourishment to make animals flourish. Her academic knowledge can provide useful information to those concerned with practical solutions to real problems.

I hope that calling for students of social movements to aspire to the same level of utility is not so easily dismissed as unprofessional or impossible. Surely, we need to understand essential questions and answers about social movements and politics if we, as citizens as well as scholars, assume our responsibility to better the world. If a social science is to mean anything, we can ask and try to answer questions whose answers would improve the world.

We must call for connections between activism and scholarship. Paradoxically, and problematically, as the study of social movements has gained respect in the academy, the accompanying professionalism has exacerbated divisions between activists and academics. To some extent, this may be unavoidable. But if such distance is the result of foregoing the exploration of important questions to focus instead on the hottest debate of the moment in the academy, we can and must do better.

We need to ask, and to try to answer, important questions, ones whose answers would improve the world. Remember, we study people who are taking risks and making commitments to do exactly that. We owe our extremely important subject comparable commitment. We need to remind ourselves that this area is *not* just another area of academic study and that successful conduct of research *could* matter a great deal.

NOTES

This introduction benefited because Colin Barker, Lynn Chancer, Manisha Desai, Fabricio Ferrier, Jim Jasper, John Krinsky, Roy Licklider, Howard Lune, John Markoff, Ann Mische, Jo Reger, Belinda Robnett, Cesar Rosado, Tracy Sefl, Jesper Sigurdsson, Chuck Tilly, Bridget Welsh, Nancy Whittier, and Elke Zuern offered helpful comments at various stages in its development. I am grateful.

1. This section draws on Meyer 1999.

Part Two

STATES AND POLICIES

Introduction to Part II

Activists and scholars of social movements share a common challenge: to identify the boundaries of the possible. Activists *can* make history, to paraphrase Marx, but not just as they choose. Activists select issues, tactics, allies, and targets, but they select from a rather limited menu. Their efforts, however, alter the options available to those who come afterward, eliminating some items on the menu, adding others.

The state is a powerful presence for all social movements, establishing constituencies or identities—more or less explicitly, delimiting potential alliances both inside and outside formal political institutions and, through policy and politics, creating both grievances and routes for redress. At the same time, the results of political contests are not completely predetermined from outside. Leadership, tactics, ideas, and alliances affect how successful organizers are in mobilizing support for their claims—that is, staging a social movement, and how actively and fully the state responds. The essays in this section start with states and policies and all show the interaction and interconnectedness of state policies and activists' efforts to promote change.

State-centered research often treats state structures and policies as constants, then runs various movements through them, comparing the differences in outcomes. Vincent Boudreau shows the necessity of taking a historical approach to the *interaction* of movements and states. His comparison of revolutionary movements in Southeast Asian states highlights the role of state repression in constraining, and thereby shaping, opposition over time. It also emphasizes the necessity of adapting political process theory, honed mostly on cases in liberal polities in Western Europe and the United States, to different patterns of contention in authoritarian states. By choosing who and how to repress in maintaining power, authoritarian leaders effectively conditioned the possible spaces for their opponents, as well as the nature of coalitions that opponents could build. In Boudreau's analysis, strategies of repression,

collective identity of revolutionary movements, and ultimate political outcomes are intertwined.

Dunbar Moodie provides a closer analysis of the interaction between state
repression and movement strategy in South Africa and challenges the reach
of contemporary social movement theory more directly. Existing theory does
not help much, Moodie charges, because of its failure to focus on interactive, or dialectical, processes. In seeking to center a meaningful sense of agency
in his analysis, Moodie emphasizes organizers' efforts to express and mobilize around the resentment and "common sense" of the workers they represented. And these workers made common sense of their observations of
changing policies not only of the South African state but also of their employers; they lodged their challenges at the state and at the workplace. Moodie
urges analysts to seriously consider social movement activists' sense of their
own efforts. For South African workers, we should examine their efforts to
reclaim "human dignity."

Manisha Desai uses a similar analytical lens but trains it on politics within
a decentralized democratic context. By addressing the development of diverse
women's movements in India over time, she shows how the issues and identities claimed by activists reflect perceived openings in government over time.
The national state, however, is not the end of the analysis, for Desai shows
that the government itself was challenged not only from within but also from
outside by the emerging international order and the World Bank's imposed
"structural adjustment" of the Indian economy. Mobilizing within the identity and infrastructure of a women's movement was the most readily available means for advancing claims about poverty and social justice—even when
those claims did not concern women exclusively. This nuanced historical
analysis demonstrates the necessity of looking beneath and beyond expressed
identities to find the sources of social movement claims.

Mary Bernstein directs attention to the interaction of a movement coalition and a subnational state on a particular area of policy. The state of Vermont presented distinct political opportunities to lesbian and gay activists.
In choosing to pursue particular claims, gay and lesbian rights organizations
effectively expressed not only what they wanted but also who they were. Given
the diverse interests of the gay and lesbian communities—even in Vermont—
selecting issues is inherently controversial within a movement coalition, and
organizers thus had to balance external and internal pressures in managing
their presentation of identity. Bernstein's analysis, which demonstrates the
connections between state policies and identities, pushes scholars to avoid
reifying collective identities as essential, rather than seeing the expression of
identity as contingent, and, as she has pointed out elsewhere (Bernstein 1997),
strategic.

Kenneth Andrews starts his overview of the influence of social movements by looking at public policy, but he then notes that this is only one dimension of influence. He argues that, in order to assess the impact of social movements, we need to examine not only the enactment but also the implementation of policy reforms and that the longer-term impact of those reforms includes changes in culture and the creation of new constituencies. His treatment of the civil rights movement, as an example, shows how much is left unsaid when a movement outcome is perceived as a discrete change in policy. He notes that changes in policy and culture afford the development of new claims and new constituencies.

These chapters cover a range of actors, causes, and contexts, but they share a concern with the interaction of challengers and authorities over a more extended time period. Each offers a processural analysis of political opportunities, politics, culture, and protest. Such approaches allow us to bound the range of the possible and develop a meaningful understanding of political agency. In short, we know that activists' efforts can matter; these authors show us when and how.

State Repression and Democracy Protest
in Three Southeast Asian Countries

VINCENT BOUDREAU

Between 1986 and 1998, three Southeast Asian dictators of long standing, Ne Win in Burma, Suharto in Indonesia, and Ferdinand Marcos in the Philippines, resigned in the face of broad popular protest. Democratization scholars, particularly those who describe recent transitions to democracy as part of a single "third wave," have viewed Philippine and Indonesian transitions as different examples of the same general political development—and the Burmese case as perhaps a near miss.[1] But were the Indonesian and Philippine transitions really similar? Did Burma miss the democratizing bandwagon by a hair's breadth or a country mile? If we attend to the processes and patterns of the struggle, instead of to the mere fact that democracy movements occurred in each place, the Indonesian, Burmese, and Philippine cases vary tremendously. In this work, I investigate the contours and causes of variation in contentious processes among these three countries. Specifically, I argue that important variations in movement identities, tactics, and influence reflected ongoing interactions between the authoritarian regimes and their societies. Those variations, and their structural roots, must be central to any explanation of the protests.

Those who have examined democracy struggles as social movements often ask what factors influence anti-regime *mobilization*, including potential movement allies, shifting policies, and changes in the likelihood or severity of repression (Hipsher 1998; Melucci and Lyyra 1998; Sandoval 1998). Mobilization levels, however, tell us relatively little about how protest drives processes of regime fragmentation and defection so closely associated with transitions to democracy. Under what conditions does protest bring down a regime accustomed to crushing dissent? One clue lies in an odd coupling of tactics and goals common to many democracy movements: essentially (or initially) *peaceful demonstrations* demanding *regime change*. In cases other than democracy movement, we are more used to seeing two different couplings of tactics and objectives: state-replacing movements adopt violent modes of struggles, whereas movements for reform embrace more peaceful protest (Zald 1988; Boudreau 1996). In the former case, the movement accumulates enough power to displace the regime; in the latter, it adopts tactics that will appeal to the regime's sensibilities. Democracy movements more generally work by encouraging loose or discouraged elements of the regime's supporting coalition to defect.

To fully understand this process, however, we need a fix on the character of potential alliances between state defectors and protesters; here, an ideational story line comes into play alongside more material factors. Patterns of state repression influence the institutions, social bases, and collective repertoires available to dissidents (Schurman 1989). Some sorts of repression drive claim makers far underground, or into radicalizing mass alliances. Other kinds of repression may decimate activist institutions and render protest tentative and cautious; still others may distinguish those who elect moderate dissent from potential radicals. Movement identities emerge in relation to such processes of contention and are not essential or fixed (Snow and Benford 1992). But the same is true of state actor identities, for modes of resistance (rather than essential hard- or soft-line orientations [O'Donnell 1989; White 1994]) surely shape how potential reformers inside the state react to dissent. Strong and vibrant anti-dictatorship movements may embolden state officials to take a reforming stance, while the absence of such movements may compel state actors to swallow their criticisms. Radicalized movements may encourage state actors to close ranks, while more moderate dissidents may invite defection. Hence, whether democracy movements and state actors are politically or physically available to one another greatly influences what modes of contention may cause defection from the regime, as well as the likely political consequences of such defections.

Political Context: State Repression, Movement Repertoires

Ne Win, Suharto, and Marcos all needed to repress dissent and resistance. I argue elsewhere that the dictators each tuned repression to thwart their strongest challengers and maximize their own strengths (Boudreau 1998). Repression, in short, was a strategic matter for these men, developed in their respective rises to power and subsequently adjusted to meet new challenges. From these patterns of repression, the new regimes took shape. In Burma, General Ne Win directed his military (the Tatmadaw) to clear the urban areas of open politics, including protest. The military hierarchy itself became the new regime's core, and ensured that civilian politicians had no role outside the Tatmadaw-dominated Burma Socialist Program Party (BSPP). Suharto took power during a furious but one-sided battle between the only two national organizations in Indonesia, the military and the Communist Party (ABRI, Angkatan Bersanjata Republik Indonesia, and the PKI, Partai Komunis Indonesia, respectively). Having physically exterminated the PKI, ABRI constructed a vast corporatist machinery and banned most forms of political organization outside that structure. Under cover of Philippine martial law, Marcos jailed many of his parliamentary opponents and chased communist insurgents into the hills—but eliminated neither. He then built his New Society regime by amassing central powers and resources and using those to limit the exercise of civil liberties, representative institutions, and legal processes that he still formally allowed.

The repressive styles at the core of these new regimes shaped political contention by conditioning the possible choices available to dissidents. Repression taught activists lessons about the likely consequences of dissident acts and helped claims makers think about how opposition might work *or* fail. Ne Win, for instance, used great violence against lowland protests but periodically allowed insurgent groups to operate under state license in distant "un-Burmese" frontiers, groups like those most under fire in Indonesia. In each setting, patterns of repression eliminated some movement organizations but left others, proscribed some activities but allowed alternatives. Repression also shaped oppositional identities by clarifying boundaries between the subversive and the innocuous and thereby shaping dissidents' programs of struggles, the social coalitions such programs would attract, and the designation of movement participants as nationalists, moral critics, revolutionaries, or something else. These identities had roots in larger structures of power but also influenced how dissidents perceived or engaged those structures. Over time, interactions between state repression and social movements created sets of *relational possibilities* between social and state actors. Repression influenced whether social allies were physically, organizationally, or ideologically available to potential state defectors. Let us examine these established relationships in each case before focusing on the democracy movements.

In Burma, Ne Win cemented his dictatorship by murdering student demonstrators at Rangoon University in June 1962 and building the BSPP as the sole narrow avenue for political participation. From then on, the military violently attacked each (admittedly rare) protest against the state (Silverstein and Wohl 1964). Dissidents escaped prison or murder by joining frontier insurgencies or forming secret underground cells. These latter institutions, however, remained largely isolated from one another, for no legal associations existed to provide them cover, and state repression severed links to the

Burmese Communist Party (BCP) in the 1960s. Protest required powerful exogenous stimuli, such as famine or currency crisis, that pushed large sections of society toward revolt—for few Burmese would risk murderous state violence unless demonstrations could threaten enough disruption to displace the state. Hence, waves of protest began as unruly and spontaneous affairs (Steinberg 1981) that grew organized as underground activists entered the fray. Burmese protest had a cataclysmic, all-or-nothing dynamic: activists working the tail end of a protest upsurge often pursued increasingly radical activities, fueled by the certainty that the state would retaliate if it survived.

By eliminating the PKI, constructing a corporatist machinery, and restricting the possibility of independent political organizations, the Indonesian state under Suharto completely reworked the conditions of political contention. Mobilizations no longer had the institutional support, guidance, or continuity that political organizations, particularly the defunct PKI, once provided. Still, because the state lay secure behind its corporatist monopoly, Suharto tolerated unorganized protest and generally did not murder or arrest demonstrators (with the important exception of separatists). The regime countered protest mainly via after-the-fact restrictions on organization forms that had been too successful, supported by conflations of *organization* and *communism* in state propaganda that invoked the New Order's baptismal slaughter. Activists quickly picked up on the new rules and responded to regime proscriptions against organization by adopting new (and often small-scale) organization forms the regime still had not banned. Activists rarely experimented with illegal organization forms, and students especially began to describe their movement as a "moral" (and explicitly not an organized "political") force. In consequence, protest remained small, rather than national; thematically limited, rather than holistic; and short-lived, rather than sustained (Aspinall 1993). Deprived of strong movement organizations, protesters eventually found careers in the country's dynamic economic mainstream, and meanwhile developed cautious modes of criticizing the regime that preserved the possibility of reengaging in the economy, and they frequently relied on support from select state actors.

In the Philippines, Marcos never eliminated either protest (as in Burma) or anti-regime organization (as in Indonesia) but sought to divide moderates from communist insurgents by coopting the former (Anderson 1998) and squashing the latter. However, Marcos's main early concern with state building (rather than decisive attacks on adversaries) provided opponents with leeway crucial to challenge his program. Almost all parliamentary opponents survived the first crackdown. They soon organized human rights associations and, by 1978, political parties. The Left insurgency weathered strong repression in the early 1970s and then steadily built a comparatively elaborate network of front organizations and underground units. Both centrist and Left groups sheltered behind civic and religious institutions, and a combination of these institutions and movement organizations supported individual activist careers for decades (far longer than in Indonesia; far more open than in Burma). Building on organizational bases that survived martial law, these opposition groups thwarted Marcos's scheme to co-opt the political center, for while promised reform often excited moderate hopes (and even triggered radical experiments with open struggle), the disappointment of those hopes (inevitable under Marcos) drove angry liberal dissidents toward radical positions and alliances. Rather than isolating the Left, therefore, regime activity underwrote stronger Center-Left coalitions. All regime opponents, moreover, developed organizations that expanded and accumulated; most adopted revolutionary ways of describing their struggle, if not radical programs for a post-transition society.

The relationship between state repression and political contention in each case varies considerably, but in each, state actors' decisions about repression condition the choices available to claim makers thereafter. Indonesia and Burma provide the sharpest contrasts. Whereas the Indonesian state eliminated forms of movement organization and then allowed protest a freer hand, the Burmese regime violently repressed protest in ways that drove dissidents into secret or distant movement organizations. The Philippine state adopted a policy eliminating neither protest nor political organization, but harassing both; the strategy was designed to preserve a liberal facade to mollify moderate opponents. Instead, it created an opposition that accumulated across the dictatorship. Table 2.1 represents the relationship between strategies of state repression and modes of political contention. We turn now to a more focused discussion of the three democracy movements.

Burma

The Burmese democracy protests of 1988 began, like every post-1962 movement, with widespread economic crisis and unorganized demonstrations. To meet massive external debt in 1987, the state cut farm-gate prices, angering rural cultivators. By October, the government announced a crushing demonetization of 25, 35, and 75 Kyat notes. In both Rangoon and Mandalay, students protested and vandalized government facilities. Similar actions occurred several weeks later in Arakan state and Pyinmana, several bombs exploded in Rangoon, and antigovernment pamphlets surfaced both there and in Mandalay. The regime closed urban universities to clear the cities of protest and sent students home, ending the protests but also spreading word of them upcountry, as the censored news media would not. Still, the 1987 protests foreshadowed more serious contention from March to September 1988, when

TABLE 2.1   Summary of Regime Repression Strategies and Social Response
in Burma, Indonesia, and the Philippines

	Burma	Indonesia	The Philippines
Dictator's initial base of power	Burmese military (the Tatmadaw)	Indonesian military (ABRI)	Philippine presidency
Major regime adversary	Urban political parties	Indonesian Communist Party (PKI)	Rival elite politicians
Mode of domination	Smothering military surveil-lance and the repression of all dissent	Strong corporatist control prevents dissent from acquiring an organized base	State attempts to divide the centrist and Left resistance by limited concessions to the former and violence against the latter
Mode of repression	Prohibition of open urban politics and the murder of demonstrators	Massive murder of PKI members and destruction of non-state organizations	Arrests scatter or detain both underground and legal dissidents, but destroys neither
Institutions of contention left by repression	Frontier insurgent armies and isolated underground cells	Loose ad hoc collectives, small-scale development agencies, and public intellectuals	Dense and expanding protest movement organ-izations, legal and illegal parties, civic groups, and an armed underground
Patterns of contention	Rare but cataclys-mic uprisings that grow more furious and organized as they progress; each ends in state violence	Limited, short-term, and episodic protests that often look to influence state policy or support reputed reformers inside the state	Sustained, organized, and increasingly insti-tutionalized protest campaigns; an expanding insur-gency; and links of support and recruit-ment between them

protests, riots, and repression shook Burma, beginning almost inadvertently
with police violence at a tea-shop fight. Before a September coup reimposed
military rule, thousands died, and Ne Win had resigned (Lintner 1990).

From March through September, the movement passed through three distinct phases, each shaped by the operation of different movement organization forms. Protest during the first stage was conditioned by the utter absence
of movement organizations or supporting social institutions. In mainly spontaneous Rangoon student demonstrations on March 12–14, protest leaders
emerged from crowds that were very nervous about government infiltration

and unequipped to screen imposters. Those who distinguished themselves by public bravery or defiant speech acquired authority. Such acts provided the best proof that their dissent was on the level, and a reckless defiance of authority became the guiding spirit for early demonstrations. After several days of loosely organized campus protests, Burmese riot police moved into the Rangoon Institute of Technology (RIT) to arrest students, but many protestors escaped. The next day, on March 16, students from the nearby Rangoon University (RU) marched toward the RIT campus but clashed with riot police crouched in ambush near a small white bridge at Inya Lake. That day's casualties exceeded 200. At this stage, broad mass outrage and violence (also unorganized) provided cover for students escaping murderous state pursuit. Three days of broader skirmishes followed in which workers, slum residents, and students fought the police and military (Sein Win 1988). On March 18, protesters burned government facilities in downtown Rangoon. Riot police attacked once more, exchanging gunfire with activists' rocks, firebombs, and other projectiles. Scores of protesters died, and the schools and universities closed.

The movement's second phase began on June 15, marked by the first signs of underground cell activity, manifest in a more explicitly political tone and a closer political, rhetorical, and symbolic association with pre-1962 organizations and traditions of struggle. These underground cells were particular creations of Ne Win's post-1962 repression: cautious, fragmented, and secret, they lay inert for years at a time but were nevertheless important repositories of movement experience. The idea of "going underground" survived from Burma's vibrant pre-1962 traditions, even as systematic state repression fragmented that underground and prevented any open dissent to which the underground could attach itself. After 1962, such cells were the fragile last ground of dissent left by Ne Win's appetite to control and repress, containing veterans of pre-coup or later protests, younger people seeking an outlet for their dissatisfaction, or, more rarely, actual BCP members. In the stifling atmosphere of Ne Win's Burma, such cells could not act except under extraordinary conditions such as those the March protests provided. Thereafter, underground activists cultivated new student leaders (to replace those arrested) and taught them to be more organization-minded.

On June 15 masked students (nobody in March wore masks) suddenly broke from a crowd milling near the RU campus center, announced a demonstration, and made a more polished political speech than anything heard in March. The next day, all of Rangoon's university campuses had protests, but leaders now devoted great energy to building committees and linking campuses. Some, like Maung Maung Kyaw, were known March leaders, but most others were not. Often, demonstration speeches announced subsequent activities. Small "lightning" rallies broke out in Rangoon's streets, where masked activists spoke for perhaps three minutes and then fled, leaving a flurry of pamphlets spinning in their wake.[2] New protests also had a broader social base than those in March. Workers, market vendors, and street gangs joined marches that often dissolved into bloody battles simultaneously in different parts of town. Activists outside Rangoon also began to weigh in, for many students sent home in March remained there and drew provincial society into the struggle. In Pegu and Moulmein, mid-June demonstrations coincided with those in Rangoon, and the Pegu unrest lasted for days after Rangoon demonstrations subsided (Yitri 1989). The June protests finally tapered off in another wave of massive arrests and shootings, and the movement lost another strata of leaders. This time, however, many surviving activists used the break to travel upcountry and to begin building new movement centers for the struggle's anticipated resumption.

On July 7, Ne Win shocked all of Burma by admitting state and personal responsibility for the March and June shootings and resigning from the party and state. His speech included broad criticism of socialist rule and introduced the idea of a referendum to decide Burma's political future. But it also contained the dark warning: "When the Tatmadaw shoots, it shoots to hit" (Lintner 1990). Moreover, he named *Lon Htien* commander Sein Lwin (the man who commanded the troops during the March repression and during repression in the 1970s and the 1962 attack) as his successor. The appointment triggered the most strongly national protests since independence. To achieve the scope and coordination of these protests, activists depended heavily on underground work under way since the June events, and others shrewdly used interviews with BBC radio reporter Christopher Gunness to announce national demonstrations on August 8 (Kyaw Yin Hlaing 1996). By August 10, protest had occurred in virtually every Burmese town of any size. Wherever populations protested, moreover, the Fighting Peacock Flag of the All-Burma Student Union became their standard, associating the movement with the nationalist struggle against British colonialism decades earlier.

After several bloody days, Sein Lwin resigned on August 12, the state apparatus pulled back from the struggle, and the movement's third period began with utter, but uncertain euphoria. Strike committees quickly became remarkably widespread, representing every conceivable constituency, from transvestites to grave diggers. Demonstrations, more like victory parades, occurred daily under strike committee auspices, and the committees also linked movement elites to mass populations. Committees published newspapers, sent organizers to smaller villages, collected food and money, secured rally venues, and established communication with other strike centers. In Mandalay, monks and lawyers organized one citywide committee that managed to produce daily, peaceful protests from August 12 onward. In all of these remarkable moves toward organization and coordination, underground activists provided the coordination and experience that Burma's repressed society could not. But they had difficulty keeping mass formations focused on the national struggle. When government officials vacated government offices, many strike committees moved in and soon bogged down in efforts to run villages. In Rangoon, those who oversaw checkpoints to collect contributions and maintain security often came from local criminal gangs and acted in frighteningly summary style. While underground activists tried to direct efforts toward movement building and consolidation, the networks they controlled proved too thin (and secret) to direct the movement. Students attempted to forge a stronger public leadership by brokering a meeting between prominent figures Aung San Suu Kyi, General Tin Oo, Aung Gyi, and former Prime Minister U Nu, launching Ang San Suu Kyi to prominence but producing no unity among the potential leaders.

In September, the democracy movement reached its apogee. Strike committees and underground cells pulled mass society into streets vacated by the dictatorship, and elite pro-democracy activists were mass leaders. Burma's brief carnival of democracy was nothing if not a movement of the whole society against increasingly isolated state authorities. The state and army, however, never split, despite rumors to the contrary. The state's withdrawal in August eliminated opportunities for contact between potential state defectors and movement leaders, much as established patterns of normal state repression had done before the protests. The pattern of Burmese repression left an insular state divided from its society and pushed dissident elites toward mass allies, away from potential reformers inside the regime. Not only did the regime not split but movement activists mistrusted any intermediate reform program and narrowed their demands to immediate regime resignation. On September 18, the military retook the country with speed and brutality. In Rangoon alone, soldiers killed thousands. They smashed strike committees, pursued students into the jungle, and enforced new and rigorous curfews and restrictions. Early estimates of those killed in September ran as high as 10,000. Subsequent estimates were closer to 3,000, still a remarkably high figure.

Indonesia

From 1988 onward, a period of *keterbukaan* or openness occurred in Indonesia. Closely conditioned by the state's decision to maintain control by monopolizing organizational power, the dissent and questioning at *keterbukaan*'s core began within the behemoth New Order apparatus, as a consequence of factional power struggles. From the early 1980s, regime members criticized government corruption, the military's established political role, and the unclear status of presidential succession (Liddle 1995). To bolster their position, some players in this struggle courted social support, particularly among students, in the process reintroducing campus institutions, like student councils and newspapers, banned since the middle 1970s. When world oil prices fell, the regime encountered its first fiscal difficulties in more than a decade, a hardship that encouraged authorities to grant nongovernmental organizations (NGOs) greater leeway to service mass communities. Broader social dissent blossomed under the influence of such changes, yet it still conformed to dynamics carved out by established state repression and bans on movement organizations. Without organizations to provide protest continuity and support—and with the ghosts of 1966 haunting thoughts of defying state proscriptions—even Indonesian[3] activists with holistic programs for political change needed to assess them in terms of their immediate, rather than long-term, promise.

This situation produced two modes of activism. First, democracy discussions, accompanied by restrained published criticism (and more pointed unpublished letters), acquired status as democracy struggle, behind a mythology suggesting that democracy occurred when democratic ideas spread. A sort of dissident lecture circuit emerged in major cities, where public intellectuals (*tokoh dari rakyat*) spoke in favor of democratic reform or against corruption, and even Suharto was compelled periodically to discuss *reformasi* (reform) and *keterbukaan* with hedged approval. Second, protest increased but remained typically localized and episodic. Students demonstrated against issues from electrical rate increases to human rights violations but seldom in broadly coordinated actions or over time. Though NGOs grew more assertive, most declined to build large networks or recruit multi-sectoral support (Bunnel and Bunnel 1996). The first independent national labor union began with symbolic hour-long national strikes; subsequent (1994) labor riots triggered enough state repression to drive workers back to local unions. Across the board, the New Order's legal and ideological constraints warned activists against building movement organizations capable of sustained national contention; the regime's history of repression ensured that most heeded that warning. Hence, small-scale and loosely organized forms of struggle, among students and in mass communities, remained more common than large-scale or sustained protest movements.

The protests that ended Suharto's rule began with a massive economic crisis that undid the work of this state repression by establishing conditions for protest across Indonesia without any explicit coordination. As the Indonesian rupiah lost value (from 2,500 to around 10,000 against the U.S. dollar), riots and protest spread geographically across Indonesia and socially among both the wealthy and the impoverished. Student and intellectual protests that regularly accompanied the special meeting of the People's Consultative Assembly (called every five years to [re]elect the president) in 1998 coincided with rural mass rioting. Elite dissidents and students never joined or enlisted this mass unrest—and indeed elites seemed to fear mass chaos so much that they intensified demands that sympathetic state actors undertake preemptive stabilizing reforms. Still, the coincidence of mass and elite unrest led military officials to try to section off dissident segments from one another. In a move that inadvertently gave student protesters their long-lost institutional base for protracted and coordinated struggle, ABRI broke a two-decade prohibition on campus protest but banned street demonstrations. The announcement carried an implicit guarantee that protesters on campuses would be safe, and soon elite alumni returned to their alma maters to join the fray. As university protests grew, the archipelago of campuses across Indonesia became apprehensible as a unified and coordinated movement. Significantly, however, the campus arena deepened the existing division between elite activists and mass demonstrators, a clear residue of the state's repressive program.

Spreading protests emboldened regime factions dissatisfied with either the status quo or their position in it, and some edged closer to criticizing the regime directly. These critical state actors picked up and amplified calls for reform issued from elite and intellectual democracy meetings and lectures. Moreover, Indonesian marines, marginalized under the New Order, now accompanied student protests, at first because their rapport with students diminished the chances of protest violence but increasingly as a token of their potential support for the reform campaign. Evidence also suggests that Suharto's son-in-law, General Prabowo Subianto, provoked rural riots to provide cover for his own power grab.[4] The regime, finally, was under strong new pressure from global financial institutions and foreign governments, both rendered far more influential inside Indonesia by the fiscal crisis; such external forces openly pushed Suharto to reform and brushed aside his efforts to evade these demands.

In this context of potential collaboration between elite democracy activists and some regime members, the new round of democracy protests took effect. At this time, the repeal of consumer price supports, undertaken to meet International Monetary Fund (IMF) demands, brought students into the streets. When soldiers killed several participants in those demonstrations, they touched off three days of rioting that left Jakarta ruined. Afterward, students left their campuses, carefully wearing colored university jackets that set them apart from mass society, and massed at the national parliament. Through the next days, activists appealed for security forces and other members of government to support political reform, for no movement organizations existed to allow these elites to mobilize and control an autonomous, mass-based movement. (In any case, mass society had just shown itself to be dangerously volatile.) After several days, a group of officials that featured the head of ABRI, the vice-president, and the Speaker of the National Assembly convinced Suharto to resign. This de facto coordination between regime defectors and protesters left most of the old regime firmly in charge—at least for the next several months. With no organizational following, and significantly afraid of mass politics, social reformers could initially do little but voice demands for the new arrangement and set about the long-deferred work of constructing the institutions of more open political competition.

The Philippines

The Philippine democracy movement rose against a regime of repression (designed to isolate the revolutionary Left by coopting the center) already imperiled by the steady accumulation of strong movement organizations among both radical and centrist dissidents. By the early 1980s, however, several exogenous developments triggered a thaw in authoritarian practice that rendered the regime's strategy even less effective. First, Marcos yielded to international and domestic pressure and lifted martial law on January 17, 1981. While carefully preserving the dictatorship's central powers (Bonner 1987), the measures expanded opportunities for legal and semi-legal anti-regime organization and protest. Shortly thereafter, a cataclysmic balance of payments crisis, brought on by the discovery of central bank fraud, halted import credits, devalued the peso, and angered the business class, providing a new and powerful group of dissidents. Inside the regime, Marcos's power base was crumbling in ways that also provided political allies for activists. Unlike Suharto, who regularly rotated senior military officers out of the ABRI hierarchy and away from power, Marcos cultivated a relatively stable inner circle that included members of the professional military (often selected by personal or ethnic connection to the president) and a cadre of civilian supporters, cronies, family members, and retainers. Rivalries between these two groups were held in check while Marcos retained clear control, but when the president fell ill in August 1982, a minor (and premature) succession crisis rippled through the regime that eventually placed Imelda Marcos more clearly in line to succeed her husband. Minister of National Defense Juan Ponce Enrile and Philippine Constabulary Commander General Fidel Ramos, representing the military's professional faction, wound up on the outs, creating the most serious potential for factionalism in the regime to that point.

Under these influences, protests, strikes, and demonstrations increased through the early 1980s in ways conditioned by martial law's original failure to eliminate either open legal or underground anti-regime organizations. In consequence, movements reacted to these new developments by expanding their existing networks of centralized organizations, capable of mixing open-legal and underground-insurgent programs in long-term struggle. Political moderates reacted to the combination of economic crisis and liberalization by adopting stronger and more organized positions, and elites among them brought vast material and organizational resources to the movement. Encouraged by this trend toward elite dissent, the underground Left began to establish semi-legal "front" organizations with stronger ties to centrist anti-Marcos groups. Hence, moderate and radical regime opponents both found themselves at the helm of ever-expanding mass organizations that often worked in consort with one another—and all anti-regime movements increasingly depicted their activity in state-replacing, revolutionary terms.

Marcos rejoined characteristically, by calling elections in 1981, 1984, and 1986, undertaking further liberalizations (such as eased press restrictions) but murdering prominent regime opponents and intensifying the war against rural guerrillas. But elections no longer posed demobilizing choices between accepting regime cheating or joining the revolution. While some activists joined elections and others boycotted, the political center had become strong enough to use election campaigns (which they also took seriously) as a staging ground for large-scale protest and refused to shrug off regime cheating or concede the superiority of the Left's boycott position. Such mobilizations threatened the regime and triggered renewed repression. Repression, in turn, encouraged further protest with broader (i.e., center-Left) political bases.

Events leading to the 1986 transition followed these patterns. Benigno Aquino, exiled moderate leader, returned home to challenge Marcos in scheduled elections and was murdered at the airport on August 21, 1983. In response, moderate and radical movement organizations joined forces in the broadest and most sustained protest to that point under Marcos. While disagreements remained within the broad antidictatorship movement over strategy and tactics, its disparate strands had each grown so strong and institutionalized that Marcos faced virtually unremitting pressure. Activists controlled strong church groups, NGOs, unions, and other movement organizations. They published magazines that sold openly on newsstands, held conferences at national universities, and marched in street rallies that only sometimes drew gunfire. When events did not excite spontaneous protest (as Aquino's funeral had) organization leaders could deploy their mass followings in command protests that kept pressure on the state. This sustained and institutionalized movement, particularly along its moderate flank, also presented increasingly attractive alternatives to both foreign observers like the United States and Filipinos in the establishment. Under duress and looking to shore up his regime in 1985, Marcos announced snap presidential elections to take place in early 1986.

The opposition campaign in those elections was better funded and more enthusiastically supported than any other under Marcos. Young military

officers, announcing their commitment to free and fair elections and a professional military, formed the Reform Armed Forces Movement (RAM). The
National Movement for Free Elections, a civic poll-watching association first
organized in the 1950s, resumed operation with strong support from the
church and the middle class. After a violence-marred campaign, the ballot
collection and counting process produced dramatic irregularities, and poll
counters (often, the wives of RAM members) stopped the process and locked
themselves up with evidence of Marcos fraud. In this highly charged atmosphere, election protests mounted, and soon military officers, representing
those shouldered aside by Imelda Marcos in the 1982 succession crisis and
featuring the RAM, moved to unseat Marcos. The regime discovered the coup
in its infancy, and the exposed dissidents holed up in one of Manila's military camps and called for help. We now know that the coup plotters did not
challenge Marcos in order to install an Aquino presidency but to establish a
military junta. Still, when nearly a million people, responding to Cardinal
Sin's call, gathered to demand that Aquino take power, and to celebrate Enrile
and Ramos as prodemocracy revolutionaries, the would-be generalissimos
reconsidered their position. From then, the protests quickly undermined
Marcos, and when ordinance from a plane sent against demonstrators landed
near Malacañang palace, Marcos understood that his chapter of Philippine
history had closed.

Comparisons

These narratives suggest a causal chain that runs from established styles of
state repression through patterns of anti-state mobilization to differences in
prodemocracy movements. In each, patterned interactions between state repression and social mobilization over the authoritarian duration shaped
movement identities and the relationships possible between state defectors
and social activists. When things started to unravel for the regime, elements
of the ruling coalition considered defecting from the dictatorship. Whether
they did or not, and the political consequences of defections that did occur,
reflected the influence of established patterns of contention.

By proscribing counterhegemonic organization, Indonesian state repression separated critical social reformers from potential mass followers. Un-
able to pursue a movement "career" within an articulated opposition structure
(as existed in the Philippines), most Indonesian activists eventually moved to
the political, social, and economic mainstream. The prospect of this move,
moreover, moderated activist strategies generally. With no organization to
mediate movement relations between social classes, critical elites could not
direct mass society and seemed rather to fear it. When the prospect of more

massive unrest dawned in 1998, elite dissidents were inclined to demand action from the state (rather than engineer a mass uprising) to avert riots in Jakarta's streets. State propaganda exacerbated the divide between elite and mass claim makers, for its mythology of Sukarno's fall spun a cautionary tale against both communism and mass chaos. No wonder, therefore, that movement identities reflected these structural influences and featured moderating ideas that protest was moral rather than political, that public intellectuals (rather than activists) were at its core, and that students needed to distinguish themselves from the *rakyat* (society).

Because Philippine activist organizations survived and expanded under martial law, political and economic crises in the 1980s drew new dissidents into existing organizations with controlling links to mass constituencies. Demonstrations typically occurred when movement leaders decided they should and depended less on exogenous provocation than did protest in Indonesia or, especially, in Burma. Moreover, the well-organized Philippine antidictatorship movement (even on its moderate flank) could make complex and protracted state-replacing and revolutionary plans. Strong links to mass organizations made movement elites less ambivalent about the opportunities in crisis than their Indonesian counterparts: bad news for Marcos was always considered good news for the movement, and mass activity was assumed to serve organization priorities. Nor did Filipinos make substantial concessions to support state reformers qua state actors: activists worked within a powerful organizational field of gravity and expected defections from the regime to the movement. Hence, when Philippine society polarized, the movement enthusiastically pushed the crisis and commanded the mass resources to do so. Standing at the helm of mass mobilizing alliances and movement organizations aimed at toppling the state, even politically moderate anti-regime activists came to identify themselves as revolutionaries, and radical tropes overlay even conservative political orientations.

Burmese state repression violently eliminated public expressions of dissent but produced small, scattered, and generally paralyzed underground cells unconnected to any larger movement organization. The clearest result of this repression was a pattern of widely intermittent mobilizations that depended on deep, widespread social dislocation to coordinate grievances and produce unrest, which in turn roused underground cells to activity. This sweeping repression also produced important and specific influences on dissident elites. Burmese intellectuals had, since the middle 1960s, no scope for critical participation in political life. The state marginalized and impoverished all social strata and more thoroughly concentrated power and prosperity among a small leadership clique than what happened in either Indonesia or the Philippines. It consequently became natural for educated activists to ally with mass society—even when no organization cemented the alliance—based on the leveling effect of their shared marginality. While 1988 protests began on campuses, participants soon moved to the streets, where workers enthusiastically joined in. The great political distance between the entrenched state and the combination of elite and mass dissidents invoked the student-led nationalist movement against the occupying British colonial regime. Thus, long before the movement demanded democratic elections or political reforms, it adopted orientations from a struggle to reclaim the nation from interlopers. While powerfully mobilizing, the nationalist identity left little room for compromise with any state actor and so exacerbated the polarization between authorities and society.

In each case, state repression shaped alliance potentials between regime defectors, reform-minded elites, and mass society. The Indonesian state divided critical elites from mass society, particularly during periods of mass anger and mobilization. Isolated from, and fearful of, mass society, dissidents who described themselves as intellectuals and moral advocates did not scare state actors into closing ranks: quite the contrary, defecting officials seemed confident of their ability to control the transition. In the Philippines and Burma, state repression produced greater solidarity between these classes—but the solidarity differed in important ways. In the Philippines, moderate movement elites had access to a degree of civil space denied those in Burma. Supported by church and civil institutions, alliance between established elites in the movement and mass members regularized and even legitimized mass activism. Hence, even as Filipino protesters called for revolution against Marcos, they did so from an establishment position so manifest as to pull many of that revolution's most fearsome teeth. In contrast, Burmese elites found common cause with the masses at the political and social margins, where they were driven by a regime policy of indiscriminate repression. The nationalist identity that bound mass and elite Burmese dissidents focused such acrimonious attention on defeating authorities in street battles and driving them from office that no moderating alliances could form between any element of the regime and the movement.

Events immediately preceding these democracy protests interacted with these more established patterns. In both the Philippines and Indonesia, larger trends toward political openness—martial law's abolition and Indonesian *keterbukaan*—set up the antistate uprisings. Each thaw moved certain activities and discourses into the realm of the permissible, broadening alliance possibilities between some state actors and the opposition. In Indonesia, *keterbukaan* introduced a rhetorical trope with currency both within the state and in society: the need for political reform and clean government. In the Philippines, expanding civil liberties, assembly rights, and formal representative institutions, helped re-center opposition activities away from the radicals, more toward political moderates, and fired moderate rage when Marcos transgressed civil norms. In both cases, new, albeit still bounded, possibilities for more legitimate dissent helped some state actors take democracy advocates more seriously. In those circumstances, defections from the authoritarian coalition became imaginable for actors somehow dissatisfied with their position in the state, whether for principled or selfish reasons.

Burma's democracy protests, however, did not occur during a liberal thaw. Although Ne Win criticized the country's economic policies, he never instituted clear political reform, nor was he pressured to from within the state. Under these conditions, dissent was neither safer nor more permissible then it had previously been, and the possibility that members of the largely unified regime would support the movement was minuscule. Without such support, either state-led reforms on the Indonesian model or defections to the movement on the Philippine, chances diminished of an intermediate regime transition, short of the full state defeat that Burmese activists pursued. The battle lines between state and society were clearly drawn, with tragic consequences for the activists and for democracy. In Burma, movement success required force massive enough to overwhelm a state still unified and committed to retaining power.

In all the cases then, movement success or failure depended on both the movement's capacity and the state's resilience. I have shown that both factors are significantly contingent on established patterns of contention, themselves influenced by patterns of state repression. This contingency helps explains a superficial paradox arising from the cases: that in its mode of struggle, the Burmese democracy movement seemed in August 1988 far closer to seizing state power outright than either Philippine or Indonesian counterparts ever would be. Certainly the Burmese underground allowed far greater movement coordination, both across territory and across classes, than ever occurred in Indonesia, particularly when one considers how Jakarta students segregated themselves from mass society. Philippine protests, while massive and organized, never developed the ferocity of the Burmese struggle, nor did the protests (as opposed to the insurgency) seize state assets and positions, as in Burma. In both the Philippines and Indonesia, however, a liberal thaw broadened the possibilities of alliance between members of the regime and democracy advocates and produced some coalition between state defectors and democracy protesters that, more than the movement's sheer power alone, displaced the dictator.

But how does one explain liberal thaws in Indonesia and the Philippines and their absence in Burma? I would start by relating these liberalizing trends to established patterns of state repression. We have seen that Marcos's decision to conciliate the political center and attack the Left both required periodic, bounded liberalizations, but that these produced social organizations capable of demanding further steps, such as the repeal of martial law. Therefore, democracy and reform became an available concept for regime members who had lost position to rivals, and the existence of established, moderate, and sociologically compatible (i.e., elite) democracy advocates allowed men like Enrile and Ramos to support the movement. In Indonesia, the construction of a massive New Order apparatus, while long an effective measure to fragment social dissent, eventually produced divisions within the vast state that paved the way for *keterbukaan*. The balance between state actors and social dissidents was, of course, different in Indonesia (where the movement had no strong organizations and ABRI retained immense powers) than in the Philippines. Yet precisely because Indonesian protesters remained weak and fragmented, members of the Indonesian state were willing to support demands for reform by pressing for a regime change they fully expected to control. Both cases contrast with Burma, where the state's decision to crush all forms of open dissent never forced Ne Win to reach any accommodation with society, so, despite the passion and duration that democracy protests achieved, they never appealed to any significant force within the state.

A host of dynamics associated with democracy protests—when protest will mobilize, whether mobilization will set a transition in motion, and who will be in control of that transition—is contingent on histories that states and movements write together, histories of state repression and movement response. Understanding how authoritarian regimes defeat, or are thrown aside by, powerful social forces requires an understanding of the historical and political context out of which those challenges and responses arise. This chapter has neither exhausted the possibilities of comparison between these important cases nor touched upon other, comparable cases. I hope, however, to have demonstrated that a habit of thinking about historic interactions between repressive states and society can illuminate the identities, organizations, and tactics that emerge in democracy protests, and, partly in consequence of those factors, the possibilities for alliance and cooperation between potential state defectors and social dissidents on which the transition to democracy, or its defeat, so deeply depend.

NOTES

I gratefully acknowledge the assistance of Mary Callahan, David Meyer, Charles Tilly, and Elisabeth Wood in the preparation and revision of this chapter. Others in the Contentious Politics Workshop at Columbia University's Lazarsfeld Center for Social Sciences also contributed criticism and suggestions that helped me sharpen this material, and they have my thanks as well.

1. In Burma, as we will see, several months of protest led Ne Win to resign and ushered in a brief period of popular rule. After little more than a month of popular rule by local "strike committees," the military reasserted its control in a

bloody attack on the movement, in which between 3,000 and 5,000 Burmese protesters were killed.

2. Much of this information differs from published accounts of the 1988 protests and is based on a series of interviews I conducted in Burma and in the United States from 1995 to 1997. I am preparing a fuller account of the movement at this writing.

3. By specifying that the protests are Indonesian, I mean to emphasize that claim makers were not challenging their inclusion in the Indonesian political community. Separatist protests from East Timorese, West Papuans, and others often were bolder and more directed at confrontation.

4. Since Suharto's fall, reports have linked his son-in-law, Prabowo Subianto, to the rural riots in Java in early 1998, to the murder of four Trisakti University students that touched off rioting on May 13–15, to that rioting itself, and to the rape of some sixty-six Chinese women during that chaos.

3

Mobilization on the South African Gold Mines

T. DUNBAR MOODIE

In August 1982, Cyril Ramaphosa announced the formation of the National Union of Mineworkers (NUM) in South Africa. South African mining is an industry composed largely of migrant workers, barracked in large concentrated compounds. Black miners typically live at mines located far from large cities, insulated from workers in secondary industry, moving from bed to heavy work to mass feeding to bed in a cycle that John Rex (1973) once called the most effective form of labor control ever invented. Conventional wisdom in South Africa was that such workers were "unorganizable." In 1987, however, only five years after the launching of the NUM, more than 300,000 black South African mine workers embarked on a legal wage strike. It was the largest black strike ever in South Africa. Black miners stayed out for three weeks before being forced back by mass dismissals. Even the failure of the strike could not conceal the colossal organizational achievement of the NUM, which has become the largest of what Eddie Webster (1988) called "social movement unions"[1] in South Africa.

When I began to study the rise of the NUM, I turned eagerly to social movement theory, hoping for a perspective to guide my understanding of actors and events. Although certain monographs were helpful, social movement theory itself was a disappointment. I turned to other, more dialectical, theoretical traditions. In this chapter, I shall use social movement theory to analyze the making of the NUM while challenging and modifying basic assumptions that haunt (and, I believe, hamper) sociological efforts to understand social movements. Three general questions set the focus here. First, what *should* social movement theory (or any other social theory for that matter) do? Second, what *does* social movement theory actually do? Third, what is it *possible* for social movement theory to do?

I assume that the proper function of social movement theory is to enable social analysts to understand social movements better. Contemporary social movement theorists, caught in a misguided effort to be scientific, try to construct general causal propositions about social movements. Our imagination has been numbed in pursuit of general propositions so abstract as to be either tautological or empty.[2] In fact, given that social movements are created in a shifting arena where strategy and opportunity are linked in particular ways, what is truly interesting about movements is their contingency. The most innovative work on social movements invokes the imprimatur of "movement theory" in a post hoc manner, rather than being driven by these theoretical hypotheses in the first place.[3] Thus, interesting work on social movements seems to emerge despite, rather than because of, social movement theory. Why?

The great promise of social movement analysis was that it originated in an effort to return agency to center stage in sociology, without ever denying the importance of structural changes. One reason much work on social movements seems formulaic is that the terminology is static and one-directional, leaving little possibility for reciprocal relationships. Thus, we struggle to express sociologically the commitment to agency that first drew us to the study of social movements. This chapter looks at how central notions for social movement theory, such as political opportunity structures, cultural framing, and mobilizing structures, have failed to grasp the experience of agency in movement practices. In the light of my work on collective resistance on the South African gold mines, I shall try to suggest how we might do better.

In the first section, I argue that the tension between structural transformations and political opportunity has been lost in the notion of political opportunity structures, a concept that elides structure and opportunity in its formulation, reducing the latter to the former, so that opportunities come to reside in structures, rather than in specific reciprocal interactions between actors and political and economic conditions. The second section argues that the notion of cultural framing implies that culture is a constant, an enclosure for action taking place "within" it. Conceptions of culture as ideology, however, flatten the dialectical and practical way in which common sense is imbricated in the taken-for-granted practices of everyday life.[4] Interests and actions sustain and modify cultures in reciprocal ways, even as they are constituted by cultural discourses. Commonsense practices work in a constitutive manner that makes "toolbox" conceptions of culture seem hopelessly self-conscious, ideological, and manipulative.[5] Moreover, because common sense maintains social order, culture may also conceal power relations. This is what Antonio Gramsci (1971) calls hegemony. Indeed, for Gramsci, social movements could contest cultural common sense by demonstrating in practice an alternative common sense that he called "counter hegemonic." His work remains in many ways the best place to start looking for a more dialectical theory of social movements.[6]

The third section examines debates on mobilizing structures and organization, suggesting that the tendency to reify movements as social movement organizations makes it difficult to specify not only what mobilization is but why it succeeds. Whereas mobilization is unimaginable without informal social networks, the historical particularity of these networks means that their relevance can usually be specified only after the fact. Only in retrospect can we pick out the networks that actually assist in the struggle from the mass of social connections to which people belong.

Finally, the chapter concludes with a return to the questions with which it began. What ought social movement theory to be doing and what is it able to do? In the course of developing concepts for the study of social movements, have we forgotten why we started? Movement theory needs to recover the sociological imagination that keeps dichotomies in reciprocal relationship, going beyond raw description without invoking static categories so abstract that they hamper understanding of new possibilities. As we remain aware of contingency in social life, we also need to grasp how the contingent, once it emerges, can be determined.[7]

Structural Change and Political Opportunity in South African Industrialization

What exogenous changes in the South African political economy sustained the rise of the National Union of Mineworkers? Jack Goldstone (1988) would no doubt point to massive population growth in South Africa during the 1960s and 1970s. As Gay Seidman (1994) has shown for South Africa and Brazil, rapid industrialization was fundamental[8]—especially after 1973 with deepening recession. South African elites were seriously divided as to how to deal with the economic crisis, as elites often are.[9] The political decision to reform South Africa's draconian labor laws was clearly fundamental. These various structural developments represented potential opportunities for the establishment of South African trade unions. Calling them "political opportunity structures," however, short-circuits the contingencies, the dead ends, and the potentials for failure that dogged actual events. Reading opportunities as structures obscures the political and interpersonal routes along which independent unions were established in South Africa.

In the first quarter of 1973 in Durban, close to 100,000 workers began a series of rolling strikes. Their action seems to have grown from informal networks in closely adjacent factories, although a student "wages commission" from the local university also had recently held meetings with a few workers. Since many Durban workers were semiskilled and a boom was on, employers granted raises in response to the strike. Slowly and laboriously (and at great risk to themselves), activists began to form trade unions, firmly based on shop floor organization. Because of state hostility to any action that overtly threatened apartheid, the early unions chose to confront employers factory by factory. In 1974, textile workers struck against Smith and Nephew, a British-based multinational. One of their leaders was Halton Cheadle, a graduate student at the University of Natal. At a cocktail party, an American diplomat mentioned recognition agreements. Cheadle, who had never even heard of recognition agreements, asked for copies of American ones, cut and pasted them, and gained recognition from Smith and Nephew. This was a breakthrough (Friedman 1987: 92–100). Afterward, seeking recognition agreements with individual companies became a major strategy of the independent union movement.

When 1979 state reforms created an industrial court, clearly designed to bring the new unions into the existing industrial conciliation system, Cheadle (by now a lawyer) and a small group of progressive lawyers and legal scholars founded the labor law journal of record and successfully argued most of the early cases before the court (Thompson 1995). In so doing, they essentially created a body of new case law establishing negotiating rights for unions and protecting strikers. The principle of unfair dismissal, which was originally written into the state reforms to protect white workers threatened by the abolition of racial job reservation, was transformed into a powerful defense for black workers, who until then could be dismissed by employers at the drop of a hat. The new labor law necessarily created a new, more liberal, system of labor relations on the ground, giving legitimacy in South African business to a new generation of industrial relations managers who set about dismantling old despotic management systems from within (Thompson 1994: 357).

The new South African labor law (and especially restrictions on unfair dismissals) was perhaps the most effective instrument of early NUM organizers confronting authoritarian compound managers about the mines. Puseletso Salae, one of the most effective organizers on the giant Anglo-American Vaal Reefs mine, remembered:

> There were a lot of complaints. People were dismissed at that time, they were dismissed almost every day. . . . I managed to get more people to join the union because all the time I was going out to fight management over dismissals and I managed to win cases all the time. The men would go around and tell other guys, "I am back! I went to the union office and now I am back." Then all the other men in his room would come and join the union immediately. (Moodie 1994: 252)

Although the law represented a useful political opportunity for mining union organizers, it cannot be seen as an independent political given. To do so does violence to the law's contingent origins in earlier labor struggles. Moreover, it was easier to implement the law in some mines than others. Management reformers in Anglo-American mines were much more willing to abide by the new law than rival mining houses. Next to Vaal Reefs on the neighboring Buffelsfontein mine, run by Gencor, for instance, Salae and the other union organizers had a much harder time of it. They were simply denied access by mine security. As Aldon Morris (1984) demonstrated so brilliantly, for the American South in the 1950s, courts, important as they are in creating political opportunities, never guarantee that movements will successfully seize those opportunities.

The general theoretical point should be clear. Movements and actors appropriate political opportunities as they take advantage of changes in social structures, but in practice those changes may stem from prior movement activity. Abstract lists of potential "changes in opportunity structure" overlook the extent to which opportunities arise only as they are recognized and created. Theory must recognize the role of imagination and initiative in strategy and not deny the dynamism and contingency that is so much the fabric of actual collective action.[10] Opportunities seized at certain junctures often create new opportunities at the next. This dialectic transforms both structures and opportunities in their mutual relationship.[11] I am not denying the importance of wider structural changes for movement success. I do want to insist, however, that opportunities do not preexist in structures. They only appear to do so in retrospect.

Ideology and Common Sense

Resource mobilization and collective identity theories pay lip service to the merits of each other and often appear together in an ad hoc manner in empirical analyses. At the theoretical level, though, they circle one another like two dogs recently met. They simply replay the traditional dichotomy between ideology and material interests. Notions of "cultural framing" permit resource mobilization theorists to talk again about ideology and its problems. In this regard, Snow and Benford (1992) and their colleagues have done us an important service, but it is a rudimentary step—at least in its rather utilitarian formulation. What we need is a terminology that can illuminate age-old dichotomies in new ways to emphasize their mutuality.[12] Gramsci's notion of "common sense," I suggest, delineates the relationship between the material, the political, and the ideological without necessitating that any one predominate.[13]

Most sociological discussions of culture fail to make Gramsci's important distinction between "ideology" and "common sense." Let me try to explain briefly, following Raymond Williams's (1981) formulation. "Ideology" in Williams's exposition is self-conscious and intellectual as well as evaluative. It consists of values set forth by actors to justify their behavior. It strives for intellectual consistency. As such, it is open to manipulation (as with Swidler's [1986] cultural tool box) or "elaboration," "alignment" and "attribution" (as with Snow and Benford's [1992] master frame). "Common sense" is different. In Williams's (1981: 110) language: "It is a lived system of meanings and values—constitutive and constituting—which as they are experienced as practices appear as reciprocally confirming. It thus constitutes a sense of reality for most people in the society." Because it is rooted in practices and taken for granted, common sense transcends the dichotomy between interests and values. Nor, in contrast to ideology, does it rely on a claim to intellectual consistency for its power. Different versions may jog along comfortably (or even uneasily) together, differently applied in different situations. More humble than a "master frame," common sense is also more tenacious. Precisely because it is confirmed as it is lived, common sense is relatively impervious to ideological attack from those who seek to change it.

Take the example of traditional migrants to the South African gold mines. The goal of a traditional Xhosa-speaker coming to work in the mines was to attain the dignity of manhood in the rural areas back home by becoming proprietor of a homestead, which would earn him the respect of his neighbors and the right to settle disputes and manage affairs with generosity and resourcefulness. This faithfulness to this rural life world kept men working in the mines and living in mine compounds, reinvesting their mine wages in rural agriculture. Working at the mines enabled migrants to achieve rural manhood, especially because, when they retired to their rural homesteads, the bridewealth system meant that wealth earned by their sons-in-law would filter up to them, maintaining them as proprietors in their old age. The incentives to maintain the system of migration were thus practical as well as ideological, material as well as moral. The notion of "common sense" respects the fact that the material and moral aspects of miners' lives depended on one another in a taken-for-granted way. Values are important for practical reasons, and interests are fundamental for the maintenance of values.

Traditional black mine migrants put up with the low wages and racial violence of mine work because of the integrity of their commonsense commitment to rural life worlds: "The pay was bad, but we liked the work. . . . Minework was our pride, a source of self-respect." The hard work and cruelty underground were extensions of character-forming activities like herding and stick-fighting in the countryside. Workers accepted mine work, with its violent aspects, because it affirmed their masculinity (Breckenridge 1998).

The benefits of rural manhood apparently outweighed the costs of racial domination, although for many workers there was a subtheme of racial resentment waiting to be tapped. One old man, for instance, said: "We would talk of the injustice of the white miners' higher pay, but we could do nothing about it since we were under them—the whites had power." Thus, traditional common sense was congruent with, but did not accept, management commitment to gold production and racial intolerance in the mines. In its stress on personal integrity, traditional common sense contained within itself the potential for counterhegemonic resistance, especially once its economic base in the homestead system had been eroded by rural underdevelopment.

As mine wages dropped relative to wages in the industrial sector and as South African reservations became less and less capable of supporting viable homesteads, mining companies moved deeper and deeper into tropical Africa to find cheap labor. Since the 1950s, labor from within the borders of South Africa had drifted away from the mines into booming manufacturing industries. By 1970, almost 70 percent of black mine workers came from outside the borders of the country, from as far afield as Malawi, Angola, and Tanzania.

In 1974, labor supply crises emerged for the South African mining industry. In May 1974, after a fatal recruiting airplane crash, Hastings Banda, the Malawian president, withdrew all Malawian labor. Within six months, the number of Malawian workers on the mines fell from more than 110,000 to a few hundred. At the same time, revolution in Mozambique reduced the Mozambican supply. The mines were suddenly in desperate need of 200,000 black workers. Since the price of gold had recently risen, the mines were able to raise wages, and they did so. Black workers poured in from South Africa's rural resettlement slums[14] (created largely by modernizing white commercial farmers pushing redundant workers off the land) and from traditional sending areas in Lesotho and the Transkei.

The new workers who came from rural slums and urban townships were both better educated and completely wage-dependent. They were also more confrontational. Mine managements had to deal with a level of militancy never experienced before. Collective protests often interfered with production. Close to 10,000 workers were repatriated to their homes after clashes with management between 1974 and 1982. Kent McNamara (1985) estimates that at least 120,000 man shifts were lost in such confrontations. Conflicts between different groups of workers along ethnic lines also multiplied.

Fearing victimization, workers refused to elect representatives to discuss issues with management. Management-initiated consultative committees failed dismally. Fixed wage rates across the industry had for years persuaded workers that wage struggles were pointless. Wage raises after 1974 were not granted evenly across the different mining houses, however, and now wages were drawn into contention. In 1982 when Consolidated Goldfields (the most conservative mining house) granted lower increases than the other companies, their mines exploded into riot and mayhem.

As for the old rural integrity, it gradually disappeared along with the traditional workers whose commitment to rural homestead agriculture had made it possible. Within five years, most mine workers were completely dependent on wages and had little understanding of old conceptions of manly dignity rooted in rural commitments. In the disorder that ensued in the mines, the union promised a new integrity based on adamant confrontation with white racism and management power. Local managements fought back, often with the support of ethnic power holders entrenched in the compound system and black team leaders who supervised underground work.

Informal networks under the old compound system were room-based. Because housing was "tribally" organized, ethnicity tended to predominate as a basis for collective action. Even within ethnic groups, however, there were divisions between educated and more traditional persons—and especially between clerks and underground workers. The union challenged all those divisions. Charles Mapeshoane, who was a shaft steward at Vaal Reefs #4, remembered that

> in the mines before the coming of the union, people [from Lesotho] tended to congregate depending on their classes—educated, traditional, etc.—although they all spoke Sesotho. But when the union came then people realized that now you have to move from up or down, meet a person where he is. Those who did not understand, also preferred to remain there on top, others preferred to remain on the bottom. The union was there to point out, to persuade people to understand that regardless of your education, you are a human being and belong to the human being class. You are the same as other people. You shouldn't regard yourself as the best person. . . . I was very careful to talk to those who respected themselves and also respected others and taught the workers respect.

The union brought a new democratic order to the decay that had set into the old authoritarian management system. According to Mapeshoane, the new norms of respect for proper procedure "did not start from the top, but grew out of discussions from below and were taken to management for discussion." Inevitably some of the representatives of the old order felt threatened. Predictably, they fell back on the ethnic bases that had served them so well in the past.

My work on the 1946 mine strike (Moodie 1986) and Roger Gould's (1991) account of the Paris Commune both make the point that informal

networks in those cases supported successful mobilization. In the South
African mines after 1982, however, NUM shaft stewards like Mapeshoane
tapped into the element of integrity in the old common sense (torn from its
precapitalist roots by the process of proletarianization) in ways that cut across
preexisting ethnic networks. Indeed, enemies of the union mobilized ethnic
solidarities (now largely based in local systems of seniority in the mine rather
than rural proprietorship) to attack it (Moodie 1994: 201–10, 283–302), and
union-bashing took on a violent and ethnic face. Union supporters turned to
violence on occasion as well. However, commitment to the union on the part
of proletarianized workers usually outweighed commitment to ethnicity.
Why? And why such firm support from relatively uneducated manual workers for whom ethnicity had been an organizing principle for many years?
Proletarianization provides part of the answer, obviously, but so does a new
fabric of common sense, which was knit together by grassroots union leaders, developing traditional ideas of justice and integrity in new oppositional
directions.

Perhaps the theme that runs most clearly through testimony from union
members themselves is Charles Mapeshoane's stress on human dignity in the
face of racist and authoritarian management. Marcel Golding, NUM assistant general secretary, put it well when he told me: "The entire tenor was
about the restoration of dignity, the rights of workers, how the mining industry had degraded people and the degradation was precisely one of the
leading causes of violence. . . . That message was activated in what the workers
were doing on the ground." The union was fighting to change the whole
authoritarian and racist system, to establish a new nonracial and democratic
order. Union members engaged in boycotts, sit-downs, marches. They met
and debated issues. They negotiated with management and confronted racist
remarks and actions that their predecessors had tolerated for generations from
white supervisors underground. They kept insisting on being treated with
respect by management and their own union officials as well. "Sometimes
workers couldn't speak English," remembered Golding, "but they were very
articulate in knowing what they wanted and they were very suspicious. Thus,
until you proved yourself you were not accepted. There was always a task to
prove that we were the right organization, we were honest, we were doing
the right things, etc."

At the insistence of local leaders, the union activated the resentment that
had always simmered beneath the terms of the implicit contract and confronted white supervisors and managers with counterhegemonic demands.
Predictably, such demands for respect were interpreted by managers as in-
subordination. And, indeed, old hierarchical forms of management really were
at risk. Workers wanted more say in safety issues, they wanted better wages,
and they expected due process in dismissal cases. In the mines, such demands

were revolutionary. Union shaft stewards developed new practices and a repertoire of collective actions that confronted the commonsense racist ways of
doing things that had been built into the old social order. They promised a
democratic alternative to the management despotism of the old system and
the chaos of the 1970s.

Many mine managers thought that the very basis of their authority was at
stake and fought back vigorously. They won some battles, but their contemp-
tuous dismissal of union demands lost the respect of workers. As Golding
said: "Sometimes these problems were very minor problems. If management
had been more astute and packaged things better, consulted, these things
would never have happened. But because of their arrogance and their refusal
to be sensitive we were able to capitalize on those issues."

As we have seen, application of the new labor law with its strictures against
unfair dismissals was absolutely fundamental. Perhaps as important, however, were the union's efforts to channel resistance into a counterhegemonic
and transethnic movement. Marcel Golding insisted that the union, too, had
to learn to respect the common sense of its own members to effectively channel collective action."

> You never go and tell workers anything. You first go and you listen,
> and then you say, "What specifically is the problem?" Having
> understood that, you say, "Where do you want to go?" Then go to
> management. Then come back and report. But never, ever, just take
> the liberty of deciding for them. They must decide what to do on
> their own and I think that was one of the good things we learned.
> That mine workers were not fools. They knew what they wanted
> despite the levels of education. They were very very determined. At
> the same time very reasonable and conservative people.

Many of the managers to whom I have spoken expressed intense frustration with NUM representatives' insistence on what they called "accountability" or "getting a mandate from the workers." After hours of negotiation
with union representatives, an agreement would be struck. At that point,
the union people would say, "We must go back to the workers." If workers repudiated the agreement, the negotiations moved back to square one.
Of course, managers believed that this was a ploy for union officials to
wriggle out of hard-wrought compromises—and to some extent it could be—
but almost all the shaft stewards and union officials to whom I spoke agreed
with Golding that workers themselves must decide what to do. Ordinary
workers had minds of their own—and their minds were informed by a common sense deeply oppositional to the authoritarian hierarchies that had set
the terms of the old system.

The union reflected, it did not merely control, the new moral order on the mines. The new common sense grew out of new material conditions, but it also grew out of different conceptions of dignity and respect and a power struggle for control of the mine and the compound. The contest was never merely over values or material conditions but intertwined both of them. Union struggles sought to institutionalize a new social order based in transethnic collective identities rooted in counterhegemonic beliefs and practices, at the same time as they sought to improve material conditions for a new, totally wage-dependent generation of workers. Whereas the language of "cultural framing" might view self-respect as a new ideology, it would overlook the fact that the new common sense was rooted in recent proletarianization as well. Moreover, it would completely fail to capture the personal commitment evoked by common sense. Conceptions of culture as a frame or toolbox fail to capture the manner in which common sense is constitutive of practices and thus is modified, even as it is used in particular political and material situations. Common sense consists of a combination of material conditions, practices, and values that are never entirely separable because they modify one another in their reciprocal relation.

Organization and Mobilization

Meanings and feelings, however powerful and deep-rooted in powers and practices, obviously do not mobilize people on their own. Organization is essential, and resistance to management injustices in the South African gold mines took place for many decades before the founding of the National Union of Mineworkers. Records of such action go back at least to 1914 (Moodie 1994: 90). Resistance was organized directly from informal (usually room-based and ethnic) social networks. Thousands of workers would gather outside the mine manager's house, armed with staves, usually after work, and shout their demands. Such "mob action" might lead to the calling of the South African police, but management always paid careful attention to demands and failed to redress them at their peril (Moodie 1994: 80–106). Such events were not unorganized or spontaneous mass collective action but rather drew on informal organization. Preexisting social networks mediated what Barrington Moore (1978) has called "moral outrage" against perceived injustices. In the face of paternalist management despotism, workers successfully appealed to an implicit contract that established an unequal equilibrium of consent. This implicit contract was always subject to collective protest on particular issues and modification in the course of such struggles.

What is fascinating from the point of view of resource mobilization theory, however, is that such collective protests were never "organized" in any formal sense. They dared not be. Indeed, such resistance remained informal precisely in order to stand up to management tactics of victimization. For example, between 1943 and 1950, an African Mine Workers' Union was formed on the Witwatersrand. In 1946, it drew on the already existing informal networks to bring out more than 70,000 black miners on strike for higher wages. The South African police literally whipped the strikers back to work (Moodie 1986). For thirty-five years thereafter, workers returned to informal methods of organizing collective action around local issues, and management was not challenged on wage rates again.

Although submerged networks never constituted formal movements, management and police records (and the testimony of retired workers themselves) demonstrate their formidable power as forces of resistance. Eric Hobsbawm, George Rudé, E. P. Thompson, and other analysts of seventeenth- and eighteenth-century English and French crowd behavior made this point long ago, and Tilly's original contributions to resource mobilization theory never made the mistake of limiting all organization to formal organizations. However, many debates about organization in social movement analysis seem to miss this important distinction. Much American work tends to model social movements on social movement organizations, which then become reified as independent actors in resistance or social change.

For many years, Piven and Cloward (1998) have argued that, at least in the United States, community organizing has shown little success in changing economic inequities. Instead, it is mass unrest that has brought poor people in the United States their most significant gains. Indeed, they say, community organizations have thrived only by piggybacking on mass movements, selling themselves to the elite as representatives of poor people and thus capable of cooling them down. Students of social movements, many of them with organizational experience themselves, are understandably offended by this point of view but have real difficulty refuting it. There is indeed little evidence that economic advances for the poor stem from independent activities of social movement organizations, at least as they are conceived by resource mobilization theorists.

Much as it rightly insists on structural preconditions for American poor people's movements, Piven and Cloward's work does surprisingly little to advance our analytical understanding of how movements of "disruptive dissensus" were actually organized. Both they and their critics implicitly assume that collective action that is not channeled through social movement organizations is not organized. Preempting the notion of "organization" for "social movement organizations" encourages analysts like Piven and Cloward to speak misleadingly of "unorganized" social movements. Early resistance in the South African mines challenges both Piven and Cloward and their critics. Apparently spontaneous collective action was invariably rooted in informal networks. It is essential to distinguish formal organization from informal networks as avenues for mobilization.[15]

Formal organization in the shape of the NUM did eventually come to the South African mines because changes in labor law made it possible and because, at least in Anglo-American mines, company industrial relations experts believed that negotiation with a representative body was preferable in the long run to increasingly violent mob actions. To understand how the NUM grew so fast in the face of stubborn local management opposition, it is essential to understand networks of recruitment and maintenance structures. Tarrow (1994: 135–36) writes of "mobilizing structures" that link informal networks and formal social movement organizations. While any movement obviously needs to coordinate a leadership cadre with its base, it is never clear from Tarrow's exposition exactly what a mobilizing structure actually is.[16] General causal theory gives us no help in understanding how mobilization works.[17] Historical analysis is asked to provide specificity where the theory has none.

In his chapter on "mobilizing structures," Tarrow (1994) implicitly stresses historical particularities over theoretical generalizations. That does not stop him from trying to generalize, however. His chapter is fascinating as an illustration of how empty the general concept of "mobilizing structures" is in illuminating processes of mobilization. After an interesting historical example, he meanders off into a dichotomy between "hierarchy and disruption" and then concludes that "there is no single model of movement organization." To explain successful social movements, Tarrow says, we must return to exogenous "political opportunities." After flirting with recognition of historical agency, he scurries back to the safety of "political opportunity structures."

What then of the fascinating task of understanding the dialectic of leading and following in all its complexity? G. H. Mead (1932: 38) rightly rejects "the assumption that it is possible to give an exhaustive account of any event that takes place in terms of the conditions of its occurrence." He refers to an "emergent event" as "the occurrence of something which is more than the processes that have led up to it and which . . . adds to later passages a content they would not otherwise have possessed" (23). The peculiarities of the rise of the NUM under the leadership of Cyril Ramaphosa could not have been predicted beforehand, yet in retrospect we do seek to explain them in causal terms.[18] We are speaking here about particular rather than general causes, however.

I take the rise of the NUM after 1982 to be an emergent event. In retrospect, we can see that political opportunities were available. They were made into opportunities, however, by Ramaphosa's organizing strategy, his ability to tap into already existing social networks, and his willingness to commit his organization to the struggle for racial dignity in the mines. None of this was obvious when he established the union in 1982. He made no reference to race, focusing on safety and dismissals, when I spoke to him in 1984.[19] All levels of management and, indeed, Ramaphosa himself expected it would take many years to get the union properly started.

As we have seen, before 1982, mobilization in the mines had always taken place without formal structures. From the outset, however, Ramaphosa, a lawyer, constituted the NUM as a formal legal entity. Constitutions do not, of course, constitute movements—or even organizations. The meteoric growth of the NUM can be explained only by recognizing the importance for recruitment and leadership of prior political traditions and networks in the mines. To understand Ramaphosa's success in getting the NUM off the ground (besides his own phenomenal hard work), one has to recall that, in addition to being a resource for rural homestead proprietors seeking to keep their traditions alive, the mines had become a political refuge for a more educated stratum of African society. More or less formal networks of these politicized workers were fundamental to the rapid growth of the NUM.

From as far back as the 1960s, African National Congress (ANC) and Pan Africanist Congress (PAC) activists, who did not end up in prison on Robben Island or in exile, sometimes found themselves in clerical positions in the mines. Even more important were young high school graduates, consciences raised in the student movements of the late 1970s, who moved to the mines as an alternative to leaving the country and joining the ANC's liberation army. James Motlatsi, NUM president, summed up how many black student activists ended in on the mines: "You have to understand, after 1976 quite a number of comrades, some ran out of the country, but others ran away from the townships to take employment in the mining industry. Because they had education, they tended to get jobs as senior blacks, as senior positions in the mining industry."

More important in Motlatsi's opinion, however, were political events in Lesotho, which guaranteed that the mines would become strongholds for seasoned politicians from the Basotholand Congress Party (BCP). Qoane Pitso, for instance, had become an opposition member of parliament during the first democratic elections in Lesotho. In 1965, he lost his seat to a cabinet minister. In 1970, he was elected again, but fearing loss of power, Chief Lebua Jonathan aborted the elections and declared a state of emergency. After a spell in prison and a failed BCP rebellion in 1974, Pitso left to work at President Brand mine. When the union arrived, he tried to keep a low profile but inevitably found himself involved at the local level. By that time on the mines, he says:

> There was strong presence of the BCP. Furthermore, from my observation, our political influence, national influence, was very strong. The black people in South Africa had never experienced democracy. People from Lesotho gave them the leadership in the

political field. Few as we are in number, you will find most of us in the key positions in the union. That is because we had had political experience already.

James Motlatsi himself had been a BCP "young lion," deeply involved in opposition to Lebua Jonathan. As he said to me:

> I was a member of the BCP Youth League. . . . I was a young star by [1970]. . . . We tried to really fight against the police—then against the army—until we were defeated and I ran to the mining industry. That's how I joined the mining industry. . . . [When the union came along] BCP had structures already in the mines . . . and it was easy to make [union] members from the BCP because they were already in a political party in a process of struggle.

Unlike the South African activists who had belonged to a number of different political organizations, BCP supporters were already organized. Indeed, Motlatsi's election to be president of the NUM at the first national congress in 1982 testifies to the strength of BCP networks in the early years of the union. Nor was it an accident that the NUM was first recognized at President Brand and Vaal Reefs West where Pitso and Salae, respectively, used BPC structures to recruit members. In the history of the NUM, then, networks of younger workers who were already politicized constituted important structures mobilizing membership for the NUM. Their political experiences and the model of the independent unions struggling in manufacturing industry made up the practical repertoire of the new union.

Many of the professional organizers for the NUM were young well-educated militants from South Africa and Lesotho who had been fired by TEBA, the recruiting arm of the Chamber of Mines, in 1982. In the first year of union organizing, they adopted a strategy of recruiting mine clerks, black personnel staff, and team leaders, many of whom had been BPC or ANC activists with their own submerged networks. As the union grew, however, less educated underground workers like Charles Mapeshoane, inspired by outrage against racial injustice and ethnic divisions, became their best recruits.

One would be mistaken, however, to attribute the success of the union merely to its ideological appeal. From the very beginning, Ramaphosa insisted on building local shaft steward structures in the workplaces. By 1984, most of the shaft stewards were lower ranked workers, many of them illiterate, but they began to take over black supervisors' functions of settling disputes and representing workers at disciplinary hearings. The mediating role of the shaft stewards was essential to the functioning of the union. Golding remembered a fundamental principle for union officials: "Always make sure that the shaft stewards agreed with what you said. You had to win over the shaft stewards before you went to the rank and file. Never go to the rank and file first. First convince the leadership that this is what needs to be done. So, when the leadership goes, they are able to take up the idea with the rank and file." Initiatives went both ways, however. "Never try to stifle what the workers want to do," said Golding:

> [The boycotts and short shifts] were all local initiatives, but under this great thrust—we've got to restore the dignity of miners. . . . All those things about restoring dignity, restoring equality, restoring fairness to people who were being unfairly treated over a century. That message was activated in what workers were doing on the ground. . . . We always said that the workers should be the organizers and that we merely bring specific sorts of expertise to bear and assist in that particular process.

The union's insistence on democratic accountability kept it close to its members. It also obliged workers to accept democratically negotiated agreements. With one or two early exceptions, if managements were willing to negotiate in good faith, the union was able to resolve conflicts. If any one factor can explain the incredibly rapid growth of the union, it is this: black workers all welcomed the establishment of a representative presence to enforce a now more equitable order in the mines. However, this democratic presence did not emerge automatically from the cultural horizon. It was nurtured and fought for by Ramaphosa and his early supporters from the BCP and the ANC in the face of strident management opposition and the impetuousness of several local leaders.

The point is that in the mines the mobilizing structures were made by people whose prior repertoires and appeal to followers rested initially on grounds other than attachment to the union. The intermediaries did not come out of nowhere, and in this case, they appealed to black miners' sense of moral outrage as well as to their stomachs. Leadership was very consultative, and union strategies shifted in response to worker demands. Mobilizing structures vary, but to understand mobilization, one always needs to examine processes of leadership and particular relations between leaders and followers (and among followers) within shifting contexts.

Conclusion

I return to the question I asked at the outset of this chapter. What can social theory do if predictability always stumbles over contingency? Why should we attempt theory at all? Let me conclude with some suggestions about an alternative way of approaching theory. First, theory should be a stimulant to the sociological imagination. We should seek to provide a more insightful interpretation of social events than the average intelligent layperson could manage. Too often, we merely provide a reclassification that makes things less rather than more clear. The best theory points to things to look for, places to start, tendencies, rules of thumb, rather than seeking a causal framework that will be reliably reproduced in reality. Rather than providing endless typologies, neatly arranged in four-by-four or eight-by-eight boxes, we need to look for open-ended starting places from which to examine particular chains of events.

Social theory often revolves around dichotomies: structure versus agency, ideology versus material reality, democracy versus hierarchy. Such dichotomies may be good ways to begin digesting empirical evidence, but analysis needs to go beyond them. Usually, one side gets overemphasized and then later the other is rediscovered with great fanfare. This process can recur too many times without generating any progress. We need to grasp both sides of our dichotomies and somehow transcend them. This seems to me the great strength of "common sense practices" as an analytical category. "Dignity" in particular can exist only as it is sustained materially in the way people interact.

Demanding dignity or maintaining integrity recurs again and again in the testimony of South African gold miners. Can one find similar motivations in other social movements? Of course, dignity means different things to different individuals in different circumstances. Seeking it may have unintended consequences for others. The very notion of dignity might be deeply problematic in some contexts. It often implies hierarchy and exclusion. Nonetheless, looking closely at struggles for dignity might bring us close to the pulse of many social movements.[20] It will not translate into a causal model, but it might be an interesting concept with which to interrogate social reality.

Given that sociology can produce only a tentative rule of thumb for causality, always looking backward because there is such unpredictability about emergence, we should aim to read history more imaginatively. We can point to interesting patterns. I advocate here two traditions in sociology. One, stemming from Simmel (1980), compares social phenomena across time and places, as, for instance, greedy organizations, or total institutions, or friendship, or what have you. At his best, Tarrow (1994) works in this tradition. The other tradition, stemming from Weber, looks back along causal chains and accidental conjunctions to divine the causal derivation of Mead's "emergent events" and Weber's (1949) "historical individuals." Weber suggests that we need to be aware always of what did not happen, paths not taken, unrealized possibilities, if we are to grasp the contingent origins of the social phenomena we seek to understand. We should study social movements not to arrive at universal generalizations but to contribute to effective history by sharing practical lessons, to enable actors better to set long-term goals for action, to alert them to successful strategies and unintended consequences, and to help them grapple with unexpected contingencies.

NOTES

This chapter was written with the assistance of a grant from the United States Institute of Peace. It has benefited greatly from the advice of the editors of this volume, especially Nancy Whittier. I must also acknowledge the editorial assistance of Benjamin Aldrich-Moodie who kept encouraging me to deepen and tighten my argument long after I thought I was done. A grant from the John D. and Catherine T. MacArthur Foundation made possible my interviews with Charles Mapeshoane and other union leaders and members cited.

1. Webster (1988) has developed the conception of "social movement" unions to describe trade unions that bridge the distinction between interest groups and social movements, with deeply committed members seeking both limited economic goals and wider political change. Such unions are often characterized by rather heterogeneous organizational components.

2. It is surely no accident that when pressed to specify suggestions for the success of movements, McAdam, McCarthy, and Zald (1996) are able to cite only three: the use of disruptive tactics, single issues rather than multiple goals, and radical flank effects. The first two were initially postulated by Gamson in 1975 (republished in 1990), the latter by Barkan in 1979, and it would not be difficult to mention counter examples for all three of them. I mention this not to "refute" Gamson and Barkan but to highlight the dead end the field has been in for the past twenty-five years. Nor do I particularly wish to single out social movement theory within sociology as such. The problem is more general. In fact, the study of social movements has been one of the most lively sociological fields since the 1970s.

3. Voss (1996) is a good example of this problem.

4. Comaroff and Comaroff (1992: 28–31) make a similar argument.

5. For a brief but superb exposition of this sort of argument, see Hall (1997).

6. I have some problems with Gramsci's elision of common sense and hegemony because this implies that common sense necessarily involves domination of a particular sort. While common sense often is hegemonic in one way or another, the type and manner of domination is a matter of investigation. Gramsci's Marxism enabled him always to measure "common sense" against "good sense." The problem is that what may seem to be "good sense" for Marxists may turn out to be "hegemony" for feminists—and for good reason.

7. The best treatment of emergence as both contingent and determined is still George Herbert Mead's difficult, but endlessly suggestive, set of lectures, *The*

Philosophy of the Present (1932). For those acquainted with Weber's methodological writings, I am suggesting here that social movements need to be treated as "historical individuals." See Weber's (1949) brilliant critique of Eduard Mayer's notion of causality in his third chapter.

8. Indeed, as Doug McAdam (1982) and Aldon Morris (1984) pointed out years ago for the American South.

9. It is difficult to think of any actual situation in which elites are not divided in some way or another.

10. This, it seems to me, is the import of Gamson and Meyer's (1996) essay, although they continue to pay lip service to the fundamentally contradictory and teleological notion of "political opportunity structure."

11. This I take to be the argument of Fantasia (1988), in a book that has been undeservedly ignored in contemporary social movement writing, precisely, perhaps, because it does not fit unilateral causal logic.

12. Perhaps the most thoughtful attempt to deal with this issue from within resource mobilization theory is Tarrow (1992), although his discussion points up the profoundly manipulative nature of "framing" as used in social movement theory.

13. In fact, of course, Gramsci, as a Marxist, tended to highlight the material as the basis of "good sense," but this very formulation points up the constitutive function of ideas in material practices.

14. Murray (1987) gives the best account of South African rural resettlement slums.

15. To his credit, Sidney Tarrow (1994: 135–36) recognizes the need to do this, as indeed do many analyses of the American women's movement. See, for example, Taylor and Whittier (1992) and Mueller (1994).

16. McCarthy (1996), who writes of "movement-mobilizing structures" as "nested" anywhere in society, is not much more help.

17. Categorical analyses of mobilizing structures (Kriesi 1996; Rucht 1996) provide typologies with little or no explanatory power for understanding the rise of actual movements. Elaborate taxonomies are futile at best and obfuscating at worst.

18. This is why Aldon Morris's account of the civil rights movement (1984) is such superb sociology as well as pathbreaking history.

19. This despite the fact that he was acquainted with a study I had conducted for Anglo-American in 1975, which did stress race as an important issue in the apartheid work place.

20. This I take to be the core argument of Axel Honneth (1996).

Multiple Mediations: The State and the Women's Movements in India

MANISHA DESAI

Should the approach of the women's organisations be one of cooperation with the state or confrontation with the State. In fact is such a distinction meaningful? ... It would be useful to distinguish between our overall perspective and understanding of the nature of the State, and the day-to-day tactics we adopt in dealing with it. We recognise that at the basic level confrontation with the State is inevitable.
—Perspectives for the Autonomous Women's Movement
in India: 23–26 December, 1985

Women within state bodies and programmes, concerned academics and activists would like to take advantage of the State's structural ambiguity and amorphousness, of the conflicting interests of the dominant groups within it and the rising consciousness regarding women's oppression. These often give women the possibility of the creation of some space for their own issues and strategies. It also carries the struggle against patriarchy into the State, where it is so insidiously installed and powerfully supported by its entire machinery. Many activists choose to selectively strategise, confront and cooperate according to the issue.
—India Association of Women's Studies, The State
and the Women's Movement in India: A Report

These quotations demonstrate the ambivalent and complex strategy of working in and against the state articulated by the contemporary women's movements[1] in India. In this chapter, I explicate this strategy in three different phases of the contemporary movement and show how the strategy has shifted

66

in keeping with the changing focus of the postcolonial Indian state. Each phase has been influenced by the earlier phase, and the latter two coexist as distinct strands, even as they interact with each other (Desai 2001).

In the first, *affiliated* phase of the movement, primarily urban and rural students and some Left and Gandhian parties organized nonparty political formations or the Indian new Left to confront the development state. The nonparty political formations were a response to the failure of the state and political parties in reducing poverty in independent India (e.g., Omvedt 1993). Women demanded land reform, minimum wages for agricultural work, and microcredit for self-employment from local bureaucracies.

In the second, *autonomous* phase, when issues of violence against women dominated the movement and the Indian state because of international commitments on women's issues, the movement emphasized the patriarchal nature of the state and confronted national and state law-making and law-enforcing bodies as perpetrators of violence against women. Through protests and working with state and national commissions, a series of legal reforms was achieved, including amendments in rape and dowry laws and banning amniocentesis for the purpose of sex selection. But, most important, the autonomous women's movement, in conjunction with the International Women's Decade sponsored by the United Nations (UN), ensured that the state recognized the subordinate status of women and gave women's issues much needed visibility.

Finally, in the third, *sustainable development* phase of the movement, as state policies focused on integrating India into the global economy, the resultant increase in poverty and marginalization of poor peasants and workers turned the movement to criticizing structural adjustment policies, a key element of what Sassen (1995) calls the reconfigured global state, and at the same time to working in partnership with the state to empower women.

I argue that this wide-ranging and changing relationship with the state is a result of the changing focus of the postcolonial state, partly in response to the women's movement and to international factors. Thus, as Jenkins and Klandermans (1995) noted, the state is simultaneously the target, sponsor, and antagonist for social movements.

Confronting the Development State

Unlike the welfare state in the West, the postcolonial Indian state defined itself as the major catalyst of change, creating state institutions to address issues of inequality. This was in keeping with the modernization assumptions of the newly emerging field of international development (e.g., Escobar 1995, McMichael 2000). Thus, in addition to initiating public sector projects to enable the economy to "take off," a package of land reform, integrated rural development, community development, and antipoverty programs formed the basis of a development state with accompanying bureaucracy at the state, district, block, and village levels. At independence, this central role of the state in eliminating poverty enjoyed universal support from politicians, industrialists, technologists, and labor leaders (Parikh 1999).

As several analysts (e.g., Frankel 1977; Kohli 1990; Kothari 1970) have observed, the Indian political elite were unusually innovative in charting such a role for the state. Hence, after two decades of state activism, when state policies geared toward capital-intensive industrialization and modernizing agriculture increased poverty among the urban and rural poor, some political actors believed they had a state mandate to highlight the contradiction between state policies and practice and to demand accountability. Such structural contradictions were recognized and articulated by a "new social class"[2] of young, educated, urban and rural men and women, influenced by radicalized factions of the left and Gandhian movements. Thus, as Moodie argues in this volume, the structure of political opportunities is not a static given but a result of actors' dynamic interpretation and articulation.

The new actors organized[3] the impoverished and alienated urban and rural people. Their focus, influenced by the *sarvodaya* (well-being of all) movement (an offshoot of the Gandhian movement), was "total revolution," involving reexamination of not only unjust economic relationships but also unequal social relationships between the upper and lower castes, as well as between men and women. Workers, peasants, tribals, and students, both men and women, organized mass protests demanding that the state live up to its promise of eliminating poverty. In this period of popular unrest, the initial phase of the women's movement, comprised of poor urban and rural women organized by middle-class women, emerged around issues of survival and gender inequality in affiliation with tribal movements and movements of peasants and workers.

The focus of the women's movement, like that of most other movements, was a challenge to the development plans of the state, which had abandoned the agrarian self-sufficiency vision of Gandhi and worked to implement Nehru's vision of rapid industrialization and modernization. Most of the affiliated women's movement criticized how the development plan had omitted women and mobilized women to access state resources, primarily in the form of employment guarantee schemes (EGS), credits for cooperatives, and land reform efforts. I provide an example to illustrate this interaction with the state.

The Chhatra Yuva Sangharsh Vahini (CYSV, or Student and Youth Struggle Vehicle) emerged in Bihar, one of the poorest states in India, in 1975. It aimed to organize the *antimjan* (the lowest of the low) as *lok shakti* (people's power) against *raj shakti* (state power) (Kelkar and Gala 1990). Composed of the new class of urban and rural students and political leaders disaffected by the ruling parties, CYSV had a number of full-time women activists who launched women's isues in the movement, such as women's rights to land and other productive resources, as well as interpersonal relationships between men and women and the institution of marriage.

I will focus on the CYSV struggle to gain women access to land in Bodh Gaya, home to many Buddhist and Hindu monastaries, temples, and institutions. The largest landowner in the area is a Hindu *math* (religious institution), which was given land rights during the Moghul and British rules. The math's estate is spread over a thousand villages covering a dozen districts. Its vast lands are administered through *kacheries* (administrative/judicial offices). The chief administrative officer of the math is also a member of the ruling Congress party; hence, the religious institution has strong political support. The math exploits both the women's labor, as poorly paid agricultural workers, and their bodies, through a system of religious concubinage (Kelkar and Gala 1990).

In response to protests all over the country, Prime Minister Indira Gandhi declared a state of emergency in June 1975 and announced several policies to address the worsening poverty of the urban and rural "masses." Three important policies enabled the activists to organize the poor and get them access to state resources. The Land Ceiling Act put a limit on how much land an individual could own and mandated the redistribution of excess land to the rural poor. A new policy mandated that the newly nationalized banks provide interest-free loans to the urban poor to start small enterprises. Finally, the EGS mandated that when fifty people approached the local state bureaucracy for work, the state was responsible for providing them employment at minimum wages.

In 1978, following these new policies, CYSV organized protests against the concentration of land by the math. A popular slogan at the demonstrations was *jo zamin ko boye jote, who zameen ka malik hoi* (those who sow and plow the land are the owners of land). In addition to the protests and strikes by the agricultural laborers, CYSV activists, with the help of lawyers, filed court cases demanding land redistribution according to state and national law. Most important, activists held meetings in every village to discuss the state's commitment to the poor and the land ceiling act, as well as the need for people to organize and act collectively. Many urban activists, unused to the rural life, walked miles and lived with the villagers in their huts to reach all the villagers and ensure their participation in the movement. Given the power of the math, the movement members faced resistance from the local bureaucrats, as well as police brutality. Initially, the movement had prepared entitlement papers only in the name of the male head of household, with widowed heads of households the only exception.

At a village meeting, however, some women peasants demanded that land be given to them as well. They argued that, because men often migrate to the urban areas, women work the land. Rural women also claimed that if land was in their names, the earnings or loan money would not be spent on drink or otherwise frittered away (Kelkar and Gala 1990). The rural women convinced the movement to fight for land in the name of men *and* women. There was much resistance from both men in the villages and the local bureaucrats. The latter agreed to give joint titles for married couples but were reluctant to give land to single women.

Ultimately, of 1,100 acres distributed to the poor peasants and agricultural laborers, only 100 acres were distributed in the name of women. Since this initial land distribution in 1981, the movement has continued to demand land for women in the subsequent land reform efforts of the state. Women have succeeded in gaining joint titles, as the national government has made that a requirement, but land in the name of women alone is still not a norm. But, as activists report a decade later, the women who did get title to land assert "we had tongues but could not speak, we had feet but could not walk. Now that we have land, we have the strength to speak and walk" (Kelkar and Gala 1990: 103).

Other elements of the women's movement used different state policies to gain access to resources. For example, Shramik Stree Sangathana (Toiling Women's Union), one of the most militant tribal women's movement groups in Maharashtra, emerged during a period of drought and high unemployment among agricultural workers and mobilized hundreds of women to take over local development offices until more work projects were sanctioned for them. They also demanded—and won—equal minimum wages for men and women and child care. In addition to these mass mobilizations, the activists also held ongoing village-based *shibirs* (camps) that served as consciousness-raising meetings to discuss tribal women's issues.

Self-Employed Women's Association (SEWA), an organization of unemployed and underemployed urban poor women in Ahmedabad, Gujarat, successfully registered these informal workers as union members and sought government funding to set up the first bank for poor women in the country. The bank provided small loans ("microcredit") to otherwise credit-unworthy poor women to start cooperatives and for other self-employment opportunities. In addition to the union and the cooperatives, SEWA has ongoing meetings of poor women to ensure their active participation in issues that affect their daily lives, such as gender, caste, and class discrimination. And SEWA is one of the few mass women's organizations that includes both Hindu and Muslim members; as such, it has played an important role in communal harmony during the Hindu/Muslim riots that have been a regular feature in Ahmedabad.

In this phase, the women's movements worked in alliance with other movements to enable poor women not only to gain access to state resources but also to empower them through active participation in the process of working with the state. This relationship, between the state and social movements, has been widely documented in the literature (e.g., Ferree and Martin 1995).

Working in and against the Patriarchal State

In the process of organizing poor, militant women, middle-class activists discovered that, despite the movement's explicit commitments to women, women's issues took a backseat to class issues in the larger social justice movement and were relegated to women activists. This subordination received further momentum when the Indian government published *Towards Equality* in 1974. This report on the status of women in India was prepared for the International Women's Year World Conference in Mexico City sponsored by the United Nations the following year. It documented the deteriorating status of women in all sectors since independence. The most shocking indicator was the sex ratio of the population. India was one of only three countries in the world where there were more men than women. *Towards Equality* galvanized activists, who began to meet in small groups to discuss the report in the context of the subordination of women's issues in movements, to read feminist literature, and to discuss the relevance of Western feminist literature to Indian realities. In 1978 about forty such small groups from around the country came together in Bombay to organize an "autonomous" movement for women and by women, in which women's issues would not be subordinated to any party or organization.

The experience of subordination in the other social movements, and the middle-class, professional, and primarily urban bias of the autonomous movement, resulted in a shift away from grassroots activism on survival issues toward public consciousness-raising campaigns (through slide shows, poster exhibitions, and street theater) and an active engagement with the state on issues of violence against women. This relationship with the state included demonstrating and protesting the patriarchal nature and actions of the state and working with state structures at different levels to influence state policy and legislation. This dual strategy of working in and against the state is evident in most women's movements around the world (e.g., Basu 1995).

These ruminations led to more visible mobilization in the late 1970s, after the government lifted the state of national emergency, when issues of police brutality and dowry deaths emerged. The autonomous movement's first national campaign was organized in 1980, around the case of a girl who was

raped while in police custody. New groups formed across the nation in response to this incident, including the Forum Against Rape in Bombay, Saheli
in New Delhi, Vimochana in Bangalore, and Chingari in Ahmedabad. Many
of these groups—small, informally structured, based on collective, participatory decision making—included activists from the earlier affiliated movement phase, as well as middle-class professional women, academics, and
women from Left parties.

The anti-rape campaign began when four law professors from the University of Delhi came across the 1977 Supreme Court judgment in a rape case
that had first come to trial in 1972. "Mathura," a tribal girl of fourteen, had
been raped by two policemen while in their custody. After initial convictions
in the lower courts, the policemen were acquitted by the Supreme Court on
the grounds that Mathura was not physically coerced, as evidenced by the
lack of bruises on her body and by the fact that she had a history of sexual
activity. The professors were so outraged by the blatant injustice of this case
that they wrote an open letter to the Supreme Court calling for reopening the
case immediately and sent copies of this letter to progressive activist groups
throughout the country. Many of the autonomous groups first came together
to discuss this letter.

The autonomous groups gathered signatures to pressure the Supreme Court
to reopen the case. On March 8, 1980, women's groups marched in protest
against the judgment in fifteen major cities in the country (Gandhi and Shah
1992; Kumar 1993). Civil liberties groups, bar associations, and other political and press organizations supported the effort. Print and television media gave
extensive coverage to the protests (many of the journalists were young women
who were part of the autonomous groups). On March 17, women's groups
in Delhi held protests outside the Supreme Court, as signatures arrived from
all across the country calling for a review of the case. When the Supreme Court
rejected the petitions, finding that the women's groups lacked "locus standi"
to file them, lawyers in several groups turned to a strategy of legal reform.

To discuss the shift to the reform strategy, the Forum Against Oppression
of Women in Bombay called a national conference on "Perspectives for the
Autonomous Women's Movement in India." Thirty-two groups from all over
India participated. For three days, women discussed topics such as the rape
campaign, the role of the state in women's oppression, autonomy of the
women's movement, and movement strategies of "case work" versus consciousness raising (Report of the National Conference 1980). These conferences have become an important venue for the articulation of theoretical
positions by the autonomous movement. The relationship with the state received major attention at this first conference, given the context of the rape
campaign. Most of the discussion in the conference report highlights how a
patriarchal state oppresses women through its definition of women as wives

and mothers, by excluding women from development programs, and by discrimination through "personal laws." Although these women's groups agreed that the patriarchal state reproduces women's oppression, they also recognized they had to work with the police, the courts, and other state bureaucracies to enable women in their struggle against violence and injustice in the wider society.

This articulation of the state-movement relationship by the autonomous movement parallels the concerns of Western feminist theories of the state at that time. As Borchorst (1999) notes, the project of building a feminist theory of the state was undertaken by Marxist feminists in Britain and the United States in the late 1970s and early 1980s. The emphasis in this phase of theory building was on the ways in which the state perpetuates women's subordinate positions in the home and family by defining them as wife and mothers, even when they participate in the paid workforce. Eisenstein (1983) and Hartmann (1981) both focused on how capitalism and patriarchy combined to reproduce a dual system of women's oppression. Although their views were not unchallenged, in this first wave of feminist state theories, scholars focused on the general patriarchal nature of the state rather than on specific policies or particular institutions. Universal theories were formulated that did not recognize the differences in the type of state even in the West (e.g., liberal versus social democratic), much less the postcolonial states in the Third World. Indian activists, while aware of and influenced by this debate in the West, consciously foregrounded the Indian reality. Thus, whereas discussions in autonomous groups reflect the state's patriarchal and repressive nature, activists clearly differentiated between a general theory of the state and the daily necessity to work with state bodies, particularly in their focus on violence against women.

At the end of the first conference, the groups agreed to seek changes in rape law at the national level, and, at the local level, to help women who were raped and faced other forms of violence with legal, medical, and emotional support through women's centers. To start seeking changes in the national law, lawyers from different groups began to circulate texts of recommendations. Activists also wrote articles in local newspapers and magazines and made rape and violence against women important issues of public discourse. In response, women members of parliament crossed party lines to support the demands of the autonomous groups to amend the existing rape laws. The government established a commission on rape to examine the existing rape laws and make amendments and gave autonomous groups an advisory role. As soon as the commission was appointed, the lawyers consulted through informal networks to work out their recommendations.

Contrary to activist expectations, the commission was sensitive to the issues raised by the autonomous groups, sought the movement's active participation, and completed its report in record time, but parliament tabled the recommendations for several months. When women's groups protested the delay, a watered-down version of the bill recommended by the commission was passed. As the experience of "femocrats" in other countries has shown, when activists are not part of the state bureaucracy, they cannot sustain their influence (Stetson and Mazur 1995). Indian feminists worked from outside the system, using their access to the state commission and sympathetic women bureaucrats and party members, but enjoyed only limited influence. As Stetson and Mazur's comparative study of wealthy countries shows, policies and structural reforms that ensure women's equality take place only when certain conditions are satisfied: when the state is defined as a site for social justice, when the state has the structural capacity to implement and institutionalize reforms, and when a wide range of feminist organizations press demands, both inside and outside formal political institutions. It would be another decade before Indian feminists began to consider working within the political system.

Even though the autonomous groups were disappointed with the outcome of the bill, they sought other levels of influence within the state. After the national bill passed, they worked at the state level to introduce training for police officers and court officials who deal with violence against women. In several states, activists succeeded in establishing women's cells in the local police departments and courts, in working with authorities in addressing women's perspectives on violence, and in ensuring that their legal, economic, and social interests were protected.

This dual engagement with the state informed the autonomous movement's other campaigns against dowry deaths, sex-selective abortions, and wife battery and led to legal and policy changes, in addition to the major achievement of making such violence a public issue. Legal changes included revised rape laws, dowry, laws prohibitions against *sati* (a widow's ritual self-immolation on her husband's funeral pyre), a new national law that investigates as murder any death of a married woman within the first seven years of marriage, and a law in Maharashtra that bans the use of amniocentesis for sex-selective abortions. Policy changes included new national and state programs and resources for addressing violence, creation of a ministry of women and child welfare, and creation of women's support groups within the criminal justice system to support abused women.

This initially successful relationship of the autonomous women's movements with the state is partly a result of the international focus on women's issues resulting from the United Nations' declaration of 1975–1985 as the International Women's Decade. As a member country, India was required to report its efforts in working toward women's equality and to create what the UN called "national policy machinery for the advancement of women."

Women's policy machinery refers to any structure established by the government to address the betterment of women's status in their society. The Indian government had made international commitments, and the easiest way to honor them—without undertaking structural transformation—was through legal reform and committing resources to a limited number of programs. The limits of the state's commitment was demonstrated when gains of the autonomous movement in the early 1980s were challenged in the mid-1980s by Hindu and Muslim fundamentalists, labeling activists "pro-Western imperialists" who threatened Indian culture.

Among the major setbacks for the autonomous women's movements in the mid-1980s was the passage of the Protection of Muslim Women's Bill in 1986. In 1985, the Supreme Court of India granted alimony to Shah Bano, a Muslim woman, overriding Muslim laws, which do not provide for alimony, in favor of secular penal laws. Her husband protested the decision, arguing no such payment was required under Muslim personal law. Muslim fundamentalist groups also protested the Supreme Court judgment as an interference in their religious matters. To appease the fundamentalists, Prime Minister Rajiv Gandhi introduced a bill in parliament that would exempt Muslim women from India's civil laws. Autonomous feminist groups organized against the bill but could not garner enough support to defeat it. Rajiv Gandhi's actions were a response to the consolidation of caste-based regional parties and the declining power of the Congress party (Yadav 1999). This period also saw the emergence of Hindu nationalism and its crystallization as a national political party with a conservative focus on women's rights (Sarkar and Butalia 1995).

Another major setback was the lack of a state response to the sati of an eighteen-year-old woman in Rajasthan state in 1987. Roop Kanwar's husband was a college graduate and her in-laws were urban, educated, and active in local politics. Yet when her husband died unexpectedly after a short illness, her in-laws coerced Roop Kanwar into becoming a sati. Although she tried to run away, ultimately she committed ritual "suicide," as villagers from miles away came to observe; police claimed no knowledge of the event and stood by as it occurred. There were protests both by anti-sati groups (mostly women's and other progressive movements) and pro-sati groups (primarily Rajasthani politicians and some Hindu fundamentalist groups), who argued that sati was their cultural/religious heritage and "right." Despite several cases against the family, they remain free and have not been convicted.

Thus, when there is a clash between entrenched political interests and women's interests, the latter are defined as issues of tradition and culture that cannot be changed but have to be honored. The cultural card has been increasingly played by governments and fundamentalist groups around the world as women's issues are being defined as universal human rights by women's movements (Desai 1996). Even as women depend on the state to enforce their interests in the face of religious traditions, political leaders need to maintain the support of organized religious groups.

Despite such setbacks, autonomous groups continue to emerge and grow and provide real services to women and, more important, an alternative discourse on women in India. Many of the groups continue to meet every three years in the national conference to discuss current issues and plan action across the country. At the same time, most autonomous groups do not work with poor women's survival issues. Since the 1990s, however, autonomous groups have become active in the international women's movement, following the world conferences organized by the UN, and are networked with groups in the North and South. As a result, activists can now use international agreements to hold the state accountable at home for women's economic and social rights. Given India's interests in participating in global trade, such efforts are difficult to ignore.

Engaging the "Global" State

India began to liberalize its economy in the late 1980s in an effort to merge into the global economy. Structural adjustment policies,[4] mandated by the World Bank and IMF for global players, resulted in increased poverty and marginalization of the urban and rural poor, as well as the emergence of several new grassroots women's movements to address survival issues. The third, *sustainable development* phase of the contemporary movement took the feminist insights of small, urban, autonomous groups to mass-based urban and rural women and applied them to issues of livelihood through sustainable development (Datar 1998; Omvedt 1993). Some of the major women's movements of this wave are the Society for the Promotion of Area Resources (SPARC), Swayam Shikshan Prayog (SSP; Self-Education Process), Stree Mukti Sangharsh (SMS; women's liberation struggle), and Shetkari Mahilla Aghadi (Farm Women's Front) in Maharashtra; the Coastal Women's Association in Kerala; and Jharkhand Nari Mukti Samiti (Jharkhand Women's Liberation Committee) in Bihar.

Livelihood issues, which combine economic and ecological concerns, are dominant in this phase, with most movement activity directed toward the state's economic and political policies. The major difference between this phase and the first phase of women's activism is that now the state sees women's movements as partners in its efforts, and these groups are involved in implementing some of the policies, rather than just accessing state resources. Most groups exemplify SPARC's belief "in enabling poor communities to gain access to state resources and in the process of bringing together communities

and policy-makers, educating and transforming both the state and women"
(quoted in Purushothaman 1998: 334).

This kind of engagement with state policies is facilitated by the state. Although early feminists in the West criticized the ability of the welfare and the
liberal state to address issues of women's equality, many contemporary feminist scholars have articulated the notion of state feminism (Stetson and Mazur
1995). In the last twenty-five years, Western and Third World states have
attempted to establish government structures, ranging from agencies to departments to ministries for women, to address issues of women's equality.
Many of these efforts were in response to the mandate of the International
Women's Decade, during which most countries signed international decla-
rations calling for women's equality.

In India, for example, the Sixth Five Year Plan (1975–1980) devoted a
whole chapter to women and allocated resources for women's issues more
specifically.[5] In 1989, the Indian government launched Development for
Women and Children in Rural Areas (DWCRA), a far-reaching policy to
support poor, rural women. Also in 1989, five state governments introduced
Mahila Samakhya, or Education for Women's Empowerment. In 1992, several states in India legislated to reserve 33 percent of the seats in village-level
self-governance (*panchayati raj*) for women. There is a bill, currently tabled
in parliament, to do so at the national level.

Following the state's lead, women's movements have worked out various
partnerships with the government. For example, SSP, a decentralized, informal network that works with 10,000 women in 300 villages across seven
districts in Maharashtra state, reached an agreement with the state's rural
development office to implement the DWCRA program in seven districts in
Maharashtra for a pilot project in 1990, but DWCRA was only a starting
point for SSP. Its aim was to get the local women's groups (*mahila mandal*)
to monitor and participate in all basic services and government programs at
the village level.

In fact, DWCRA seemed the most strategic program to work with, as it
was based on providing poor women's groups with funds to start economic
activities and provide training. It also had machinery at the district and local
level that could be readily tapped by the mahila mandals (women's groups)
and women's nongovernment organizations (NGOs). Some NGOS and mahila
mandals submitted several proposals for the program; by 1994, sixty-four
mahila mandals were funded at close to a million rupees for economic activities, which ranged from tailoring to producing files, chalks, or envelopes, to
production of foods and spices, as well as to operating plant nurseries and
tea stalls.

At the state level, through the lobbying efforts of the network, DWCRA
was extended to six more districts, and 300 new women's groups have ac-

cess to government funds each year. In these six districts, government personnel and infrastructure were created to handle program implementation. In response to SSP's lobbying, the state government issued thirty-two new directives to tailor the program more carefully to suit women's local needs, including making literacy part of the training, so women can process their own applications; making the group size requirement of fifteen to twenty more flexible to accommodate smaller and larger groups; and providing child care and traveling stipends.

Through the network's intervention, village women became exposed to the programs, the state machinery, and the process of writing and thinking through proposals. During the pilot period, SSP also undertook political education of village women, so they could understand how the government bureaucracies and banks functioned. Women were actively involved in negotiations with officials at the village, district, and state levels, giving them firsthand experience in political empowerment. As SSP coordinated this program throughout the state, rural women from many different groups were able to take advantage of government resources and learn political lessons as well. In addition, SSP focused on building the capacity of women's collectives, peer learning exchanges, initiation of savings and credit groups, training, establishing linkages, creating information networks, and searching for alternative frameworks for women's economic empowerment and advocacy (Purushothaman 1998: 117).

Furthermore, SSP not only provided employment to women at the local level but also empowered them politically and socially to work together through the state and the local communities to address inequalities more generally. This multipronged strategy illustrates the basic principle that "poor people can and must organise themselves, develop skills, and create sustainable processes and institutions in order to participate in decisions which affect their lives."

In addition to implementing state policies for poor women, women's movement groups from both the autonomous phase and the sustainable development phase are working together to challenge the economic liberalization of the Indian economy at the macro level. In preparation for the Fourth World Conference on Women at Beijing, a nationwide process of meetings among women's groups resulted in a critique of the UN's Draft Platform for Action. Activists

> recognise[d] the structural nature of poverty that affects women,
> economically and socially marginalised people, and indigenous
> communities. The gender subordinating structures that ensure
> women's persistent and growing poverty worldwide are exacerbated
> by current political, macro-economic policies, programmes and

structures. Economic growth not directed toward social development
on a sustainable ecological basis exacerbates both poverty and
environmental degradation. (Krishnaraj 1995: 131)

The women's movement critique of the new economic policy in India
documents the large-scale loss of livelihoods for women around the country,
loss of common property resources, and loss of the meager social supports
for food, health, and education formerly provided by the state. It shows that
women, in particular, are being forced into more and more temporary, low-
paid, and insecure jobs. In the household, women are bearing a greater burden of liberalization by spending more time in procuring food and fuel,
providing care, and spending fewer and fewer resources on themselves.

In addition to this critique, the national committee of women's movement
groups that came together for the Beijing Fourth World Conference also issued an alternative plan of action that announced its goals clearly:

Reject: the theory that the market is the sole arbiter of human
existence.
Assert: the rights of nations and people to choose their own path of
development free from the pressures of imperialist dominated
agencies and financial institutions.
Demand: not structural adjustment but structural transformation.
(Krishnaraj 1995: 123)

The alternative plan demands land rights for women, rights to common
property resources, and also the rights of such basic needs as potable water,
sanitation facilities, housing, clothing, health, and education for all. Following the Beijing conference, women's groups formed the National Alliance of
Women (NAWO) to implement the agenda from Beijing, to keep the pressure on the Indian state to honor its international commitments, and to coordinate the efforts of local grassroots groups and make them an integral part
of the ongoing international process for women's economic and social rights.

Such attempts to work in and against the state are also evident in the
movements' efforts to capitalize on the bill reserving 33 percent of seats in
local government for women. While a few elite women have been engaged in
formal party politics since the establishment of the Indian National Congress
in 1885, under Mahatma Gandhi's leadership, large numbers of women participated in the nationalist movement and made women's enfranchisement
an issue that the nationalist elite had to address. Activism from this group of
women resulted in constitutional equality for women at independence. In the
first election after independence, many women contested, and won, positions
in recognition of their role in the nationalist movement. As the initial enthu-

siasm waned, however, women's political participation deteriorated. Beyond tokenism, no party, including the Left parties, has made any effort to fulfill the constitutional mandate. In the 1996 elections, only thirty-six women were elected to the 545-member parliament.

The autonomous women's movement had shied away from electoral politics to avoid being coopted and to be able to confront the state and party politics on violence against women. Only in the early 1990s, primarily in response to the state's initiatives, but also in response to setbacks experienced by the autonomous movement, did women's movements begin to address political empowerment. Other factors contributing to this shift to working within the political system are economic liberalization and the increasing communalization of politics and social and political life in the country (Desai 1997). At the same time, with the international focus on women's issues, political parties are also taking women's agendas seriously, and activists recognize the opportunity to work both within and outside the system to influence the economic and social rights agenda. At a seminar held in Mumbai in 1996 to discuss women's movements and formal politics, activists noted that it is not enough to have women as tokens in planning commissions or nominated to the upper house of the parliament (Rajya Sabha). Women also need to enter the political arena and ensure the accountability of politicians to the the women's movement.

The most important factor, however, that has led to working for electoral politics is the passing of the 73rd and 74th amendments to the constitution in 1992, resulting in the Panchayati Raj Act (ratified by all states by 1994), which provided for progressive decentralization and devolution of power to village communities. The act defines a three-tier system that, with some variation, includes a village *panchayat* (council), the *panchayat samiti* (council of a cluster of villages), and *zilla parishad* (district council). The most radical aspect of the act was that it reserved 33 percent of seats for women (irrespective of population), 33 percent for scheduled tribes (proportional to population), and 33 percent for scheduled castes (proportional to population). The reservations for the scheduled tribes and castes are time-bound, whereas those for women are not, and women may also contest the nonreserved seats.

This effectively provides for the exercise of decision-making power by an average of 2,250,000 people at the local level, 51,000 at the intermediary level, and 4,750 at the district level. As a third of these seats are reserved for women, there are about 750,000 seats at the village level, 17,000 at the intermediary level, and 1,583 at the district level reserved for women. Further, as the act also ensures that a third of the positions available as chairpersons in all the three tiers be reserved for women; women should head 75,000 village councils, 1,700 intermediary councils, and 158 district councils. In Maharashtra, at least 99,140 women will have decision-making powers (Poonacha 1992: 22).

In light of this enormous potential, women's groups have begun to take electoral politics seriously. Although some women's groups are still opposed to electoral participation, as they see it as another form of co-optation by the state and another means through which class differences will be perpetuated, in general, most agree that "in the wide-canvas of interrelated long and short-term strategies, reservation of electoral seats for women is but a part. It is of importance because it combines possibilities of struggling from within and the provision of services which will strengthen women's struggle for survival" (Gandhi and Shah 1992: 139).

Hence, many women's movements' groups, particularly in the rural areas, have actively begun to mobilize female candidates to stand for election. This is an enormously difficult task. Village women are reluctant to stand for elections as most of them are illiterate, do not know the system, and are pressured by the men in their families and their communities and social norms to stay away from the public arena, defined as a male space. Therefore, women's movements in Maharashtra have coordinated efforts to organize political literacy camps for women. Although women are articulate and express opinions during the camp sessions, outside the camp setting, women are constrained by the heavy work burden, social pressures, and lack of information and knowledge about the political system. But, despite such obstacles, with the support of women's groups, village women have been standing for and winning local elections. In Maharashtra, there are several all-women panchayats.

But standing for elections is only half the battle. As the experiences of many women's groups and several studies show, elected women face enormous difficulties in carrying out their political duties. Male members of the panchayat resist elected women's participation. They hold meetings without them, misinform them, refuse to serve under them, make them sit on the floor instead of a chair, and continue to intimidate them and humiliate them if they insist on participating in the affairs of the panchayat. Often women are fronts for the agendas of their male relatives and come to the meetings only to sign the muster and then leave all official business to the men. In other cases, men attend the meetings on behalf of their wives or with their wives (Datta 1995; Poonacha 1997).

Despite such hurdles, in many cases elected women have made a difference. Women focus on issues of community survival in general rather than the monetary well-being of a few. They have gained new authority in their homes and in the community. Working to bring changes like running water in the village or another teacher gives them a great sense of achievement. In villages where women are part of movements or where there are movement groups or NGOs, women members are more active and not as easily intimidated. Although the potential of reserved seats for women's empowerment is enormous, given the inequities of caste and class, gender quotas alone are not enough.

Recognizing this, movement activists have begun to work on several fronts. They have organized women to make the political parties more responsive. In the 1991 elections, seven national women's organizations undertook a door-to-door campaign to sensitize women voters on the need to choose candidates based on what they would do for women. Activists are also highlighting factors such as corruption, criminalization, and nepotism that keep women out of politics and are engaging in grassroots efforts to transform the political culture. They hope that women, together with the women's movement, can create new relationships of feedback, accountability, and responsibility with the electorate, which can be put forward as an alternative to the existing distanced and once-a-term contact (Gandhi and Shah 1997: 137).

In addition to attempting to transform electoral politics, the women's movements are continuing their efforts in outlining an alternative politics. For example, in 1996, the Women's Manifesto and Charter of Demands was formulated by the National Alliance of Women after a series of grassroots meetings organized by a network of regional groups (NAWO 2000). The manifesto defines politics from women's perspectives and expresses concerns about economic liberalization and communal politics. It demands a restructuring of society on the principles of justice, equality, and political will to stem the tide of violence against women and a new politics for introducing ecological limits and social responsibility in an era of globalization. It declares:

> At the heart of this new global politics is how to reinvent the state and make it different from the centralized bureaucratic and controlling state that had taken away the functions and roles of civil society. . . . Freedom from want, from hunger and homelessness and the denial of basic needs is the most fundamental freedom without which there can be no other. How this freedom will be ensured by a deepening of democracy, strengthening of civil society and the creation of a different kind of state is the project of democracy in our times. (Shiva 1997: 43–44)

Thus, women's movements in India are working with state policies while simultaneously challenging the state's economic and political agenda, as India is turning away from domestic concerns to compete more effectively within the global economy.

Conclusion

The contemporary women's movement in India has engaged the state in different ways at different times, depending on what the Indian state is doing. It

has accessed state resources for poor women, confronted the state's patriarchal laws and practices, and even implemented the state's economic and
political policies. The Indian experience offers several insights for state and
social movement relationships in general and feminist state theories in
particular.

First, the experience of the women's movement in India demonstrates the
dynamic two-way relationship between the state and social movements. The
women's movement in each phase engaged women in interpreting and trans-
lating state policies into economic and political empowerment. This is not
just a case of SMOs using available resources and opportunities to mobilize
people. Rather, activists in India organized women to engage state bureaucracies effectively, while at the same time transforming those agencies. The
active and transforming process in which movement activists engage is often
missed in the instrumental focus on resources and political opportunities—
even though social movement scholars today focus on both resource mobilization and cultural work (e.g., McAdam, McCarthy, and Zald 1996a, Tarrow
1998). At the same time, the Indian women's emphasis on the active engagement and empowerment of women whether in small, autonomous groups or
in mass-based urban and rural groups demonstrates that the issue of participatory process is not limited to new social movements based on identity
politics. Rather, in India, and in the Third World more generally (e.g., Escobar
and Alvarez 1992), it is an important component even in mass movements
focused on "old" issues and the state.

The state, in turn, also responded to the movement in several ways: it
provided activists with access to some policy-making processes, such as an
advisory role in the rape commission and other commissions related to dowry
deaths and violence against women; it undertook legal reforms, however limited; it formed partnerships with the movements to implement state programs
and altered those policies in response to movement experiences. But the Indian case also demonstrates the limits of the state-movement relationships.
When women's interests clash with other, more entrenched, political interests, they take a back seat.

Second, the Indian case also highlights the importance of international
influences on state feminism in the era of globalization. As Sassen (1995)
argues, the process of globalization does less to diminish the state than to
reconfigure it. In this reconfiguration, the state is much more susceptible to
international pressures and agreements. This can work against the interests
of domestic actors, as in the case of structural adjustment policies. In the case
of women's rights, however, many states have had to enact policies and
institute structures to address women's equality in response to the UN's International Women's Decade and its commitment to women's equality. Furthermore, movements can also use international agreements to make the state

more accountable and responsive at home—as women's groups are doing in India and elsewhere. This global dimension, while important in the transnational social movement literature (e.g., Smith 1998), is missing from most feminist theories of the state in the West—even as women's groups in the West are using such international agreements to hold their own states accountable and working in international networks with groups from the global North and South.

NOTES

1. I use the plural to indicate the different strands of the movement. The main strands include the autonomous women's movement, which identifies itself as feminist; the Left party–affiliated movements; the women's movement organizations that are associated with *dalit* (lower caste), peasants, and workers' movements; and women's professional organizations, development NGOs, and research and documentation centers. This chapter is based on over a decade of research on the women's movements in India in the form of participant observation, interviews with activists, and collection of movement documents and papers.

2. Unlike the new social classes in the West, the new class in India did not move away from old class issues but instead reinterpreted them to include caste and gender inequality.

3. It is important to distinguish between organizing and mobilizing as Payne (1989: 897) does in describing the work of Ella Baker in the civil rights movement in the United States. "Mobilizing is more sporadic involvement of large numbers of people for relatively dynamic activities, organizing involves creating ongoing groups that are mass based in the sense that the people the group purports to represent have a real impact on the group's direction."

4. Structural adjustment policies include a range of reforms, such as privatization of health care and education, removing government subsidies from the agricultural and industrial sectors, and opening Indian markets to other countries.

5. However, as Bina Agarwal noted at the workshop on the relationship of the state to the women's movement, the Sixth Five Year Plan (1975–1980) devoted an entire chapter to women, and the issue of land rights for women was a central feature of policy. In the Seventh Plan, however, the chapter was dropped, and in the Eighth Plan, concern for women was again part of the welfare and disabilities chapter—where it was in the First Five Year Plan (India Association of Women's Studies [IAWS] 1995).

5

The Contradictions of Gay Ethnicity:
Forging Identity in Vermont

MARY BERNSTEIN

When one is presented with a stigmatized identity, it makes sense to
challenge the stigma surrounding that identity. This serves, ironically, to
reinforce the solidity of that identity even as the stigma is rejected.
   —Shane Phelan, "(Be)Coming Out: Lesbian Identity and Politics"

The rise of so-called identity politics or new social movements over the past
four decades has raised intense debate among both social movement scholars
and activists over the merits of pursuing a "politics of recognition" (e.g., Bower
1997; Currah 1997; Vaid 1995). Many queer theorists, poststructuralists, and
feminists argue that to gain recognition for a constituency, activists narrowly
and naively rely on fixed or essentialist notions of identity (e.g., Bower 1997;
Phelan 1993; Seidman 1993). By advocating for rights based on an identity
such as "woman" or "gay," identity movements reinforce the identity on
which the movement is based and, as a result, fail to recognize diversity,
homogenize and ignore differences within the identity category, and inhibit
the creation of a "politics of commonality" (Gitlin 1994, 1995; Kimmel 1993;
Phelan 1993)[1] among diverse groups. Engaging in politics based on identity
categories shores up the category itself and sets up invidious distinctions,
reinforcing a normal-deviant dichotomy (Phelan 1993). Cultural transformation is sacrificed for narrow political gains.

   I ask, in this chapter, to what extent do activists naively and narrowly
adhere to and rely on fixed or essentialist notions of identity (an ontological
move, rather than a strategic claim [Phelan 1993]) in order to gain recognition for that identity? Does a politics of recognition require that activists rely
on a fixed notion of identity? Could demands for recognition in fact be stra-

tegic, given certain political contexts? Are identity politics that demand citizenship rights necessarily exclusionary, and do they solidify an essentialist, exclusionary identity?

I address these questions by examining the development of the lesbian and gay movement in Vermont. I first examine why lesbian and gay activists in Vermont pursued a politics of recognition, seeking to pass legislation that defined them as a discrete and insular minority, and, second, whether their political pursuit reinforced fixed, fundamentally exclusionary notions of identity. I then argue that the politics they pursued, rather than deriving from a fixed notion of identity that straightforwardly translated into claims for citizenship rights, resulted from complex interactions with the state, the opposition, and with other social movements, as well as activists' strategic choices. The identities produced in Vermont's campaign for lesbian and gay rights were fraught and negotiated. I argue that pursuing a politics of recognition does not necessarily result from, or rely on, essentialism, nor do identity politics necessarily reinforce the identity on which the movement is based. The questions, then, are how interactions with the state and the broader political environment channel political action and how movements manage difference within political campaigns.

New Social Movement Theory and the Limits of Essentialism

According to new social movement theorists, identity movements seek to transform dominant cultural patterns, or gain recognition for new social identities, by employing "expressive" strategies (Cohen 1985; Melucci 1985, 1989; Touraine 1981). Such movements challenge dominant cultural norms, seek to democratize relationships, and operate on a different logic from "instrumental" movements (Cohen 1985). The development of NSMs is "ultimately rooted in structural and cultural transformations that characterize all Western European countries" (Kriesi and Giugni 1995: xxi), implying that new identities are either chosen or result straightforwardly from the declining significance of class, religion, and family ties in a "postindustrial" society (Kriesi and Giugni 1995; Touraine 1981). Yet the processes by which these identities are constructed and why they often take contradictory forms remain unclear. In contrast to NSMs, instrumental movements are said to be externally oriented, aimed at achieving concrete goals, rather than challenging dominant cultural patterns or seeking the recognition of new identities (Duyvendak and Giugni 1995). This characterization of movements as instrumental or expressive stems in part from the conflation of goals and strategies (i.e., that instrumental strategies are irrelevant to cultural change, while expressions of identity cannot be externally directed) (Bernstein 1997). This distinction assumes a priori the role of identity for different types of social movements, ignoring the different constructions of and roles played by identity within the same movement.

Studies of the lesbian and gay movement similarly distinguish between "ethnic-identity" and "queer" strategies. Ethnic-identity strategies rely on fixed notions of identity and seek to secure recognition for that identity in the political realm (Altman 1982; Epstein 1987; Escoffier 1985; Gamson 1995; Paul 1982; Seidman 1993; Vaid 1995). Queer theorists, post-structuralists, and many feminists (Bower 1997; Seidman 1993) decry what they see as the reliance of identity movements on fixed fundamentally exclusionary, notions of identity. Essentialism homogenizes groups of people who often have little in common either politically or otherwise when differences of race, class, gender, and sexual style are taken into account. For example, the category "women" typically ignores differences of race, class, and sexual orientation. Others charge that identity movements and their reliance on essentialism inhibit coalitional politics and even blame such movements for the decline of the Left (Gitlin 1994, 1995).

Queer strategies, on the other hand, are "antinormalizing." Rather than shoring up identity categories through engagement with the state and the law, such politics take place in the streets and in the malls, aimed at deconstructing the very categories on which the movement is based (Bower 1997; Gamson 1995). Queer politics, unlike ethnic-identity politics, are said to be transformative (Bower 1997; Phelan 1993; Seidman 1993). In practice, however, queer politics often reinforce an identity and exclude those who are not white and middle class.

In short, distinctions between "ethnic identity" and "queer" strategies needlessly reify the political practices of lesbian and gay activists and thus inhibit an understanding of the role of identity in specific social movement contexts. Elsewhere (Bernstein 1997), I argue that identity has three dimensions in social movements: identity for empowerment, identity as strategy, and identity as goal. When identity is a goal of social movements, activists may either seek recognition for a new identity or work to deconstruct identity categories such as "gay/straight," or "man/woman" (see also Gamson 1995). In this chapter, I consider the third dimension of identity and examine the conditions that produce politics of recognition, the role of essentialism within that pursuit, and whether such politics reinforce a stable identity.

The Law, the State, and the Construction of Identity

The fluid role of identity in social movements is shaped by the interaction of activists and the broader political environment, including the law; and the law shapes the values, beliefs, and preferences of activists (Katzenstein 1998). When activists have recourse to the law, their agenda narrows as they pursue a conventional "politics as usual." Similarly, Calhoun (1993) argues that "states are institutionally organized in ways that provide recognition for some identities and arenas for some conflicts and freeze others out. States themselves thus shape the orientations of NSMs as well as the field of social movements more generally" (387). Valocchi (1999) argues that in addition to external pressures, identities are constructed as a result of "internal processes of network building, culture making, and consciousness raising" (207).

But activists also deploy identity in self-conscious, strategic ways when pursuing political and cultural goals. Polletta's (1994) discussion of SNCC shows that in fighting to enfranchise poor, rural, uncredentialed African Americans, activists sought not only to secure recognition of a new identity but to transform dominant political and economic structures. Polletta's work shows that constructions of identity can be strategically chosen for political and instrumental goals. The relationship between internal struggles, the political context, and the opposition led activists in Vermont to pursue human rights legislation. This pursuit may have consolidated an identity but did not dictate its content or rely on an essentialist understanding of that identity. While lesbians and gay men claimed rights based on a particular identity, knew that this identity was partially imposed from the outside, only provisionally adopted by activists, and did not adequately represent their constituents.

Data and Methods

I focus on Vermont for several reasons. First, Vermont is a small state, with a relatively young lesbian and gay movement (see table 5.1). As such, we can trace the development over a period of twenty years of a political consciousness among those who shared a same-sex desire. Vermont's small size makes examining internal differences and strategic choices easier. Because Vermont is also a relatively homogeneous state, differences by race do not appear as significant as in more heterogeneous locales, which is one potential limit of the data. But even within a relatively homogeneous population, differences were not subsumed by appeals to essentialist visions of lesbian and gay identity. Nonetheless, the processes outlined in this chapter may be more complex in more diverse locales.

Research for this case study involved triangulation of data. I examined movement documents such as press releases, position papers, and newspaper accounts from lesbian and gay and mainstream presses. I supplemented the written material with interviews with nine selected informants. The type and

TABLE 5.1   Timeline

1983	First Lesbian and Gay Pride March held in Vermont, held annually from this point on.
	Vermonters for Lesbian and Gay Rights forms.
1985	Governor Kunin recognizes two liaisons from the lesbian and gay communities.
1986	*Out in the Mountains* begins publication.
	State ERA is defeated.
	Vermonters for Lesbian and Gay Rights no longer exists; Vermont Coalition of Lesbians and Gay Men is formed to emphasize statewide representation.
	Attorney general's office agrees to record complaints of discrimination based on sexual orientation.
1987	First statewide lesbian and gay rights bill is introduced in the state legislature.
1989	Second statewide lesbian and gay rights bill is introduced in the state legislature. Hate Crimes Act is introduced in the state legislature. A series of four public hearings is held around the state.
1990	Hate Crimes Act is passed and signed into law by Governor Kunin.
1991	Third statewide lesbian and gay rights bill is introduced in the state legislature.
1992	Third version of the bill, an "Act to Prohibit Discrimination on the Basis of Sexual Orientation," is passed and signed into law by Governor Dean.

extent of opposition is investigated through secondary sources and activist accounts.

Identity and the Construction of a Social Movement

The term "lesbian *and* gay" is now so commonplace that it is easy to forget that it is not simply one identity but a tenuous coalition. The lesbian and gay male communities in Vermont remained relatively distinct until the start of the 1980s. Although the lesbian community organized around feminist issues, neither community specifically organized around lesbian and gay concerns. In this section, I consider how Vermont's lesbians and gay men came together to form a political alliance. I examine the role of activists' self-understandings of identity in forging a cross-gender alliance. The next section examines why this alliance pursued lesbian and gay rights legislation.

The development of the lesbian subculture in Vermont mirrored the national development of feminism and feminist organizing but did not rely on a fixed notion of "lesbian" identity that carried a specific content. In recounting her experiences in the "lesbian community" in Vermont, one informant expressed her frustration at academic reductionism of lesbian culture(s), suggesting diversity in what constituted a "good" lesbian:

I read different things about the seventies. Sometimes I read we all wore flannel shirts and had no sex and sometimes I read we were all

promiscuous and, but anyway I was in a group, that was the other thing I was in. I was in a group of lesbians that called itself the— well—the nonmonogamy group and we were kind of politically committed to being nonmonogamous and having these open rela- tionships and we got a lot of flack for this . . . [but] the people that I knew were thinking why should lesbians repeat male patterns.
(P. Luhrs, interview)

In part, she was reacting to the portrayal of 1970s lesbian feminism as asexual, monogamous, and even puritanical. "Lesbian" does not capture the plural- ity of meanings attached to the term by those who adopted the label, nor does it represent the fraught and contested history of the term. In Vermont, many women with same-sex desire defined themselves as lesbian, whereas others saw themselves as bisexual. Some believed that being a lesbian was a choice; others thought their sexual orientation was immutable. Some believed separatism was the best strategy for pursuing feminist goals; others thought that working with heterosexual women or gay men was beneficial (Luhrs, B. Lippert, Russell interviews). So, rather than operating from a fixed understanding of iden- tity, the lesbian community was diverse, with frequent struggles for the hegemony of one strategy over another, or one lifestyle over another. But es- sentialism was not foundational and did not straightforwardly determine lesbian politics in Vermont. Identity and strategy interacted in complex, context-specific ways.

Coalitions between feminists who identified as lesbian and those who iden- tified as heterosexual were also tenuous and provisional. In the early 1970s, lesbians and straight women began working together on issues of abortion, rape, and other types of male violence against women. They created rape crisis centers, battered women's shelters, hotlines, and health clinics. Consciousness- raising groups, an integral part of the subculture, created emotional bonds among participants, and many feminist organizations emerged as a result of these networks. Schisms between lesbians and straight women emerged periodically; straight women would try to purge lesbians from their organi- zations. Alternatively, many lesbians chose to work in separatist groups, and often women who lacked adequate "lesbian credentials" were unwelcome. At other times, straight women and lesbians worked together. Throughout the 1970s, at least three women's centers existed in Burlington, the state's largest and most liberal city, where much social movement activism was cen- tered (Luhrs interview). Thus, the "feminist" category was also contested.

The majority of lesbian organizing centered on feminist issues; organiz- ing as lesbians was limited to sponsoring dances and social events. On occa- sion, lesbians and gay men united strategically on issues of common concern, for example, in response to gay bashing (Russell, Luhrs interviews). Yet beyond creating "women's spaces," public demands for policy change were almost never made on behalf of lesbians (Luhrs interview).

Until the 1980s, the gay male subculture was less political than the lesbian community. Unlike other locales, Vermont never developed a large commercial infrastructure of bars and bathhouses. In the 1970s, an inn catering to gay men, run by a gay male couple, gained visibility and may have had a positive impact on public attitudes in one working-class Vermont town, until it gained notoriety as the alleged site of male prostitution. Yet, for the most part, gay men in Vermont remained isolated. In the early 1970s, at least one gay male discussion group existed, providing a safe social space for gay men where personal (and political) issues about homosexuality, such as coming out, relationships, and feelings of isolation, could be discussed (Russell, Lippert interviews). But like lesbians, gay men had not organized as gay men on behalf of gay issues; unlike lesbians, gay men were not politically organized as a community.

The desire for public recognition of lesbians and gay men came from internal dynamics, resulting from both prior political experience and personal and organizational networks of the activists. In 1983, several lesbians organized Vermont's first Lesbian and Gay Pride March and rally (see table 5.1). In the words of one organizer: "It became strikingly obvious that Burlington ought to have its own Lesbian and Gay Pride Day—that we never celebrated ourselves as queers publicly in Burlington, although we did march and demonstrate for every other radical and progressive cause" (Wittenberg 1986: 4). Lesbians who had been involved with *Commonwoman* newspaper did the bulk of organizing for the first march (Russell, interview). Through personal contacts, several gay men also helped organize the march. In contrast to other cities and states, where political organizing emerged as a result of precipitating events such as police entrapment or brutality (the most famous being the raid on the Stonewall Inn in New York City), internal organizing created the fledgling lesbian and gay movement in Vermont. When asked why the first march took place in 1983, Howard Russell, one of the organizers, said that it grew out of a sense of entitlement, of a critical mass within the community (interview). The march was certainly intended to create a sense of pride in one's same-sex desire but was not designed to segregate lesbians and gay men from other political causes, as the campaign for the Equal Rights Amendment (ERA), discussed later, illustrates. Although an essentialist understanding of one's identity may have been a factor for many, it was not the only motivating factor. Activists had not yet turned to the state for recognition.

Whereas lesbian and gay pride parades are certainly public exhibitions of identity, the strategy can be antinormalizing and is not necessarily essentialist, though it might well have reinforced, for some, a stable identity based on sexual orientation. According to Russell:

> [I was] talking with lots of gay men who were just so angry that I was involved in organizing. They said that people were going to get hurt—this is crazy, why are you doing this? . . . What was really powerful for me over the first several years was seeing some of those very people who were the most angry get out there and march. . . . It brought this tremendous conversation out into the open about people's fear, about stepping forward, people's anger at people who did step forward, people's anger at themselves at being angry at someone, for not stepping forward. It was unreal upheaval. I think it was really the launching of the more public gay community in Vermont. (Interview)

The pride march challenged the status quo by making visible hitherto invisible communities but demanded neither acceptance nor rights from the heterosexual majority. Activists did not demand validation for a nondeviant status but began to challenge, if not transform, dominant cultural values. To publicly claim one's same-sex desire marked a departure from the norms of self-hatred and fear. The ensuing dialogue within the lesbian and gay communities underscored the ways anti-lesbian and anti-gay discrimination, a reality regardless of whether one viewed one's own sexual identity as fixed or mutable, had negative repercussions on their lives and gave people a sense that political action was possible.

The success of that first march, despite fears that no one would show up (Wittenberg 1986; Russell interview), provided the impetus for organizing on specifically lesbian and gay issues. Vermonters for Lesbian and Gay Rights (VLGR), the first self-consciously organized gay and lesbian political organization in Vermont, emerged soon after the march. Yet gender differences produced tensions in the newly formed VLGR.

Together with the pride march, VLGR served as the catalyst from which Vermont's lesbian and gay political infrastructure emerged. Groups such as OUTRIGHT, an organization to assist lesbian and gay youths, Vermont's first lesbian and gay newspaper, and many of the major Vermont AIDS organizations later formed as a result of these organizational and personal networks. The pride march organizing committee for the next several years was essentially VLGR (Russell interview). The inspiration for these organizations came less from a reliance on a naive essentialism than from a recognition of discrimination and, in the case of AIDS, the need for treatment and care.

External Processes of Identity Construction
Opposing Movements

External attacks on Vermont's lesbian and gay community spurred activists to pursue a formal politics of recognition from the state. The interactions with the state, as well as with "opposing movements," which I define as two protest movements engaged in the same issues but on opposite sides (Bernstein 1994; Meyer and Staggenborg 1996), pushed activists to assume a public lesbian-and-gay identity, even while the movement itself avoided dictating the content of that identity. Homophobic attacks on lesbians and gays by ERA opponents in Vermont, as well as the response of the women's movement, helped to sever lesbian and gay identity from feminist identity, and activists responded accordingly. Thus, the process of creating an ostensibly "ethnic-like" identity was not predetermined or predicated on an essentialist understanding of a sexual identity but on interactions with anti-gay activists and other social movements.

In 1986, lesbian and gay rights became the Achilles' heel of the feminist movement when conservative opponents waged a virulent campaign to defeat Vermont's statewide ERA. Feminist groups around the state, as well as the Governor's Commission on the Status of Women, had been working for years to pass a statewide ERA, which was coming up for a vote in 1986. The opposition, led by Phyllis Schlafly and her STOP ERA organization, sought to link abortion and lesbian and gay rights with the passage of ERA. Even more egregiously, they linked passage of ERA with the spread of AIDS (Colby 1986), distributing brochures entitled "ERA/Gay/AIDS connection." Proponents of ERA alternately ignored the issues of AIDS and lesbian and gay rights, sought to hide lesbian and gay activists from the public eye, or simply claimed that the issues were unrelated. In 1986, Vermont's statewide ERA was defeated (Anderson 1986). The failure of feminists to recognize diversity among their own members and to address the issue of sexual orientation, not lesbian and gay assertions of an essentialist identity, led to the fragmentation of the pro-ERA coalition. The anti-gay attack by ERA opponents ultimately led lesbian and gay activists to pursue rights in their own name.

Whether sexual orientation was essentialist or socially constructed was less a focus of the anti-ERA campaign than portraying the content of lesbian and gay identity as sick and immoral. According to the *Vanguard Press*, the anti-ERA campaign spewed "the most negative, misleading and downright sleazy commercials, brochures and advertisements in the history of Vermont politics" (quoted in Anderson 1986). Anti-ERA advocates trotted out the usual anti-gay myths (Herek 1991), claiming that in addition to supporting an

unhealthy "lifestyle" (implying choice) that causes disease (i.e., AIDS), passage of the ERA would lead down a slippery slope to "homosexual" mar-
riages (Colby 1986), presumably threatening the stability of mainstream
America. The pro-ERA coalition responded by stating that it supported all
people's civil rights and then dodged the lesbian and gay issue (Livingston
1986). In reality, "most of our liberal/feminist friends sought only to distance
themselves from us, instead of speaking out forcefully in defense of our basic
humanity" (Anderson 1986: 1).

Lesbian and gay activists were enraged at being used to defeat their allies.
Howard Russell, one of the organizers of the early coalition meetings, put it
this way:

> I remember the coalition meeting we had right after the ERA was
> defeated and people were . . . just enraged, so angry and that was the
> first time that on a serious level people said we need to go for it
> here. . . . If you want to attack something with gay and lesbian
> rights, here's a bill on it. It's going to be in the legislature. . . . If we
> need to pass a lesbian and gay civil rights bill to get that issue out of
> the ERA issue, then pass [it]. (Interview)

The rage also arose from perceptions in the lesbian and gay communities
that they had been abandoned by feminists. Self-recriminations by lesbian
and gay activists who had accepted dominant ERA strategy abounded. According to longtime gay and Democratic Party activist Terje Anderson,

> While many of us were involved in the campaign [for ERA], doing
> the drudge work, by and large we bought into the larger strategy of
> "stay quiet, don't mess this up." Those who did speak out forcefully
> were snubbed and privately censured by the ERA leadership. For
> better or for worse, we accepted without much argument the idea
> that we were a liability in this campaign and that the most valuable
> role we could play was an invisible one. (1986: 1–2)

The combination of fury at being used to defeat their allies and the lack of a
coherent feminist response to the conservative opposition underscored the
need for a separate lesbian and gay rights bill. Ironically, the invisibility and
absence of a well-organized, self-identified lesbian and gay movement with
clearly defined goals helped derail the ERA because no consistent response
to the opposition existed.

The anti-ERA campaign also provoked an increase in anti-lesbian and anti-
gay violence, or at least the perception of an increase.[2] The year after the ERA's
defeat, lesbian and gay activists asked their allies in the legislature to intro-

duce the first lesbian and gay rights bill into the Vermont state legislature. So regardless of one's view about the causes of same-sex desire, the structure of the opposition, as well as the feminist response, catapulted lesbians and gay men into creating an "identity-based" movement.

The State

In 1983, the newly formed Vermonters for Lesbian and Gay Rights had no clear political agenda. Recognizing that discrimination based on sexual orientation was a reality, members began tentatively by polling candidates for their views on sexual orientation policies but received no responses at all. Recognizing the need for reliable communication, political legitimacy, and ongoing visibility that went beyond the annual pride marches and rallies, members wrote and received a grant to start a lesbian and gay newspaper, entitled *Out in the Mountains* (OITM). In 1986, when activists repeated their survey, candidates were told that results would be published in the lesbian and gay community's statewide newspaper. This time, virtually all responded (OITM 1987a).

When activists began seeking funds for OITM, they also sought official contact with the governor's office. In 1985, activists took advantage of the openness of the Vermont polity and benefitted from the inside expertise of openly gay state and national Democratic party activist Terje Anderson (OITM 1986b). Beth Dingman, a longtime member of a women's press collective (OITM 1986a), and Anderson were chosen by the lesbian and gay communities to serve as official conduits to the governor's office. Largely at Anderson's request (M. Hurlie interview), liberal Democratic Governor Madeline Kunin officially recognized the two as liaisons from the lesbian and gay communities. After the 1986 lesbian and gay pride march, Governor Kunin asked to meet four times a year with the liaisons (Trebitsch 1986). By 1986, Vermonters for Lesbian and Gay Rights, as a result of debilitating attempts to impose structure, had faded away. Activists attempting greater regional representation formed the Vermont Coalition of Lesbians and Gay Men.

After the defeat of the ERA, lesbians and gay men in Vermont felt threatened as a result of a perceived increase in anti-gay violence and homophobia. The incipient lesbian and gay political organizations enabled activists to respond to the threat, by seeking passage of the lesbian and gay rights bill. The anti-ERA campaign had placed the issue of lesbian and gay rights on the political agenda, independently of lesbian and gay activism in Vermont. Politicians were forced to take positions on the ERA and, by implication, on lesbian and gay rights. So, in 1986, partly through Anderson's influence as chair of the platform committee of the state Democratic party and partly in response to the anti-ERA campaign, support for lesbian and gay rights was included in the official platform of Vermont's Democratic Party (OITM 1986c). Governor Kunin also spoke in support of both ERA and lesbian and gay rights. Representatives from the liberal Chittendon County and Burlington areas were persuaded to introduce the statewide anti-discrimination bill in 1987.[3]

Initial interactions with state authorities over the statewide anti-discrimination bill led activists to frame their claims in ethnic-like identity terms. During committee hearings on the first bill in 1987, it became clear that documentation of discrimination was necessary. Although VLGR had conducted its own survey of discrimination based on sexual orientation in Vermont, judiciary committee members wanted documentation from more "credible" sources. Lesbian and gay activists turned to the state for assistance. They contacted members of the attorney general's office who agreed to record and file allegations of discrimination. The absence of legal protection based on sexual orientation precluded actual investigation of complaints (OITM 1987b). Vermont's Human Rights Commission also became involved in collecting statistics, at least as early as 1988 (S. Sussman interview).

The language of the law helped construct identity and gave activists a template by which to work. In 1989, a hate crimes bill to enhance penalties for bias-related violence was introduced into the Vermont legislature as a result of cooperation between the attorney general's office, the Vermont Human Rights Commission, and the Anti-Defamation League. Sexual orientation was included in the bill. According to Susan Sussman, then director of the civil rights division of the attorney general's office and later director of the Vermont Human Rights Commission, it was never a question in either office whether sexual orientation would appear in the Hate Crimes Act. In 1989, the Human Rights Commission held a series of four public hearings around the state on hate crimes. According to Sussman, "The vast majority of the testimony collected at those hearings had to do with examples of gay bashing and violence against lesbians so that was the overwhelming testimony that we received and so it gave us even more support for lobbying for the bill" (interview). The Human Rights Commission worked with the Vermont Coalition of Lesbians and Gay Men to spread the word throughout the community, using OITM, phone trees, and mailing lists. The attorney general's office also included the Vermont affiliate of the American Civil Liberties Union (ACLU) in drafting the Hate Crimes Act to ward off potential constitutional challenges to the bill (Sussman interview). Therefore, a second piece of legislation that defined people who shared a same-sex desire was introduced, this time independently of organized lesbian and gay activism. The structure of the law, in conjunction with interactions with the state, and the opposing movement that defined lesbians and gay men as a recognizable minority, all pushed activists into pursuing political recognition from the state, regardless of how lesbians and gays defined themselves.

Opposition to the hate crimes bill coalesced around inclusion of sexual orientation. Unlike anti–gay rights campaigns in other states run by groups like Colorado for Family Values, opposition was less visible and less organized in Vermont (OITM 1990). In a divide-and-conquer approach reminiscent of the anti-ERA campaign, one oppositional group distributed cutouts of masquerade ball masks, claiming that the Hate Crimes Act was a "mask" for gay rights (Sussman interview). Thus, once again, the lesbian-and-gay identity was underscored and reinforced by the opposition, in a bill championed by a coalition, one part of which consisted of lesbians and gay men.

The tide turned against the bill when Roger Macomber, a gay man, was beaten nearly to death outside a gay bar in Burlington. A rally attended by approximately 700 people followed at a local church to express outrage over the attack. Governor Kunin, in a completely unprecedented move, testified at a public hearing in support of the Hate Crimes Act. A civil rights commissioner who was an out gay man also gave persuasive testimony (Sussman interview). The Hate Crimes Act was passed and signed into law in 1990.

The forging of a public lesbian-and-gay identity was a complex process only minimally related to the possibly essentialist self-perceptions of lesbians and gay men. The pride marches represented an attempt by lesbian and gay communities to celebrate themselves and disrupted the participants' self-perceptions and even self-hatred, a fundamentally antinormalizing goal. Antifeminist, antigay, and antilesbian forces helped solidify an active and public lesbian-and-gay identity more than the internal community push toward organizing. Seeking to affect policy, activists deferred to authorities in shaping their goals and tactics, requiring evidence of discrimination based on sexual orientation, providing language in the form of preexisting rights legislation in Vermont, and modeling hate crimes legislation after similar laws passed in other states.

Constructing Identity and Managing Difference

Queer theorists often assume that interactions with the state require wholesale acceptance of the argument that sexual orientation is immutable, whether determined biologically or set very early in childhood socialization. They also assume that, in pursuing rights from the state, activists will ignore differences within the community for the sake of achieving narrow political gains. But the lesbian and gay rights campaign in Vermont casts doubt on these reductionist accounts of lesbian and gay politics and, at the least, suggests that pursuing a politics loosely based on identity does not necessarily lead to excluding differences. In Vermont, activists employed strategies to contest stigmatized identities and to advocate for rights but relied on neither an essentialist nor an exclusive understanding of that identity. Organizers recognized the diversity within their communities in terms of gender, views about the mutability of sexual orientation, and sexual style. Vermont's lesbian and gay activists pursued an inclusive grassroots strategy in their attempt to pass the Hate Crimes Act and, later, lesbian and gay rights legislation.

For hate crimes, activists set out to show that not only was discrimination based on sexual orientation a serious problem but violence against lesbians and gay men was prevalent, even in serene, rural Vermont. Hate crimes were not predicated on the victims' understandings of their identity; in fact, antigay hate crimes are sometimes perpetrated against heterosexuals presumed incorrectly to be lesbian or gay. Together with lesbians and gays, the attorney general's office, the Human Rights Commission, and other minority communities actively lobbied for the bill's passage.

In 1990, the hate crimes bill was passed and signed into law, marking a turning point for Vermont's lesbian and gay movement. Because the likelihood of success had been so high for passage of hate crimes legislation, the lesbian and gay rights bill was temporarily overshadowed. Once the bill passed, the Vermont Coalition of Lesbians and Gay Men returned to its original goal of passing lesbian and gay rights legislation.

The coalition was a loose, unstructured organization that existed largely through the efforts of a few committed activists. By 1990, two of the early organizers, Terje Anderson and Howard Russell, had become involved in other concerns; AIDS work occupied more of Anderson's time and Russell had decided to run for the state senate. The bulk of the organizational responsibility had also rested on former liaison Heather Wishik and current liaisons Holly Perdue and Keith Goslant. According to Mary Hurlie (interview), who became politically involved in 1990 and later went on to become cochair of the coalition,

> It seemed to me incredibly more difficult than it needed to be
> because . . . they had no resources, it's amazing they were able to do
> the work they did back then, but what would happen would be there
> was going to be a public hearing, this tremendous phone tree of the
> state would start but it was this frenetic kind of energy that would
> have to happen every time we needed to have someone call because
> they were the swing vote on the bill, in this committee or we'd have
> to call so and so because he said he hadn't heard from anyone in his
> district and there seemed to be this sort of frenetic sort of scrambling
> to get the word out to people. There was no sort of structure . . .
> even loose network, if you will, doing that—so it seemed real
> inefficient to me, and it seemed like, maybe it wasn't reaching as
> many people in the state as it could.

Hurlie, a management consultant who became involved in the drive for the anti-discrimination bill as a result of her involvement in Russell's state senate campaign, set out to make structure palatable (interview). Yet it was the grassroots nature of the campaign that led to inclusivity in a way more difficult for formal organizations to achieve.

Identity can be deployed strategically in political campaigns in order to criticize the values, norms, and practices of the dominant culture, or to educate by dispelling stereotypes about the minority (Bernstein 1997). In 1990, prospects looked bright for the bill's passage, because it enjoyed the support of the governor and leaders of both legislative houses, among others. Thus, activists did not consider educating the public, criticizing dominant values, or empowering activists to be priorities. Public education was fine, but the idea was to stay focused on the legislature. None of the activists I interviewed remembered discussing the use of confrontational tactics at this time. I would argue that the openness of the polity, and particularly the accessibility of public hearings, mitigated the need for militancy. Anyone could come to the hearings, sign up, and have their say. Activists also believed that they would never win on the basis of numbers alone, comprising at most an optimistic 10 percent of the population. Instead, lesbians and gay men chose to put themselves on the line. In Hurlie's (interview) words,

> It's an intellectual debate in the state house or in Washington, or city hall . . . about gays and lesbians. . . . It seems very very easy for privileged, the white heterosexual men particularly to have that debate . . . and just speak from the head. . . . We realized that wasn't going to work. We're going to lose that one every single time and we decided to put a face on it.

They decided to activate friendship, organizational, and professional networks (lesbian, gay, and straight). Through these networks, friends and colleagues would hold coffee "klatches." Ten to fifteen people would invite their elected state official over for coffee to discuss the anti-discrimination bill. They dispelled legal myths such as fear that passing an anti-discrimination law would lead to affirmative action for queers (Hurlie interview). Legislators who feared support for the bill would harm their reelection campaigns were reminded of past supporters who had been reelected. Fact sheets dispelling myths about gays as child molesters were distributed to each state senator and representative (P. Olson interview). Activists initially targeted swing votes on the judiciary committee so the bill could reach the floor, successfully swaying some votes (Hurlie interview).

Those opposed to the bill constructed homosexuality as a choice or a practice—learned behavior that by implication could be changed. For example, attorney Duncan Kilmartin testified that bill "S. 131 could give a preferred status to practicing homosexuals given to no other category of human beings. S. 131 affirms and approves criminal conduct, immoral conduct and high risk conduct for the individuals involved and society at large." For the opposition, that "practice" consisted of alleged sexual behavior (both public and private) with no less than 500 partners per year, as well as with animals. The opposition depicted these images in lurid, graphic detail during the hearings (e.g., Kilmartin 1992) and claimed that lesbians and gay men were out to recruit the state's children into "homosexuality." Other opponents expressed fears that half of San Francisco (portrayed as menacing men in leather) would move to Vermont upon the bill's passage. The opposition also quoted scripture to justify opposition to the bill. In the words of lesbian activist Linda Hollingdale, "the con side was definitely religious, moral, really sick stuff, I mean it was almost a sit down and cry over what they would bring up as arguments" (interview). The Right's strategy, however, backfired. According to Peggy Luhrs (interview):

At first the right wing was really vicious to the legislators, called them up . . . intimidated them, but then after a while, it got them mad, you know, and legislators who had been opposed to gay rights started seeing how vicious the opposition was and started saying I didn't believe before there was this much discrimination against gays but now that I see this, I do and I'm voting. So they really won it for us, in a way.

Other lesbian and gay activists I interviewed said that by focusing so much on the alleged sexual practices of lesbians and gay men and behaving emotionally and unprofessionally, the opposition showed "themselves for being the lunatic fringe that they truly were. That what they were responding to was an issue of personal fear and personal belief rather than having any substantive piece of information and that became very clear when you sat in those hearings" (K. Goslant interview).

In response to these vicious attacks, it would have been easy as well as strategic to claim that sexual orientation was immutable, to omit bisexuals from the bill (because bisexuals seemingly have a choice over intimate partners), and to disavow any connection with leather or other "deviant" sexual practices. Instead, the lesbian and gay leadership did not dictate the content of the identity that would be deployed at the public hearings, and all members of the lesbian and gay communities were encouraged to attend (Hurlie, H. Perdue, Goslant, interviews). No one was censured by the lesbian and gay leadership. People simply told their stories.

In contrast to the significance attributed by academics to essentialism as a determinant of lesbian and gay politics and strategy, most activists saw the immutability issue as a red herring, recognizing that the origins of homosexuality are contested by scientists and community members alike. For example, during one of the coffee klatches, state senator Ruth Stokes asked why lesbians and gay men needed protection if sexual orientation was a choice. One person responded with a question, asking "Ruth, would it matter if it weren't a choice? Would you vote differently?" (Hurlie interview). Stokes was also reminded that religion was a choice protected from discrimination. Hurlie recalls testifying at the hearings that she felt sexual orientation was not a choice for her, but if it were, she would still choose it. Although activists consciously dispelled myths about gays and lesbians as child molesters, the campaign for lesbian and gay rights did not itself solidify a particular construction of identity. "The thing was, the Right portrayed us so much as sexual beings where our testimony was so much, you know, the rest of our lives, where we were being discriminated against" (Perdue interview). According to liaison Goslant (interview), "actually, our community at times would come back saying that it was for them very empowering to sit in this room and hear people stand up and say this is who I am and I make no excuses for it and I'm just as deserving of protection."

According to Perdue, supporters of the bill showed up for the hearings nicely dressed, in clothes many probably had not worn since their first job interviews. Lesbian and gay activists perceived that the religious opposition's credibility with legislators was harmed by Bible thumping and emotional outbursts. As a result, decorum prevailed among lesbian and gay activists and their supporters. So while combating dominant constructions of gender was not prevalent during the hearings, it was a strategic move brought about by positive responses from legislators and a desire to distinguish themselves from the religious opposition. Bisexuality presented the most difficulty because, at the time, there was no organized bisexual contingent. Legislators expressed their confusion, thinking that "bisexual" meant that one had to have twice as many partners as heterosexuals. Activists simply replied that bisexual meant attraction to both sexes.

Many accounts of lesbian and gay politics document how bisexual and transgendered people, as well as the leather community, are shunned by lesbian and gay political leaders, in an effort to make the movement appear "normal" and nonthreatening to government and the public (e.g., Bernstein 1997; Bull and Gallagher 1996; Halle 2001; Marotta 1981). What accounts for the different strategy used in Vermont? In part, both in contrast and response to the exclusive leadership in places such as Oregon and Colorado, already legendary for having divided the "good queers" from the "bad queers" (Bernstein 1997; Bull and Gallagher 1996), as well as their own experience in the ERA campaign, the Vermont liaisons pointedly included diverse segments of the lesbian and gay communities. Perdue (interview) recounts that

measures were taken to ensure that all parts of the community were represented. At a gay pride rally, for example, men from the leather community
would be asked to serve donuts and coffee. Although he did not think that
the leather community was very strong in Vermont, Goslant (interview) elaborated on the coalition's philosophy:

> If we were presented with we know that this person is going to
> show up in full leather or this person is going to show up in drag,
> I'm not sure we would have opposed it, because one of the things
> that we have said consistently is that there is no part of it that's
> unacceptable and we're all in this together. We're talking about our
> community and not just a select group of people because, you
> know, we can dress Republican and we can smell sweetly. We're
> not into being correct.

Perdue (interview) echoed similar sentiments: "We were real clear that the
fairies and the bull dykes and the radical lesbians . . . and the leather boys
and the leather women are all part of our community and nobody is going to
pit one of us against one group, one subgroup against the other. . . . [None-
theless] word was out that if we came out looking like our stereotypes that
we would make people afraid." Perdue went on to explain that the leather
group still felt included because they were invited by the coalition to participate in public events such as Coming Out Day. "Just by having them in a
public forum that says Vermont Coalition of Lesbians and Gay Men spon-
sors workshop by—their names were out there and they were a piece of us."
The strategy proved successful, and the bill passed in 1992.

Eight years after the passage of Vermont's statewide anti-discrimination
bill, Vermont, in response to a recent court case that declared it discriminatory for the state to deny marriage licenses to same-sex couples, passed a "civil
union" law that grants same-sex couples the rights to which married couples
are entitled, but reserved the term "marriage" for opposite-sex couples
(Bernstein and Reimann 2001). The care activists in Vermont took to represent the diversity of their communities was important in discussions about
same-sex marriage. According to Hurlie (interview):

> Our decision-making process on the board is consensus and we are,
> our fall back is voting. . . . We've recently been debating [same-sex
> marriage] and we reached consensus at our board meeting that . . .
> we as a coalition absolutely support the legal right to marry. And the
> second paragraph of our position statement will talk about we also
> strongly believe that the institution of marriage tends to marginalize
> people in our society, that we believe that everyone ought to have

access to all the financial and legal protections that anyone who chooses not to couple [has].

So essentialism is once again not a determining factor; rather strategy and attending to diversity influence the political stands of Vermont's lesbian and gay activists.

Conclusion

The pursuit of lesbian and gay rights cannot be reduced to an easy reliance on fixed notions of identity or to activists' proximity to the law. Vermont activists made strategic decisions based on their own and others' past experience that took into account the diversity of lesbian and gay communities. Although activists did indeed contest the stigma associated with homosexuality, what constituted that identity remained fluid. Although internal moves toward asserting identity helped to politicize a community based on a common sexual orientation, what defined that identity was both fraught and negotiated. The opposition, mobilized against both the ERA and lesbians and gays, helped impose an identity from which activists constructed, at least in part, their political agenda. The lack of a feminist response helped to sever a lesbian-and-gay identity from the women's movement. Both the law and state authorities provided blueprints for how to proceed in the quest for citizenship rights, demanding evidence of categorical discrimination. So whereas activists provided the state with evidence of discrimination, such evidence was based less on their own experiences of their identity than on the discriminatory responses to their (perceived or actual) same-sex desire by others. As the case study of Vermont illustrates, it is a mistake to reify the political practices of lesbian and gay activists. Whereas both internal and external processes influence the construction of identity and identity politics, it is also the result of activists' strategic responses to interactions with the law, the state, and other social movements. The open polity and grassroots style of organizing encouraged a fluid construction of lesbian and gay identity.

NOTES

I would like to thank Nancy Naples, Nancy Whittier, and David Meyer for their comments on earlier drafts of this chapter.

1. See Currah (1997) for a discussion of the "communitarian" critique of identity politics.

2. During the 1980s, homophobic hate crimes appeared to increase, although it is unclear whether the number of such hate crimes increased, or whether the rise

reflected increased reporting of incidents and better record keeping (Jenness and Grattet 1996).

3. Two bills to protect people from discrimination on the basis of HIV antibody status were also introduced in the state legislature in 1987 and passed in 1988. Vermont's legislature operates on a biennium system, so the bill was successful after its first introduction. A statewide bill specifically using the words "sexual orientation" had yet to be passed.

6

Creating Social Change: Lessons from the Civil Rights Movement

KENNETH T. ANDREWS

The civil rights movement has had a lasting impact in the United States through its influence on social policies, political alignments, public opinion, and other social movements. Even though many of its fundamental goals were never realized and other gains have been rolled back, the civil rights movement is still viewed as one of the most influential social movements in U.S. history. For example, Aldon Morris, in *The Origins of the Civil Rights Movement*, argues that the civil rights movement had "a profound impact on American society" (1984: 266). Similarly, Dennis Chong points to the movement as "the quintessential example of public-spirited collective action in our time" that "spark[ed] radical changes in American society" (1991: 1).[1] Nevertheless, our understanding of *how* the civil rights movement (and movements more generally) brought about change is limited.

I use the civil rights movement to demonstrate the theoretical insights that emerge from a closer analysis of the process by which movements generate change. In short, I argue that our understanding of the cause and form of movement impact is underdeveloped. In this chapter, I will compare explanatory strategies that focus on the organizations and the public activity (e.g., demonstrations, boycotts) of movements and propose that organizations and movement activity may work together to bring change. I begin by addressing general questions about movement outcomes. Then, I describe causal mechanisms through which movement organizations and events can produce broader changes. I illustrate these dynamics using examples from the civil rights movement from my own research on the Mississippi movement and from the broader scholarship on this influential case.

Outcomes, Organizations, and Events

How do we decide what counts as an outcome or consequence of a social movement? In some cases, scholars have attempted to measure success— whether a movement achieves its goals (Burstein, Einwohner, and Hollander 1995; Gamson 1990; Giugni 1998; Mansbridge 1986). This strategy faces several difficulties, however. As we know from many social movements, goals shift over time, and there is often low consensus within social movements about the exact form success would take. Even more important, focusing on success does not allow room for the unintended impact of social movements on social structures (Kriesi, Koopmans, Duyvendak, and Giugni, 1995; Snyder and Kelly 1979). As a result, scholars' more common strategy is to examine outcomes, allowing greater flexibility to consider a broad range of movement effects. These impacts can include collective benefits relative to a movement's constituency, as well as unintended effects of the movement, both positive and negative (Amenta and Young 1999b; Edsall and Edsall 1991; Kriesi et al. 1995; Snyder and Kelly 1979).

Social movements attempt to bring many different types of change. For example, in recent years feminists have attempted to develop parallel organizations, raise consciousness, change public opinion, reform mainstream institutions, and promote nonsexist language and informal behavior. If we considered the unintended consequences of movements, the list would grow even longer (Tilly 1999). Most of the examples that I use are dimensions of political change including agenda setting, policy enactment and implementation, and the acquisition of political power. Nevertheless, my discussion includes social and cultural impacts as well, because these types of changes are intertwined with and can mediate between social movements and institutional change (Rochon 1998; Wirt 1997). The main challenges to studying the impacts of social movements are the same, regardless of whether one is studying political, social, or cultural impacts.[2] There is a clear theoretical advantage to studying as many types of outcomes as possible, because it allows for comparisons of the conditions that facilitate movement impact across different institutional settings.

The most common issue raised in discussions of movement outcomes is the methodological challenge of "nonspuriousness." For example, Amenta, Caruthers, and Zylan (1992) note that "in the strongest form of this argument, opportunity structures determine both movement formation and what may be perceived as gains won by the movement" (310). The list of potential exogenous factors is quite long, including repression, allies, economic conditions, and so on. There are a variety of strategies, techniques, and specific measures to assess the relative significance of external factors in relation to movement factors. Some scholars elevate this methodological problem to make the broader claim that "movements succeed or fail as the result of forces outside their control" (Tarrow 1998: 24; see also Kitschelt 1986). From this perspective, all perceived movement impacts are spurious. This conclusion is a bit hasty, as numerous studies have demonstrated the independent influence of social movements.[3] I address these factors only tangentially in this chapter, even though a complete analysis would require a more detailed treatment (see Giugni 1998 for a more complete discussion).

In this chapter, I move from the conventional question of *whether* movements have an impact to *how* movements have an impact. Clearly, these are interconnected questions; however, the second question has been neglected. In answering the question of how movements create change, I begin by examining the role of movement organizations and protest events. Paying attention to these issues will lead inevitably toward more complex theories of movement trajectories to determine whether certain organizational forms and strategies are more influential in some political contexts than others.

Movement Organizations

Efforts to explain the influence of social movements often begin with an analysis of the formal organizations making claims on behalf of a broader movement constituency (Gamson 1990). Although a broad range of studies focuses on organization, there is no clear consensus on the organizational factors associated with movement impacts. Several characteristics appear in organization-based explanations, including leadership, organizational structure, and resources. Organizations can facilitate movement impact in several ways. I begin by delineating some of the most common organizational processes.

Often we think of social movements as making claims to which political authorities respond. Hence, a main impact of social movements is on the agenda of established institutions. Movements may achieve such institutional change in various ways. Organizations that achieve *access* may parlay their legitimacy into substantive influence through negotiation. For example, antitoxic activists have attempted, with some success, to participate in regulatory bodies (Rochon and Mazmanian 1993). In this vein, Diani (1997) argues that "social movement outcomes may be assessed in terms of the movements' capacity to achieve more central positions in networks of social and political influence" (1997: 133; see also Laumann and Knoke 1987). On the other hand, movement organizations may achieve leverage without directly bargaining with state actors or other authorities (Schwartz 1976). The presence of movement organizations can encourage authorities to make preemptive concessions.[4] Movement organizations can also influence policy through sponsorship and coordination of disruptive or persuasive protests.

Many movements, however, attempt to play a more direct role in the implementation of change by establishing parallel institutions or intervening more directly in state activities. Movement organizations may directly institute changes that benefit their constituency, or they may co-opt state institutions and use state resources and authority for movement purposes. For example, feminists have built numerous community institutions to sustain the movement's infrastructure and address gender inequities in the broader society (see Ferree and Martin 1995). Within the Catholic church, for example, feminist activists have developed their own ritual and liturgy (Katzenstein 1998). Movements can employ organizational models of change with little protest in the form of large demonstrations (Katzenstein 1998). In addition, organizations may allow movements to persist through periods when opportunities for influence are minimal (Andrews 1997; Taylor 1989).

Quantitative studies of the southern civil rights movement's impact have typically employed an organization-based explanation (Andrews 1997; Button 1989; Colby 1985; James 1988; Matthews and Protho 1966; Stewart and Sheffield 1987; Timpone 1995). These studies have examined whether communities with greater organizational capacity had more substantial changes in the acquisition of political power and the implementation of social policies. In my case studies of Mississippi communities, I found that organizations played key roles in responding to repression and sustaining confidence in the efficacy of protest (Andrews 2000; on the latter point, see Klandermans 1997). The size of civil rights organizations had a positive impact on the election of black candidates to office and the distribution of poverty program funding (Andrews 1997, 2001).

The Consequences of Movement Action

Another strategy for explaining how social movements promote institutional change examines the effects and characteristics of movement action or protest events such as riots, demonstrations, boycotts, and other public action. Protest can have effects on elected officials, courts, third parties, and countermovements. These effects can derive from specific, targeted campaigns or can be the cumulative result of widespread protest. Further, protest may be influential by creating a sense of crisis, disruption, or threat to authorities, by persuading third parties, or by creating sympathy for a movement's constituency or claims. These alternatives suggest different mechanisms whereby protest has a lasting impact. In addition to its direct effects, protest can facilitate periods of organizational innovation as new groups attempt to implement or extend movement claims. Those organizations can extend or protect movement impacts through the processes outlined in the previous section.

Arguments about the influence of protest have been most thoroughly developed in the "protest event analysis" tradition, in which scholars use accounts of collective action (from newspapers or other sources) to create an index of the amount and form of movement activity. Protest event studies have examined a number of characteristics including size, duration, and intensity of collective action. In some cases, these measures are combined—a good example is measures of strike volume that combine duration and size to assess working days lost.[5] Indices based on newspaper accounts recognize the importance of media coverage of movement events. Rucht, Koopmans, and Neidhardt, note that "the first hurdle for successful protest is erected by the mass media" (1998: 8). The media can advance the movement's agenda by conveying a movement's demands and social criticism to the broader public (see also McCarthy, McPhail, and Smith 1996).[6]

One group of scholars treats protest events as the key determinant of movement influence, but there is significant disagreement about what makes protest influential (Gamson and Schmeidler 1984; Morris 1984; Piven and Cloward 1984, 1992, 1993). The causal mechanism tends to be either disruption-threat or persuasion-sympathy. For example, some scholars argue that protest that is portrayed favorably in the media and that resonates with widely held values enlists other more powerful actors on the side of the movement. In this argument, "third parties," "bystander publics," or "conscience constituents" are critical. Lipsky, in a classic essay, argues that "the 'problem of the powerless' in protest activity is to activate 'third parties' to enter the implicit or explicit bargaining arena in ways favorable to protesters" (1968: 1145, see also Wilson 1961).

In contrast, some scholars argue that protest that is disruptive and threatening to elites prompts a rapid response—typically either concessions or repression. Movements exert pressure through negative sanctions. Piven and Cloward argue that "the most useful way to think about the effectiveness of protest is to examine the disruptive effects on institutions of different forms of mass defiance, and then to examine the political reverberations of those disruptions" (1977: 24). The first explanation proposes that protest can mobilize sympathetic third parties who carry forward the movement's agenda by exerting influence on political elites, either directly or indirectly through public opinion.[7] The second emphasizes disruptive, sometimes violent, action forcing a reaction from political elites. Following either line of argument, some scholars observe specific constraints on protest effectiveness. For example, neither demonstrations nor media coverage can convey the nuances of specific policy preferences (Walton 1988). Protest may be limited as well by its short timespan, making it difficult for activists to sustain mobilization throughout the slow machinations of the policy process.

Organizations and Events in Explanations of Outcomes: Illustrations from the Civil Rights Movement

I argue that we need to focus on the relationship between organizations and events in our analysis of outcomes because each provides partial insights into how movements create change.[8] In the following sections, I explain key theoretical claims about how organizations and events produce social change, with illustrations from the civil rights movement.

Movement Organizations Implementing Change

Organizations are significant not just because they increase movements' legitimacy or take advantage of access to policy makers but because they may directly implement change themselves. During the civil rights movement, the protest-based model sought to influence external institutions through sit-ins, freedom rides, marches, and demonstrations. But at the same time, movement organizations sought directly to improve conditions and develop their own institutions. These efforts provided a basis for movement collaboration with and pressure on nascent federal programs. For example, in many parts of the rural South, movement activists attempted to establish economic cooperatives (Marshall and Goodwin 1971). The War on Poverty became one of the most significant battlegrounds for civil rights organizations as activists attempted to shape its structure and content. The Child Development Group of Mississippi (CDGM), the first statewide Head Start program in Mississippi, provides an example of how movement organization was important for the implementation of such programs. The CDGM formed close alliances with established civil rights groups, and, as a result, it formed projects in virtually all of the Mississippi counties that had had sustained civil rights activity in the early 1960s (sixteen out of nineteen counties). In contrast, among the thirty-five counties that had no organized civil rights activity during the early 1960s, only two counties had CDGM Head Start centers.[9]

How did CDGM emerge so quickly and become so closely connected to local civil rights movements? Organizationally, the structure of the Mississippi movement became much more decentralized rather than federated following the 1964 Freedom Summer. Thus, even though some state movement leaders were opposed to working with federal poverty programs, they could not prevent local leaders from participating in CDGM. In addition, diffuse networks of activists across county lines would allow for communication about the new program. Significantly, some of the CDGM's state leadership—Tom Levin, Art Thomas, Marian Wright—had direct ties with local leaders throughout the state.

At the local level, the affinity between CDGM's program and the move-ment-sponsored Freedom Schools was clear. Freedom Schools were central to the community organizing of the early civil rights movement. They included programs for literacy, "citizenship" training, and general education.[10] Both CDGM and earlier Freedom Schools emphasized educational enrichment and participatory democracy. In many cases, the same personnel were involved. In addition, CDGM brought considerable resources that could allow local movements to upgrade and expand their existing programs.

Moreover, local movements had a point of leverage over the new pro-gram. The movement was the only group positioned in 1965 to provide an infrastructure for Head Start centers. For the most part, public school boards were unwilling to provide access to their facilities, staff, and resources. The few proposals submitted by Mississippi school boards were typically rejected by the Office of Economic Opportunity (the federal agency administering poverty programs) because they made minimal efforts to generate white par-ticipation and did not include significant participation of parents or other community members, two goals central to the War on Poverty.[11] The move-ment could offer access to the community centers and supportive black churches in Mississippi where the emerging program could develop. This combination of forces favored the expansion of CDGM through local civil rights movements in Mississippi. This brief discussion shows a process driven by informal ties among activists and the interorganizational ties among civil rights–affiliated groups.

Organizational Sponsorship of Protest

Many scholars have argued for a positive, if complex, relationship between organizations and events (McAdam 1982; Oberschall 1973; Tilly 1978). Aldon Morris's (1984) analysis of the civil rights movement makes the stron-gest case for the positive influence of organizations on protest activity. Spe-cifically, Morris traces the relationship of the movement's organizational basis in the black church, its mobilization of the church's resources, and its deploy-ment of those resources in protest campaigns throughout the South. For the Birmingham campaign of 1963, Morris (1993) makes a persuasive argument that the strong organizational capacity of the local movement facilitated effec-tive strategy and tactics that had an independent effect on political change. He provides one model for analyzing movement organization, political action, and impact.

Even if Morris is correct for Birmingham, all organizational infrastruc-tures need not produce effective protest activity. Are there organizational forms that dampen the protest activity of a movement and lessen the movement's efficacy? Organizational infrastructures support mass mobilization to vari-

ous degrees. In Birmingham, movement organizations' strong base in indigenous institutions enabled them to recruit and mobilize participants effectively.
Further, the protest activity undertaken in Birmingham was decidedly not
spontaneous; confronting the machinery of segregation required intense coordination, planning of actions, rules about when to withdraw, and support
services both during actions and for those arrested afterward. The organizational forms that emerged, combining charismatic leadership—to promote
mobilization into high-risk activities—and strong networks of bridge leaders (Robnett 1996)—to provide coordination on the ground—were effective
in promoting protest. In different contexts, and with different organizational
forms, the relationship may not be so straightforward. During the civil rights
movement, mass protest was less viable when organizations were weaker,
organizations depended on local authorities, or conflict among organizations
undermined effective coordination (e.g., Keiser 1997).

Moreover, even when organization does facilitate protest, those organizations that engage in mass protest are also more likely to be targeted for
repression and least likely to secure external resources (Haines 1984; Jenkins
and Eckert 1986; McAdam 1982). Debra Minkoff's analysis of women's and
racial-ethnic organizations finds that those that "follow an accepted course
of institutional challenge based on moderate objectives and targeted at nonpolitical arenas" are more likely to survive (1993: 903). If our analytic questions concern the impact of movements, then we must ask whether these
organizations can protect or extend political gains achieved during periods
of broader protest. This is one question I turn to in the next section.

Protest Facilitating Organizational Expansion or Innovation

We have asked what role organizations play in initiating and sustaining protest. However, we can reverse the relationship, asking questions about the
impact of protest activity on organizational processes (Minkoff 1997). If an
upsurge in protest leads to expansion within established organizations or the
founding of new organizations, Minkoff argues that this "may encourage
multimovement coalitions that can position supporters inside the political
system thereby maintaining readiness for future protest" (1997: 796). The
decline in mass protest after the heyday of the civil rights movement has captured the attention of many observers. Yet, at the local and national level,
there were a greater number of social movement organizations after the
movement than there were before it (Andrews 1997; Minkoff 1997). These
changes in the structure of black advocacy can be considered an intermediate outcome of the movement. More important, these actors were in a position to challenge reversals in political or cultural change.

Similar arguments have been made about the increasing number of African Americans, such as black elected officials, who have achieved positions inside mainstream institutions. Do these individuals and organizations press forward goals and maintain ties to a broader social movement? Some evidence suggests they do (Andrews 1997; Carson 1986; Santoro 1998; Santoro and McGuire 1997). For example, Wayne Santoro has used a two-stage analysis of U.S. cities to assess the impact of protest on the election of black candidates to office and the impact of those elected officials on the extent of affirmative action programs. In both cases, he finds a positive relationship. Civil rights protest, thus, had an indirect impact on the institutionalization of municipal affirmative action programs through promoting the expansion of blacks holding office.

Periods of mass protest, then, can facilitate organizational expansion and the entry of movement participants into positions of influence within mainstream institutions. This allows the movement to continue to exert its influence, even as mass mobilization dies down. Protest is influential, in other words, not just because of its immediate effects on policy and institutions but because of its effects on the long-term organizational strength of the movement.

Targeted Campaigns or Widespread Mobilization?

Arguably, the central goal of the civil rights movement was increasing black access to the vote and, consequently, increasing black political participation and electoral influence. In the wake of the movement, these changes undeniably occurred. However, competing explanations have been developed to account for the increases in black political participation following the civil rights movement. The most influential argument identifies a causal sequence with three main "moments": (1) black-led mobilization throughout the South in the early 1960s, creating the momentum for (2) significant federal initiatives to guarantee black political participation, followed by (3) dramatic increases in black voter registration and (presumably) influence. David Garrow's study, *Protest at Selma*, develops this thesis systematically.[12] He summarizes his argument as follows:

> The political sagacity of Martin Luther King, Jr., and his aides, . . . was demonstrated by their very deft creation in Selma of events that spurred support in Washington and across the country for more stringent voting rights safeguards to be enforced not by the federal courts but by the federal executive branch. . . . From their efforts in those early months of 1965, as well as from the efforts of Johnson, his men at Justice, and certain members of Congress, sprang a legislative enactment that was to stimulate as great a change in American politics as any one law ever has. (1978: 235–36)

This view has been echoed many times over. In an impressive analysis of legal change, Rosenberg claims that "there can be no doubt that the major increase in the registration of blacks came from the action of Congress and the executive branch through the 1965 Voting Rights Act" (1991: 61; see also Alt 1995). I argue that this is the dominant narrative because it can be found most clearly in popular presentations of the civil rights movement such as documentaries, widely read historical studies, and textbooks.

Several empirical expectations are embedded in this narrative. First, voter registration increases should follow the 1965 Voting Rights Act rather than precede it. Second, increases in black political participation should follow immediately rather than gradually. Third, black political participation should increase where federal intervention is greatest. Timpone (1995) calls this the "government intervention" argument because of the key role attributed to federal legislation. Social movement activity plays an important role but only through a momentary impact on the legislative process. In addition, the key social movement actors are the strategists who direct national organizations that are positioned to shape legislation.[13]

In contrast, some scholars have developed an alternative account that places greater emphasis on the cumulative and incremental impact of "mass mobilization" on black political participation and officeholding (Andrews 1997; Rochon and Kabashima 1998; Rosenstone and Hansen 1993; Santoro 1998; Timpone 1995). The first empirical difficulty faced by the "government intervention" argument is the increases in black voter registration that preceded passage of the Voting Rights Act in 1965. As the federal intervention argument suggests, there was an upsurge in black registration in the mid-1960s. However, there was also a steady rise in black voter registration over the twenty-five years preceding the Voting Rights Act. In addition, Timpone found that the upsurge in registration began between 1962 and 1964. He infers that the electoral competition around the 1964 elections and the Voter Education Projects (grants administered by the Southern Regional Council to local voter registration campaigns by civil rights groups) spurred an increase in black registration before the passage of the Voting Rights Act.

These accounts diverge on key points. Yet some points of convergence suggest how national legislative victories are related to the efforts and achievements of local movement groups. For example, the successful implementation of national legislation may depend on more modest, local victories before and after major legislative gains. Similarly, major legislative changes may serve to institutionalize the impacts of local campaigns. To understand outcomes, then, we should expand our focus on major legislative gains at the national level to incorporate changes in individual and group behavior (e.g., changes in black political participation) and variation over time and place. These relationships point to the complex interconnections between grassroots organizations, the protest events they organize, national organizations, and the state.

Conclusion

In this chapter I have proposed a more explicit focus on the causal relationship between movements and outcomes that goes beyond the initial question of *whether* movements have impacts. Building on arguments that link organizational and event processes to movement impact, I have illustrated how social movements influence the extent and form of social change. This type of analysis is important because the civil rights movement has provided a model for our understanding of legal, political, and social change more generally. Asking these questions allows us to address more refined questions about the temporal pattern of change, the relative importance of watershed events or the accumulation of mass protest, and the interaction between events and organizational processes.

Rather than proposing a holistic theory of movement impacts, I have attempted to shed light on a neglected set of questions concerning the consequences of movements and to demonstrate the theoretical payoffs that emerge from addressing those questions. I have suggested directions for analysis of outcomes. First, movement organizations are important not only for their ability to gain access and pressure authorities but also for their efforts to implement changes directly for their constituencies. Second, movement organizations and protest events interact, each potentially facilitating the impact of the other. An organizational base can be important to sustaining protest under some conditions, and, conversely, periods of extensive protest may encourage the formation of new organizations that can outlast the protest wave. Third, the temporal dimension of social change is crucial, and the accumulation of mass protest and watershed events can interact in producing major changes. Analyzing these types of processes for the civil rights movement and other movements, and comparing them across movements, will lead to more complex and powerful theories of movements and their consequences.

NOTES

I thank Roberto Franzosi, David Meyer, Ziad Munson, Michael Schwartz, and Nancy Whittier for comments on earlier drafts of this essay.

1. Surprisingly, there has not been more substantial research and debate about how the movement produced such far-reaching impacts. The "origins" or "emergence" of the movement has produced a more lively debate (see Carson 1986).

2. I disagree with Rochon's (1998) argument that political impacts face greater methodological difficulties than cultural impacts. The key differences concern the types of evidence that would constitute an outcome.

3. For examples, see studies cited throughout this chapter and recent literature reviews by Burstein et al. (1995) and Giugni (1998).

4. The presence of movement organizations can also trigger efforts by authorities to increase their surveillance and repressive capacity.

5. Studies examining the effects of protest events on outcomes have often used a simple count—the number of events in a particular temporal or spatial unit (e.g., Burstein and Freudenberg 1979). Fording (1997) argues that counts are highly correlated with more refined measures producing substantively comparable results when used to predict outcomes. However, researchers are likely to continue measuring specific characteristics of events in outcome studies because it allows them to test more refined hypotheses. For example, studies of media bias show that size has an important effect on coverage (McCarthy, McPhail, and Smith 1996: Rucht and Neidhardt 1998).

6. This methodological argument for using media coverage to measure protest events contains a specific model of movement impact. Rucht and Neidhardt extend this argument: "Insofar as we are interested in those protests which are an input for the political system, media-reported protests have a higher validity than the whole range of actual protests" (1998: 76). Testing this argument would require an independent measure of protest activity and outcome measures.

7. This argument assumes a democratic regime where elected officials will have some incentive to monitor and respond to constituent preferences. As O'Keefe and Schumaker (1983) argue, protest takes on the form of a "two-player game" between the state and protestors in authoritarian regimes.

8. The separation of organization- and event-based explanations is most obvious in quantitative analyses. Laumann and Knoke (1987) provide one model for examining questions about organizational processes, event processes, and the intersection between them.

9. My analysis of CDGM and the Mississippi movement is documented more systematically in my forthcoming book; see also Dittmer 1994; Greenberg 1969; Payne 1995; Quadagno 1994.

10. The literacy and "citizenship" training classes were an outgrowth of voter registration campaigns. Mississippi law required that registrants fill out an application and interpret a section from the Mississippi constitution. Local registrars applied these rules so that it was often impossible for blacks to register, regardless of their literacy. Nevertheless, local organizers continued to operate literacy programs and bring qualified applicants to the courthouse. Moreover, literacy classes were an organizing tool for the movement, creating local networks of grassroots leaders (Dittmer 1994; Payne 1995).

11. Local agencies submitted applications to the Office of Economic Opportunity to administer various poverty programs such as job training or Head Start projects.

12. Burstein (1985) argues that protest increased the salience of civil rights in American public opinion, rather than changing the direction of public opinion, and that movements probably cannot to have such a substantial impact on opinion. Rather, within a favorable context, movements can move an issue higher on the political agenda (Burstein 1999). Examining the 1964 Civil Rights Act, Burstein (1993) argues that protest has an effect on agenda setting but not on other outcomes, such as the development of policy alternatives or legislative enactment.

13. This narrative does not directly address the relationship between voter registration and the actual political influence of black voters. However, the argument does imply that political influence should flow from the newly acquired access to the ballot.

Part Three

ORGANIZATIONS AND STRATEGIES

Introduction to Part III

The chapters in this part highlight the importance of activists' identities and ideologies to the study of social movement organizations (SMOs) and dynamics. These identities may be shaped by previous social movement events or social-structural and cultural changes. "Standpoint," ideology, and identity are critical to our understanding of how participants in social movement organizations create shared meanings, develop effective strategies, and reach agreements about obtainable goals. Each of the authors tackles this problem through analyses of micro, meso, and macro connections.

The part begins with an overview by Suzanne Staggenborg, who provides an insightful analysis of the field, emphasizing meso-level analysis and the importance of submerged networks of organizational and unaffiliated activists. In her study of the Bloomington, Indiana, ERA movement, Staggenborg emphasizes that neither a macro-level focus on political opportunities or culture nor a micro-level focus on "individual enthusiasms" can fully explore this movement's emergence. Most important, she argues, is how these macro and micro conditions are mediated by meso-level structures. Staggenborg suggests how we might study these linkages, arguing that analyses of framing, mobilizing structures, and activists' connections can lead to greater clarity in the empirical case, suggesting a new emphasis for theory on social movements.

Simliarly, Colin Barker and Michael Lavalette's study of intergenerational conflict between older and younger union members on the Liverpool docks lends insight into the connections between identity, movement organizations, and past as well as present political and movement outcomes. They highlight activist agency in interpreting political opportunities, arguing that how activists decide what to do, and which strategies to use are intrinsically bound with identity and past political experiences. Barker and Lavalette view strategizing as a process that includes rational and cultural elements and is bound up in the possibilities of the moment, in light of interpretations of the past. Understandings of past political outcomes converge with present identities and frame activists' interpretations of current political opportunities to affect decisions about movement strategies and goals. Barker and Lavalette's analysis raises provocative questions about our conceptualization of an SMO's ability to frame strategies and the relationship to agency and structure.

Mildred Schwartz's and Jo Reger's studies provide excellent examples of the meso-micro linkage. Unlike previous studies of factionalism in social movements, Schwartz's study of factions in the Canadian New Democratic Party and Reger's study of the New York City National Organization for Women (NOW) chapter emphasize that factions offer positive, as well as negative, outcomes. Factions, they argue, often enhance the bridging capacity of organizations to link political, structural, and cultural change with individual motivations to act. Both studies also show the impact of collective identity on social movement organization and vice versa.

In Schwartz's study, ideological disputes and power struggles arose between groups who had different interests. Farmers, academicians, and industrial workers vied for power within one political organization. Although Schwartz emphasizes the difficulties of organizations within a multiorganizational field, the field is defined by the "social location" of the activists. Each organization struggles to gain ideological and strategic influence in shaping the meaning of its efforts among diverse participants. The contest over meaning is important because it becomes the vehicle for explaining the macro-level social, cultural, political, and economic conditions to the citizens at the grassroots. In this way, the political party serves as a meso-level link between its purported constituents and the system it challenges. Social location, then, becomes central because the meaning imparted by the party must resonate with its constituents. Schwartz shows that while the New Democratic Party was never able to satisfy all of the factions—many left the party—the battles over meaning forced the organization to modify, clarify, and redefine its positions. Thus, factions enhance the bridging capacity of meso-level organizations by expanding their mass appeal.

Whereas in Schwartz's study, the battles over ideology resulted in organizational splintering, Jo Reger's study shows how an organization can use factions to build unity, resolving ideological and identity rifts through structural accommodation. The New York City NOW chapter opted to split the ideologically opposed factions into two groups housed in the same organization. This accomodationist stance of providing space for those committed to political change as well as for those more in support of consciousness raising led to a mutually beneficial, if sometimes strained, relationship. As in Schwartz's study, these factions broadened the base of NOW.

Finally, Rebecca Klatch offers an analysis of the impact of political, social, and cultural change on a cohort of youths. The same broad external events produced radically divergent ideologies and organizations, as they were mediated by the social location of the incipient activists. Her analysis of members of the Students for a Democratic Society (SDS) on the Left and Young Americans for Freedom (YAF) on the Right illustrates the convergence of external and internal factors as mediated through political organizations on the development of political consciousness and identity. Klatch, like Barker and Lavalette, emphasizes temporal processes, arguing that political consciousness and identity evolve over time. Individuals' identities are critical in determining whether they became activists, and whether on the Left or Right, but subsequently experience with the organization influences their sense of self and political activities.

Clearly, linkages between the micro, meso, and macro levels are affected by identity, ideology, and framing. Social location and identities are shaped by larger social-structural, cultural, economic, and political forces and are critical to the processes by which meso-level organizations operate. All of these studies suggest the necessity of seriously considering the connections between identity, agency, structure, and framing in the context of social movements and collective action.

7

The "Meso" in Social Movement Research

SUZANNE STAGGENBORG

Beginning in the 1980s, many sociologists began to call for theories that connected micro-level interactions with macro-level social structures and changes (cf. Alexander et al. 1987; Huber 1991; Knorr-Cetina and Cicourel 1981). Scholars also became interested in making connections among levels of analysis to develop more complete theories of social movements. In an influential review of the field, McAdam, McCarthy, and Zald (1988) examined some relationships between macro- and micro-level dynamics and called for more research at the intermediate "meso" level of analysis. In the past ten years, a number of theorists have heeded their call to better conceptualize the meso level and link levels of analysis in social movement research, but we still need to do more of this type of theorizing.

My goal in this chapter is to encourage new research on meso-level structures and processes that mediate between the micro and the macro in social movements. I begin by discussing promising approaches to linking micro and macro dynamics. I then illustrate how meso-level research and connections among levels of analysis are important to explanations of movement emergence, maintenance, and outcomes and provide examples of the type of research needed.

Approaches to Micro-Macro Linkages

Using a variety of definitions of "micro" and "macro," researchers offer different approaches to the combination of these levels of analysis (see Münch and Smelser 1987 for a review). Most analysts recognize, however, that levels of analysis are continuous rather than discrete and "that in any kind of social organization we can observe an interpenetration of these analytic levels"

(Smelser 1997: 29). Micro-sociological analysis involves study of individual behavior and patterns of interaction among individuals, whereas macro-sociological analysis focuses on large-scale and long-term social processes (Collins 1981). The meso level of "structural but subsocietal phenomena," such as organizations (Smelser 1997: 1), bridges these levels of analysis.

Researchers seeking to integrate levels of analysis have adopted various approaches (see Ritzer 1996: 507–9). One approach is to examine the connections among variables at different levels of analysis. Opp and Gern (1993), for example, use both micro and macro (which actually includes meso) variables to explain mobilization in East Germany in 1989. Zuo and Benford (1995) analyze a combination of macro, meso, and micro mobilization processes in explaining the Chinese student movement of 1989. In a study of political violence, della Porta (1995) argues that each level is central at a different stage in an evolving cycle of violence. At the start, large-scale political and social conditions influence the development of the meso-level movement and micro-level perceptions. Once meso-level groups have emerged, they influence individuals and political opportunities. Later, when the movement is in decline, micro-level processes become most important in keeping militants active.

Some researchers begin with the level of analysis most appropriate to their research problems and then make connections to other levels. Randall Collins (1981) focuses on micro interactions and how they affect macro phenomena. (Of special interest to social movement theorists is Collins's emphasis on the emotional energy generated by interaction rituals.) Bert Klandermans (1997) begins with the individual in explaining participation in collective action but examines individual decisions within the context of organizational characteristics and political opportunities. William Gamson (1992a) is similarly interested in linking individual behavior to sociocultural levels. He specifies "bridging processes," such as the development of collective identity, solidarity, and consciousness, and identifies different "mobilizing acts" during face-to-face encounters that link individual and cultural levels.

Although all of these strategies for combining micro and macro have merit, I prefer to begin with the meso, and make linkages to the micro and macro levels of analyses (cf. Hage 1980). In line with this approach, Neil Smelser (1997) views social movements as meso phenomena, and McAdam et al. argue that "the real action in social movements takes place at some level intermediate between the macro and micro" (1988: 729). They develop the concept of the "micro-mobilization context" as a meso-level linkage between macro and micro processes. Gerhards and Rucht (1992) elaborate on this idea in their distinction between "micro-mobilization" actors, which mobilize individuals, and "meso-mobilization" actors, which coordinate groups and networks. Both types of actors are part of "the intermediary structure that is a fundamental part of the micro-macro bridge" (Gerhards and Rucht 1992: 559). McCarthy (1996) also elaborates on the "micro-macro bridge" in conceptualizing various formal and informal "mobilizing structures" through which people organize for collective action.

Elaborating the Meso

To link the micro and macro through a meso focus, we need to continue to elaborate the ways in which mobilizing structures vary over time and across movements, both cross-nationally and within single countries (cf. Tarrow 1998; Zald 1992). This means expanding our conception of the meso beyond the most obvious forms of organization, recognizing that, in some movements and at some stages of movement development, political social movement organizations (SMOs) may be scarce or peripheral. Instead of acting largely or solely through SMOs, movements can be embedded in informal networks, cultural groups, institutions, and everyday life. Zald (2000) suggests that we should broaden our conception of movements by conceptualizing them as "ideologically structured action." To do so, however, we need to think about all of the places in which such action occurs, including political parties and government bureaucracies, as Zald suggests, as well as other structures such as alternative and mainstream institutions (Katzenstein 1998).

Of course, organizations *are* important to social movements, and we need to continue to examine the effects of SMOs and other formal organizations in different cultural and political environments. We also need to continue to look at internal organizational characteristics of SMOs and changes over time in organizational structures, comparing different types of SMOs. At the same time, we must recognize that the meso-level of a movement is much more complex than a collection of SMOs and must consider the internal dynamics and functions of all mobilizing structures.

The notion of "social movement communities" (see Buechler 1990; Staggenborg 1998a; Taylor and Whittier 1992) is particularly helpful in capturing the diversity of meso structures. Social movement communities include SMOs but also networks of individual movement adherents who do not necessarily belong to SMOs, institutionalized movement supporters, alternative institutions, and cultural groups. Movement communities may be local, national, or international in scope. Their connections to protest cycles, bases of constituent commitment, connections to other movement communities, linkages between groups at different levels (e.g., local and national), number of movement organizations, extent of centralization, and extent of institutionalization vary (Staggenborg 1998a). They likely look different in different cultures and political systems. For example, Jane Jenson (1982) argues that the women's movements in Italy, France, and Great Britain took different forms as a result of different political contexts, including different relationships to Left parties.

In addition to varying across political contexts, movement communities change shape over the course of a social movement. During a protest cycle, they are highly visible and often overlap with the communities of other movements in the same "social movement family" (della Porta and Rucht 1995). After the cycle of protest subsides, the shape of the movement community will depend on the particular environment of the individual movement and on the movement's constituency. Some movements, particularly those facing countermovements, maintain themselves with professional SMOs (Staggenborg 1988). Movements with limited constituencies may survive the "doldrums" with an elite-sustained organizational structure (Rupp and Taylor 1987; Taylor 1989). Some mass movements become "submerged" (see Melucci 1984, 1989, 1996), engaging in actions that are ideologically structured but not politically contentious (cf. Klandermans 2000; Zald 2000).

Focus on the meso-level structures of social movement communities is critical in explaining movement processes. Mobilizing structures affect micro-level interactions, motivations, and perceptions of macro-level political and cultural opportunities. The actions of meso-level actors can sometimes bring changes in large-scale political and cultural conditions. In the following sections, I discuss the importance of meso-level structures, and their connections to the macro and the micro, for the key issues of movement emergence, maintenance, and outcomes.

Movement Emergence

In the early 1970s, a campaign to pass the ERA got off the ground in the United States. The ERA movement emerged at a time of widespread, visible movement activity, particularly among feminists. In my research on the early women's movement in Bloomington, Indiana (see Staggenborg 1998b), participants in the ERA campaign described rallies and street festivals, tables at the local mall, and intense discussions about new possibilities for women. Few talked about the fact that the Indiana legislature in the early 1970s was staunchly conservative and not about to pass the ERA. When I asked one informant if she was discouraged by the political obstacles, she explained that she was busy going to rallies and talking to people like herself, who were excited by the possibility of change rather than to stubborn legislators. To be sure, some politically astute leaders were well aware of the intransigency of the state legislature and worked to change its composition later in the decade. But they would never have imagined doing so had there not been a supportive feminist community.

We cannot understand the emergence of a movement, or of a specific campaign within a movement, by looking at political opportunities and large-scale structural and cultural changes alone. Nor can we understand movement emergence by looking only at individual enthusiasms. Both large-scale conditions and micro-level motivations and interactions are mediated by meso-level structures. We must examine the structure of the movement community and how it influences perceptions of large-scale trends and individual motivations and interactions. In the case of the Indiana ERA campaign, the movement community in the early 1970s was energetic and expanding, with an active NOW chapter, a women's center, and numerous groups engaging in visible collective action. Interactions in this vital movement community, rather than the political opportunity structure, fed mobilization.

Macro conditions create the potential for mobilization through their impact on organization, resource bases, and grievances (cf. Tilly 1978). For example, urbanization and other socioeconomic changes strengthened organizational bases like the black churches for the American civil rights movement (McAdam 1982; Morris 1984). Large-scale changes such as women's entry into the labor force created the potential for organization among women (Freeman 1975; Klein 1984). In explaining how macro potentials lead to mobilization, theorists have argued that political opportunities motivate entrepreneurs and other participants to originate movements by creating expectations of success (e.g., McAdam 1982; Tarrow 1998). Some theorists have also noted that threats, rather than opportunities, can lead to collective action; as Koopmans argues, "threat will increase the likelihood of collective action because it increases the relative costs of not acting" (1995: 26). However, both political opportunities and threats must be perceived and interpreted (see Klandermans 1997).

To bridge the macro-micro gap, we need to look at both meso-macro and meso-micro linkages. The notion of collective action framing is particularly helpful in connecting all three levels of analysis. Collective action frames, produced at the meso level, allow groups and individuals to interpret political opportunities and threats (cf. Snow and Benford 1992). A number of studies have shown how movement organizations engage in frame alignment to link individuals to movements (cf. Benford 1993; Snow and Benford 1988; Snow, Rochford, Worden, and Benford 1986; Swart 1995). Gerhards and Rucht (1992) reveal how "mesomobilization actors" connect master frames to the concerns of particular constituents, helping to link different groups in collective action campaigns (see also Carroll and Ratner 1996).

Other studies have focused on the meso-micro link by examining the processes through which meso-level micro-mobilization contexts provide networks, information, and organizational settings for recruitment. Potential organizational resources are mobilized into movements through meso structures. Klandermans (1992, 1997) stresses the connections between characteristics of multi-organizational fields, such as the number and type of organizations allied with the movement and processes of resource mobilization.

Movement culture produced within meso structures is important in binding individuals to movements. Movements form and people join them because they are excited about the cause and hopeful that they can bring about change through collective action. However, the emotional energy needed for the emergence of movements must be generated within movement communities. Taylor and her collaborators (Taylor and Rupp 1993; Taylor and Whittier 1995) point to the importance of group ritual and emotion in binding individuals to collectives. Jasper (1998) stresses the effects of emotions generated within movement culture and through movement networks on individual motivations and movement mobilization.

Compared to meso-micro connections, the macro-meso link has received less attention. We must study the characteristics of meso structures and cultures that make them capable of converting large-scale potential into commitment. What structures and cultures are able to exploit potentials created by macro-level political, social, structural, and cultural patterns? How are political opportunities and threats made apparent within social movement communities? Or, as in the case of the Indiana ERA movement, what types of meso structures and cultures encourage collective action against the political odds, perhaps ultimately creating political opportunities?

One approach to meso-macro linkages is suggested by Carol Mueller (1994), who uses Melucci's theories about the construction of collective identity at the meso level in her analysis of the origins of the U.S. women's movement. Although large-scale socioeconomic changes helped to create public support for feminism among both men and women, a feminist collective identity among women was forged within submerged networks. Mueller adds, however, that feminist collective identity picked up force as a result of large-scale structural changes, resulting in "a massive shift in consciousness among both men and women" (1994: 252). The new collective identity of women became part of public discourse, and this large-scale change in consciousness then affected political outcomes. Thus, we need to analyze how meanings created in movement communities are enhanced or altered by large-scale trends and then examine the effects of the resulting changes in public discourse.

Another approach to macro-meso connections is to compare the ability of different types of mobilizing structures to harness the potential of large-scale changes. In a study of political commitment in environmental groups, Paul Lichterman (1996) shows how different movement organizations utilize particular cultural skills and lifestyle patterns. He distinguishes between two political styles, the communitarian and the personalized, which are linked to large-scale class and cultural patterns. He found that activists from the "new class" sector of the professional middle class were drawn to movement organizations with a personalist style of activism that encouraged individual expression, allowing them to use the cultural skills that they valued. Community-based activists, such as African American residents of a city, were more likely to be mobilized by structures that built on existing cultural and religious traditions and ties. Similarly, Harris (1999) shows how African American religious culture within a variety of mobilizing structures motivates political activism among blacks. Thus, different movement organizational structures exploit different large-scale socioeconomic and cultural patterns.

Different structures within movement communities can also be linked to the perception of political opportunity that can mobilize activism. One important structural variable is the extent to which individual movement communities (e.g., feminist and environmental) overlap. During a cycle of protest, information about political opportunities spreads rapidly, through overlaps leading to the emergence of some new movements. In the 1960s, the movement to legalize abortion, known then simply as "the abortion movement," emerged in a context in which numerous movements were demanding "rights," and the civil rights movement in particular had demonstrated how the courts could be used to establish these rights. The abortion movement was a loose collection of small groups and entrepreneurs with connections to civil liberties, civil rights, and family planning groups, as well as to the emerging women's movement (see Staggenborg 1991). Through these connections, activists learned of legal precedents, including *Griswold v. Connecticut*, the 1965 contraceptive case based on the "right to privacy," which suggested abortion could be legalized through litigation. Moreover, through connections to civil liberties lawyers, the abortion movement gained access to the resources needed to take advantage of political opportunities. Access to these resources and the perception of opportunity, as well as the energetic support of the new women's movement, allowed the abortion movement to spread.

Thus, connections among activists from different movements are an important feature of meso organization that can lead to awareness of political opportunities, resources, and the growth of a movement. But, as the Indiana ERA example shows, expectations of success are not necessarily based on assessments of the external structure of political opportunity. Instead, they can be generated through interactions with like-minded persons in a social movement community. During a cycle of protest, activists involved in a number of different movements typically interact. Even in the absence of real political opportunities, the sheer volume of protest encourages the belief that real change is possible. Even if the movement fails to achieve its goals, it may produce outcomes that aid future rounds of protest (see Mueller 1987; Staggenborg 1994).

Movement Maintenance

In the late 1970s and early 1980s, the women's movement in Bloomington, Indiana, like the movement elsewhere in the United States was quite active (see Staggenborg 1996, 1998a,b). One important focus of activity was the ERA; although Indiana had passed the amendment in 1977, many groups, such as the Bloomington chapter of NOW, continued to work for the national ERA campaign. Another focus of activity was abortion rights, which were under strong attack in the late 1970s and early 1980s, with the passage of the Hyde Amendment denying funding for abortions to poor women, Supreme Court decisions upholding funding cuts, and the election of an anti-abortion President Ronald Reagan (see Staggenborg 1991). However, the deadline for the ERA ran out in 1982 and the period of intensified threat to abortion rights ended with the tabling of anti-abortion legislation in Congress in 1982 and a Supreme Court ruling reaffirming *Roe v. Wade* in 1983. Then the period of highly visible feminist political activity ended.

After the early 1980s, the Bloomington feminist community experienced stretches of time with little visible political activity and had great difficulty in maintaining movement organizations like Bloomington NOW. Many activists were exhausted by the ERA campaign and disillusioned regarding the possibilities for change in the Reagan era. At the same time, there were often no acute threats around which to mobilize an issue campaign. In this political context, many Bloomington feminists, particularly lesbians, chose to put their energies into cultural activities such as the annual National Women's Music Festival (NWMF), a feminist chorus of the Unitarian Church, and other feminist writers' groups and reading groups.

Nevertheless, feminist networks in Bloomington were activated from time to time to support collective action. Most notably, when abortion rights were again under attack in the late 1980s and early 1990s, local feminists became involved. During the anti–Gulf War movement of 1990–1991, a number of feminists who had been participating in largely cultural activities joined in the antiwar activities. In response to a gay-bashing incident in Bloomington in the early 1990s, lesbian feminists joined gay men in testifying before a city human rights commission and forming an explicitly political organization to fight for gay and lesbian rights.

The surge in mobilization around abortion rights was a response to counter-movement threats to legal abortion centered around the Supreme Court's 1989 *Webster* ruling, which made the abortion issue "hot" throughout the United States (see Staggenborg 1991). In Bloomington, these national developments made many students and other local feminists concerned about abortion rights, but campaigns supporting the issue did not simply organize themselves. They built on the existing women's movement community and were limited by its resources and structure. For instance, some women's studies students, eager for activism because of their perceptions of threats to abortion rights, fumbled around trying to figure out how to begin an organization or campaign. They initially contacted the local NOW chapter, thinking they could become a student caucus of NOW, but the organizational disarray of the chapter soon discouraged them. With advice from a veteran feminist on the staff of the Office for Women's Affairs (an institutional outcome of earlier feminist mobilization and a part of the movement community), the students finally formed an independent group called the Women's Student Union. But they were still uncertain about how to get started until an organizer from the national Fund for a Feminist Majority located them through the women's studies department and involved them in a campaign against parental consent laws in the early 1990s. Thus, mobilization was aided by institutionalized elements of the local women's movement community—women's studies and the Office for Women's Affairs—and by national support that overcame the weakness of other elements of the local community.

We can see a similar process in the case of renewed gay rights activism in the early 1990s. A local gay-bashing incident, in which a young man was nearly drowned, provided the spark for the formation of a group called the Gay, Lesbian, Bisexual (GLB) Coalition in Bloomington in 1992. Organizers of the group saw the local incident as part of a larger pattern of right-wing assaults on gays and lesbians throughout the United States. At the same time, a key organizer noted that the 1992 presidential election also encouraged their action, saying "everybody felt more energized once we got the Republicans out of government" (interview 6-15-93). Although perceptions of opportunities and threatening events provided an impetus, the state of the local movement community influenced mobilization. Organizers found that many of the lesbians and gay men who showed up at coalition meetings had previously been involved in movements like the women's movement and the abortion rights movement. At the same time, it was not easy to get everyone in the lesbian-feminist community involved. Some longtime activists participated, others did not, and a GLB organizer believed that they were not reaching many longtime lesbian-feminist activists. She noted that personal contact was important in persuading such women to come to meetings and that some thought they had paid their dues and preferred social and cultural activities to renewed political activism. For those who did become involved, ties to one another and to gay men were important.

As this account suggests, we should closely examine how movements emerge out of "submerged networks," pursuing both meso-macro and meso-micro connections to explain movement maintenance. Large-scale cultural and political conditions, including both political opportunities and threats to values and rights, such as abortion rights and gay rights, clearly influence mobilization. Frequently, critical events provide the impetus for political action (see Staggenborg 1993). How people react to such events depends on their previous political experiences and on meso mobilizing structures (see Staggenborg 1996, 1998; Woliver 1993). Characteristics of movement communities, including internal networks, central gathering places, SMOs, ties between national and local activists, and overlaps with other movement communities, affect the mobilization of a new campaign in response to critical events.

McAdam, McCarthy, and Zald (1988: 716) focus on the role of SMOs, arguing that formal SMOs typically maintain movements and that informal micro-organizational contexts are rarely sufficient for movement survival. But in some movements, such as the Bloomington women's movement, SMOs may be relatively unimportant during certain periods, and it is even possible, as Piven and Cloward (1977) have argued, that movement organizations sometimes hasten movement decline. Because SMOs have high maintenance needs, movements may survive the doldrums through the more informal submerged networks of movement communities. Under what conditions are SMOs critical to movement survival? How do other types of structures, including cultural groups, connections among movements, and institutionalization, maintain movements and support renewed collective action from time to time? We need to answer these questions.

Macro-level political and cultural features, such as the extent of opposition or support for a movement, affect the types of mobilizing structures needed to maintain movements. Because SMOs are likely particularly important to the maintenance of movements that face countermovements, they must remain vigilant on a number of fronts for many years. In the American pro-choice movement, formalized SMOs with professional leaders kept the movement alive during times when it was difficult to keep supporters focused on the abortion issue (Staggenborg 1988, 1991). After a huge victory like legalization of abortion by the U.S. Supreme Court in 1973, it is difficult to maintain a high level of grassroots involvement as supporters turn their attention to other causes. But attacks by countermovement forces require ongoing vigilance, and formalized organizations and professional expertise allow movements to continue to solicit money through direct mail, monitor developments in the legislatures, and file lawsuits. Movements that face specific attacks over long periods of time likely develop formalized organizations that maintain the movement and battle the opposition in institutional arenas (Staggenborg 1988).

Movements that lack extensive support for their goals or face a hostile political climate may also require one or more strong organizations to sur-

vive for many years. Rupp and Taylor (1987) show how the women's movement was maintained after the passage of suffrage through the National
Women's Party (NWP), an "elite-sustained" organization (see Taylor 1989,
1994). The NWP was not the sole carrier of feminism after suffrage, but it
was the core of a movement based on tight friendship networks and strong
leadership, which kept the goal of passing the ERA alive when there was little
support for this goal. Because the movement lacked the large numbers necessary for tactics such as demonstrations, it engaged in institutionalized tactics
like lobbying and letter writing (Taylor 1994: 292), which are best coordinated by movement organizations. A strong organization was important in
providing leadership and centralization to a movement sustained by a small,
elite group of women rather than a mass base.

Thus, different movement organizations can be critical to the survival
of movements under various political conditions, including the presence of
a strong countermovement and the absence of a mass base. However, movement organizations do not always play such a central role in sustaining
movements. Movement *campaigns*, which typically involve a complicated
array of meso actors, are particularly important to movement maintenance
(cf. Kleidman 1993; Oliver 1989). Although movement organizations are
often central to campaigns, unaffiliated individuals and other groups are also
involved in issue campaigns. Often a coalition of groups is involved, and sometimes a new umbrella organization forms to lead a campaign. Tensions between grassroots groups or individual activists and professional organizations
and leaders may make it difficult for SMOs to control strategy (cf. Kleidman
1993). For example, NOW took a lead role in the ERA campaign, but many
other groups participated, and NOW could not control the arguments and
actions of many individuals and groups (see Mansbridge 1986).

In examining meso campaign structures, we can make connections to both
large-scale factors and micro-level perceptions. Building on an array of meso
structures, campaigns respond to threats and take advantage of political
opportunities. The political opportunity structure facilitates and constrains
actions and can also be changed in typically small but significant ways by
movement actions (Oliver 1989: 12). Meso actions also affect micro interactions, bringing about changes in individual perceptions. By observing and
taking part in successful actions, participants find opportunities for new
actions, learn new ideas, develop commitments, and come to believe in the
efficacy of collective actions. When movement actions stop producing gains,
"people's estimates of the probability of success decline and collective action
begins to taper off" (Oliver 1989: 16).

Movements temporarily lacking campaigns of their own can survive slow
periods through connections to other movements with compatible goals. As

David Meyer and Nancy Whittier (1994) have shown, overlaps between social movement communities allow movement "spillover." Issue-specific political opportunities or threats may make one movement "hot" just as another movement suffers from the doldrums, but spillover of activists from one movement to another allows a larger movement community to survive. By participating in the campaigns of ideologically compatible movements, activists remain involved even when their "home" movement is in decline.

Gerhards and Rucht's (1992) study of "meso-mobilization" in West Germany shows how diverse groups from different movements were brought together in protest campaigns in response to critical events. They describe a wide range of "micro-mobilization groups" including "loose circles of politically engaged individuals" and "religious groups," as well as SMOs. To mobilize these groups for collective action campaigns, networks of activists formed special task forces or coordinating bodies. In the two cases of meso-mobilization that Gerhards and Rucht studied, the networks were strong and there were many politically active groups to organize.

The meso-mobilization process might look quite different, however, if movement networks are weaker and less visible. Some movements may be able to survive for a time without strong SMOs and without visible political campaigns. Those with extensive constituencies and broad goals, like the contemporary women's movement, can likely survive unobtrusively (cf. Katzenstein 1990, 1998). During slow periods, a movement community might consist largely of committed individuals who attempt to advance movement goals in their everyday lives (cf. McAdam 1988b; Whittier 1995), through institutional support, and in cultural types of movement activities. To explain how collective action campaigns emerge under such conditions, we need to look closely at characteristics of movement communities.

Movements can maintain themselves through micro-mobilization processes that continue to involve veteran activists in new campaigns, as the examples of abortion and gay rights campaigns in Bloomington show. The structures of a movement community are important in determining whether previous activists will join in a new campaign. In a loosely connected movement community, individuals who interact with activists less frequently and are asked to participate less often are most likely to cease active participation (see Klandermans 1997: 107). In addition, meso mobilizing structures may be more or less compatible with the motivations and lifestyles of individuals. In an analysis of personalist activism in the environmental movement, Lichterman (1996) found that individuals who were motivated by a search for self-fulfillment through political action tended to maintain their activism even as individual movement organizations failed. Often, such activists take jobs and otherwise organize their lives to allow for ongoing activism. Groups that attract people with personalized commitments encourage individual expression and participation. In the Bloomington women's movement, numerous people fit this profile of ongoing activism and personal commitment. Others had jobs and lifestyles that were not compatible with full-time activism, yet they retained connections to the movement community and occasionally participated in limited ways.

Movement Outcomes

The United States and Switzerland are both federal systems, but Swiss women did not win the vote until 1971, over fifty years after American women. In a comparative study of the women's suffrage movements in the two countries, Lee Ann Banaszak (1996) argues that the outcomes of the two suffrage movements were influenced not so much by resources and political opportunities as by the *use* that each movement made of resources and opportunities. The U.S. movement used strategies and tactics that were successful in winning suffrage. Swiss activists could have used many of the same strategies and tactics effectively but failed to do so. Although characteristics of the Swiss political system played some role in constraining the activities of Swiss suffrage groups, Banaszak argues that the movement missed many opportunities because of values and beliefs that affected activists' perceptions of political opportunities and their strategic decisions. In particular, the Swiss suffrage movement never adopted values that would challenge the "status quo" belief in "the positive worth placed on the use of existing channels when participating in politics and the condemnation given to attempts to challenge status quo institutions" (Banaszak 1996: 35). As a result, Swiss activists failed to use tactics that could well have helped them achieve suffrage much sooner.

In contrast, the American movement rejected the status quo value of working through the system and pursued a broader range of strategic and tactical options, including those that directly challenged the government. The values and tactics of American suffragists were strongly influenced by their extensive ties to other movements, such as the abolition and temperance movements. Within the American suffrage movement, extensive networks and overlaps in personnel also linked state and national suffrage groups. These linkages among movements and among suffrage organizations and activists at different levels provided American suffragists with ideas and information about effective tactics. The Swiss movement lacked both the ties to other social movements and connections among groups within the movement that could have altered values and beliefs and provided information necessary to the adoption of particular tactics.

Banaszak (1996) argues that values come from macro social structures, meso interactions between groups, and micro interactions among individuals. The Swiss and American suffrage movements differed most strongly at the meso level. If we start with meso differences, we can explain why the two suffrage movements perceived large-scale opportunities differently and adopted disparate values and beliefs and, consequently, different tactics. As Banaszak concludes, the perceptions of movement activists are understudied (222). Outcomes are influenced not only by political opportunities but also by the ability to recognize and take advantage of opportunities. This is widely acknowledged among social movement scholars (e.g., Tarrow 1998), but we have not conducted enough close-up studies to determine the connections among large-scale opportunities, mobilizing structures, and individual perceptions that affect movement outcomes.

As with mobilization, movement outcomes are influenced by a combination of large-scale opportunities, meso organizations, and micro perceptions. Although theorists have focused on the influences of macro opportunities on meso organization and resources, less attention has been paid to the ways in which meso structures can alter perceptions of political opportunity and lead to collective action that creates new political opportunities. How do varying characteristics of movement communities affect outcomes?

Movement communities differ in their internal and external ties. In some instances, particularly during cycles of protest, movement communities within the same social movement family overlap a great deal, leading to mutual influence. Within a specific movement community, there may be stronger or weaker ties among individuals and groups. As Banaszak's study demonstrates, these characteristics of movement communities then affect values and perceptions, which affect strategies and tactics and influence outcomes.

In addition to altering perceptions of political opportunities, meso structures may encourage collective action that changes the political opportunity structure (cf. Gamson and Meyer 1996). In the ERA campaign in Indiana, the political opportunity structure was discouraging in the early 1970s, but a lively movement community encouraged collective action. Although the early activity was unsuccessful because of the negative political opportunity structure, the show of support for the ERA had an impact. The existence of a strong feminist community encouraged political activists to believe they could change the composition of the Indiana legislature to enable passage of the ERA. Activists worked through the Democratic Party and an ERA coalition to elect sympathetic legislators, and the ERA passed in Indiana in 1977 when there was a Democratic majority in the state legislature for the first time in the decade.

Broadbent (1998) provides another example of how collective action can alter political opportunities. In his study of environmental politics in Japan, he finds no sudden opening in the political opportunity structure to explain environmental protest. Rather, grievances led to protest, which altered the political opportunity structure as activists worked to elect mayors and governors from opposition parties, leading the ruling party to respond with anti-pollution legislation (Broadbent 1998: 112). The nature of the protest was limited by preexisting structures of Japanese society, which kept the movement localized, but movement actions could gradually help to create the meso structures needed for long-term national social movements (Broadbent 1998: 361).

Conclusion

Theories of movement emergence, maintenance, and decline, as well as outcomes would benefit from greater attention to the connections among processes at different levels: macro-level social-structural and cultural changes and political opportunities that encourage movements and affect outcomes, meso-level organizational bases and culture, and micro motivations and recruitment processes. If we start with the meso, we can examine the ways how characteristics of movement communities influence individual commitment and how meso structures are altered by leaders and activists (the meso-micro link). We can also examine the ability of different mobilizing structures to exploit, and sometimes create, political opportunities and large-scale changes, as well as the ways in which large-scale changes alter mobilizing structures (the meso-macro link).

A focus on social movement communities allows us to expand our view of meso structures and the ways in which they aid or hinder activist responses to political opportunities. Movement communities differ and change over time in ways that affect how participants perceive large-scale opportunities and changes and how effective movements are in generating new opportunities. Networks among activists, overlaps with other social movements, connections between local and national groups, bases of activism, and institutional ties are among the variables that affect perceptions of opportunities, values, and tactics.

During cycles of protest, movement communities help to engender new movements and attract new participants because activists are energized by critical masses of participants in visible actions and movement centers. During the doldrums, the action is less visible, and the movement community may be decentralized. But community structures, particularly cultural manifestations of movements, such as women's music festivals, help to sustain movements by keeping activist networks intact, maintaining collective identity, and generating emotional energy. As a result, the movement can erupt into political action from time to time, particularly when critical events occur. Movement community structures and values facilitate some tactics and constrain the use of others, producing different outcomes even in the face of similar political opportunities. We need more empirical studies to show how different types of meso-level movement communities are related to individual leaders' and participants' perceptions of political opportunities.

8

Strategizing and the Sense of Context: Reflections on the First Two Weeks of the Liverpool Docks Lockout, September–October 1995

COLIN BARKER & MICHAEL LAVALETTE

The Start of a Dispute

Late on the afternoon of Monday September 25, 1995, a group of young Liverpool dockers were told to work an extra hour at the end of their shift. Their company, Torside, subcontracted their labor to the main docks employer, the Mersey Docks and Harbour Company (MDHC). The instruction breached existing union agreements. Men required to work overtime were supposed to be given notice two hours before the end of a shift and to be paid in two-hour blocks. But that afternoon the young Torside dockers were given just half an hour's notice and told they would receive only one hour's pay. Five men refused, stating that they had already made arrangements for the evening (one, for example, had to pick up his children). In any case, they argued, agreements were being breached. At the end of the shift, these five walked off the ship they were working. They were met by James Bradley, Torside's managing director, who immediately sacked them. The other fifteen workers on their team left the ship to find out what was happening. They were told to return to work immediately. When they refused, Bradley sacked them as well.

The Torside stewards' committee called a workforce meeting in the canteen for 8 A.M. on Tuesday. Five Torside dockers, working elsewhere in the port, were given permission by their foreman to leave their ship to attend. At the meeting, the stewards advised that the matter could be negotiated and that the remaining Torsiders, sixty of them, should go to work while talks proceeded. However, before any decision could be taken, the meeting was interrupted. Bradley appeared at the canteen door at ten past eight with his personnel manager. The two men walked from table to table through the whole canteen, writing down workers' names and sacking them all for not already being at work.

Shocked and angry, the Torsiders had to decide how to respond.

"What Is to Be Done?": Strategizing and Social Movement Theory

Deciding what to do—*strategizing in collective action*—recurs as a problem for movement participants. Social movement scholars, however, have paid it relatively little theoretical attention (Barker 1997). Yet what movement actors decide to do, and how they do it, has significant effects. There are "strategic hinges" (Kimeldorf 1988) where immediate decisions shape the pattern of the future. Thus, strategizing is an important topic, raising core questions about the relations between agency and structure that go beyond this chapter's scope.[1]

To explore practical strategizing is to open questions not fully addressed within either political process or collective identity theories. Political process theorists have focused attention on factors shaping movement emergence and development, notably political opportunities, resources, and mobilizing structures. This largely structuralist schema has been enriched by the addition of framing, a concept denoting the work of movement activists in defining movement goals and rationales (McAdam, McCarthy, and Zald 1996). Meanwhile, collective identity theory has focused more on the symbolic processes by which actors perceive themselves as sharing common interests and goals (e.g., Cohen 1985; Melucci 1989, 1996). Strategizing is problematic for both paradigms.

First, "opportunities," "resources," and mobilizing structures" clearly affect what movement actors decide to do but only to the degree that actors *recognize* them as such and employ them. Such factors possess an inherently *interpretive* aspect, for they must be *socially constructed* to be activated (e.g., Kurzman 1994, 1996), and different constructions are open to contestation. Movement action involves elements of "seizing the time" or "opportunism" (in a nonpejorative sense), "resourcefulness" (Ganz 2000), and "social appropriation" of existing network and organizational structures (McAdam 1999). Once opportunities, resources, and mobilizing structures are grasped as themselves interpretive, then a notion like "framing" needs to be greatly extended.

Second, collective identity is both a relational and a practical matter. It involves questions not just about who actors *are* and about their relationships with others but also about what they *should* and *can do*. Movement identities shape participants' understandings of what they can achieve and embody narratives that explain why. Identity construction is not peculiar to "new" movements but is an inherent and central aspect of all movements and forms of collective action, just as problems involving strategizing regularly appear in all forms of movement. Thus, the seeming choice offered by Cohen (1985) between "strategy *or* identity" can be supplanted, in the context of decisions about collective action, by significant questions about strategizing *and* identity.

We should not conceptualize strategizing activity solely in terms of some narrow, economistic weighing of risks, costs and benefits or following a purely instrumental model of human action. Both the development of strategies and their enactment engage the whole personality, involving—like language—various evaluative registers and tones, including the emotional, the moral, and the aesthetic (Barker 2001). To strategize is to mobilize the *will*, to energize and commit the self, simultaneously placing body, social career and standing, credibility, and identity at risk. Nor, in considering what strategizing involves, need we suppose that actors carefully think through every element, for there are taken-for-granted aspects to strategic assessments. However, although not all the elements in strategizing are necessarily immediately explicit, we can hypothesize a general logic whose parts represent issues that actors may need to articulate.

"What is to be done?" is the fundamental strategic question. To answer it, actors must define themselves, the situation, and relevant purposes as well as the means to achieve them.

To act, we must have some sense of who we are, of our social and personal identity. Identity, a relational and situational concept, tells us "what we are" in relation to others, notably, to opponents and potential allies, whose own identities are part of the concept sets that define our own. Our sense of what "we" and "they" are—and might become—shapes how we construct relevant goals or demands. We make conditional predictions about what may happen if we act—"If we do this, they might do that"—and thus evaluate what we can hope and work for.

To achieve our ends, what can and should we do? In practice, actors innovate within known "repertoires of contention" (Tilly 1993, 1995b; McAdam, Tarrow, and Tilly 2001). But actors also have to *select* from within these repertoires (Crossley 1999). Suitable and possible ways of pressing their claims—picketing, petitioning, occupying premises, and the like—depend on their estimation of the situation and its participants. Likewise, actors draw on known "repertoires of organization" (Clemens 1996) to determine how to organize themselves and mobilize others. In turn, these decisions are shaped by "repertoires of interpretation" (Mooney and Hunt 1996), larger frameworks of understanding or perspectival lenses. For instance, a pacifist, a Marxist, or a social democrat will "see" a situation's possibilities and limits somewhat differently.

Each element in strategizing is potentially open to *contention about contention*, or "discord" (Zirakzadeh 1997). Movements are fields of argument, where the meaning of such apparently structuralist entities as "opportunities" is open to debate. The prospect that strategizing will be followed by actual physical *enactment*, when actual collective action will unleash a chain of unknowable consequences, places a serious "disciplinary realism" on strategizing.

The activities of others, who also strategize for themselves form an essential aspect of the context of strategizing. Indeed, those others and their activities provide the most immediately relevant parts of a given context. Opponents can innovate, learning new ways of responding to our strategic moves, reducing their own vulnerabilities and blunders, and countermobilizing against us in unexpected ways (Jasper and Poulsen 1993).

Two significant consequences follow. First, strategizing is an *interactive* or *relational* process: what we decide to do is affected by what others are deciding and doing. Second, strategizing is a *temporal* process. What we decide has an impact on them and their sense of context, reconfiguring their situation and demanding their response. In turn, their response reconfigures the situation again for us, demanding a "re-strategizing" to deal with the altered context. This interactive process continues throughout the life of a contentious episode, in something like a developing "conversation" in which forms of expression include bodies and brickbats, as well as words.

How we define ourselves and others in contentious interaction is not just a matter of constructing the present and future but also the past. What seems desirable and possible depends on what we think we and they are and what we and they have been. Perhaps they have been powerful while we were weak and deferential, but now we see cracks in their armor and sense our new strength. Or the reverse—once we were giants, now we are pygmies. Likewise with allies: those who were unavailable to us can now be won, or our former allies now are unreliable.

How we define the context, finally, involves the immediate situation and the sense we make of the larger social environment, in which other actors like ourselves, our opponents, and potential allies are also present. The sense we make of that wider context—which has its own historicity—can have energizing or depressive effects on what we think we can do. Thus, larger "cycles" of protest and containment can themselves play their part in strategizing.

To return to the Liverpool dockers and explore what they decided to do, we need to know about their previous experiences of contention, particularly the sense they made of these experiences and how they fit them into a picture of existing society and its possibilities.

Liverpool Dockers: A Heritage of Struggle

In the postwar decades, dockers in Britain were counted among the most militant groups of workers. This reputation owed little to their main trade union, the Transport and General Workers Union (TGWU), but to a tradition of "unofficial" strikes and tight workplace organization. They were central to the major industrial battles of the later 1960s and early 1970s, most famously in 1972, when five London dockers were jailed during a struggle over control of new container technology, unleashing a wave of unofficial action and a consequent Trade Union Council (TUC) threat of a general strike, all of which won the five dockers' rapid release.

By the 1980s, however, the "cycle of protest" had ended. An employers' offensive across major industries, coupled with rising unemployment, produced significant defeats for union organization in steel, newspaper printing, car manufacture, and, most notably, coal from 1984 to 1985. Increasingly confident port employers pressed the Thatcher government to reintroduce casual working and denationalize the dock industry, which would allow them to break the TGWU in the ports. Legislation to that effect was introduced in 1989. The TGWU botched official resistance in a particularly inept fashion (Lavalette and Kennedy 1996b: 27–31). There were unofficial strikes in major ports. In Hull, Bristol, and London, these were defeated, shop stewards were sacked, and union organization broken. Only in Liverpool, after a six-week strike, did the employers concede anything: no one was sacked, and permanent employment for existing dockers was maintained along with union recognition.

However, MDHC management worked to ensure that the Merseyside workers' victory was shallow. Immediately after the strike, the dockers were "put to the brush," sweeping the entire area of the port several times over, in an act of ritual humiliation. Disciplinary regimes were altered. "Written warnings" were used increasingly for infringements of working rules. Shop stewards lost control of health and safety issues to company safety officers. Candidates for a union steward's post had to sign an "accreditation" form promising they would do nothing to harm the company.

Between 1989 and 1995, using redundancy compensation, MDHC cut its directly employed workforce from 1,100 to 324. It took on new workers, though no longer in its own name, but through subcontracting labor supply companies: Nelson Freight (a part-owned subsidiary of the MDHC) and Torside. These new workers were required to work "flexibly" across the whole port area and endured worse pay and conditions.

The formation of Torside, in particular, seemed ominous. Some older dockers were initially very suspicious of these new young workers: they were working on "casual" contracts, on less pay than themselves; surely they threatened a further undermining of conditions and pay. Management probably hoped eventually to secure a more amenable workforce by gradually replacing the older men with new young workers who lacked the older dockers' militant traditions and by minimizing work contact between the two groups. However, if this was management's hope, it was soon disappointed. The young Torsiders joined the TGWU and proved if anything more militant than their war-weary older brethren. They elected shop stewards, who coordinated their activity with the MDHC stewards in a joint committee.

From 1994, MDHC enforced new work contracts. Dockers now had to work on three-week cycles, during which any particular day's work could last from four to twelve hours. "Rota days off" were liable to sudden change. All were required to be "on call" during their days off, placing dockers permanently at the company's disposal. The impact of these new arrangements on family and social life was grievous (Lavalette and Kennedy 1996a). MDHC used TGWU officials to police the new arrangements. The union seemed more concerned with maintaining presence and membership on the Liverpool docks than with protecting, let alone advancing, workers' conditions.

But if management appeared to have the upper hand, the dockers continued to organize and resist (Lavalette and Kennedy 1996b: chapter 2). The company paid for two full-time stewards, no doubt hoping they would act as additional means of containment. However, the two stewards, in conjunction with the rest of their committee, used their position to minimize the isolation of different groups and to maintain a sense of unity as a single dock workforce. In one notable incident in 1992 at the P&O ferry port for Ireland, management attempted to bring in their own cargo handlers. When the ferry gate came down, dockers stormed onto the ship and there was a furious confrontation. This brief skirmish secured an agreement that unloading P&O ferries would continue to be Liverpool dockers' work. In the aftermath, MDHC tried to dismiss a steward for pushing a port policeman during the battle for the ferry. There was an immediate unofficial walkout across the whole port area, involving all groups of dockers in a notable show of solidarity. The steward was reinstated.

A supposed agreement equalizing Torside workers' pay and conditions with those of the MDHC dockers was slow to bear fruit. On three occasions the Torsiders balloted for official strike action, in support of their expectation of equal pay and an equivalent work regime. The young workforce often came to be seen not as the individualistic, overtime-chasing wedge of anti-unionism some older dockers had feared but rather as "impetuous young lions," especially ready to take collective action. Mostly in their twenties, they had not

directly experienced the defeats of the 1980s and the consequent cautious-
ness and even fatalism of older workers, reinforced continuously by the official machinery of the TGWU. Their direct experience had shown that collective
action could work. As late as August 1995, they had balloted to strike against
threatened redundancies, which were then withdrawn. By comparison, the
older MDHC dockers and their stewards tended toward greater caution. They
saw themselves as fighting to maintain a deteriorating position, had a strong
sense of the limited possibilities, and felt pressure from the TGWU not to take
undue risks.

    In autumn 1995, the dock workforce was thus composed of three groups:
324 dockers, employed directly by the MDHC, were now concentrated and
isolated from the rest of the workforce in two locations: in the Canada and
Royal Seaforth Docks. Working separately across the rest of the port area
were 11 workers employed by Nelson Freight and 80 employed by Torside.
These last young dockers were sacked on September 26.

Strategies in Contention

Faced with their sudden and unexpected sackings, the Torsiders responded
by immediately setting up a picket line at their usual dock entrance. They
displayed TGWU strike placards, left behind from a previous dispute. Meanwhile, several MDHC stewards, who had been present at the Torside canteen meeting that Tuesday morning, contacted the TGWU local docks official,
Jack Dempsey, seeking talks to resolve the issue. Dempsey drove down to
the picket line. Once there, he objected to the use of TGWU placards, on the
grounds that the dispute was "not official," and tried to grab them away from
the pickets. In the resulting scuffle, one of the dockers' shirts was ripped. One
of the bigger dockers physically lifted Dempsey back into his car.

    That struggle on the picket line on the first day of the dispute symbolized
a strategic issue at the heart of contemporary trade unionism. Who "owns"
the unions—the officials or the members? Who controls the use of a union's
name and its insignia? The matter involves not simply the immediate officials and members of unions but government and the law as well. The force
behind Dempsey's bizarre behavior was not simply some personal quirk, but
"legal terror." If MDHC could show that the TGWU was involved in an
"illegal" picketline, then the union's funds might be sequestered in court and
its organized presence on the docks jeopardized. A crucial effect of the anti-
union laws of the 1980s was to demand that unions deny their members the
use of their own machinery. The TGWU, like many other unions, submitted
to this logic and would continue to do so throughout the 28-month dispute.
Better to make concessions to employers than risk losing everything.

However, the Torsiders found themselves in conflict over strategy not just with their paid officials. There was also disagreement between them and the main body of shop stewards representing the MDHC dockers. The stewards' committee suggested they "keep a lid" on the dispute, while seeking a negotiated resolution, but the young Torsiders argued that this would achieve little and that their action should be spread to the whole body of Liverpool dockers. That, for them, was the lesson of the 1992 P&O dispute in which the successful walkout included all groups of dockers.

On Wednesday, the Torside picket line stopped the eleven Nelson Freight workers going to work. The eleven were immediately sacked by MDHC, on the grounds that they were engaging in "illegal secondary action." This only raised the temperature further.

The Torside and Nelson men decided to try to bring out the main body of MDHC dockers. Their informal strike committee prepared a leaflet, explaining to the MDHC men what had happened. It said that, unless the dispute was settled, they would form a picket line at the MDHC entrance the next morning, Thursday, September 28. A delegation went to the TGWU offices to arrange the printing of this leaflet, only to be told that they could not use union facilities. They instead went to a local unemployment center, paying to produce the leaflet. By the evening, the leaflet was in the hands of the MDHC workers, who knew that, next morning, they would have to decide how to respond to a picket line. The main stewards' committee advised the Torsiders to proceed carefully, to leave space for negotiation through the union. Meanwhile, MDHC let it be known through Jack Adams, a more senior official of the TGWU, that any MDHC man who refused to cross a Torside picket line would be assumed to have sacked himself. The Torsiders discussed the situation and concluded they had no choice but to go ahead with their picket.

The Torside leaflet threw the MDHC workers, and their stewards, into deep uncertainty. Indeed, some told us they had privately decided, after a sleepless night, that they would ignore the pickets and go in to work to permit a negotiating strategy to proceed. But on that Thursday morning, faced with the actual presence of a picket line, the overwhelming majority of the MDHC workers refused to cross. Their whole history of struggle over the years militated against any other possibility. Some of them, in fact, were facing a picket line including their own sons.

When the Torside and Nelson men announced, in advance, that they would mount a picket line on Thursday morning, they were launching the most powerful sanction available to them, to *compel* the MDHC stewards and dockers to join them, even though the employers had announced that respecting the line would mean the sack. That Thursday morning picket line had an almost sacred quality. On one side of the line, as the Torsiders had drawn it, stood honor and tradition, the very meaning of working-class struggle. To cross would be polluting. The fact that, for some dockers, the line was manned by their own sons only added to its symbolic power. Whatever their personal estimates of the situation, whatever private thoughts they wrestled with the night before, in the event they could not cross. Better the sack than the dishonor. Only thirty of the MDHC workforce crossed the picket line, to calls of abuse.

Through the rest of Thursday, Friday, and the weekend, the whole Liverpool port was on strike, including numbers of white collar and ancillary workers, who had a long tradition in Liverpool of solidarity with the dockers. During these days, the dockers held meetings in the local social club. They were barred from meeting in their own union's offices. The TGWU officials feared that union funds could be attacked if illegal strikers were permitted to meet on union premises.

The shop stewards attempted to open negotiations, but MDHC refused to meet them. The company did meet with Jack Adams, but these talks achieved nothing. There was a seeming standoff for several days.

Then, on Sunday evening, October 1, MDHC sent letters to the homes of every docker, using motorbike and taxi messengers. The letters took two forms. About half the MDHC dockers were told not to bother attending work on Monday, since they had engaged in an illegal "secondary" strike in support of workers from a different employer and were no longer employed. (Some of these letters were delivered to the homes of workers on vacation.) However, 180 men, including the thirty who had crossed the picket line on Thursday and Friday, received a different letter. This stated that, in the light of the illegal strike, existing contracts had been revoked, and the company no longer recognized the union. The 180 were offered new personal contracts and told they must report for work on Monday morning or be deemed to have sacked themselves. Not one shop steward received this second letter.

At the dock gates on Monday morning, only the same thirty dockers crossed the picket line. At a mass meeting, the other 150 publicly ripped up the offers of personal contracts in a nonunion regime. It was soon revealed that MDHC had entered into a contract with Drake International, a London-based employment agency, who began bringing in a replacement workforce from London, Ireland, and elsewhere. The scabs were initially housed on the docks in portakabin accommodation. The company advertised job vacancies on the Liverpool docks in the local press. The dispute was now, manifestly, a union-busting lockout.

A Double Deferral

As we noted earlier, strategizing is undertaken not in a social vacuum but in the face of the actions and words of others. From the beginning, the docks dispute was shaped by the intersection of two opposing strategies, employers' and workers'. Management's strategy was aggressive and offensive. Relatively unconcerned about winning "ideological" battles for public opinion, managers relied on the brute power of the sack as their main weapon. If they were resolute and unyielding, they could win: the state was on their side; union militancy was at a low level nationally. The employers, seeking a new, compliant and nonunion workforce, aimed to abolish any form of organized resistance to their power.

This fact was confirmed on Monday October 9, two weeks after the initial Torside sackings. Organized by their stewards, all the sacked dockers, on the advice of the TGWU legal department, turned up that morning to offer themselves as available for work. The MDHC men were met at the locked gates by a force of police with Eric Leatherbarrow of MDHC, who said, "I don't know what they're doing here, they don't work here, I want anyone who steps on this property arrested for trespass." As for the Torsiders, they marched in to their old canteen, where they had a confrontation with Bradley. Chief steward Bob Ritchie asked Bradley: Were they all sacked? *Yes, you're all sacked.* What about me, who was on holiday? *You're all sacked.* What about the five men who had permission to attend the meeting? *You're all sacked.* What's the future of the Torside company? *What the fuck's that got to do with you?* Bradley asked the port police to escort them off the premises. Following TGWU advice that there should be no violent confrontation, no occasion for them to be disciplined, they departed.

Management's initiatives in sacking the dockers and hiring scabs reconfigured the situation, compelling the dockers to formulate new strategies on a less familiar terrain. Now the question was posed: what to do *next*? And who should decide? The dockers were less unified than the employers in views of what should and could be done. Three potential strategies were in contention, and the interrelations between their proponents would prove decisive.

The first was that of TGWU officialdom, whose disbelief in the practical possibilities of collective action was palpable.[2] In the 1980s their strategic stance was given the name of "New Realism." Under the Tories, union leaders reasoned, the boot was now firmly on the employers' foot. Anti-union laws made militant resistance impossible. To maintain any kind of industrial presence, unions must be ready to make concessions and seek to show they could be helpful to managements. Members should be attracted not by the fighting power of unionism but by such inducements as credit cards and other benefits. In the Liverpool docks, after 1989, the TGWU bent its efforts to persuading MDHC to continue recognition, hoping that in better times it could win back its former place as the union for dockworkers. If, meanwhile, that meant concessions on workers' conditions, the price must be paid. Faced with the actual sacking of its members, the union acted chiefly to distance itself from their "illegal" action. It urged workers not to take collective action, dissociating itself from them when they did. Initially, the union denied the dockers the use of union premises, only allowing them the use of office facilities *after* securing a statement from MDHC that it would not sue the TGWU for supporting illegal strike activity.

Representing a quite different strategic pole from the TGWU—indeed, in active and open conflict with the union's officials—were the young Torsiders. By the start of the dispute, they had become the most radical group on the docks. Their response to the employers' offensive was, immediately, to establish a strike committee, organize a picket line, and call on other workers to join them. If union officialdom got in their way, they pushed them aside and ignored them. They determined for themselves what tactics were appropriate in the face of management's onslaught, relying on their own collective strength and that of the other dockers, in whose solidarity they (correctly) believed they could trust. The threat from MDHC to sack all the dockers did not deter them. There was, as one of their stewards explained, "nowhere else for us to go" but to demand active support from the MDHC men.

However, having once activated the main body of MDHC workers and their stewards, the Torsiders also handed over the power of initiative to them and demanded, even deferred to, their leadership. Within the whole body of the dock workforce, the stewards' committee was the natural, and acknowledged, leaders. The more prominent stewards were all respected militants, some with more than two decades of experience of trade-union struggle in the docks. In contrast to the TGWU, those stewards' foremost concern had been to defend organization and conditions on the docks, often against serious odds. From the second week, therefore, it fell to them to determine how the dockers as a body should respond to the new situation.

The stewards' committee organized picketing of the dock gates. However, the contrast between picketing in the first and second weeks is sharp. On the first Thursday, the Torsiders deliberately unleashed the full symbolic power of this element of their repertoire of contention. But during the second week, the pickets were few and made no significant effort to turn back transport. They were "token." Throughout the whole course of the dispute, the dockers were somewhat reluctant to use mass pickets. It was as if the dockers distinguished between themselves as "true believers," for whom the line's forbidding power was undeniable, and other workers, whose beliefs they never put to a full test. While they believed the solidarity of Liverpool dockers was an unimpeachable fact, they doubted that other workers shared their faith enough to respect the same line. Yet many of the drivers going in and out of the docks were themselves members of the TGWU. And there were large concentrations of TGWU members in local workplaces, some of them directly dependent on the docks for both supplies and exports.

The stewards did not issue a call to other workers for practical as well as financial support. A militant former Tilbury docker visited Liverpool during this second week, urging a mass occupation of the Liverpool docks and a spread of the dispute to other major local workplaces, to pressurize the port employers to negotiate. But his advice was ignored. The stewards made no public challenge to the TGWU's policy of shutting them out of union premises. Rather, they relied on the TGWU officials to attempt negotiations with the employers who were sacking and replacing them.

Any other tactics, of course, would have posed the question of breaking the law: secondary action, secondary boycotts,[3] and mass pickets were all potentially illegal. The TGWU officials would have strenuously opposed any such moves. Yet these forms of action, along with independence of union officialdom and defiance of anti-union laws were all part of militant dockers' historical repertoire of contention and indeed were part of the personal traditions of many leading stewards. But now, they believed, these things could no longer be done, even though they had, themselves, struck illegally on September 28.

Here the stewards' beliefs about the nature of the "period" played their part. The defeats of the 1980s left their mark on a generation of working-class militants. The experience of the past weighed on the brains of the living, in the shape of depressive doubt that impulses from below, historically the major source of initiative and innovation in the workers' movement, could be mobilized to turn the tide. How could other workers be asked for practical solidarity, when they had been cowed and fragmented by the Tories' attacks and their organizations shackled by anti-union laws? The effect was fatalism about the limits of working-class solidarity.

Such fatalism is by no means the same as ideological acceptance of a state of affairs but can involve an angry, if highly frustrated, sense of practical impotence in the face of what is felt as manifest injustice. Fatalism involves a living, felt contradiction between the normative and the pragmatic, between a sense of what is just and what is (currently) possible. As such, fatalism is a potentially highly unstable, "conditional" amalgam (Bagguley 1996). Nonetheless, its immediate effects are conservatizing. In the dockers' case, it meant accepting *part*, though by no means all, of the same New Realism as the TGWU's full-time apparatus. Had they simply agreed with the TGWU officials, the Torsiders would have been sacked without a struggle, or the dockers would have accepted a settlement with the company when it was first offered. Fatalism in the dockers' case meant not that they would refuse to fight on but only that they believed they must fight alone. So far as Britain was concerned, all they could *demand* of other workers was financial aid and occasional token demonstrations of support.

The defeats of the previous decade, in their view, had affected everyone but themselves—and perhaps some dockers abroad. It had affected every other dock in Britain, every other workplace, every other group in the TGWU, where at best only a minority of stewards could be relied on to provide support. The Liverpool dockers, with their particular traditions, could rely on themselves. But they must stand alone, prepared if necessary for a bitter if hard-fought defeat. The outcome was a *modus vivendi* between militant solidarity and accommodation to New Realism, which could not overcome their opponents.[4]

Thus, there was, during the first two weeks, a "double deferral" process. The young Torsiders, who were ready to reject the union officials' authority, compelled the older dockers to join them, but then allowed—indeed, effectively demanded—that the joint stewards' committee, in which they were a minority, take over the leadership of the dispute. Their last independent initiative was the Thursday picket line. They deferred to the senior stewards, with their long record of organizing resistance to the employers. In turn, the stewards deferred to the TGWU, not openly criticizing the officials and accepting much of the union's definition of the possible limits of struggle. In this way, initial antagonisms and differentiations within the dockers' movement were smoothed over. A kind of homogeneity of response was produced, or—to put the matter another way—one view became hegemonic. Potential contention about the possibilities of contention was contained.[5]

The Limits of the Possible?

For the next two years, the Liverpool dockers' lockout continued. The very reasons that the stewards and the TGWU officials had for advocating caution—namely, the impossibility in the present period of effective militancy—became a self-fulfilling prophecy. Believing that more militant tactics could not win, they did not pursue them; yet the nonmilitant tactics could not win. The TGWU continued to view the dockers' struggle as an unofficial dispute, for which strike pay was not available, although at times the TGWU made some *ex gratia* payments. Though union rules allowed it, the TGWU did not provide "lockout pay" to its members. The MDHC refused any further meeting with the stewards, while occasionally agreeing to fruitless talks with full-time TGWU officials.

The Liverpool dockers became, for many workers and socialists, public heroes: a group of workers who would not sacrifice their principles, who not only refused to cross a picket line but went on to reject offers of tens of thousands of pounds in redundancy money rather than give up their fight to preserve their own and their sons' jobs and to maintain the principle of the right to union organization at work. That heroic stature—reflected back to them in applause, admiration, and praise wherever they spoke as they traveled the country (and indeed the world)—was earned in the most extraordinary way. Yet, at the same time, the image developed, both among the supporting public and even among themselves, of the dockers as heroes-who-could-not-win, men[6] of astonishing courage and tenacity, but also ultimately lacking in efficacy. They became "tragic heroes," symbols of defiance but also of defeat, heroic martyrs rather than leaders whose example showed the way to victory. They embarrassed but did not directly challenge union officialdom. Their struggle came to be emblematic of a whole period, representing in microcosm a larger set of class relations and practices and, like all emblems, open to different readings.

Their heroism was always ambiguous in its meaning for the wider working-class movement. Alternative strategic lessons could be, and were, drawn. The "militant" lesson was that the stewards' approach was doomed to fail; hence, a different one ought to be applied. The second, New Realist, lesson was that, whatever tactics they followed, collective action was bound to fail.

Yet, even if most challenges from below were limited, passivity and defeatism were not universal. Some strikes during the same period succeeded, including an illegal Glasgow engineering occupation that forced management to withdraw redundancies. The Liverpool docks dispute itself lasted for twenty-eight months, thanks entirely to the commitment and energy of the dockers themselves and their wives and girlfriends. It owed little to the official trade union machinery, whether within the TGWU or other unions in Britain. The Liverpool dispute reflected, and itself contributed to, a particular "balance" within the forces of working-class resistance in Britain, with many parallels in other countries. That balance is not simply struck between the forces of capital and labor but also within the labor movement itself, between confidence and fatalism, between militancy and moderation. Labor movements, like others, are anything but homogeneous entities; they include complex networks and tendencies, which contend among themselves over the identity of the movement itself, its strategies and policies.

Context and Agency

Does "the period" explain the dockers' strategy and their ultimate heroic defeat? Not adequately, we suggest. Here, the literature on "cycles of protest" is relevant, provided we read it in a nondeterministic fashion. That literature rests on a well-founded historical observation, that industrial and other forms of protest come in "cycles" or "waves" (e.g., Cronin 1979; Harman 1988; Haynes 1985; Kelly 1998; Markoff 1996; Shorter and Tilly 1974; Tarrow 1989a, 1989b, 1993, 1998). Official statistics reveal that, in Britain as elsewhere in advanced capitalism, a rising "wave" of strikes and other forms of protest associated with "the sixties" was followed by a "downturn" (Cliff 1979) and a subsequent "trough," when the numbers of strikes and of workers involved in them were much lower, and when—though this is harder to quantify—workers' victories were harder to obtain.[7]

To date, however, the "cycles" literature has focused more attention on the upsurge and peak aspects of wave movements than on downturns and troughs. The latter pair are marked not by the total absence of protest activity but by its relative *practical containment*. Indeed, we might equally speak of "waves of containment," sometimes mistakenly identified in conservative thought with "normality," when ruling-class hegemonic efforts are relatively successful, for example, when "employers' offensives" bear fruit for their initiators (e.g., Cliff 1970; Fantasia 1988; Saville 1960; Voss 1996). In such periods, movements experience sequences of defeats punctuated only occasionally by victories, and opportunities appear less open.

Tarrow (1993) offers a brief characterization of a "cycle of protest" (or upsurge and peak), whose features include an overall heightening of the level of protest, geographical and sectoral diffusion of forms of contention, contests between "old" and "new" organizations, emergence of new frames of meaning, and elaboration of new repertoires of contention. In troughs, we can witness the same features but in a negative mirror image. Here, the overall level of manifest protest is contained. Overt collective conflict is confined within particular sectors, since the efforts of those seeking diffusion are relatively unsuccessful. Established organizations limit the influence of new impulses, inhibiting the influence of their more radical critics. Although new frames of meaning may emerge, their bearers have difficulty expressing them in widespread collective action, instead developing them in "submerged networks" (Melucci 1989) and in "abeyance structures" (Taylor 1989). If new repertoires of contention develop, they do so sectorally without generalization across different fields of protest.

There is a difficulty: these broad-brush portraits of contrasting development patterns can seem inevitable. Activists might think that what they can do is entirely determined by the period in which they are (un)fortunate enough to be working, reducing them to puppets driven by cycle phases. "Upsurges" and "downturns" take on almost magical appearance. Upsurges appear "spontaneously," as Goodwyn (1991) usefully reminds us, which usually means that the analyst does not know what actually happened and who did what. Downturns are determined by mysteriously proverbial rules like "What goes up must come down" or "Every joy must turn to sorrow." Such essentially conservative notions fail to explain why some popular upsurges end in revolutions whereas others fizzle out and provide no indication of the activities that turn upturns into downturns, or that lift movements out of troughs. "Responsible agency" disappears from view.

To avoid such traps, we must remember two points. First, if peaks and troughs seem opposites, they share common features, even if in different balances. In both, we see movement contests between radicalism and moderation, between fatalism and optimism, cognitive encumbrance and cognitive liberation. In both, ideas about the possibilities of collective action fluctuate and shift in the light of new arguments and practical experiences, as the elements of opportunity that appear volatile and stable also fluctuate (Gamson and Meyer 1996).

Second, contrary to some earlier theorizing about "cycles," neither upsurges nor downturns follow ineluctable developmental paths. Instead, they are marked by sequences of situational dilemmas that actors may resolve in different ways and with different outcomes. The practical agency of small minorities, and even individuals, can sometimes be decisive (Barker, Johnson, and Lavalette 2001). Certainly, the period actors find themselves in does set constraints of varying rigidity, but constraints are not fates, only frameworks of necessity within which actors assess their room for maneuver in contradictory ways.

The dock stewards' strategic reading of their situation was relatively "encumbered" (Voss 1996), involving the kind of "pessimistic realism" that tends to inhibit action. They expressed some of the rhetorics that Gamson and Meyer (1996, citing Hirschman 1991) identify as undergirding arguments for relative inaction: a sense of the futility of making demands on other workers for collective action, a desire not to further worsen relations with union officialdom, a concern not to put older dockers at physical risk on picket lines. A practical challenge to that case—involving arguments for more boldness, for more open challenges to the TGWU, and for a greater sense of urgency—would have implied a challenge to the senior stewards' leadership and to the dockers' existing identities. In theory, such a challenge might have come from a rival grouping within the strike leadership, knowingly posing ideological alternatives, or it could have arisen "spontaneously" if the Torsiders, with their "impatience of the young," had maintained their own distinct momentum. In the Liverpool case, neither of these possibilities occurred, but only a relatively small, but determined minority might have made a difference. By posing alternative logics and arguing for the enactment of a different set of strategies, such a minority could have altered the history of the Liverpool lockout.

NOTES

Our thanks to Paul Brook, Alan Johnson, John Krinsky, Sidney Tarrow, and Charles Tilly for criticism of earlier drafts.

1. See Barker, Johnson and Lavalette, forthcoming.

2. In the aftermath of the final defeat of the dockers, in January 1998, the *Guardian* published an angry exchange in its letters column. Bill Morris, TGWU general secretary, attacked the journalist John Pilger for the crime of "raising the hopes" of the dockers in the possibilities of success.

3. Such secondary boycotts, or "blacking," would have entailed workers in other industries refusing to handle goods brought in through the disputed Liverpool docks.

4. See Lavalette and Kennedy (1996b) and Kennedy and Lavalette (1997) for further critical discussion of the dockers' overall strategy.

5. Some dockers did worry that the stewards' tactics were insufficient. See the interesting interviews conducted after the dispute by Greg Dropkin (1998) and published on the Internet at www.labournet.co.uk.

6. And women, too. The "wives, partners, sisters, and daughters" of the dockers formed their own organization, Women of the Waterfront, in October 1995, campaigning tirelessly (Lavalette and Kennedy 1996b: 45–65).

7. This was the background to the proliferation of theories of "the death of class" (e.g., Pakulski and Waters 1996), the displacement of labor by "new social movements." For a general critique, see Barker and Dale 1998.

9

Factions and the Continuity of Political Challengers

MILDRED A. SCHWARTZ

Dissatisfied persons who believe that existing political parties cannot solve their problems may join others in protest movements. Sometimes those movements attempt to influence the course of government directly by nominating candidates for office, or by exacting pledges of programmatic support from candidates who run under an existing party label. These actions express a conviction that participating in elections and in legislative bodies can produce change. To distinguish them from other political movements, I label them *party movements*.

Political movements face a hard road, subject to constraints arising from inadequate resources, efforts at suppression, and the inertial forces that work against mobilizing support. Yet they may still endure. What is it about the movements themselves that might contribute to their continuity (Whittier 1997: 760)? Here, I look at the strategies and tactics movement leaders and activists use. I take the position, like the authors of a broad survey of literature on social movements, that "movements may largely be born of environmental opportunities, but their fate is heavily shaped by their own actions" (McAdam et al. 1996b: 15).

I claim that one factor that promotes continuity is factionalism, even though that seems antithetical.[1] Factions are groups that reject current leadership, tactics, or interpretations of core beliefs. A frequent characteristic of party movements, factionalism results from power struggles, ideological disputes, and efforts by external enemies to promote dissension. It appears often enough to lead to the easy assumption that it is a principal cause of movement decline or death. In this chapter, I argue that, instead, factions may help movements survive. I examine the sources of factionalism, the impact of factions on solving party movement problems, and the ways in which factions can be vehicles of continuity.

Because even participants in factions are wary of negative connotations of the label, factionalism, they are more likely to emphasize the positive aims of their actions, that is, the ongoing reform and redirection of an existing organization. Yet to accomplish their aims, they must form a new group—or faction. By deliberately challenging the status quo, factions generate conflicts that will almost inevitably alter a movement. Intentionally or not, they may even invite the destruction of their host. In this chapter, however, I focus on their impact on continuity.

I illustrate through the case of the Cooperative Commonwealth Federation (CCF) and its successor, the New Democratic Party (NDP), carriers of social democracy in Canada. The CCF/NDP, the designation favored by most political scientists, has a long history full of factional tension, making it a strong example.

Factions in the Cooperative Commonwealth Federation and the New Democratic Party

The Setting for Factions

The CCF began in 1932 in Calgary at a meeting of the Western Conference of Labour Political Parties to which farm groups had been invited. Participants from labor parties in the four western provinces included the Socialist Party of Canada, along with the United Farmers of Alberta, the United Farmers of Canada (Saskatchewan Section), and the Canadian Brotherhood of Railway Employees (McHenry 1950: 23–25).[2] The research committee of the League for Social Reconstruction, mainly university-based intellectuals, was then called on to help draft a constitution and a policy statement, both subsequently adopted at a convention in Regina in 1933 (McHenry 1950: 265). The CCF was now set to work for a planned economy. Its first major victory was winning governing office in Saskatchewan in 1944.

Through the 1950s, the promising future of the CCF was never realized, despite its provincial success. Trade union leaders came to believe that there was an uncomfortably narrow social base for the party, even in Saskatchewan. In 1958, the Canadian Labour Congress issued a call for the formation of a new party, one that would include the CCF along with organized labor, farm interests, professionals, and other "liberally minded" persons (Morton 1986: 20). After the CCF's dismal showing in the 1958 federal election, the party reformed as the New Democratic Party in 1961. The NDP would give a new place to nationalism and offer a more decentralized and cooperative conception of federal-provincial relations. It also showed a new awareness of Quebec's special position and aspirations, the latter a response to the desire to make electoral headway in that province (Whitehorn 1992: 50–61). Trade unions were given a more prominent role, and union locals, in particular, were encouraged to affiliate with the party (Horowitz 1968: 202–5).

By labeling the CCF/NDP a party movement, I touch a sensitive cord among Canadian political commentators, many of whom are also its supporters. Some unequivocally consider the party a social movement (Avakumovic 1978: v; Morton 1986: 3; Wiseman 1979: 28; Young 1969: 3). Others complain that the CCF/NDP is no longer a movement, but merely another political party that emphasizes the consolidation of power (e.g., Zakuta 1964). Still others reject the social movement characterization for its emphasis on organizational failings and lack of sufficient attention to a hostile environment (Whitehorn 1992: 23–29). In my approach, however, there is no basic dichotomy and no value judgment. The CCF/NDP's party status is manifested in its search for government office. In addition, it continues to conform to Tilly's model of a social movement by offering "a sustained challenge to power holders" (1999: 257) through electoral protest (Carty, Cross, and Young 2000: 48), and through close ties to historically disadvantaged groups that support its claims to moral rectitude and a sizable following and that provide avenues for less institutionalized protest. The CCF/NDP demonstrates movement characteristics, as well, in its unifying programs and identity and its encouragement of commitment through a shared ideology. For those attached to it, the CCF/NDP represents a way of life (Schwartz 1994: 23).

The Variety of Factions

Multiorganizational Fields. The history of the CCF/NDP is rooted, like other party movements, in its location in a multiorganizational field (Curtis and Zurcher 1973). That field may include other protest movements, established political parties, interest groups, and issue or advocacy groups, organizations not always clearly differentiated (Clemens 1997: 1–2; Tarrow 1995b; Thomas and Hrebenar 1995). As they interact, they may provide necessary resources but also create lines of fissure out of which factions can emerge. For instance, factional divisions in the CCF/NDP's multiorganizational field include those between farmers and labor and between intellectuals and workers.

Although the CCF's origins began with a merger between farm and labor groups, the latter represented different and often competing interests (Melnyk 1985: 52). For example, in Manitoba, one founder was the Independent Labour Party (ILP), composed mainly of British-born workers who followed a moderate, non-Marxist form of socialism. The ILP's success in urban areas contrasted with experiences in other western provinces, where the principal party movement was the rural-based United Farmers, also partners in the CCF's creation. Given the ILP's small size and the importance of agriculture in Manitoba, the CCF wanted to expand its connection with farmers in that province as well. For the most part, however, ILP members were suspicious of allying with rural progressives, excluding United Farmers from membership. They believed farmers could not be true socialists (Wiseman 1985: 20). Organized labor, in turn, remained a suspect partner in the provincial CCF, where the formation of the NDP was opposed on grounds that labor would acquire too much control (Wiseman 1985: 152).

The CCF/NDP has been a welcome opportunity for those whose adoption of socialism stems more from intellectual commitments than experience. From the outset, the university-based League for Social Reconstruction provided organizing and ideological resources. But their middle-class status has also been a point of contention, especially among workers. For example, in British Columbia, there was reluctance to admit members of the league into constituency groups because they would dilute the CCF's working-class nature (Melnyk 1989: 135–36). But neither the CCF nor the NDP has ever been essentially class parties, yet the tension between workers and intellectuals continues.

Institutions.   At least two institutional bases are relevant to the emergence of factions in the CCF/NDP. One involves the pull from federal versus regional forces in Canada. The second, more general to any party movement that enters a legislature, arises from conflict between governing and organizational goals.

In Saskatchewan, the farmer-labor alliance was initially more congenial than in Manitoba (Lipset 1968: 99; Spafford 1968) and led to the formation of the Farmer-Labour Group (FLG), "de facto, the Saskatchewan CCF" (Sinclair 1973: 422). This meant that the FLG was in charge of local organization. The FLG retained its autonomy and kept its own name until 1934, when it first contested office. But even when it did finally change its name to the Cooperative Commonwealth Federation, Saskatchewan Section, closer ties across federal levels did not appear. When the Saskatchewan party won office in 1944, it "operated on its own as it had always done, changing CCF policy to suit what it saw as the Saskatchewan conditions" (Young 1969: 109).

The formation of the NDP was not a welcome move in Saskatchewan, where the party continued to call itself the CCF Saskatchewan Section of the NDP (Morton 1986: 22). According to former Premier Allan Blakeney, it did not officially change its name to the New Democratic Party of Saskatchewan until the convention of 1968,[3] a change that would not alter the aim of distinguishing itself from its federal counterpart. For example, the federal NDP's attack on Prime Minister Trudeau's Liberal government's anti-inflation policy of wage and price controls met a much more measured response from the new premier, Allan Blakeney, since his government was also pledged to planning and controls, a move that infuriated trade unionists within the province

(Avakumovic 1978: 224–26). The Blakeney government also assumed a new direction as a defender of provincial rights, primarily in the form of western Canadian autonomy (Carty and Stewart 1996: 75). This put it at odds with the traditional CCF/NDP stance of advocating greater centralization.

In a parliamentary system of government, authority rests with the cabinet. Opposition parties expect to rely on their caucus leaders to formulate policy positions as well. In a party movement, in contrast, adherence to policy goals formulated by an active membership is essential. In Saskatchewan, according to Eager, expectations that the organizational wing of the CCF would be paramount were unmet: "From the time that the CCF came to power in 1944 the administration exercised the traditional prerogatives of government of the British parliamentary system. Premier Douglas was no more restricted in his actions than his counterpart in any other party" (1963: 128). Lipset (1968: 258) suggests a more influential role for the party conventions and for the Legislative Advisory Council but, in general, he too acknowledges the reality of parliamentary ascendancy. Tension remained between the federal and regional wings. Moreover, it is a continuing tension, reflected most recently in changes in leadership selection (Archer and Whitehorn 1997; Carty et al. 2000: 124).

Ideology.   Most critically, ideology affects factionalization, whether as a historical component of a party movement or a newly developing system of meaning. Ideology spells out beliefs about how to understand the political world by attributing blame and offering a blueprint for action. It links a party movement's identity—what it stands for—with the frames adopted by individuals to make sense of their environment (Hunt, Benford, and Snow 1994: 190–91; Klandermans 1997: 43; McAdam et al., 1996b: 5). Because ideology is central to defining a party movement, it is also often a source of dispute. Whose interpretation of ideology is correct? Can more than one ideology coexist within the party movement? Whose commitment is less than wholehearted? Such questions generate passionate responses. If the party movement succeeds, its ideology is worth fighting over, even inside the movement.

Over the years, the most troubling ideologically based factions in the CCF/NDP related to doctrinaire forms of Marxism or to Trotskyist variants. Some of these factions have arisen within the movement, others from outside, like those from efforts of the Communist Party to infiltrate and take over the CCF/NDP. In either case, the debate is over the kind of socialism appropriate for a movement that truly represents the working class. Although the CCF's official position was to exclude members of the communist party or related organizations, it was not always possible to do so. For one thing, local branches did not necessarily agree with the policy. For another, the positions of the CCF and the communists seemed sufficiently similar to many CCFers, who were particularly open to the communist messages (Wiseman 1985: 39; Young 1969: 280). Among the critical incidents in this ongoing faction battle were the dissolution of the first Ontario chapter of the CCF and later expulsions of members in Ontario and Manitoba for ostensible connections to the Communist Party (Morley 1984: 201–10; Wiseman 1985: 37–62; Young 1969: 265). However, the CCF was considered the most undisciplined and Trotskyist in British Columbia (Young 1969: 277).

A more recent factional development by a group within the party incorporated a number of ideological themes. In 1969 the "Waffle" drafted the Manifesto for an Independent Socialist Canada. The Waffle apparently got its name from Ed Broadbent, then a young political scientist who would later break with the faction and eventually become the national party leader. For him, the manifesto was to be a rejection of "concessions to consensus radicalism: if it waffled, it would 'waffle to the left'" (Morton 1986: 92).

The manifesto linked Canadian independence, meaning independence from the United States, with the prospects for socialism. In the past, some of the CCF/NDP's continentalism had come from the affiliated trade unions, many themselves components of international unions. Brodie points out how "the industrial unions of Ontario's manufacturing heartland such as the Steelworkers and the United Auto Workers, were dependent on American capital both for their organizational existence and their members' well-being" (1985: 209). The Waffle was then also taking on trade union power within the NDP. In addition, the manifesto criticized the bureaucratized nature of the NDP and advocated both greater member participation and greater reliance on direct action (Gordon and Watkins 1970: 103). These uncompromising positions meant that some support dropped away, yet ninety-four supporters were willing to sign it before it was presented to the NDP leadership convention in October 1969. Even though the manifesto failed to win majority support, it generated strong interest and turmoil among the convention delegates.

In Saskatchewan, the Waffle divided the NDP. Delegates returned from the 1969 Winnipeg convention with enough enthusiasm for the Waffle's agenda to dominate the provincial executive and the leadership convention (Morton 1986: 107). In this effort, they were aided by the support of the provincial NDP leader, Woodrow Lloyd, for the Waffle manifesto. When Lloyd decided not to stand for reelection, a convention was called in 1970 and the Waffle offered Don Mitchell as a candidate in a tightly contested and bitter race (Morton 1986: 108). When Allan Blakeney, a mainstream candidate, won, some delegates refused to vote. According to one source, "Hardcore Wafflers, they insisted that there was really no choice" (Morton 1986: 108). When the 1971 provincial election approached, Mitchell stipulated that his group's support would come only if the NDP upheld the Waffle agenda

(Morton 1986: 130). Subsequently, the Waffle remained as a faction concerned with nonelectoral activity (Brodie 1985: 213).

In summary, the location of party movements in a multiorganizational field, the institutional context in which they operate, and the ideological perspective they bring to all stimulate the emergence of factions. Of the three, ideology is an intrinsic attribute of all party movements. Ideological themes, in fact, also animate factions that stem from multiorganizational connections and institutions. Internally, ideology is the element that unifies. Yet it also has the capacity to divide and create factions. In this way, the CCF/NDP is much like other party movements.

Adapting to Problems

All the factions described have been noticeably disruptive. Yet instead of destroying the party movement, they encouraged the CCF/NDP to change, I argue, because the same factions represent avenues through which a party movement can adapt to recurring problems and altered conditions. These problems are common to all organizations (Scott 1998: 10), including party movements. At the same time, the adaptations factions stimulate do not necessarily lead to resolution of the factional conflicts themselves. Nor do all forms of adaptation work in positive ways. But because positive outcomes are both so impressive and unexpected, they invite careful examination. These outcomes affect mobilization, recruitment, resources, ideology, goals, and alliances.

Mobilizing Participation

Organizations need to stimulate participation to ensure that jobs get done, a task particularly important for party movements, which depend entirely on the active participation of their members. Factions are a way of expanding opportunities by introducing new actors and events into the life of party movements (Coleman 1990: 390–93). Factions aid continuity because they value the party movement itself, encourage opponents to voice their positions, and, above all, persuade members not to exit.

These elements are well illustrated by the ILP, which expanded the CCF's constituency in Manitoba and enabled it to take advantage of the ILP's existing organization. The ILP leaders were able to give even more visible leadership to the CCF. When disputes arose between the groups over ILP autonomy, those same dissident leaders insisted that the ILP resume its affiliation with the CCF.

The enthusiasm among factional supporters is contagious, raising the energy level for the whole movement. Eve and John Smith, early activists and socialists in the British Columbia CCF, describe this phenomenon: "If the CCF had been a religious movement, we would have been considered the fundamentalists. The Regina Manifesto [the original statement of the CCF's position and the only one that directly mentioned socialism as part of its goals] was our Bible. We didn't believe winning votes was the most important thing" (quoted in Melnyk 1985: 151).

Factions produce committed participants, who not only arouse others with similar perspectives but also help crystallize opposition. Opponents, in turn, are important because they ensure that existing party movements can continue, despite factional inroads. In general, all these examples of factions illustrate how opportunities for participation expanded, even when groups battled each other.

Recruiting Participants

All organizations need to recruit, train, and replace participants. Because individuals typically play many roles, problems can arise when organizations try to impose either too many or too few restrictions (Katz and Eisenstadt 1960). If party movements engage in uncontrolled recruitment, they may suffer engulfment and lose control of their organization. If they overcontrol recruitment, they may remain insulated from their environment. There is an active dilemma here, stemming from conflicting requirements. On the one hand, party movements should vigorously recruit supporters to extend their influence and demonstrate that they must be taken seriously. At the same time, party movements must forge and protect a unique identity, which can be sustained only after the full socialization of members, an easier task if those members are initially similar (Schwartz 1996). In sum, party movements that are hosts to factions must fight against engulfment by dissidents while not resorting to tactics that insulate them from growing trends.

An example of these dilemmas is illustrated by Arthur Turner, an early CCF member of the British Columbia legislature. He used assumptions about the association between social class and political disposition to examine the socialist worth of prospective members. He was particularly cautious in admitting middle-class intellectuals from the League for Social Reconstruction, an organization that included founders of the national CCF.

> They wanted to join the CCF right from the start, but we felt shy of them. They had to sort of beg and plead for us to let them in. . . . We felt we were lowering our socialist status by letting the middle-class bourgeoisie—the people we considered to be part of the exploiting class—come in. We didn't want our socialist ideas diluted too much, and we were afraid that they would so impress the CCF that we

would become more like what we refer to nowadays as a left-wing
liberal party. We also felt that they were coming in to show the
workers that it wasn't all working-class people who were doing this.
(Quoted in Melnyk 1989: 135–36)

Successful recruitment can set aside some of this reluctance over time.
Factional disputes in the Manitoba CCF stimulated the party movement to
broaden its social base by the 1970s, to include not only farmers and labor
but also a more varied ethnic mix along with elements of the middle class
(Wiseman 1985: 150). The Waffle mobilized the young, encouraging their
membership or support, brought a more middle class face to the NDP, and
highlighted the role available to intellectuals. Even after Waffle members were
expelled or left, residues of the new connections it represented could still be
discerned in the NDP (Brodie 1985: 213).

In general, when party movements steer clear of engulfment by factional
recruits, they benefit from a degree of openness. They are rewarded when
factions help broaden party movements' social bases to better reflect current
concerns.

Gathering Resources, Providing Meaning

Party movements often struggle to find participants with the skills and talents to present their message, enlarge their core of workers, and find the fi-
nancing to pay for the trappings of a physical presence. An even more essential
resource is legitimacy, fundamental to any organization (Pfeffer and Salancik
1978: 193–96) but most problematic for party movements, because of their
newness and their challenge to established institutions.

For party movements, legitimacy means acceptance by the broader community, manifested in the ability to attract supporters, sympathizers, and elites
prepared to defend them. Factions can contribute to a party movement's legitimacy by adding to these elements. We can trace additions to the CCF/
NDP's legitimacy through the factional mobilization of farmers, unionists,
young people, intellectuals, the middle class, and legislators. For example, in
a survey of delegates to the 1971 leadership convention, "one-half of the
Waffle supporters were under 30 years of age, almost one-third were students
or academics and one-fifth were teachers or professionals" (Brodie 1985: 212).
In contrast, trade union delegates were older, less well-educated, and solidly
working class. Newcomers were then giving the NDP a more contemporary
appearance.

Party movements provide a system of explanations for events and conditions (Klandermans 1989: 9–10)—what we also call ideology. When the larger
community is prepared to acknowledge that a party movement has something

relevant to say, legitmacy follows. Factions raise questions about ideology that challenge and expand existing meaning systems. Their actions clarify a movement's ideology even when the message they bring is ultimately rejected. For example, each time a faction has pressed the CCF/NDP to take a stronger position on socialism, the movement has had to grapple with the symbolism and content of socialist theory. If responses abandoned traditional socialist positions, they were formulated in light of opposing views (Schwartz 1994: 23–28). Of the ideological factions, communists and Trotskyists were purged and the Waffle withdrew, but they all stimulated the CCF/NDP to reexamine itself. The results were more complex and more nuanced than their opponents wanted, yet they were partly a consequence of dealing with factions. Morley (1984: 201–20) concludes that these particular factional struggles made the CCF/NDP more mature and resilient.

The CCF/NDP cases illustrate how factional challenges to ideology resulted not in a single system of meaning but an expansion in the ideologies available to the party movement. In adding to the movement's repertoire, this advantage ties even more supporters to the movement.

Defining Goals

Defining goals, necessary for any new organization, is especially pressing for party movements challenging the status quo. At the same time, like all organizations, party movements must expand resources on their own maintenance, a task that frequently leads to downplaying goals (Scott 1998: 10). Factions spotlight political goals and require that old goals be reexamined and redefined. Both the provincialist faction and the Waffle helped redirect the NDP by forcing a reconsideration of its positions on nationalism, the rights of Quebec, and provincial autonomy. These goal redefinitions were intended to restrain internal and external criticism and to attract and satisfy supporters.

Some factional influence on goals is less clear but may still have long-term implications. For example, the organization faction—that is, the wing of the movement concerned that power remain with the organizational apparatus and its members, not solely with its legislative component—has had a difficult time asserting its control. Still, only through its efforts can the social movement activity associated with rank-and-file participation continue to survive. Similarly, although the Waffle did not resolve questions about the positions taken by trade unionists in the NDP, it helped stimulate the subsequent nationalization of the Canadian Auto Workers Union that had earlier appeared so dependent on its U.S. connections.

The ILP faction's efforts to promote industrial socialism and virtually dismiss its agrarian counterpart would soon founder. Before long, the CCF, nationally as well as in Manitoba, downplayed its commitment to socialism, at least as a concept. Certainly in Saskatchewan, but even in Alberta and British Columbia, the CCF's initial ties with rural residents and primary producers were critical to its growth. But, in the long run, the ILP's conception of the future for a social democratic movement was closer to the way Canadian politics actually evolved. An emphasis on urban interests, links with trade unions, and concerns for workers were, in fact, themes that would bring the CCF its greatest support. Exactly these kinds of interests and sectors led to the founding of the CCF's successor, even though the ILP was no longer on the scene.

Later, the Waffle was no more successful than the ILP in reinvigorating enthusiasm for socialism. Yet it did introduce to the NDP additional concerns associated with the New Left, including ones relating to discrimination, racism, and to lifestyle issues. That is, it gave issues already prominent in the New Left a political focus and an arena that would give them the potential to become the subject of political action.

In sum, factions can have at least two connections with goals. They can challenge the party movement to clearly focus on goals, and they can add to or change goals. In either case, they can help the party movement to enhance its appeal.

Managing Alliances

Social democratic party movements tend "to exist in a world of natural friends and enemies whose role is dictated by ideology rather than by shifting interests" (Schwartz 1994: 12). The major enemies of the CCF/NDP are in the business community, although, in the past, the Roman Catholic Church was also a vocal opponent. Traditional friends are found among unionized workers, farmers, the poor, pacifists, and, more recently, advocates of rights for women, gays, and lesbians, as well as environmentalists.

The task for the CCF/NDP is to neutralize enemies and expand and intensify ties with friends. Factions can be helpful when they increase the network of alliances by encouraging support from sympathizers without necessarily recruiting them into the party movement. For example, the Waffle expanded the NDP's network by bringing ties to the student movement and the New Left.

More generally, factions have the potential for increasing sympathetic alliances essential for party movement continuity and expansion through their own connections with groups and interests that can then be extended to the party movement.

Factionalism is not only—or always—helpful to a party movement. Indeed, factional conflict can overwhelm a party movement. Scarce resources can be diverted to infighting. Dissension can undermine legitimacy and embitter participants. The introduction of new ideologies or reinterpretations of old ones can solidify irreconcilable differences. Conflict may lead to breaking away of splinter groups and a decrease in resources. Allies important to the party movement may prove unstable and become bitter critics when they are dissatisfied. Yet the formation of factions is compatible with party movements' continuity when factions add excitement and resources with new, more committed actors, leaders, and allies and when they provide focus and clarification for goals and ideology.

Contributions to Continuity

Is It Worth the Struggle?

The positive consequences of factional actions are not primarily an unintended result but a direct outgrowth of tactical choices. Forming a faction, or, more neutrally, a challenging group, is a strategic choice for changing a party movement and passing on the challenger's message. To participants, no amount of disruption may be excessive as long as the message comes across. But what if the faction itself is weakened or even destroyed? Is there still something to be gained from factionalism? To answer these questions, I examine the judgment of participants in the Saskatchewan Waffle.

John Richards, a former Member of the Legislative Assembly (MLA) and Waffle supporter who advocated separation of the Waffle from the NDP and left the NDP to sit as an Independent Socialist, evaluated the effects of separation on the NDP: "Across the country the quality of internal debates became flat and listless; policy debates seemed irrelevant to the direction pursued by the leadership of the party" (Richards 1981: 73). Peter Prebble (1981), an NDP MLA from Saskatoon, and a critic of his party from the Left, expressed his disappointment that the NDP had not been prodded to take more consistently left-wing positions, something he thought would occur if there were more of a radical faction within the party movement.

More optimistically, Don Mitchell, a founder of the Waffle, evaluated the merger of old and new Left in the Waffle as a plus for the NDP: "We were able to confront, because of our political and economic framework, a rather tired and, I think, a rather drifting New Democratic Party" (1981: 86). He concluded:

> I believe that the theory and analysis of the Waffle is sound, that
> there is a common basis of unity in that theory in the province, and
> what we need is a re-organization of the Left and a co-ordinating
> function by a group like the Waffle that learns from the experience

of 1969 to 1971 how to bring those various groups together and to
avoid the wasted energy of internal struggles within the NDP.
(Mitchell 1981: 91)

Recognition of the Waffle's influence is even implicit in the assessment
offered by Lorne Brown (1981), a labor historian and a Waffle member. In
his commitment to Marxist-socialist ideals, he perceives the need for an active faction as a part of an electorally involved party movement, although
the NDP is no longer his venue of choice. In sum, factional representatives
want to bring change to the party movement and are pleased when change
occurs, even when it jeopardizes the continuity of the faction.

Surviving Factionalism

Given continuing encounters with factionalism that produced serious conflicts, only some of which were illustrated here, how did the CCF/NDP manage to survive? Aside from such factors as its inclusion in the Canadian party
system and its organizational resources, I see independent contributions to
survival from the very factions that otherwise appear so destructive.

Because factions affect political goals and meaning systems, factions forced
the CCF/NDP to keep examining both. This kind of self-examination is in-
vigorating and keeps a party movement from stagnating ideologically or
organizationally.

Like other party movements, and many organizations in general, the CCF/
NDP has many inner contradictions, two of which I discussed under institutional sources of factionalism. On the one hand, carrying out its agenda requires a unity of purpose that encourages centralized control. On the other,
it is committed to membership participation and consensual decision making. Factions highlight these contradictions and push the CCF/NDP toward
accommodations that value decentralization and loose coupling. The more
successful the party movement in adopting these organizational forms, the
more it can minimize factional stress (Scott 1998: 158–61).

All party movements operate in a volatile environment where conditions
and interests change. If existing movements become overinvolved in maintaining themselves, factions alert them to new issues and new constituencies
ready for mobilization. Factions have played this role for the CCF/NDP by
focusing attention on changes in the economy and the country's demographic
composition. The enthusiasm of new participants then reawakened the commitment of earlier adherents.

Finally, we have seen how ideology runs through the relations between
factions and party movement continuity. At one level, ideas are a critical
impetus for factions. At another, they are tied to the basic problems every

party movement faces so that factions' ideas bring become part of the currency with which problems are faced. But, most significantly, they are the substance of continuity, for factional participants seek to perpetuate ideas. Waffle members reported that, organizationally, the NDP was a vehicle for spreading and acting on ideas. When factions can bring fresh ideas and reinforce old ones, they promote the party movement's continuity.

Carty and his coauthors (2000: 94) report that the NDP grew increasingly suspicious of relations with social movements advocating progressive causes in the 1990s, at least of those that are part of its multiorganizational field and potential factions. And NDP officials attribute recent poor electoral showings to the instability of support from would-be allies. But perhaps the NDP's failures are also attributable to its own inability to use factional alliances resourcefully.

Factions are so prevalent in party movements that one could define their presence as a characteristic of party movements. It could be tempting to blame factionalism for the short history of party movements. Factionalism is a risky encounter for party movements, as the case of the CCF/NDP so richly illustrates, yet factions can make important contributions to party movement endurance. When party movements survive the turmoil, they emerge stronger and more focused.

NOTES

1. In ongoing research, I examine five strategic responses. In addition to factions, these are purges, mergers, makeovers, and dormancy or abeyance. That research was initiated by a grant from the Faculty Research Program of the Canadian Embassy and later expanded by a Senior Fellowship from the Canadian Embassy. Collection of Canadian data was made possible through a grant from the Social Sciences and Humanities Research Council of Canada. Co-investigators Frederick C. Engelmann and Kenneth Carty contributed in hiring and supervising outstanding research assistants Maria Greene, Csaba Nikolenji, Emma Cross, and Miriam Koen.

2. The railway representative was the sole official one, and his actions were troubling to his home union (Melnyk 1989: 48–49).

3. I am indebted to Professor Howard Leeson for tracking down this information. There is some dispute as to when the change actually took place.

More Than One Feminism:

Organizational Structure and

the Construction of Collective Identity

JO REGER

Conventional wisdom holds that organizations need homogeneity to avoid internal conflict and factionalism. Scholars argue that the more diverse a group's membership, the higher the risk of factionalism (McCarthy and Zald 1987). Others argue that organizational structure is the key, with less formalized collectivist groups more susceptible to factionalism over new political ideas, beliefs, or goals (Staggenborg 1989, 1995). By examining the link between structure and culture, I argue that groups can accommodate diverse ideologies or identities and not suffer from divisive factionalism. Groups will adjust to new, seemingly oppositional political beliefs if the organization gains significant advantages. The resulting accommodation provides a structural "niche" for the formation of a new activist identity, which minimizes conflict between identities through boundary construction. Therefore, factionalism, when accommodated, can simultaneously preserve group diversity and organizational integrity.

Because of its history of contested definitions of feminism and organizational factionalism, the contemporary women's movement provides an excellent location to examine the link between culture and structure (see Arnold 1995; Davis 1991; Ferree and Hess 1985/1995; Freeman 1973, 1975; Friedan 1977). In a case study of a National Organization for Women (NOW) chapter, I found that to increase member recruitment and commitment New York City (NYC) NOW feminists modified the chapter's structure to accommodate the process of consciousness raising (CR).[1] In doing so, members created a site for the construction of a new feminist identity. To decrease intragroup conflict, the new identity is structurally segmented from the rest of the chapter.

Although this case does not represent all grassroots social movement organizations, it shows the relationship between the construction of an organization and the creation of activist identities. I first examine factors shaping organizational structure and then discuss the process of collective identity construction and the role of boundaries. After presenting a brief history of NYC NOW, I describe how structural development and collective identity construction are linked in this chapter and how its infrastructure and organizational profile are shaped by the construction of collective identity.

Construction of Organizational Structure and Collective Identity

In part, resources, the political environment (Gamson 1975/1990; Gelb 1987; McAdam 1982; McCarthy and Zald 1977, 1987), and movement ideologies (Arnold 1995; Carden 1974; Martin 1990; Riger 1984; Rothschild-Whitt 1979; Thomas 1999) shape organizational structure. Initial structures may be shaped by the availability of "mobilizing structures," but once a movement is active, it is the "organizational profile of those groups purporting to represent the movement that become important" (McAdam, McCarthy, and Zald 1996a: 13). Organizational profiles, including strategies, tactics, and targets, are shaped by movement ideologies, which in turn influence the construction of organizational structure. Once an organization has emerged, competition among social movement organizations may cause the group to adapt to survive (McCarthy and Zald 1977; Zald and Ash 1966). In particular, the need for stable resources can pressure an organization to routinize its resource-gathering processes and formalize its systems of authority (Gelb 1995; Knoke 1989; McCarthy and Britt 1989; Wilson 1973).

In the early years of the women's movement, feminist visions of an ideal society influenced organizational structure (Carden 1974; Evans 1979; Riger 1984). Women's rights organizations, such as NOW, created centralized formal organizations to pursue equality through institutional and state-directed channels. By adopting a structural form resembling those of the institutions targeted, women's rights organizations promote change though having a formal division of labor and identifying a clear chain of authority (Ferree and Hess 1985/1995). In contrast, women's liberationist groups developed loosely structured, decentralized collectivist groups focused on interaction and consensus as a means for women's personal transformation and community building (Cassell 1977; Evans 1979; Rothschild-Whitt 1979).

When individuals come together and interact within a social movement context, they construct a collective identity that serves as the basis for collective action (Johnston, Laraña, and Gusfield 1994; Melucci 1985a, 1989;

Taylor and Whittier 1992). This collective identity is a "shared definition of a group that derives from members' common interests, experiences and solidarity" (Taylor 1989: 771) and articulates the groups goals, beliefs, and visions of social change. Collective identities are not static but change as activists, external factors (i.e., access to resources, the political climate) (Whittier 1995, 1997) and collective action goals change (Johnston et al. 1994).

Activists define collective identities in opposition to other groups in society, including targeted groups such as the state or countermovement groups. In other words, groups enact boundaries to distinguish between members and nonmembers (Taylor and Whittier 1992). This differentiation from the rest of society allows members to create a "free space" or social movement community, in which to define their culture, ideologies, and collective action goals (Buechler 1990). Boundaries can be symbolic marked through use of language, signs, symbols, artifacts or, as I argue, can be delineated through organizational structure. In sum, culture and structure are linked through the reciprocal construction of both an organizational profile (building on resources and movement ideology) and collective identities (fostered by the construction of symbolic and organizational boundaries).

New York City and the National Organization for Women

The National Organization for Women is the largest feminist organization in the United States, claiming more than 500,000 members nationwide (NOW 2000). Created in 1966, NOW was a major participant in the campaign for the Equal Rights Amendment (ERA) in the 1970s and 1980s and is currently involved in struggles for abortion access and subsequent legislation, lesbian rights, and women's economic equality. The organization operates on several levels, with a national level that oversees regional, state, and local chapter activities. Here, I examine the NYC chapter, founded in 1967. The NYC NOW was the first local chapter to form and continues to be one of the largest, claiming more than 3,000 members in the late 1990s (NOW NYC 2000). The chapter grew quickly, its presence enhanced by its location in a national center of activism, politics, and media.

The NYC NOW has been active on a variety of national and community issues. Situated in NYC, the chapter is adept at drawing national attention for its actions. For example, a protest of sexist advertising by a Manhattan jewelry store, Tiffany's, brought national attention in the 1970s. The chapter also played a central role in the campaign to pass the ERA. Other issues included a battle against Operation Rescue (a nationwide anti-abortion campaign that attempted to close women's health clinics), the support of political candidates, and protesting the welfare reform acts of the 1990s. The chapter continues to focus on both national and community issues. For example, in August 2000, members raised funds for domestic violence programs, protested police inattention to attacks on women in Central Park, and denounced sexist ads by People for the Ethical Treatment of Animals (PETA).

Over its long and active life, NYC NOW has experienced a number of clashes over goals, strategy, and structure; its persistence reflects its ability to manage these conflicts. In 1968, a group criticized the organization's formal hierarchical structure and eventually split off, forming a women's liberation group called The Feminists. Radical feminist ideology and a collectivist structure were incorporated into the chapter in 1972 when, after repeated requests by women both in and outside the chapter, leaders agreed to the formation of a CR committee. Consciousness raising is a process begun by decentralized women's liberationist groups in which women experience empowerment through discussing their personal experiences and linking it to societal oppression in an egalitarian setting (Ferree and Hess 1985/1995).

Structural Development

Two intertwined factors shape NYC NOW's overall organizational structure. First is the influence of the national organization with its adoption of a more formal structure. Second is the need for continuous resource acquisition within a specific institutional environment. Because of the latter, the chapter has undergone structural adaptations throughout its history. The most striking and permanent adaptation is the formation of a decentralized CR committee within a hierarchical and formalized organizational structure.

Soon after its formation, the NYC chapter developed a formal centralized structure, modeled largely after the national structure. The original structure was also a response to the competitive NYC movement community, where a developed infrastructure (including multiple phone lines and a centrally located office) could sustain recruitment and fund-raising efforts. One activist recalled how this competition began in the early years of the movement: "There are lots of different women's groups. . . . You have upper crust ladies' clubs with all the trappings of feminism. You have the National Women's Political Caucus. So even from day one . . . NOW in this town competed with a variety of other women's groups and so it was always differentiated."

To sustain the chapter's infrastructure and influence policy makers and legislators, members developed a formal leadership system and committee structure. The chapter's leadership system has a clear chain of authority established through a hierarchy of officers: president, multiple vice presidents, a secretary, a treasurer, and a board of directors. The chapter also has a system of ongoing and active committees and subcommittees. Committees tend to focus on issues, whereas subcommittees concentrate on sustaining the infrastructure. Regular chapter committees include family relations, consciousness raising, lesbian rights, media reform, psychology, fund-raising, and reproductive rights. Subcommittees include groups working on programs like communication and media, producing leaflets, tabling at different locations in the city, and coordinating volunteers.[2]

Consciousness raising is one of the chapter's oldest committees. The chapter institutionalized CR in 1972 when it began to hold sessions in the NOW office in response to member demand and public interest.[3] At this time in the women's movement, women's rights groups began to bring CR into their organizations as a recruitment device and to help women rethink their lives and understand the importance of feminist organizing (Carden 1974). The committee continues to be one of the largest and most active in the chapter.[4] But the introduction of CR into NYC NOW posed a dilemma in terms of chapter structure and ideology. Women need to experience the CR process in a decentralized and nonhierarchical setting, an organizational context not found in NYC NOW's main infrastructure. To be true to the process, CR committee members had to adopt a more decentralized style with no official leader. In return, the chapter leaders had to accommodate an organizational style that countered the rest of the chapter.

This accommodation, negotiated by maintaining boundaries between the CR committee and the rest of the chapter, resulted in the committee becoming separated and somewhat alienated. As the CR committee became established, members began to distinguish between CR feminists and feminists in the rest of the chapter. One CR committee member characterized the relationship with the rest of the chapter as an "us versus them" situation. Another bitterly described how CR committee members were perceived: "The CR group was a fringe group of touchy feely people who didn't really understand what the issues were and that you really had to do all this marching and organizing and whatever. They didn't have a legislative analysis. They, the CR group, weren't doing real work. There was a very clear feeling about that." By incorporating CR into the chapter in the form of a committee, members found a way to accommodate new ideas, goals, and members into the chapter, increasing its vitality and avoiding factionalism.[5]

Collective Identities in the New York City Chapter

Organizational structure shapes, and is shaped by, the construction of each distinct feminist identity in the NYC chapter. Situated within different structural bases, these identities draw on separate groups of activists and embrace different beliefs about accomplishing social change. Situated in the chapter's main infrastructure, one identity embraces the ideas of liberal feminism[6] and works within the chapter's main infrastructure to make legislative and policy level changes. Situated in the CR committee, the other identity focuses on CR principles and works within a decentralized committee to change society through personal transformation. These identities are constructed, in part, through the development of structural boundaries.

Both groups of activists define their identities as "feminist," but their definitions of feminism vary. I label them according to the goals expressed by the activists. "Political feminists" use state-directed legislative strategies; "empowerment feminists" focus on CR and women's transformation. This label reflects descriptions of feminism as a means to "empower" women to create new communities. These identities overlap, with empowerment feminists working and interacting outside of the CR committee. Some empowerment feminists "cross" over and become political feminists, but none of the women interviewed moved from political feminism to empowerment feminism—although one straddled both identities and went from the CR committee to become a chapter leader and then back to facilitating CR groups.

Political Feminists

The chapter's centralized, formal structure with set authority systems and differentiated tasks and responsibilities is supported by a belief that equates structural development with goal accomplishment. Members believe that a developed infrastructure is a source of efficient activism, membership retention, and leadership development promoting organizational continuity. They perceive organizations lacking formalized structures and procedures as short-lived and ineffective.

Many of the interviewees recounted stories of decentralized women's groups that eventually disappeared from the NYC scene. These stories took the tone of "cautionary tales" that emphasized the transient nature of informal and consensus-based groups, as one member's story of joining NOW reflects. Originally a member of a decentralized group, she joined NOW after working in an abortion rights coalition with NYC NOW members. She remembers realizing that the decentralized group with "its structure-lessness was not going to be able to do anything to save legalized abortion and I could see in my contacts with NOW that they were going to. They had an organization with structure." She moved from a decentralized organization, in which no one held leadership positions and everyone got two minutes to speak, to an organization with officers, committees, and meetings conducted through by parliamentary procedure. In her view, formal structure was necessary for action. She continued: "If you don't have any structure, you spend more time. No one is designated to pinpoint [a] vision

. . . and then there is so much infighting. There is even more infighting than when you have structure."

The Women's Action Collective, formed in NYC during the 1992 Anita Hill–Clarence Thomas hearings was the subject of another cautionary tale. The decentralized group drew hundreds of women to its first few meetings but soon ceased meeting because of infighting and disagreements about the group's goals. One NYC NOW member described the group as "imploding because they hadn't thought through their feminism."

These tales reconfirmed NYC members' belief in their chapter's structure. One member described how a formalized structure kept the chapter going: "We are very structured. We have a president. We have a board. It is not [a] free floating equal chaos and that really does a lot to keep us in line. . . . That kind of structure—people with roles, people with elections—that really keeps us going." Political feminists reported that a developed organizational structure also aided in membership retention, an advantage the chapter enjoyed over less structured groups. A president during the late 1980s and early 1990s recalls the state of the chapter during a period of intense pro-choice mobilization: "We had stuff going on so that when people came to the chapter and wanted to be involved, it was kind of a bustling place. There were people around. There were a few different committees active and that was always a good thing."

Members also perceive formalized structure as an important element in leadership development. In NYC NOW, the chapter's structure provides a "training ground" for women to become leaders. This view is based on a belief that society constructs barriers that keep women from leadership and, therefore, equality. Consequently, a hierarchical structure offers women a place to acquire important leadership skills (see Halcli and Reger 1996; Reger 1992). According to one member:

> You do get self-confidence and I see really an enormous blooming of women in NOW where they come in sort of mice, and they leave like tigers. . . . It's a tremendous change that I've seen in some women. [It is] just unbelievable what happens. I mean it is very positive for a lot of women. . . . It's the structure and always the leadership. You do something and then something happens. It really does change their lives.

Chapter hierarchy and structure then facilitate women's leadership and, therefore, change society. Chapter presidents have gone on to hold legal and political positions, including elected office and administrative positions in government. One member called the presidency of NYC NOW a career stepping stone to "something high profile."

Women who constructed a political feminist identity come to NOW to find women with similar political beliefs. For example, one member described the chapter as "a place where you know that you're not going to make best friends with someone and then have someone say 'Oh yeah, I think abortion is wrong.'" In addition, the chapter also serves as a site for women to learn how to be a part of a group. Members described themselves as a group of women brought together by "desire to bring about change" and as a "fighting bunch." According to one woman, participating in the chapter shows women they are not alone and that there are ways to fight together. She described this feeling of being part of a group: "Once you've learned how to fight as part of a group, and you know that they are out there, it's a whole different feeling than feeling like you don't know people. You don't know where to go. You don't know what to do."

Engaging with the state is the primary goal, and members work for equality by challenging preexisting legislative, economic, and social systems. According to one member, NOW members have a "strong sense that women need some fundamental empowerment that we don't have." However, acknowledging discrimination is not enough. Members must believe that change is possible and that NOW is the key to affecting change. A longtime member noted that in her experience NOW members believe in "a cause": challenging patriarchy and inequality in society. One member described what she saw as the chapter's goals: "I think what NOW does when it does the right things, it challenges male authority, male laws, with the idea that you can make a difference. You can bring about change."

One way political feminists create a group feeling is to select women with different ideas about organizational structure and social change. Several of the interviewees noted that some new members, uncomfortable with the complexity and form of the chapter's organization, eventually left. When asked what NOW members had in common, one former president replied:

> [Laughing] I do think it has something to do with being comfortable with a kind of hierarchy, I think ours is a useful hierarchy. I mean I think it should be required reading for every feminist at least coming into NOW to read Jo Freeman's "Tyranny of Structurelessness." . . . I think you don't necessarily need to know the NOW history but there is a bit of hierarchy which I think gives us enough structure to have lasted for thirty years.

Understanding the reason for the chapter's structure fit with a second criteria members used to screen out those who did not "get" the political feminist identity. Women needed to understand that political feminists define the group primarily as a political organization. One leader explained: "I think all women in NOW share a vision. I think they all know that something is not right out here [laughed] and that something is sexism. . . . The difference is people who really get the political stuff versus those who don't. Some people just don't get it."

This implicit process of screening, through self-selection, encourages both diversity and coherence in collective identity construction. The belief in structure becomes a boundary enacted by political feminists. Accepting the chapter's structure by joining and maintaining affiliation marks an understanding and commitment to the goals and means of the group. Political feminists' emphasis on political and legislative change is not only a strategy; in the chapter, it becomes an essential component of their constructed identity.

By drawing clear boundaries between themselves as political feminists and other forms of feminism, members construct a feminist identity that promotes goal-oriented political action over personal empowerment. However, not all NYC NOW members embraced this definition of feminism. The CR committee constructs a different feminist identity and has a different relationship to the chapter's organizational structure.

Empowerment Feminists

The CR committee's organizational profile reflects the group's belief system and shared feminist identity. Members structure the committee in a non-hierarchical manner, and no formal leaders or "experts" emerge to direct the sessions or the committee.[7] Whereas political feminists avoid socializing and sharing, CR committee members are encouraged to bond as a form of political empowerment. In addition to building communities among women, empowerment feminists perceive the committee as the source of the chapter's emotional "character."

Within the committee, members focus on sharing life experiences and emotions as a key to transform women's visions of the world. This emphasis on the personal led one woman to call the committee the "emotional infrastructure" of the chapter. Another woman who entered NOW through the CR committee describes it as one of the most "memorable and transforming experiences in my life." A former committee member offered this description of consciousness raising: "I think CR allows women to understand the commonality of their experience and . . . to get in touch with, and create an analysis and critique that then comes out of your own experience. It grounds it [personal experience] and makes it more powerful. It is not analytical."

Many of the women in the committee talked about the transformative effect of CR. A younger woman in the committee said, "I think CR has been important to me in helping to realize the different ways in which our rights and assumptions operate." However, CR is not seen as therapy for women. Instead, its goal is to create feminists who understand their own lives in the context of a sexist and discriminatory world. One woman described her experience: "I had been in therapy for some time at that point and therapy is really about fixing yourself and there were a lot of things that came to me in the course of the CR group that weren't me. They were about the world outside of me." Members view CR as essential to the chapter and to NOW's goals. One longtime organizer in the committee responded to the question of how she saw CR fitting with the rest of the chapter: "I think it has got to be key. The personal is political and getting people to see that [is important] because it [sexism] is very subtle these days. . . . CR makes people feel much clearer focused and centered in their beliefs . . . and makes them stronger."

Within the committee's boundaries, drawing on the belief that CR transforms society, members construct an empowerment feminist identity. The committee and the empowerment feminist identity offer women a different, more emotion-rich location wherein to explore feminism. In particular, it appeals to women seeking a certain sense of connection. Several women recounted stories of seeking a community of women when social events enraged or disturbed them. One woman remembered why she came to the committee:

When the Anita Hill incident took place in this country, I was watching it on television. I felt . . . rage. It was so blatant and powerful that I needed to be, to partake in a larger experience with it and I called NOW. . . . I attended [a meeting] and it was [a] tiny room filled with at least 200 women who felt exactly like I had. . . . There was this new community for me—ready to bond with, to share and to become an activist with.

She said the experience of watching Anita Hill testify about sexual harassment made her want to be with other women and do something constructive with her rage. She continued, "I felt a need personally to connect and do more and feel like I wasn't just sort of out there as an individual dealing with this stuff." Another woman, who had begun CR before joining the chapter, interpreted her involvement as an ongoing search for community and sisterhood among women. She said, "I had begun to understand and see that I needed women, but it wasn't still something I could tell consciously." By bringing women together, the committee becomes a place where women felt free to explore their lives. One member stated that, through the committee, "NOW has given me the environment to transform myself."

Empowerment feminists believe the only way to achieve liberation in society is to first undergo consciousness raising. One young woman described the process: "I think it is essential. I believe that the only way for women to heal, to try to give birth to a new self, and to bond and create a community that bonds differently . . . can only take place with consciousness raising. . . . Consciousness raising is a tool to create new communities with new dynamics." She believed that the movement could not thrive and be productive without CR. She said, "Without CR sort of grounding you and your own experience, it becomes incredibly intellectual and incredibly analytical and I think that is unbelievably destructive of the movement."

Just as political feminists screen out women who do not "get" the organizational structure, empowerment feminists construct boundaries between those who understand the process of CR and those who do not. This boundary is primarily enacted between the committee and the rest of the chapter, creating a sense of opposition between political feminists and empowerment feminists. Political feminists participate in this boundary construction by viewing CR as "immature" and nonpolitical. One political feminist, who had done CR outside the chapter, explained why she did not join the committee: "I guess maybe I was too far past it. I think there's a lot of good in it but I think some of it's a little [she paused] touchy feeley kind of stuff." Many of the political feminists interviewed saw CR as an initial step to understanding feminism but not as a solution to women's inequality. Also, political feminists choose not to enter the committee, barred by their belief that building a woman's community is apolitical. In response, empowerment feminists tend to view the rest of the chapter as misguided for emphasizing political gain. One longtime committee member said bluntly, "We are so fucking busy with the legislation that we lose sight of the woman." In her view, CR helped women "connect in a very basic way" necessary for women's liberation. She added, "That is why I say with all the legislation in the world [women's equality] is not going to happen. It is not going to help."

Even though their identity is different from that of political feminists, empowerment feminists belived themselves to be important members and participated in maintaining the chapter. One member reflected on what she saw as the purpose of the committee as opposed to the rest of the chapter: "We have different goals. We have the goals of bringing women into the chapter. We have the goals of giving them the opportunity to relate the personal and the political in their lives that is, of course, the major goal." One advantage of the committee is that it provides an "entryway" for women to become active in NOW. One CR committee member noted: "Since I have been involved we've attracted quite a number of women to other things in NOW through consciousness raising. We kind of sold them on the other activities in NOW and they got involved. So we have been fairly successful as a recruiting vehicle for the chapter."

A member active in the 1990s noted that about a third to a fourth of the women continue to do some sort of NOW-related activity after participating in a CR group. One member who "crossed" described that process: "After my first consciousness raising group, I was really ready to throw myself into sort of the pragmatic of strengthening NOW." However, "crossing" does not weaken the boundaries between the groups but instead serves to reaffirm them by acknowledging their existence through negotiation.[8]

The willingness of empowerment feminists to negotiate boundaries has not gone unnoticed by others in the chapter. One former president acknowledged the importance of the committee to the rest of the chapter: "It is important. We get activists out of it. . . . If you sit and look at the board there are any number of board positions, at any one time, that are being filled by women who come out of the CR committee and they are doing stuff."

However, as a political feminist, the same leader saw the committee as removed from the chapter. To her, the committee was unpredictable, meaning it sometimes participated in chapter events but other times retreated from chapter business. She recalled a particular event: "The CR committee bought an entire table at an event we were doing. No other committee came even close. . . . On the other hand, the CR people do go off and into their own fucking world. [I] cannot tell you how many times they have been totally out of touch with what's going on in the rest of the chapter."

One reason for empowerment feminists' willingness to negotiate boundaries and interact with the rest of the chapter emerges from their understanding of the multiple definitions of NOW. Several women from the CR committee discussed different types of feminism existing within NOW. One woman noted:

> I think that for a lot of people what being a feminist, being a NOW member, meant was making a financial contribution and . . . going to a meeting every once in a while. . . . Then there were women who felt that being part of NOW meant demonstrating, being part of demonstrations and going to Washington to march and doing the clinic vigils and that kind of stuff. . . . And then there was a group that thought it was about CR.

Another woman echoed her statements, calling NOW an "umbrella organization" embracing feminists with a range of beliefs and ideas. By acknowledging that different forms of feminism need to co-exist, empowerment feminists are able to stay connected and engage with the rest of the chapter membership.

Conclusion

This chapter illustrates how organizational structure shapes, and is shaped by, activist identity construction through boundary creation and provides an important theoretical bridge linking structure (represented by organizational structure) and culture (represented by collective identity) in social movements. The NYC NOW case study shows how this link between structure and culture allows groups to diversify ideologically and still remain organizationally coherent. Therefore, factionalism, when structurally and culturally accommodated, brings significant benefits to an organization.

This chapter illustrates how organizational benefits include continued mobilization, managed conflict, and infrastructure maintenance. In NYC NOW, two feminist identities offer potential recruits different definitions of feminism, casting a "wider net" for continued mobilization. The construction of interorganizational boundaries, although building on in-group hostilities, also manages conflict by creating structural spaces for both groups and decreasing the need for groupwide power struggles. In other words, each identity has a spatial domain in which to carry out a feminist agenda without interference from the other. In addition, continuity of the organization is enhanced through the construction of a political feminist identity, which views structural development and maintenance as a key aspect of its goals. In sum, by drawing from both the women's rights and women's liberation branches of the movement, structurally and culturally, NYC NOW creates an organizational environment that sustains member commitment and organizational structure, aiding continuity.

NOTES

The author would like to thank Nancy Whittier, David Meyer, Carol Mueller, and Dawn Cooley for their comments and support of this work. An Elizabeth D. Gee Fund for Research on Women grant at the Ohio State University, Columbus, Ohio, funded this study.

1. My analysis draws on two types of data. First are documents, dating from 1966 to 1995, from NYC NOW, which provide information on the chapter's history, organizational activities and events, members' personal reflections on feminism and NOW, and information on organizations and institutions with which chapter members interacted. The second major source of data is thirteen in-depth interviews with leaders or core activists from the chapter. Interviewees provided information about their own experiences and also served as informants about the state of the chapter. The interviews were open-ended and semistructured and lasted between thirty minutes and three and one-half hours. To gain a broader understanding of the community environment and political context of the chapter, I interviewed six key informants in NOW at the national and state levels.

2. *NOW-NYC News*, February 1990. Files of the New York City NOW chapter.

3. *NOW York Woman*, July 1972. Files of the New York City NOW chapter.

4. In 1996, the committee had nineteen members and conducted two ongoing CR sessions throughout the year. *NOW News*, January/February 1996, Files of the New York City NOW chapter.

5. The CR committee is prominently listed on the chapter's web site under the heading, "For Women to Get What We Want, We Need to Get Together." (*NYC NOW*, October 1999. "NYC_NOW's Committees," online, Internet.)

6. Radical and liberal feminists identify different sources of women's oppression, means for social change, and visions of an ideal society. Liberal feminism advocates working within social institutions as a means to end men's unjust societal advantages and increase women's civil rights. Radical feminism focuses on women's personal transformation as a form of liberation and the creation of a new system, rejecting the "male" world (Ferree and Hess 1985/1995).

7. Jo Freeman (1972/1973) warns against characterizing decentralized groups as "structureless." She maintains that all organizations have some sort of structure whether formal or informal.

8. This insight is draw from Barrie Thorne's (1997) analysis of gender boundaries between elementary school girls and boys.

The Development of Individual Identity
and Consciousness among Movements
of the Left and Right

REBECCA E. KLATCH

This chapter examines the effects of internal and external factors on the de-velopment of individual political consciousness and identity, as well as on the mobilization and course of social movements. I analyze the effects of these factors on movements of the Left and Right by considering activists involved in two predominant groups of the 1960s: Students for a Democratic Society (SDS) on the Left and Young Americans for Freedom (YAF) on the Right. This chapter is part of a larger project that compares women and men who were active in SDS and YAF, tracing their paths from early childhood, through the radicalizing events of the 1960s, up to their adult lives (Klatch 1999). Other studies focus on the collective identity of social movements; this study focuses on the formation and development of *individual* consciousness and political identity. Also, studies within social movements often focus on a single case; this study compares movements of the Left and Right, allowing for analysis of the differences as well as the parallels and overlaps in the devel-opment of consciousness and identity of activists in opposing movements.

In examining external factors, I use Karl Mannheim's theory of genera-tions to understand how historical location and differences in social back-ground generated two opposing wings of the 1960s generation, with divergent political consciousness and identity. I analyze two internal factors: the im-portance of peers in solidifying commitment to a movement and in helping articulate and develop a broader analysis or framing of issues, and the effect of an organization's size on activists' experiences and views and the develop-ment of a movement.

Discussing internal and external factors separately, however, implies that they are distinct categories. Yet, as we shall see, external and internal factors often interact in influencing political consciousness and the course of movements. In the 1960s, both the media and government repression interacted with the internal dynamics of movements of the Left and Right, fundamentally altering the direction of SDS and YAF. Media coverage of SDS changed the organization's size and group life. Government repression provoked a process of radicalization for both leftists and libertarians in YAF, leading to a shift in consciousness and identity, and also providing an opening for the overlap between the worlds of the Left and Right.

Both SDS and YAF were founded in 1960. Both were also youth groups stemming from older organizations of the Left and Right.[1] SDS was more well known and visible during the 1960s; YAF was the most prominent student organization on the Right and served an important role as a training ground for a whole generation of conservative leaders, some holding positions of political prominence today (Andrew 1997; Klatch 1999). In my work, I was interested in the interorganizational similarities and differences between the two groups as well as the intraorganizational differences within YAF and SDS. For example, within YAF there were crucial differences between traditionalists, who adhere to a religious and social conservatism, and libertarians, who believe in the free market and individual liberty. Such differences proved critical to YAF's history (Klatch 1994, 1999). These differences between traditionalists and libertarians, as well as the radicalization of libertarians during the late 1960s, also resulted in a congruence in the identity and consciousness of libertarians and the Left.

This study is based on two sets of data: field research based on in-depth life histories of seventy-four SDS and YAF activists as well as participant observation at reunions of 1960s activists, and archival analysis of the organizational materials of these two groups.[2]

External Factors Shaping Political Consciousness and Mobilization

Generational analysis provides one framework to understand how external factors affect the development of political consciousness and the mobilization of social movements. Karl Mannheim (1952) argued that, during times of radical social change (war, depression, or mass migration), youths may form a generation with a shared consciousness. Like class consciousness, based in a common social location, Mannheim's generational unity is based in a common historical location. "Generation-units" (in Mannheim's terms) are people who share a common historical location and who experience dramatic social changes at the same time. Although many analysts used Mannheim to understand left-wing movements of the 1960s (DeMartini 1983; Fendrich 1974; Fendrich and Lovoy 1988; Fendrich and Turner 1989; Jennings 1987) or, more recently, the feminist movement (Schneider 1988; Whittier 1997), a portion of Mannheim's theory was overlooked. Mannheim proposed that social background may lead individuals to "work up" their experiences of social change in different ways, resulting in different generation-units forming at the same time. These intracohort units then perceive the world differently. For Mannheim, such generational-units are locked into an antagonistic, forever intertwined relationship due to their common historical experiences.

Mannheim's theory points to the significance of historical factors in political mobilization and shaping a generational consciousness. In the 1960s, such historical realities as the cold war, the civil rights movement, and the Vietnam war were fundamental in mobilizing youths. Yet different units of this generation perceived these historical forces differently. For example, the founding statements of SDS and YAF and interviews with activists who attended the founding conventions of each organization[3] reveal that the cold war shaped beliefs, but in divergent ways. For the Right, communism and the cold war not only provoked fear about the loss of freedom but also symbolized the loss of American status and disillusion. Having grown up believing America was good and great and powerful, youths on the Right saw a disjuncture between this belief and the reality of a weakened America. Juxtaposed against this image of America was the reality of a rapidly expanding Soviet empire, an empire that represented bleak totalitarianism. In contrast, for those in SDS, the shadow cast by the cold war did not originate in the Soviet Union. They viewed the Soviet system less as a threat than as a dinosaur, an overcentralized, encrusted bureaucracy. Rather, just as youths in YAF encountered a disjuncture between their ideal image and the reality of a weakened America, so, too, youths in SDS were provoked by the hypocrisy they perceived between the ideal of the United States as leader of the Free World, upholder of equality and justice, and the reality of America in the 1950s, a nation still ridden with economic and racial inequality. The cold war represented nuclear annihilation rather than Soviet expansionism, and the deterioration of civil liberties during the McCarthy period, not the loss of American power. In short, same historical forces shaped both generation-units differently.

These contrasting perspectives are rooted in differences in social location, which Mannheim argues result in the formation of antagonistic generation-units. I analyze the backgrounds and upbringing of YAF and SDS activists to show how these individuals followed parallel (but divergent) paths to becoming committed activists. Overall, SDS members came from more privileged backgrounds in terms of parents' education and occupation, although these differences are fewer between SDS members and libertarians or women in

YAF. Also, SDS activists tended to come from either Jewish or Protestant homes, whereas YAF members were predominantly Catholic or Protestant. Within YAF, libertarians tended to be white, Anglo-Saxon Protestants from old-lineage families; traditionalists were more likely to be Irish Catholic and first- or second-generation American.[4]

Further, individuals do not independently decide to participate in activism or choose their own political beliefs from an array of possibilities. Rather, the majority of activists on both the Left and Right were born into politically oriented families; only a few activists departed from their parents' political orientation toward the Right or Left. Youths in both SDS and YAF also typically grew up in communities that shared their families' ideological orientations. SDSer Jeanne Friedman, for example, grew up in a Bronx Democratic working-class community in which all the kids on the block stuffed envelopes at the local Democratic headquarters. Jeanne comments: "You were born a Democrat. There was no choice involved. . . . It was like being born Jewish. There were certain things you had to do. You had to be interested in politics and . . . you had to regard the unions as the absolute savior of the working class."[5] Meanwhile, YAFer Marick Payton grew up in Kansas in a community he describes as "midwestern common folk conservatism." He explains: "There was a paranoia and I certainly did share that. There was not merely the fear of an internal communist revolution, but a great distrust of the federal government, and a great threat that the federal government would launch a sort of socialist welfare state. FDR was seen as the great bogeyman."[6]

In addition to the political beliefs of parents and the surrounding community, religious and moral upbringings shape political consciousness. These varying backgrounds and upbringings, combined with critical experiences in high school—such as significant teachers, inspiring books, participation in student government or debate teams, school papers—are all critical to the formation of political consciousness. In short, by the time these activists reached the door of YAF or SDS, they already had firm ideas about the social and political world; many had also been politically active for years before joining YAF or SDS.

Many social movement analysts have focused on the issues that lead individuals to join a particular movement and the social networks that draw individuals into a social movement organization. But political consciousness also grows from the multitude of forces which exist *prior to* participation. The essential process of "cognitive liberation" (McAdam, 1982) occurs long before an individual is exposed to a formal organization or even a network of other activists. A complex array of external factors—social background, parental ideology and values, the political climate of the community, the influence of teachers, leaders, or books—intertwines with individual personality and experiences during childhood to create an affinity toward the political world. This orientation, combined with critical historical and political events, propels individuals to put their beliefs into action. Thus, structural factors as well as individual experience and personality shapes political identity and action.

Internal Factors Shaping Political Consciousness, Commitment, and Organizational Life

Much recent work within social movements focuses on the development of the collective identity of a movement (see, for example, Friedman and McAdam 1992; Gamson 1992; Melucci 1995; Taylor and Whittier 1992). Far less attention is paid to the formation and development of individual identity within the context of a social movement. Although people who enter social movement organizations typically already have formulated political beliefs, once they become active, their consciousness and political identity develop further through participation and interaction with peers. Once activists became involved with SDS or YAF, their beliefs evolved over time. In particular, interactions with peers and the size of the organization were essential to individual experience and orientation.

Peers play a key role in building solidarity within a movement as well as in educating activists about a more complex political ideology. Activists on both the Left and Right say that interaction with peers furthered their commitment to the movement and taught them a deeper understanding of the political world. Being with those who shared similar views and values provided support, and reaffirmed activists' subjective view of the world. They confirmed that participants weren't alone in acting on their convictions, that they were doing the right thing. As SDSer Dorothy Burlage put it, "All along the way there were people who would get me to the next step. . . . They validated what we were doing."[7] Peers also fostered collective enthusiasm that sustained morale during the long months of organizing.

In addition, peers played an important role in pushing forward an activist's beliefs. Those who had been involved longer served as role models and educated others about issues and theory. YAFer Don Ernsberger says the people he met during the Goldwater campaign were already reading Ayn Rand and "were primarily more libertarian than I was and they pulled me that way. . . . We used to argue things and [they] eventually pulled me into a more consistent position."[8] Experienced activists provided a vocabulary that solidified an activist identity and deepened commitment to the movement. Through daily social interaction and conversations, peers construct a larger framework for individual issues, working out the details of political ideology and of identity.

SDS member Bernardine Dohrn recalls the impact of friends she made at the University of Chicago: "I fell in with a lot of people who were from Left families, a lot of New Yorkers and a lot of people who were politically active. It took me quite awhile to even know what they were talking about. They had a whole frame of reference. . . . Immediately it was a very political world. . . . So immediately my frame of reference broadened enormously."[9] Other respondents discuss how particular friends challenged their beliefs or exposed them to new ideas or writings, opening them up politically and intellectually, teaching them a "way of seeing." In this way, activists were educated in a political perspective. The ideas they brought with them were further shaped through their interaction with others. Through their peers, activists on both the Left and Right learned a framework for understanding injustice and articulating who or what is responsible for social problems, as well as strategies and goals for social change. As Klandermans puts it, "Collective beliefs are created by individuals not in isolation but in the course of communication and cooperation"(1992: 83). Through shared experiences and ongoing conversations, activists reaffirmed and extended their own political ideology and identity.

Besides interactions with peers, a second internal factor that shaped the experiences and orientations of activists in YAF and SDS was the size of the organization. Within SDS, the experience of early activists (those who entered SDS from 1960 to 1964) was fundamentally different from that of later activists (those who entered SDS from 1965 to 1968). Early activists were involved in a small, tight-knit organization in which face-to-face interaction was common. The earliest members were even hand-picked by founding members to fit into the group. As pioneers speaking out in a time of general apathy, early SDS members relied on each other and welcomed others of like mind. Bound together in a beloved community, a type of gemeinschaft, people knew each other and worked together as a circle of friends.

In the aftermath of SDS's success in organizing the first large national antiwar march in Washington in April 1965, media coverage of SDS led to a dramatic increase in membership. Consequently, the fundamental experience of being in the organization changed.[10] As SDS grew, it became more diverse, with conflicting ideological tendencies. People were no longer hand-picked to fit into the group. The expansion of SDS also meant that people no longer knew everyone in the organization. The vast majority of activists did not become involved on a national level; at best, they knew most members of their chapter. In addition, the growing factionalization and impulse toward ideological purity that characterized the later years of SDS led to a lack of cohesion, a fragmentation of the organization. Thus, the bonds of gemeinschaft were broken, as the sense of community no longer superceded the differences between members. Helen Garvy speaks about how SDS's growth changed the nature of group meetings:

> A lot of the change . . . had to do with the [fact that the] groups got larger. Then it becomes much more shouting matches. People who are good orators and were not intimidated about getting up on speaking platforms tend to become much more important than when the national council meeting is in a room this size and everybody knows each other and . . . respects the work that the other people are doing. It's real different. . . . I always felt that people respected me because they knew what work I did. They could see it.[11]

In addition, later activists were less invested in maintaining organizational unity because they were not the founders of SDS. No longer were activists single voices speaking out in the darkness. By now, multiple organizations existed on the Left; one could choose among an array of possibilities for involvement, and the survival of SDS itself seemed less central. In short, the increase in size of SDS led to the development of "micro-cohorts" (Whittier 1995) in which activists experienced the organization in different ways.[12] The development of these micro-cohorts, in turn, was accompanied by differences in individual identity and consciousness that also contributed to divisiveness within the organization.

On the other hand, YAF experienced no parallel dramatic rise in membership. Members of YAF struggled together in a relatively small movement throughout the 1960s. Like early SDS they were pioneers bound together in common cause, happy to find others of like mind. Unlike SDS, however, as the 1960s progressed, YAF activists *increasingly* became a minority voice speaking out during a liberal era. This sense of alienation in YAF grew throughout the 1960s, particularly as the New Left gained in strength and number. Members of YAF felt more and more ostracized for holding unfavorable views. This only intensified their sense of mission. Lee Edwards explained how ostracism strengthened people's commitment:

> My God, to be a young conservative in the sixties was to be . . . an untouchable, a pariah, a Jew in Syria, a black in South Africa. . . . So we fought back. . . . Your abilities—intellectual abilities, political abilities—are all heightened in that kind of an atmosphere. We were in the front lines of political and philosophical debate and activism in this country. And we were very good at it or else we would have been demolished. . . . We were determined not to be silenced . . . not to be defeated. There was a sense of a crusade, a mission.[13]

This sense of marginalization, due to YAF's size and the ostracism YAF members faced, affected the consciousness and individual identity of activists, solidifying commitment and identity with the organization and reinforcing common beliefs.

In sum, peers act within a movement to solidify commitment, pulling people further into the movement, and helping to articulate a larger frame of understanding. Size of a social movement organization is also important in shaping individual experiences, in building solidarity, and in affecting the tone and style of the organization. The changing organizational environments within SDS and YAF affected activists' consciousness and identity. On one hand, YAF's small size and marginalization increased solidarity, intensified commitment, and particularly heightened traditionalists' conviction that they were right. In SDS, on the other hand, the growth of the organization resulted in a decrease in solidarity and divisions in political identity. Accompanying the dramatic increase in membership was a loss of unity, intensified factionalization and infighting, and a less welcoming and inclusive style. Yet the size of SDS was itself directly affected by external relations with the media, illustrating the interaction between internal and external factors in influencing social movement dynamics and the consciousness of activists.

Internal-External Interactions

External and internal factors interact in shaping the course of a movement, the relations among members, and political identity. Two external factors—media coverage of movements and the degree of repression used against them—fundamentally affect the internal dynamics and the career of a movement, sometimes in unexpected ways.

Media coverage of SDS had critical repercussions for the internal life of the organization. In the aftermath of the April 1965 anti-war demonstration organized by SDS, in which unexpectedly large numbers of people protested, there was heightened interest in SDS from the national media. Not only did media exposure dramatically increase SDS membership; it also brought new constituencies to the organization, with many new members from different social backgrounds than earlier activists (Gitlin 1980; Mankoff and Flacks 1971). Differences in background and orientation, combined with the shift within SDS as it became a mass organization, resulted in increased factionalization, ideological conflict, and generational strain within the organization (Gitlin 1980). The media both produced and magnified differences among SDS members, as activists argued over the best response to the media. Tensions escalated over the creation of "movement stars" and over some activists' attempts to grab more media attention by engaging in outrageous actions. This heightened militancy brought on police suppression and created a cycle of escalating movement anger and paranoia, followed by more police reaction.

Thus, increased media attention toward SDS provoked increased membership, fundamentally altering the nature of the organization. Media coverage interacted with size in generating internal division and ideological conflict, escalating the militancy of some activists, which, in turn, also escalated repression against the movement.

Police reaction and, more generally, government repression is a second external factor that interacted with the internal dynamics of the movement. But this time there were unintended consequences for both the Left and Right. There were significant differences between Left and Right activists' encounters with repression. The FBI counterintelligence program aimed at the New Left during the late 1960s, COINTELPRO, meant that more and more SDS members experienced incidents of FBI surveillance, harassment, and encounters with infiltrators. Compared to libertarians and traditionalists in YAF, SDS activists encountered the greatest resistance from authorities and therefore paid the highest costs for political involvement. Not only did SDSers face tear-gas and police brutality; they also were more likely to be arrested, jailed, and put under surveillance or harassed by the FBI. In addition, two SDSers in the study were expelled from school as a result of their participation, and two other activists went underground by the end of the decade. And SDS members were also much more likely than members of YAF to encounter strained relations with parents as a result of their activism, as well as to face obstacles in employment due to their activism during the 1970s and 1980s.

In contrast, traditionalists in YAF were the least likely to face any organized resistance by government. They held demonstrations and marches, but none reported any negative consequences in terms of being arrested or jailed, beaten by police, harassed by the FBI, being expelled from school, or facing obstacles to employment due to their political histories. Thus, the costs incurred were relatively small, requiring few risks.

In contrast, libertarians in YAF *did* engage in high-risk activism. As more and more libertarians during the mid- to late 1960s became active in antiwar protests, they were exposed to individuals willing to take higher risks and directly encountered repression. At least half of the libertarians interviewed were involved in demonstrations in which they were tear-gassed and witnessed police brutality.

As a result of witnessing government repression and police brutality, both SDSers and libertarians in YAF became radicalized, through what Klandermans (1992) refers to as "consciousness-raising during episodes of collective action." In 1967, for instance, Bill Steel, a libertarian YAFer witnessed the police beating demonstrators during a Vietnam War protest at Century City. He was shocked into feeling he had been "supporting the wrong side," and shortly afterward he began campaigning against the draft and became more involved in anti-war protests as well.[14]

Integral to this radicalization process was a shift in identity, a re-labeling of the self. Just as many activists on the Left went through a process by which they changed from calling themselves liberals to leftists to Marxists, Maoists, anti-imperialists, or simply "radicals," so, too, did libertarians experience a parallel transformation. Accompanying their turn against government, by the end of the decade over half of the libertarians interviewed shifted their identification, using the term "anarchist" to describe themselves politically. These labels not only capture a shift in world view but also convey identity and commitment to those outside, locating individuals within a larger community. For both the Left and Right, these new names signified a similar process of radicalization.

Government repression also had serious consequences for SDS as an organization. Repression, and the resulting radicalization of activists, contributed to a heightened sense of militancy in the organization during the late 1960s. As conditions seemed to worsen and no change was evident, activists grew tired and frustrated; many came to believe that more extreme actions were needed to stop the killing and to create social change. The paranoia provoked by government harassment also increased activists' insularity. The need to establish trust meant that activists became more concerned with surrounding themselves with others like themselves and excluding those with opposing views. This combination of the need for trust, insularity, and the belief that it was necessary to be full-time revolutionaries created a social movement dynamic that fostered dogmatism. Individuals felt continuous pressure to act in the correct political manner. The urgency of events pushed people to militancy as other activists in the movement pulled them into it. As Andrea Cousins explains:

> There was . . . a kind of ethos . . . that you're supposed to be politically active all the time, that if you were serious about [politics] you . . . put that first. . . . And if you weren't doing that, you were really being self-indulgent and you were not doing the right thing. . . . We oppressed each other with a tremendous sense of moral principle. We were in such a kind of straitjacket, having to prove to each other that we were doing the right kind of political work, and thinking the right way. . . . There was such a hierarchy . . . with people who were right and people who were wrong, tremendous self-righteousness.[15]

Dogmatism led to polarization.

The escalation of militancy was also intricately bound to the ideological divisions within SDS during the late 1960s. Like many social movement organizations, SDS succumbed to factionalization, with each sect demanding ideological purity from its adherents.[16] The polarization resulting from these divisions furthered the insularity of activists, as people sought out others aligned with their position. This, too, increased militancy.

Peers were critical in moving activists to a more militant position. Peers acted as a means of social control to keep activists in check, to bind them to the movement, and to ensure ideological purity. Although social movement communities provide a sense of shared beliefs and experiences, forging bonds of solidarity within a movement, group bonds can also become stifling. As William Gamson writes, "At some point, social support can become social pressure"(1992: 64–65). For SDS during the late 1960s, political events were urgent and unending: the assassinations of Martin Luther King, Robert Kennedy, and Malcolm X; the killing of Fred Hampton; ghetto riots; the confrontation between protestors and police at the Democratic National Convention; the trial of the Chicago Eight; the student take-over of Columbia University; the escalation of fighting in Vietnam; and the events in France in May 1968. These events, combined with the acceleration of government repression against the Left, exacerbated internal pressures from peers within the movement. These internal pressures and deepening ideological divisions within SDS resulted in an explosive national convention in 1969, and eventually led to the demise of the organization.

Although government repression was not aimed at YAF as an organization, libertarians' experience of repression and their observation of police brutality did lead to a widening gap between traditionalists and libertarians. During the late 1960s, libertarians and traditionalists took opposing sides on the Vietnam War and on government repression of protestors. Libertarian Dave Schumacher discusses the disillusionment he felt toward government as a result of the repression he observed:

> [At] the march on Washington I can remember going underneath the Justice Department and [Attorney General] Mitchell standing out there on the balcony and watching . . . and there were helicopters and the police. . . . I reacted very, very negatively to the way the government was responding to protestors. There was a lot of suppression—you know, the flag burning and draft card burning—the government responded to those in a fascist way. . . . I just never could understand why other people in YAF didn't see that association. . . . When you see the way the administration responded to opposition to the war and the things that were going on—domestic surveillance and the efforts to control personal behavior. . . . It was objectionable.[17]

Whereas traditionalists remained hostile to the anti-war movement and to student protest on campuses and supported measures to maintain order, lib-

ertarians were radicalized by the repression and brutality used against protestors.[18] Libertarians' increasing opposition to government further separated
them from traditionalists and brought libertarians into common cause with
the Left. In short, there was a growing distrust between libertarians and traditionalists as their interests diverged. Traditionalists viewed libertarians as
flag-burning, dope-smoking leftist sympathizers; libertarians viewed traditionalists as law-and-order, drug-suppressing authoritarians obsessed with communism at the expense of civil liberties.

The examples of media coverage of SDS and government repression against
protestors demonstrate how external factors affect the internal dynamics of
a movement. Although media coverage (or the lack of coverage) did not have
any visible effect on YAF, the shift in media coverage of SDS during the mid-
to-late 1960s led to a change in the size and nature of the organization and
subsequently resulted in growing division, distrust, and the escalation of
conflict within the organization. In turn, as a result of media coverage, SDS
experienced further conflict over tactics for dealing with the media, with some
activists escalating tactics to gain media attention. Thus, the nature and course
of SDS as an organization was altered by relations with the media. The harsh
reaction by authorities to leftist protest dramatically affected both the Left
and libertarians of the Right by exposing them to high-risk activism. Repression also led to activists' radicalization, a shift in consciousness and identity,
a poignant illustration of how external factors can affect individual identity
and the construction of meaning. Repression additionally contributed to
heightened militancy and increased distrust of authorities and outsiders and
fostered dogmatism within SDS. The radicalization of leftists and libertarians also resulted in a growing overlap between the worlds of the Left and
Right.

The Overlapping Worlds of the Left and Right

The shifts in belief among leftists and libertarians signified an opening between the worlds of the Left and Right, a convergence between elements within
YAF and SDS that indicated overlapping interests and values. As a result of
government repression and the radicalization of libertarians, the gulf between
traditionalists and libertarians grew wider, and the identity and consciousness of libertarians and sectors of the New Left converged. Unlike traditionalists in YAF who saw no common ground with SDS, by the late 1960s many
libertarians found common cause with the Left, and some even began working in coalition with SDS in organizing moratoriums, teach-ins, anti-war
protests, and campus demonstrations against the Reserve Officer Training
Corps (ROTC).

The congruence between libertarians and sectors of the Left grew as both felt a common hostility toward the state. Libertarians, radicalized by opposition to the war, government repression, police brutality, and legislation against drugs, began to perceive government itself as the enemy. This view further exacerbated tensions between traditionalists and libertarians. Whereas traditionalists continued to believe that communism was the main force of evil, libertarians began to view the U.S. government and domestic fascism as an equal or even more dangerous threat to individual liberty.

As more and more libertarians began to see the state as the enemy, they discovered common ground with the New Left. Both feared Big Brother, believing the government had no business interfering in people's personal lives. Both decried the fate of the individual living under the shadow of the corporate state. Both worried that government had become uncontrollable, veering toward totalitarianism and intervening both internationally and domestically in areas where it did not belong. Both believed that government, rather than offering solutions, had become part of the essential problem.

The shared antagonism that libertarians and the New Left felt toward centralized authority was connected to a common belief that people should control their own lives. Both opposed the growth of bureaucracy and sought to return power to the individual. Libertarians shared the New Left ideal of building "a new community which will reaffirm the dignity of the individual in the face of the corporate state."[19] Both sought to replace the centralized, hierarchical, top-down power structures of the state with decentralized, self-governing communities. In place of mass society, they called for a society of decentralized institutions in which individuals participated in decisions affecting their lives. Both libertarians and the New Left advocated neighborhood government, local control, and community policing. Both were skeptical of the paternalistic welfare state and supported self-help and self-determination in poor and black communities. Both sectors also ardently defended civil liberties. They opposed government restriction of abortion, drug use, pornography, and mutually consensual sexual acts.

In short, as the worlds of libertarians and traditionalists moved farther apart, the worlds of libertarians and the Left grew closer together because of both internal ideological factors and the impact of external events. By the late 1960s, more and more libertarians felt alienated from the conservative movement and charged YAF with being run by reactionaries and bigots. They accused the Right of being a "wasteland of authoritarianism," bordering on fascism.

As with SDS, YAF too went through an explosive national convention in 1969. The ideological divisions between libertarians and traditionalists escalated and led to the purging of libertarians before, during, and after the convention. Demonstrating the divisions in the organization, libertarian platform resolutions calling for immediate withdrawal from Vietnam, legalization of marijuana, and denunciation of domestic fascism were defeated resoundingly while traditionalists successfully passed resolutions calling for an end to East-West trade, support for South Africa and Rhodesia, victory in Vietnam, opposition to campus radicals, and domestic law and order.[20]

The issue that finally broke the convention into two hostile camps was draft resistance. Two draft resolutions were proposed. The first, called the Goldwater plan, promoted a volunteer army and the gradual abolition of the draft. The other resolution advocated active resistance to the draft by illegal or legal evasion. The delegates endorsed the Goldwater plan, but traditionalists added a clause to condemn draft resistance and the burning of draft cards. In response, one libertarian stepped forward and declared it was the right of every individual to defend himself from violence, including state violence, and burned his draft card in the middle of the convention floor. The meeting erupted into an angry mob. One group of libertarians stormed out of the meeting, denouncing domestic fascism and calling for resistance to the Vietnam War, legalization of marijuana, and unity with SDS.[21]

The aftermath of the convention and the subsequent purges of libertarians resulted in the formation of an independent libertarian movement. Dozens of libertarian chapters withdrew from YAF, no longer wishing to associate with the conservative movement, and formed new libertarian organizations. The libertarian movement blossomed across the country. By 1970, in addition to a multitude of libertarian groups, there was an array of libertarian journals including *Left and Right: A Journal of Libertarian Thought*, *The Match*, *Man and State*, *New Individual Review*, and *The Libertarian Forum*. At the end of 1969 and during the early 1970s, libertarians also initiated meetings and conferences of the Left and Right, trying to build a common movement (Klatch 1999). Although no enduring coalition between libertarians in YAF and the Left survived, the Libertarian Party was formed in 1971 and still remains a vibrant third party in the United States, continuing to draw adherents from both the Left and Right.

This unique intersection between the Left and Right speaks to the peculiarities of American political ideology in which suspicion of authority, opposition to government, and the ideals of individual freedom, decentralization, and community control are core values for segments of both the Left and Right. Yet it also illustrates the unanticipated outcome of the interaction of external and internal factors on social movements. In particular, government repression led to a shift in consciousness, a changed understanding of self and society for activists on both the Left and Right. As a result of the crackdown against protestors, both sectors grew more distrustful of government, increasingly critical of the state itself. Both leftists and libertarians went through a process of radicalization in which their identity as activists and their own ideology changed, signified by the adoption of words such as "radical," "revolutionary," and "anarchist" to indicate their new understanding of the world and of their own role as creators of social change. These parallel processes also brought together segments of the Left and Right in an unexpected alliance. The radicalization of libertarians also resulted in a growing schism within YAF, organizational conflict, and eventually the purging of libertarian members. Thus, external forces have profound effects on individual consciousness, on the internal dynamics and the course of movements, as well as on the possibility of bonds between movements across the political spectrum.

Conclusion

Comparing the cases of the Left and Right during the 1960s illustrates the complexity of analyzing external and internal factors as discrete influences on social movements. On the one hand, external factors, such as generation and social location, and internal factors, such as peers and the size of an organization, are important on their own in the development of political consciousness, the formation of individual political identity, and the mobilization and course of social movements. Growing up during the same period, these youths were motivated to action by similar historical events but, based on their different social locations and upbringings, they developed divergent interpretations of these events. Internal relations among peers are significant in movements both for solidifying commitment and furthering beliefs, as well as in acting as mechanisms of social control, constraining independent belief and action, and enforcing political conformity. Size of an organization also fundamentally affects degree of solidarity or division within activists in a social movement organization.

On the other hand, often internal and external factors interact in affecting political consciousness and the dynamics of social movements. In SDS, external media coverage resulted in an explosion in the size of the organization, which, in turn, led to "micro-cohorts" within the organization, ideological division, and less solidarity. Another external factor, government repression, also had unexpected consequences for both the Left and Right. Repression and police brutality led to the radicalization of both leftists and libertarians in YAF, clearly demonstrating how external factors affect individual consciousness and identity. This radicalization process, combined with libertarians' shift against the Vietnam War and their affinity with the counterculture, led to an opening between the worlds of the Left and Right.

This unexpected overlap of interest between segments of the Left and Right during the late 1960s and early 1970s challenges any static notion of a social movement constituency, demonstrating the shifting nature of movement communities even across the political spectrum. This overlap between Left and Right also challenges any simple assumption of movement/countermovement cycles. Even who is defined as an opponent to a movement changes over time. External factors of state repression and harassment, and the consequent delegitimation of authority, played a key role in fostering this alliance between the Left and Right and in reconfiguring the political landscape. In short, we must analyze both internal and external factors, as well as the interaction between them, to understand the development of individual consciousness and the nature, scope, and life course of social movements over time and across the political spectrum.

NOTES

1. YAF was formed at the estate of William F. Buckley in Sharon, Connecticut, in 1960; SDS began as the Student League for Industrial Democracy, a youth affiliate of the League for Industrial Democracy, an old Left organization dating back to 1905, when it was originally called the Intercollegiate Socialist Society.

2. The sample of former SDS and YAF activists was selected based on the following criterion: all people chosen were active for at least two years in SDS and/or YAF. The final sample of activists contains 34 female activists, equally divided between SDS and YAF, and 40 male activists, 19 from SDS and 21 from YAF. Although a serious attempt was made to diversify the sample in terms of race, because both organizations were composed primarily of white activists, all activists interviewed are white except for 3 black activists in SDS and 1 black activist in YAF. Activists were also chosen to get a mix of both leaders and rank-and-file activists. In SDS, the sample contains 24 rank-and-file members and 12 people who were part of national leadership and/or were at the Port Huron conference, 6 of whom were women (50 percent); the YAF sample consists of 23 rank-and-file members and 15 members who held national office and/or were at the founding Sharon conference of YAF, 2 of whom were women (13 percent). However, among the rank-and-file activists, some in the sample were leaders of local chapters.

In addition, the sample was chosen to reflect the ideological differences within each group. The YAF activists include 25 traditionalists and 13 libertarians. The SDS sample includes 5 Progressive Labor members or sympathizers, 5 Weathermen members or sympathizers, and 2 Revolutionary Youth Movement II members or sympathizers; the majority of SDS activists were either unaffiliated with any factions during the 1969 splits (12 activists) or were uninvolved in SDS politics by 1969 (12 activists).

Further, given previous research on the New Left, which indicates differences in background and upbringing between those who became active in the early 1960s and those who were drawn in during the mid to late 1960s, the SDS sample also contains a mixture of activists who joined from 1960 through 1964 (17 people) and those who were drawn in from 1965 through 1968 (19 people). For a complete discussion of the methodology of this study, see Klatch (1999).

3. The founding statement of YAF, the Sharon Statement, came out of the founding conference held at Sharon, Connecticut, in 1960. The Port Huron Statement, SDS's founding statement, was issued in 1962 at the Port Huron convention.

4. For a detailed discussion of the backgrounds and upbringings of SDS and YAF activists, see Klatch (1999, chapter 2).

5. Interview with Jeanne Friedman, October 27, 1990.

6. Interview with Marick Payton, January 30, 1990.

7. Interview with Dorothy Burlage, July 23, 1989.

8. Interview with Don Ernsberger, November 19, 1989.

9. Interview with Bernardine Dohrn, September 12, 1990.

10. Whereas SDS membership in December 1964 (before the march) was 2,500 with 41 chapters, by October 1965 (after the march) membership escalated to 10,000 with 89 chapters. From this point on, SDS membership continued to escalate. By October 1966, SDS claimed 25,000 members and 265 chapters, and by June 1968 membership was estimated to be anywhere between 40,000 and 100,000 with 350 chapters (Sale 1973: 664).

11. Interview with Helen Garvy, October 23, 1990.

12. These varying experiences of SDS by early and later activists had particularly important repercussions for women in the organization. See Klatch (1999, 2000).

13. Interview with Lee Edwards, July 11, 1989.

14. Bill Steel, quoted in Lowell Ponte (1970: 72).

15. Interview with Andrea Cousins, July 25, 1989.

16. For a more detailed discussion of the splits within SDS during the late 1960s, see Klatch (1999); Gitlin (1987); Sale (1973).

17. Interview with Dave Schumacher, September 1 and September 7, 1989.

18. Besides the Vietnam War and reactions to government repression, a third factor that contributed to the widening gulf between libertarians and traditionalists was the counterculture. In brief, while traditionalists abhorred the counterculture, libertarians embraced it both ideologically and in their own lifestyle. In particular, the use of drugs brought libertarians and the Left together. It was not only the actual use of drugs but also government repression faced by "freaks" that led to a questioning of authority and cemented bonds between libertarians and the countercultural New Left (Klatch 1994, 1999).

19. Quote from "State of the Student, State of the University: Corporate Liberalism on Campus," from SDS chapter at Indiana University, SDS Papers, n.d.

20. See J. M. Cobb (1970); Jerome Tuccille (1969); and Jerry W. Venters (1969).

21. See Tuccille (1969); for a full account of the 1969 YAF convention, see Klatch (1999), chapter 7.

Part Four

COLLECTIVE IDENTITIES, DISCOURSE,

AND CULTURE

Introduction to Part IV

Activists in social movement organizations and communities construct rich internal cultures that help to maintain solidarity and commitment (Johnston and Klandermans 1995; Lichterman 1996; Taylor and Rupp 1999). They construct collective identities, group definitions through which they understand themselves, their connection with one another, and their political place in the world (Bernstein 1997; Melucci 1989; Taylor and Whittier 1992). They develop frames and discourses for understanding their issues, which they deploy publicly to gain recruits and bring about change (Benford and Snow 2000; della Porta 1995; Snow et al. 1986; Steinberg 1998). Yet they do none of these things in isolation. Movement participants construct collective identities, frames, and discourses within the context of the dominant culture and structural inequalities.

The chapters in this part highlight the connections between how activists conceptualize themselves and their worlds and the external structures and dominant cultures in which they operate. Contributors develop analytic tools for examining these intersections, showing how movements draw on both dominant and oppositional cultures, how structural inequalities shape collective identity and movement culture, and how external contexts affect the interpretation and implementation of movement frames and discourses. They build connections from social movement theory to feminist theory, discourse analysis, and intersectional theories of race, class, and gender. They bridge culture and structure, internal and external levels of analysis, and political opportunity and collective identity theories.

The four chapters present different perspectives on how external cultural and political contexts intersect with and shape movement discourses and collective identities. Nancy Naples examines the intersections between movement frames, dominant culture, and political structures. She argues that the

frame of community control of schools emerged within a movement to improve schools in black and Latino neighborhoods by giving power to local
parents. This frame had political meaning within the discourse of civil rights
and economic equality but quickly lost its progressive political meaning,
however, as it was co-opted, first by those who supported administrative decentralization of schools as a cost-saving measure, and later by parents who
advocated for parental local control to exclude curricula they deemed anti-
Christian or pro-homosexuality. Drawing on materialist feminist theories of
discourse, Naples shows that while frames emerge in a movement context,
they acquire meaning within external discourses and structural relations of
race, class, and gender. Her chapter thus draws on both cultural and structural analyses to show how the internal discourses and frames of a social
movement interact with their external contexts.

Marc Steinberg takes up the question of the sources and meanings of
movement culture and discourse. He argues that movement frames are neither separate from dominant discourses nor straightforward and unified. Like
Naples, Steinberg draws diverse theoretical perspectives into social movement
theory—in this case, the dialogic theory of Bakhtin—to show how movements'
oppositional discourses intersect with dominant cultures. Movements both
appropriate and redefine dominant discourses, and discourses acquire multiple
meanings as they are expressed and interpreted in contexts. Collective actors
such as the Spitalfields silk weavers thus recombine elements of dominant
discourses according to changing events and contexts. Steinberg's chapter
gives us a fuller understanding of how movements and their cultural and structural contexts intersect.

Belinda Robnett also emphasizes the effects of external contexts on movement culture, but she turns from discourses and frames to collective identities. Robnett argues that the civil rights movement's initial losses and gains
in institutionalized politics (specifically, the rejection of the Mississippi Freedom Democratic Party at the 1964 convention and the passage of the 1964
Civil Rights Act) directly affected the movement's collective identity, as many
participants came to believe that educated, middle-class African Americans
might achieve recognition, but the masses would not. As activists interpreted
these events, they constructed a new collective identity that rejected nonviolence and integration and a newly militant Black Power movement. This new
collective identity, however, was linked to hierarchical and exclusive organizational practices that led to a decline in participation. Robnett thus shows
that collective identity is shaped not just by internal processes but by the
impact and interpretations of external events. Like Naples, she emphasizes
the impact of external hierarchies of gender, class, race, and education on
individuals. Thus, she argues that external political events, internal collective identity constructions, organizational practices, and mobilization are

inextricably linked. Robnett brings together theoretical perspectives in this argument, including black feminist theories of race, class, and gender, as well as theories of political opportunities and collective identity.

Finally, Rhys Williams contends that movements necessarily draw on the dominant culture in fashioning their own rhetoric and frames. Like Steinberg, Williams shows that available meanings constrain movement frames, yet can be turned to movement ends. By contrasting how the civil rights movement and the religious right use religious discourse, Williams shows that an influential dominant discourse can lend itself to multiple interpretations. The variations are not endless, however, but draw on available traditions and "symbolic repertoires." The civil rights movement drew on elements of religious discourse that emphasize "opening" of political and cultural space to diverse groups, whereas the religious right drew on those that emphasize "closing" of discourse and possibilities. For both movements, religious rhetoric was effective because of its powerful resonance in American culture. Williams's chapter, then, brings cultural theory and debates into social movement theory in order to enrich our conceptualizations of how movements' internal cultures and cultural contexts shape each other. Together, the chapters in this section offer synthetic tools for understanding the interpenetration of movements' insides and outsides and for bridging theoretical approaches to social movements.

12

Toward a More Dialogic Analysis
of Social Movement Culture

MARC W. STEINBERG

For years now many social movement scholars have been chanting a theme: bring culture back to our analyses. Increasingly, we've focused on collective identities, media events, rituals, ideologies, and narratives to understand how culture helps shape organization and action. Despite this array of cultural forms and activities, however, most analysts using the political process and resource mobilization perspectives have fixed their attention on framing. In this chapter, I argue that framing analyses have unduly narrowed our understanding of social movement culture. Most such studies see social movement culture as instrumental, deliberately produced (often by social movement organizations or key activists) to maximize mobilization or influence.

I offer an alternative perspective that questions these largely instrumentalist assumptions. From a *dialogic* perspective, I argue that cultures constructed through contention are only partly the product of calculated action. Discourse (for both SMOs and activists) is partly bounded by the cultural practices available for them to make meaning. First, this means focusing on the discourse through which people can make claims, articulate senses of justice, and express their identities. Further, I will argue that we must understand this process as *relational*. Rather than analyzing the culture of contention as divided between discrete dominant and dissident spheres we need to analyze how both are partly products of the other. Challengers often create oppositional discourses by borrowing from the discourses of those they oppose; in protracted conflicts, both dominant and challenging discourses can mix together. This give and tug of meanings in ongoing dialogue can have unanticipated, and sometimes contradictory, consequences for movement development. I take a group of early-nineteenth-century English workers as an example of this dialogic alternative. I examine how these workers opposed domination by their employers partly by borrowing and refashioning employers' discourses legitimizing their power.

In an insightful discussion of framing literature, Robert Benford defines framing as "signifying work . . . the processes associated with assigning meaning to or interpreting relevant events and conditions in ways intended to mobilize potential adherents and constituents, to garner bystander support, and to demobilize antagonists," and frames themselves as "emergent action-oriented sets of beliefs that inspire meaning and legitimate social movement activities and campaigns" (1997: 416). Most social movement analysts have focused on framing as multilevel strategic persuasive communication by which activists or social critics make an issue ideationally and empirically salient to potential supporters and bystanders and thus create a sense of actionable injustice and identity. Frame analysts also argue that, in producing collective action frames, activists draw on existing elements within some larger cultural system, such as ideologies, cultural themes and counterthemes, or master frames, which are more generic framings of injustice that span a cycle of protest (Babb 1996; W. Gamson 1995, 1998; Johnston and Klandermans 1995; McAdam, McCarthy, and Zald 1996; Rochon 1998; Snow and Benford 1988, 1992).

A fundamental problem in many framing studies is the underlying conception of challenging groups create meaning. Most studies implicitly assume a representational-responsive understanding of meaning production (Billig 1991; Petrilli 1993; Shotter 1997). Under such assumptions, actors are said to create meanings, such as frames or identities, which they transmit to others through shared discourse. From this implicit assumption another often follows: meanings and understandings conveyed through a discourse are largely self-evident and unchanging. However, culture through this perspective runs the hazard of being seen as a thing apart, divorced and abstracted from complex ongoing processes of producing meaning during conflict. Frames, identities, and other cultural practices often are depicted as discrete, internally cohesive packages of meaning readily passed between actors. Challengers' shared understandings of the conflict can be too readily assumed, rather than perceived as an ongoing and problematic achievement (Benford 1997; but see Gamson 1995; Gamson and Meyer 1996; McAdam, Tarrow, and Tilly 1997). As Francesca Polletta (1997, 1999) has argued, this can falsely divide the strategic from the symbolic aspects of challengers' actions.

This objectification leads to related recurrent problems. Some analyses, including framing studies, operate with an implicit cognitivist understanding of cultural processes, viewing culture as something that we individually carry around in our heads (Jasper 1997; Johnston 1995). Analysts thus often depict framing as a market activity in which frames are pitched to potential adherents or sympathizers through "alignment" processes, demonstrating how a movement frame fits with other discrete ideas target audiences believe (Klandermans 1992; Snow et al. 1986).

Likewise, when movement participants engage one another (as well as outsiders) in a shared discourse, we often assume they all are articulating the same meanings because they use a common vocabulary (Benford 1993b). From this perspective, the relative success and endurance of framing, collective identity, and other cultural practices can be unnecessarily reduced to individual conscious decisions about desirability and utility. Cultural practices can be reduced to individual strategic actions, abstracted from the relational actions, networks, and group processes in which they occur. In addition, the waning persuasiveness of frames is often sought outside of framing practices themselves, in external transformations of political opportunities or insufficiently specified shifts in wider "cultural environments" (Babb 1996; Gamson 1992b; McAdam 1994; McAdam et al. 1997; Schneider 1997). Analysts therefore look for the changing power of culture in individual consumption or the political environment, but rarely at the discourse processes themselves as bearers of meaning.

Through such depictions, frames, movement discourse, identities, and other cultural practices are deemed parallel to other material resources vital to collective action (Bernstein 1997; Fine 1995; Friedman and McAdam 1992; Williams 1995; Williams and Kubal 1999). However, such parallels suggest an excessive voluntarism—that people can control, create, and distribute meanings much as they do material resources—and thus pays insufficient attention to cultural meanings' structural characteristics independent of actors' control (Carroll and Ratner 1994; see also Masson 1996). Cultural practices do not have the same "thingness" that lends to their acquisition, exclusivity of control and dispersion that material resources have (Jasper 1997; Kniss 1996; Steinberg 1998).

Finally, although a number of analysts recently have emphasized that cultural practices have a constraining and enabling duality, this is rarely demonstrated (Gamson 1992a, 1998; Goodwin and Jasper 1999; Jasper 1997; Ray 1999; Williams and Kubal 1999). Moreover, by ignoring the *multivocality* of social movement discourse, the ways in which words and phrasing can be interpreted in different ways by different people, framing studies often overlook the often dialectic or "two-sided" nature of culture (Billig 1991; Billig et al. 1988; Polletta 1998a; Silverstein 1991; Williams and Blackburn 1996). Practices of cultural domination are never so monolithic that they foreclose all creativity and resistance. Artful challengers can partly transform discourses of domination into cultural weapons of critique. A dialogic perspective helps us understand more clearly how this process works.

Dialogic Analysis

Rather than viewing culture as a thing apart with embodied, stable meanings, dialogists start with the assumption that culture includes sets of ongoing social practices (Ponzio 1990; see also McClellan 1990). Frames, identities, and the discourses through which they are conveyed have meaning only as they are used in relations *between* people in communication (Petrilli 1993; Volosinov 1986). When dialogists speak about communication between people, they mean it in a very wide sense. Face-to-face interaction is one form of relationship, but so is a writer conveying a message through a printed text, or an artist offering a political message through a poster. From this perspective, cultural meanings are relational practices or processes, and their reality lies not within individual minds nor in ideology, but within ongoing social action itself (Shotter 1997).

Dialogists develop multiple interpretations of the relational nature of cultural practices, both through social action and discursive structures. If cultural meanings arise between people in social action, then discourse itself has a double directionality, simultaneously a territory for shared understandings and one of difference and contention (Bell 1998). Discourse therefore is best perceived as a *multivocal* practice; any communication likely has more than one meaning for the participants (Huspek 1993; Volosinov 1986).[1]

Because many social practices are routine and directed toward common goals, people frequently engage in discourse with mutually shared or parallel meanings. M. M. Bakhtin, the originator of much dialogic theory, argued that the patterned nature of social life paralleled a similar patterning of discursive practices, called *speech genres* (Bakhtin 1986). Bakhtin viewed genres as patterned mutual understandings that develop over time, that change with the organization and practice of social life, and that can proliferate as spheres of social life become more varied and complex (Sampson 1993: 119–22). Ian Burkitt conceptualizes genres as "given sets of statements involving positions, world-views, ideologies, and linguistic styles which usually find their expression in certain practices in the everyday world" (1988: 164).

Genres are never self-contained units or packages, replete with wholly evident meanings. Rather, the meanings of any one genre are partially a product of their use in relation to other genres in a particular *discursive field*, the mutually recognized sets of genres through which people communicate intelligibly about a social situation or issue. Thus, the construction of fields involves widely recognized cultural assumptions as to how and when a genre can be applied to a social situation, the extent to which it can relate to other genres, institutional rules for its use (especially in relation to other genres), and the relations between the actors themselves (particularly in recognized hierarchies and power differences) based on past and ongoing practices

(Crossley 1999; Ray 1999). As in Tilly's (1995a, b) concept of "repertoires of collective action," dialogists argue that "each different sphere of human activity will have its own repertoire of genres" (Burkitt 1998: 165).

The discursive field concerning labor conflict in early-nineteenth-century England contained genres of economics (how people can and should relate to one another through market practices), religion (the moral and ethical precepts by which people should act as good Christians), and politics and nationalism (the ways in which people should be guaranteed certain rights as citizens of England). As we will see, in historically defined ways, all the actors involved understood these genres to relating to one another as they communicated about the pertinent issues. This configuration of genres both facilitated and limited the ways in which labor conflicts could be conceptualized and articulated. As Anna Clark (1995), Sonya Rose (1992, 1993), and others have noted, the genres in this discursive field shared assumptions about gender hierarchy and the places of men and women in these conflicts. Because the genres within the field shared embedded constructions of women's subordination (rather than being at odds with one another and highlighting the issue for communication), it was difficult, if not impossible, to construct labor conflict as a women's issue, though women as a group were often the most exploited workers.

Dialogic repertoires are thus relational practices given the who, what, when, where and how of a conflict. Parallel to the concept of political opportunity structure, discursive practices depend on the who and how, that is, which actors are possible participants and how their defined relations with each other provide opportunities to communicate meaning. Mutual appreciation of the applicability and interpretability of a genre for a conflict, as well as a shared recognition of the actors' capacity to use these genres, also play a part. Repertoire development also depends on which genres can be combined to provide mutually interpretable meanings and how this combination can be accomplished in a given field. Discursive practices have the potential to evoke certain mutually understood meanings (McClellan 1990; Petrilli 1993). In some cases, for example, genres of religious sanctification might have mutual interpretability with genres of citizenship rights, but in other contexts they might not. The construction of a discursive field also depends on historical time and place and how discourses have been used in the memorable past.

No genre or field is ever a tightly policed or structured whole, given the multivocal nature of discourse (Hoy 1992). Because repertoires of genres and the fields in which they are located are dynamic social practices, their boundaries are blurry (Burkitt 1998; Ponzio 1990; Williams and Kubal 1999). Thus, within a given genre or field, actors have the creative capacity to detect contradictions or gaps in meaning, as well as silences where they can produce new (and possibly oppositional) meanings (Steinberg 1999b).

For dialogists, discourse is both enabling and constraining. Discourse is enabling because through it we give the social world meaning for action; it can provide opportunities to create new meanings leading to new forms of challenge. But actors cannot make meanings just as they would wish, because discursive practices necessarily limit the vision of what is necessary, plausible, and justifiable.

Finally, dialogists find constraint in discursive practices of power and dominance (Burkitt 1998). More powerful actors, within the boundaries of a field or genre, can exert control over the who, what, and how of meaning, making discursive practices more *monologic*. As Chik Collins observes, powerful groups attempt to mask diversity and conflict "by inhibiting the development of meanings antagonistic to their own, and by devaluing, ridiculing and marginalizing hostile meanings where they do develop" (1996: 76; also see Shotter and Billig 1998). Monologic practice in this sense is akin to the Gramscian concept of hegemony, the process of making powerholders' ideological views into generalized common sense (Brandist 1996; Gardiner 1992; Steinberg 1998). However, as hegemony theorists suggest, such domination can never be total. Because of the blurry boundaries of fields and genres and the multivocal nature of discourse itself, potential for resistance and subversion remains (Baldridge 1994; Pollock 1991).

Thus, dialogism offers a more fully relational and contingent analysis of cultural practices than framing studies. Rather than looking for distinct frames or ideologies that challengers pit against dominant frames, or assuming that resistant cultural practices are harbored in a detached subversive subculture, dialogic analysis argues that much contention occurs within a discursive field heavily structured by the dominant genres. New genres can emerge through resistance, but only as the end product of a process of ferment within dominant ones (Burkitt 1998). Further, these partially transformed genres do not have wholly stable meanings or represent end states of consensus building. As challengers seek to transform existing meanings in discursive practices to articulate senses of injustice, make claims, and establish alternative visions, they also remain bounded by the field and the genres within which they struggle. Moreover, as Mary Pollock (1991) argues in the case of feminist discourse, since discursive resistance is always a dialogue with domination, for the latter can always talk back; even the successful appropriation and reworking of discourse in one context contains the potential for resurgent hegemonic meanings in another.

Finally, if challengers generally remain partly captive to some hegemonic meanings, then to characterize that over which actors cannot maintain exclusive, stable control remains problematic. And since discourse is multivocal and the boundaries of fields and genres are dynamic, the meanings that activists and SMOs seek to establish through persuasion always have the potential for being transformed by supporters and sympathizers.

The Case of the Spitalfields Weavers

This section illustrates a dialogic perspective through a look at the discursive repertoire of the silk weavers of London's Spitalfields[2] district in early-nineteenth-century England. I emphasize the dynamics of repertoire construction. The analysis demonstrates how the weavers struggled against power holders within dominant genres of political economy, Christian piety, and nationalism. They refashioned these discourses of domination in their justice claims. By drawing from within these genres, however, their discursive repertoire channeled and limited their options and desired outcomes.

By the 1820s, more than 14,000 silk weavers populated the five eastern plebeian parishes traditionally designated as London's Spitalfields district. From the perspective of London's manicured, Spitalfields swelled with lowly commoners (Spitalfields Benevolent Society Report 1812: 5–6). The silk weavers lived in distinctive enclaves, and by the 1820s they constituted between a fifth to a quarter of the laboring population (McCann 1977: 3; LSP 1823, CLVI: 23; PP 1835, VII: 11: PP 1834, XXIX, App. A, Pt. III: 115A). Silk weaving itself was a patriarchally structured domestic industry; many women had entered it in a subservient position. Within the family workshop, the average male weaver worked and supervised between two or three looms, as well as his wife and children on ancillary tasks. Weaving basic silk broadcloth was a routine skill, but the weavers retained respectability because of the more complex production of fancy goods, such as satins and brocades. Most weavers' pay was well below that of London's craft elite, though their incomes certainly elevated them among Spitalfields' common laborers (Jordan 1931: 12; *Letters* 1818: 11; LSP 1823, CLVI: 86, 125; Porter 1831: 222–3, 274; PP 1818, IX: 40, 44, 46, 141, 148, 188; PP 1832, XIX: 209, 213, 285, 299, 488, 716, 725; PP 1835, VII: 10–11).

The weavers' respectable status was enhanced by their reputation as literate and cultured and their relative peacefulness during London radicals' mobilizations in the 1810s. Additionally, over the decades they had been among the most consistent working-class payers of parish taxes, were characterized as disdainful of parish relief, and had established symbiotic relationships with the petty bourgeoisie and tradesmen who dominated parish politics. The weavers parlayed this reputation within the parish into favorable impressions among local authorities, middle-class interlopers, and elite commentators (Hammond and Hammond 1919: 212–13; LSP 1823, CLVII: 16; Manchee 1913: 332–33; McCann 1977: 3; Partington 1825: 38: PP 1817, VI: 31; PP 1818, IX: 42, 160; PP 1832: 714; PP 1834, X: 320).

Above all, the weavers' distinction as respectable artisans rested on the foundations of the Spitalfields Acts. Originally born from Parliamentary reaction to silk weavers' violent strikes in the late 1760s and early 1770s, the

Acts loomed large in the conduct of the local trade. They applied only to the district; among the important clauses were prohibitions on masters from employing cheaper labor outside the district, restrictions to two apprentices for all masters, and the adjudication of all pay disputes between masters and journeymen by local magistrates. Most significantly, the Acts mandated the fixing of piece rates through negotiation between the two groups, with binding arbitration by magistrates as the fallback. Additionally, the Acts prohibited the importation of foreign silks, partly protecting the trade from foreign competition, though smuggling became an increasing worry (Bland, Brown, and Tawney 1919: 547–51; Clapham 1916: 460–62; Plummer 1972: 327–29).

Throughout the eighteenth century and into the early nineteenth, the trade had been dominated by small masters who had traditionally apprenticed. Based in the district, they generally organized the production of between ten and forty looms and often tried to maintain steady relations with a core set of reliable journeymen. Because small masters rose from the ranks (and sometimes found themselves returning due to the cyclical nature of the trade), they seem on the whole to have supported journeymen's efforts to maintain the Acts (Jordan 1931: 2; Rothstein 1977: 286; LSP 1823, CLVI: 20, 22; PP 1818, IX: 185, 197; PP 1832, XIX: 715). The independent masters, in turn, depended for materials on the silk merchants and manufacturers who brokered materials and finished goods and funneled this production into national and international markets. As opposed to the small master, these large-market entrepreneurs typically lacked experience in production and resided outside of the district (George 1925: 177; Plummer 1972: 319). They themselves began to get a foothold in production in the 1810s, and by the early 1820s, a trade observer noted that "the silk trade is very much under the influence of a few leading houses, who are extremely active, and distinguished for their zeal and perseverance." One prescient master, forecasting a silk trade without protection of the Acts, predicted "there will be but Two Classes, the great Capitalists and the Labourers" (British Library, Place Coll., Set 16, v. 2, f. 32; LSP 1823, CLVI: 101; Plummer 1972: 319; PP 1818, IX: 59, 157).

Large manufacturers came to see the Acts as antiquated fetters on the business. From the middle 1810s, they started public grumbling about the Acts, which by the 1820s had turned into a declarative roar for their repeal. They were abetted by political economists, their allies in Parliament (among them the reigning Tory government) and many in the press (Claeys 1989: 144; Gordon 1979: 19; Hilton 1977: 312). Throughout the contest to repeal the Acts and then into the 1830s, the silk weavers found themselves battling this imposing phalanx. Male weavers also faced the erosion of their patriarchal privilege in the workshop and household. From the advent of the battle over the Acts in 1823, portions of the weavers engaged in a cycle of collective action to stave off mounting degradation and misery. The collective action repertoire of the weavers was sophisticated and varied, encompassing petitioning, lobbying, meetings and demonstrations, strikes, and even property damage. In the post-repeal period, they pursued a pattern of alternating targets between manufacturers and the government. The silk weavers fashioned a discursive repertoire in the field through which their opponents sought to monologically define the trade. The chief genre they sought to appropriate and transform was political economy, though they also drew on Christian genres and a genre of British nationalism and citizenship. In the following sections, I explore the dialogic development of this repertoire as the weavers developed it in interaction with power holders and over changing circumstances. I also consider how the discursive field imposed boundaries on how the weavers could articulate their senses of injustice and their claims for redress, ultimately limiting their contentiousness.

The Manufacturers' and Weavers' Discursive Repertoire

The 1810s witnessed efforts by bourgeois moral crusaders to proselytize among the silk weavers, concerned that periodic bouts of economic distress might stir radicalism. They made frequent visits during depressions, dispersing food relief, Bibles, and heavy doses of what they hoped were mollifying inspirationals (McCann 1977; *Philanthropist*, v. 2, no. 6, 1812, no. 7; *Report of . . . the Spitalfields Soup Society for 1811–12*, Soup Society, 1813). The messages directed to the weavers emphasized Christian resignation and patriotic loyalty to face their travails. One moral crusader scripted an idealized pronouncement for weavers tempted by radicals:

> We are poor and industrious men, and cannot be expected to be conversant in politics, or the science of government. We are Christians, and are instructed to fear God, be subject to the higher powers, and not to meddle with them who are given to chance. It does not become us therefore to agitate a subject of which we are necessarily ignorant. (Brock 1817: 9)

For Hannah More, an evangelical Anglican and literary queen of deferential didactics for working people, the Spitalfields weaver was a recurring character. In "The True Rights of Man; or, The Contented Spital-Fields Weaver," the weaver lyrically recounts the virtuous worker's discourse:

> That some must be poorer, this truth I will sing,
> Is a law of my maker and not of my King:
> And the true Rights of Man, and the life of his cause,
> Is not equal possessions, but equal just laws. (1819a: 151)

Pamphleteers and parliamentarians were also reconstructing the discursive field in which definitions of political and trade citizenship, standards of justice, and the rule of law increasingly depended on economic liberalism and bourgeois individualism. This was a far-reaching effort to make political economy a generic common sense, and the acts were a prime target. Against their protectionism, the large manufacturers and political economists proffered a concept of negative rights. Freedom was founded in the minimal intrusion of government on matters of individual choice. As a critic of the Acts noted, "Government should in no case interfere to adjust the gains and losses of its subjects. Its business is to remove every obstacle which may stand in the way of accumulation of wealth and the development of powers and resources of talent and industry,—not certainly to pamper and enrich one class of producers at the expense of the community" (*Edinburgh Review* 1819, 32: 64). His sentiments were echoed by a major tract condemning the Acts: "[T]he object of all political institutions is negative rather than positive. . . . The security of the property, life, and freedom of the subject, at the smallest possible expense of the revenue, is, or ought to be the ultimate end of all governments" (*Observations* 1822: 66). This vision was embedded in the large manufacturers' petition to Parliament in May 1823 to repeal the Acts,

> as to be exempted from the arbitrary, injurious, and impolitic
> enactment which prevents them, while they continue to reside within
> certain districts, from employing any portion of their capital in such
> other parts of the kingdom as may be deemed most beneficial;
> thereby depriving them not only of the fair exercise of their privi-
> leges as free subjects, and totally preventing public benefit that
> would arise from a competition between the London and the country
> manufacturers, but depriving them also of all hope of ever partici-
> pating in the foreign trade of the Empire. (*Hansard's Parliamentary
> Debates* [hereafter *Hans*] n.s., 1823, IX, c. 148–49)

At the heart of the assault against the Acts was the genre of political economy, which maintained that the market provided the natural mechanisms for the organization of production, the value of labor, and its products and trade prosperity. The silk weavers' labor was cast as a commodity whose value could be established only by market forces. "Dr. Adam Smith," remarked one critic, "has so clearly illustrated the connection between the wages of labour and the fund out of which they are paid, that if reason governed the world, all controversy on the subject would be set for ever. . . . The price of labour varies with the market; the interest of both parties is consulted by the variation; competition acting on each side, neither is oppressed; and the market rate of wages is uniformly and precisely what it ought to be" (*Obser-*

vations 1822: 23–24, 38; see also "Verax" 1822: 42). In the end, market forces assured a just harmony: "The great objects of the manufacturer are or ought to be, to extend the market for his commodities and increase the amount and productiveness of his capital; and the real interests of the labourer are secured exactly in proportion as these objects are accomplished . . . there is in the long-run a perfect identity of interests between the two classes" (*Observations* 1822: 23).

The weavers thus found themselves in a struggle in which the discursive field was defined by the "weaving" together of the dominant genres of Christian piety, nationalism and citizenship, and political economy. Over the decade and a half of a concerted, though losing, battle to first retain and then revivify protection, they dialogically engaged these genres, developing a complex repertoire through processes of appropriation of these discourses and discourses of radical politics propagated by the increasing tide of radical reformers. This repertoire had an improvisational quality, shifting partly with their claims and targets. The multivocal nature of key terms within these genres—such as "justice," "right," "freedom," "property," and "value"—posed opportunities for the weavers to contest and transform the discourses.

Early in their campaign, the silk weavers and their allies countered the attacks on the Acts by emphasizing the positive functions of government. They also highlighted the collective citizenship rights of workers, a notion of the common good focusing on the contributions of producers, an interventionist concept of the state, and an understanding of freedom markedly at variance with the discourses of their opponents. As the activist John Poyton stated, government "was designed at the first formation of civil society, for the mutual protection of the community at large" (British Library Add MSS 27805, *An Account* 1823: 60–61). John Powell, a radical supporter of the weavers, extended this line of reasoning:

> What is the end of all legislation, and even all human labour? Is it not regulation? Can that which is so useful in all other things become worse than useless in its application to labour? What principle of regulation, so equitable, so efficacious, so conformable to the genius of British legislation, and so calculated to secure the first principles of a well-regulated society, as the Spitalfields Acts? . . . But competition sustained at the expenses of the working classes will derange all legitimate interest in society, which interest can only be secured by the principle of the Spitalfields Acts. The insatiable avarice of many of the rich, into whose hands the power of legislation has fallen, has in all ages led them to adopt artificial arrangements further to separate labour and profit. (British Library Add MSS 27805, Powell 1824: 4–5; see also *Letters* 1818: 42–43; Hale 1822: 6)

In a dialogic fashion, a Coventry weaver seized on the notion of individual freedom proffered by the manufacturers and deftly sought to expose the class biases that it contained: "But what sort of freedom is it that they advocate? Why a freedom the very reverse of the thing they pretend; it is nothing more nor less, in application to the productive classes, than freedom for the powerful to oppress and defraud the weak" ("Coventry Freeman" 1824: 5).

In their fight against repeal, the weavers linked a concept of positive rights and justice conferred to a group of citizens for the protection of property, which political economists were keen to assert. Appropriating the idea of property, they asserted,

> It has been stated to the committee of the lords, "that no interference of the law in labour is just." Not just, Sir, why not? is not all acquired property protected by law, and is not that just? Why then should it not be just to protect natural property which is labour. Labour is the only property a poor man has, which is the root and origin of all the riches of the great and mighty, who are able to protect themselves, while the poor have neither the means nor the power of self-defense without the assistance of the law. (*An Account* 1823: 60; see also Powell 1824: 6)

Arguing to retain the Acts, the male weavers drew on the nationalist genre that the government used when it sought defenders for the nation. Spitalfields had been a prime recruiting ground for the Navy during the Napoleonic Wars, and the weavers deployed concepts of patriotism to pursue their collective citizenship rights (LSP, CLVI, 1823: 30). They structured their demands for protection in terms of the quid pro quo with the state: "[O]ur trade was shielded by a generous Parliament, and thereby inspired with true loyalty. We left our looms in defence of our much beloved King and country, and are always ready to do so again" (*An Account* 1823: 45, see also 28–89 and Place Coll., Set 16, v. 2, "Silk", fo. 66).

The weavers drew on the discourse of biblical morality used by bourgeois proselytizers to articulate claims of the common good. In an anti-repeal circular distributed to MPs, they observed that "[i]t may be said of the weaving business, what Solomon said of husbandry—'the profits of the earth are for all'" (*An Account* 1823: 25). A weavers' leader, in an open letter to manufacturers, warned of damnation for those pursuing profit at the weavers' expense:

> The Lord will pour out his vengeance on the oppressors of the poor and needy, that keep back the hire of the labourer by fraud and violence, which (by the by) is entered into the ears of the Lord of the Saboath, whose voice is, "go to now, ye rich men, howl and weep, for

the miseries that shall come upon you. Your riches are corrupted; your gold and silver is cankered; and the rust of them shall be a witness against you, and shall eat your flesh like fire, and be as burning metal in your bowels" (James v. 3, 4). (*An Account* 1823: 62)

The weavers forestalled the repeal of the Acts in 1823 but were defeated the following year. From 1825 onward, they conducted a cycle of collective actions that focused alternately on the manufacturers and the government. Having established a discursive repertoire that highlighted the duties of government, in the late 1820s they began to incorporate the genre of political radicalism stemming from the campaign for parliamentary reform and a developing working-class popular politics (Tilly 1995b). Such discourse excoriated the government for being the preserve of a corrupt and self-indulgent ruling oligarchy. Though propagated by radicals as a critique of political corruption, the weavers used it to condemn government for failing to protect their collective economic rights. In a petition to the Parliament in 1827, they boldly pronounced:

The petitioners are well aware that the misery of the times . . . is the result, the natural result of laws emanating from the House, such having arisen solely from the want of a fair and equal representation of the people in the House; and that, therefore, the petitioners earnestly and urgently implore the House, in its wisdom and clemency, to do something (and that promptly) to benefit their unhappy and wretched condition. (*Trades' Free Press*, July 1, 1827)

They closed with a plan to restore protection derived from this political critique, calling upon the House "to take into its early and serious consideration, to institute the best means to accomplish that most important and desirable of all requests,—viz. an effectual and real Reform in the House, the want of which has been the principal cause of the wretched and miserable state of the petitioners, whose rights and liberties have from time to time been bartered away, and sacrificed, like cattle in Smithfield. From the want of Reform has originated all their grievances" (*Trades' Free Press*, July 1, 1827).

As they incorporated the genre of radical politics into their repertoire, other genres, such as that of Christian piety, were displaced. Discursive conflict focused more completely on issues of political rights and economic exploitation, given the institutional arenas of the struggle and the larger contemporary political context. These political and economic critiques could be relationally linked within the discursive field of the late 1820s, given the other ongoing struggles in which workers participated.

Silk weavers and their allies sought to counter the genre of political economy both by appropriating key elements of the discourse and exposing its class-interested bases. They offered a popular perspective on exploitation based in a labor theory of value and a diagnosis of unemployment and economic distress as partly due to underconsumption. The market, they pronounced, was no fair arbiter. As one sympathizer argued during the Repeal debate, "Human labour is the real standard of value, and it is in the interest of the capitalist, the agriculturalist, the merchant, and the manufacturer, that it should never be exchanged for less than its real worth" ("Coventry Freeman" 1824: 4). Seeking to establish moral high ground within the discursive field, the weaver ironically quoted Adam Smith to validate this theory of exploitation: "Adam Smith, an authority our great pretenders are fond of quoting, says, 'the prosperity of a country consists in the comforts and enjoyments that the people, both rich and poor, possess beyond the common necessaries of life'" (Powell 1824: 5). One sympathizer stated that, with repeal, "the very principles of sound political economy have been violated. Dr. Adam Smith says, 'a man must always live by his work, and his wages must be at least sufficient to maintain him" (Hale 1822: 41).

In late February 1828, a general meeting of the silk weavers assembled to approve a petition to Parliament. The chair announced, through a well-developed appropriation of political economy: "They found, generally, in all situations where capital was employed, the individuals so employing it sought the Legislature to protect that capital. If he understood the business which had called them together, it was for the protection of capital; that capital which was the most valued in all states—it was labour" (*Trades' Free Press*, Feb. 23, 1828). Discussion was wide-ranging and drew from a variety of dominant genres and radical political discourse. The litany of causes of their circumstances well represented the strands of their repertoire, drawing prominently on transformations of radical politics, nationalism, and political economy: they blamed their poverty on

> the long misrule, which has been pursued by legislators,—from the manifestly erroneous policy of our commercial transactions,—from the cruel, overreaching and tyrannical conduct of certain unprincipled, greedy, and speculative employers,—from the dangerous tendency of the pestilential dogmas of certain professors of political economy,—from the unjust and oppressive exactions of the lords of the soil and the loom,—from the cold and stoical indifference manifested in the great mass of public men as to the welfare of their fellow creatures." (*Report . . . for a Wage Protection Bill* 1828: 31)

Now standard features of their repertoire, the weavers use a refashioned discourse of economics to discuss the role of government and the necessity of law to maintain harmony between the classes (ibid.: 7, 12–14, 24). To counter the foil of political economy, the weavers proposed "the indubitable laws of social economy," a genre of popular working-class economics that increasingly was a staple of many working peoples' struggles. This was constructed partly by drawing on political economy's own labor theory of value.

> An equitable reward for labour is best adapted, and is indeed indispensable to secure the greatest quantity of wealth in any country, and to promote the legitimate interests of all classes of society.

> 1st. Because it is labour which gives value to land and raw material for manufactures. "The labour of the country is the wealth of the country" (Adam Smith), and in proportion as the wages are high or low, the value of wealth of such country is increased or diminished.

> 2nd. Because the great majority of the people of every country is necessarily composed of those whose sole property is their labour, by securing therefore to labour an adequate reward, the positive comfort of the greatest possible number would be secured also; and, as Labourers form the base of society, all the other classes must be benefited in due proportion. . . .

> 6th. Because an inequitable remuneration for labour necessarily diminishes the means of purchasing the products of labour, in a greater degree than the reduced price of commodities tends to increase the means. (*Report . . . for a Wage Protection Bill* 1828: 14–15)

The silk weavers' struggles thus illustrate several facets of a dialogic perspective on collective action discourse. They developed their conceptions of injustice, diagnoses of their problems, and vision of equitable resolution substantially within a hegemonic discursive field. That field was defined situationally and composed of dominant genres of Christian religious piety, nationalism and patriotism, and political economy. Each genre contained multivocal possibilities for the weavers to seize on key words and phrases and transform their meanings for their own claims. They deftly created an oppositional voice *within* them. Key terms such as "justice," "freedom," "property," and even "capital" were used to create a voice identifying injustice. At each point in the cycle of their struggle, they engaged in improvisational efforts to expose how the "truths" of large manufacturers, parliamentarians, and pundits of political economy were ideological exercises of power.

Through their protracted battle, the weavers constructed a dynamic repertoire of discourses, containing a weave of several genres, and its composition changed with the shape and context of the conflict and the discursive field. Certainly, this repertoire was partly strategic, but it was never simply instrumental. For the Spitalfields weavers, their discourses voiced powerful and righteous truths, whose moral authority partly rested in the truths offered by the dominant discourses that they used for their own ends.

As I have argued elsewhere (Steinberg 1995, 1999b), the generic roots of this repertoire created a conundrum of legitimacy when, in 1829, the weavers destroyed the broadcloth and looms of a number of their peers, who continued work at the height of a strike for higher piece rates. Having articulated a collective identity as deserving citizens and emphasizing labor as the source of value and a form of property, the weavers in such collective violence severely undermined their claims of entitlement to governmental assistance. Such violence could be only dubiously justified by their discursive repertoire, since they had used concepts of citizenship and morality within the dominant discursive field to articulate their claims, and their nemeses were able, from within the same field, to denounce their actions. Moreover, unlike many of their London counterparts, the weavers were only marginal players in a growing cooperative socialist movement in the period, and as new forms of union militancy emerged in the 1830s, they remained entrenched in a clearly lost struggle for protection (Steinberg 1995: 76).

Perhaps their discursive repertoire limited their field of vision for these alternatives. After partly constructing their vision of justice through a refashioned capitalist discourse of economics, for example, they found that moving on to cooperative socialism was problematic. Finally, the male weavers' citizenship claims reinforced dominant notions of patriarchy within the household, which, as Anna Clark (1995) argues, became increasingly central to working-class radical discourse starting in the late 1820s. For female weavers, the cost of the struggle for collective economic security was the legitimation of their silence and subordination (Steinberg 1999b).

More generally, we can see how the weavers' discursive struggle, while concerted and often ingenious, nonetheless left them partly captive to the truths of dominant genres. In appropriating elements of political economy, they simultaneously retained a vision in which larger processes of capitalist production remained unquestioned. Their nemeses, the large manufacturers, retained their collective identity as legitimate masters of production and distribution, a status predicated on their continued exploitation of the weavers. The weavers' partial appropriation of the discourses of Christian evangelicalism and bourgeois citizenship likewise retained underlying conceptions of hierarchy in which the weavers remained legitimate challengers so long as they were deferential underlings. They could press their claims only by implicitly affirming their inferior status, and recourse to radical or violent means of redress thus undermined their legitimacy.

Thus, in this history discursive repertoires should not be viewed exclusively as a resource. Certainly, the weavers strategically created their discursive repertoire. However, by operating within the dominant discursive field, they never wholly controlled the discourses by which they asserted their claims for justice. Their claims, identity, and actions were still partly morally measured by the truths of dominant genres through which they gave meaning to their collective voice, and this created unseen but real disadvantages as well. As borrowers and refashioners of these genres, the weavers never controlled their meanings. In later years, as the trade was transformed and the weavers increasingly slipped into poverty, their public identity became one of impoverished and degraded second-class citizens, and their claims were largely ignored.

Conclusion

To fully comprehend the dynamics of social movements, we need to analyze carefully how culture infuses meaning into collective action. Challengers are strategic actors, but even the most calculating plans are based on some moral vision of the world, collective identity, and shared understandings of how these can be realized. Framing analysis and other recent work on the cultural dimensions of social movements have persuasively brought such concerns to our attention. However, what they often lack is a concept of social movement culture as a dynamic and relational process.

A dialogic analysis focuses our attention on culture as a set of practices that occurs *between* power holders and challengers, sympathizers, authorities, and other groups (as well as between actors within those groups themselves). Dialogism offers a specific framework for a more dynamic analysis of collective action discourse. It focuses on the discursive repertoires produced by challengers within specific fields often greatly defined by power holders. Dialogic analysis explores how these repertoires often are fashioned through the partial reworking of dominant genres, as well as the continual uncertainties and challenges that these repertoires pose for all involved. By artfully transforming the meaning of the discourses used to dominate them, challengers both provide their claims with credibility and cast doubt on the often assumed truths power holders voice through these words. The Spitalfields weavers' case has demonstrated how developing such a repertoire works. Over the course of a movement, challengers create a repertoire of discourses to articulate their purposes and visions and also adapt smaller improvisations to meet the changing exigencies of conflict. And as the weavers' case has shown, the creation of any such discursive repertoire not only facilitates collective action; it imposes constraints on how challengers can construct their claims and legitimate their identities.

Long ago, V. N. Volosinov mused that the "word is a two-sided act" (1986[1929]: 86). He and many dialogists have since argued that this "two-sidedness" of discourse redounds as cultural practices both enable and constrain actors, particularly the subordinated when they attempt to speak truth to and *through* power. Social movement participants continually engage these issues throughout the course of contention, and dialogism offers us a conceptual tool to deepen our understanding of this complex cultural process.

NOTES

1. A parallel argument can be made concerning identity construction. As Jennifer de Peuter observes, "Selfhood is less a property of mind than it is a dialogue on the boundaries of selfhood and otherness. . . . The dialogical-narrative self is not a fixed text, but is a multitude of situated, re-interpretations, re-ordered with each telling and hearing in changing social contexts" (1998: 39, 45; see also J. Gamson 1995; Taylor and Whittier 1992; Tilly 1998).

2. I examine this case more extensively in Steinberg (1999a), chapters 3–6.

13

Materialist Feminist Discourse Analysis and Social Movement Research: Mapping the Changing Context for "Community Control"

NANCY A. NAPLES

How do progressive frames achieve wide acceptance and become institutionalized in social practices but lose their critical feminist or progressive intent? Examples of this process can be found throughout feminist praxis, from the transformation of "battered women" into the "battered woman syndrome" to the depoliticization of "sexual harassment" (e.g., Loseke 1992; Walker 1994). My goal in this chapter is to demonstrate the value of a materialist feminist discourse analysis for explicating how social movement frames gain wide appeal but, over time, can lose the progressive formulation that incited their production or can even be used to counter progressive goals.[1] I incorporate discursive, cultural, and structural factors in social movement research (see, e.g., Gamson 1988; McCarthy 1994; Taylor and Whittier 1995: 185; Steinberg 1999b). A materialist feminist approach focuses on the social and political context, subject positions, and power relations through which social movement frames are generated, circulated, and then reinscribed within different discursive and institutional practices (e.g., Landry and MacLean 1993; Ramazanoglu 1993), as well as the shifting *discursive fields* surrounding the production of specific movement frames (also see Donati 1992).

Materialist feminism has intellectual roots in Marx's historical materialism but is informed by contemporary debates in feminist epistemology that view knowledge as mediated by positionality, discourse, and power (see, especially, Hartsock 1983; Smith 1987, 1990). The concept of "positionality" argues "that gender is not natural, biological, universal, ahistorical, or essential and yet still claim[s] that gender is relevant because we are taking gender as a position from which to act politically" (Alcoff 1988: 433). Materialist feminist scholars argue for an intersectional approach to gender, race, class, and sexuality and resist abstracting gender from other dimensions of social identity (Brenner 2000; Hennessy and Ingraham 1997). Materialist feminism is also informed by Foucauldian analysis of discourse (Foucault 1972). According to Dorothy Smith (1989: 47) we draw on "discourse institutionalized in relations and apparatuses of ruling" to interpret the world around us. Social movement actors do not operate outside these interpretive processes and institutional practices. Although social movement actors are not free to choose the discursive frames through which they articulate social movement goals, some actors are situated in positions of power to control the production of particular frames.

Discourse limits what can be discussed or heard in a political context and is not necessarily tied to particular organizations. Dynamics of gender, race, class, and region, among other structures of inequality, shape whose voices are represented and heard in public policy debates, as well as in a social movement context. I illustrate this process with reference to the *community control* frame popularized during the late 1960s. As Howard Hallman (1969: 1) notes, the call for community "control emerged as a demand of black nationalists as a means of achieving 'black power,' a slogan that gained popularity during the Meredith Mississippi Freedom March of June, 1966." The community control frame continues to resonate for residents in communities across the United States and has expanded from the 1960s usage by black power activists and urban minority parents to members of the religious right, residents of suburban communities, and community police. Community control resonated with civil rights activists, as well as policy makers of diverse political perspectives, low-income women of color in poor neighborhoods, white middle-class parents, and the religious right, who now use the frame to justify demands for teaching creationism in the public schools and banning books like "Heather Has Two Mommies" from the school library (e.g., Berliner 1997). The diverse political constituencies who use the community control frame for contradictory purposes illustrate how movement actors can lose control of a movement frame over time (also see Tarrow 1992). Analysis of the political, economic, and social context surrounding the development and wide acceptance of the community control frame demonstrates the inherent contradictions in the discursive field from which it was drawn.

I draw on data from a case study of women community activists employed in community action agencies who struggled for "community control" of schools and other community-based institutions in New York City.[2] I gathered focused life histories from women who were employed by the community action programs in Harlem and the Lower East Side of Manhattan and

Bedford-Stuyvesant to examine their motivation for community work, the political analyses and political strategies they developed over time, and the ways in which the changing political economy influenced their work. I focus on the narratives of activists involved in the community control of schools struggle in New York City during the late 1960s and early 1970s. I also draw on newspaper accounts and archival data, annual reports, and minutes from monthly board meetings, as well as relevant secondary research for this analysis.

Materialist Feminist Discourse Analysis

A materialist feminist social movement analysis uses Foucault's (1972) discourse analysis to reveal how movement frames contest, reproduce, or participate in relations of ruling. Discourse organizes relations among and between movement actors and others; gender, racial-ethnic, and class inequalities infuse subject positions within the discourse. Thus, movement organizations do not produce their frames self-consciously; existing discourses and power relations constrain them. When they do successfully produce oppositional frames, movements can lose control over how these frames are appropriated and reinscribed over time. As Patrick Mooney and Scott Hunt (1996: 188) conclude from their study of the U.S. agrarian movement, "movements are shaped by a repertoire of interpretations in which the alignment of master frames varies with changing socioeconomic and political contexts" (quoted in Benford 1997: 417). From a materialist feminist perspective, we can analyze how movements construct their frames within the discourses that organize, and are structured by, ruling relations. These discourses are embedded in everyday activities. As Dorothy Smith (1999: 94) explains, a materialist feminist approach "would extend people's own good knowledge of the local practices and terrains of their everyday/everynight living, enlarging the scope of what becomes visible from that site, mapping the relations that connect one local site to others."

Collective action frames can also resist domination or at least demonstrate the cracks in the dominant discursive field (see Katzenstein 1999). Ruling relations and resistance are evident both in the processes that generate a particular social movement frame and how the frame is circulated, interpreted, reinscribed with alternative meanings, and taken up by potential allies as well as opponents. Social movement framing and less visible discursive realms intersect, at times creating contradictory constructions of political action as the political context and constituency shift. I now turn to a discussion of the community control frame to illustrate how a materialist feminist discourse analysis helps us understand these processes.

The "Community Control" Frame

In 1990 in the suburban town of Joshua Gap, California, a group of residents called for the removal of *Impressions*, the multicultural reading series published by Harcourt Brace Jovanovich, from the local elementary school. The protesting citizens claimed that this series presented ideas and values that were at odds with the traditional values of their community. David Post (1992: 676) found, in his insightful analysis of this struggle, "that in Joshua Gap the concept of the community, like that of the nation, was itself imagined and constructed by members" many of whom had only recently moved to the town. Across the United States, numerous conservative and, in some cases, reactionary and racist calls for community control of schools are reported in news items and opinion columns, as well as in scholarly accounts. This development might not seem strange if one took the call for "community control of schools" out of the context in which it was originally expressed. However, in many ways, the call for community control of schools in the second half of the 1960s contained within it the contradictions revealed in the protest by elementary school parents in Joshua Gap. To delineate the contradictions of this movement frame, I begin by discussing precursors of the community control of schools movement, then focus on the discursive, political, and social context in which it arose in New York City. I shift then to the standpoint of women living and working in low-income New York neighborhoods who participated in the movement for community control of schools. I conclude by illustrating how the discursive themes evident in its construction and political implementation laid the grounds for the cooptation of the frame for conservative, racist, sexist, and homophobic ends.

Precursors for Community Control of Schools

Alan Altshuler (1970: 64), who chaired the Academic Advisory Committee on Decentralization in New York City in 1968, defined community control as "the exercise of authority by the democratically organized government of a neighborhood-sized jurisdiction." It includes political decentralization, although for Altshuler communities would remain accountable to "higher levels of government—just as are the charters of cities and suburbs today" (64–65). Community control, in the sense that members of the low-income communities of color in New York City understood it, included both political and administrative decentralization. However, few legislators or public officials who supported administrative decentralization included political decentralization and community control in their vision.

In Altshuler's (1970: 12) view, "neighborhood democracy has few precedents—that decentralization and widespread citizen participation have not been characteristic of American cities in earlier historical periods." As late as 1962, he notes, no obvious "demands for neighborhood government or community control" were evident. Even though activists did not call for community control in earlier periods, large city bureaucracies like the public school system adopted strategies for decentralizing much earlier (Cronin 1973). The few early experiments designed to expand participation in public school governance emphasized administrative decentralization more than community control or political decentralization. In 1950, New York's city planning commission proposed the establishment of sixty-six districts to plan and coordinate schools, hospitals, recreation facilities, and streets (Cronin 1973: 190). The following year Manhattan Borough President Robert Wagner set up twelve planning districts in Manhattan. Only a few years later, the Board of Education, itself, determined that some decentralized system of decision making was needed to facilitate the administration of the New York City public schools. As Melvin Zimet (1973: 9) observes, "the concepts of administrative decentralization and community control gathered momentum and converged on a collision course" around 1967 when the Mayor's Advisory Panel on Decentralization of the New York City Schools (1969) released their report. Although that report's discursive framing of the importance of local participation in planning and decision making was a far cry from black power activists' radical call for community control, it did emphasize the link between civic participation and public education.

Mapping the Discursive, Political, and Social Context

In the context of the civil rights movement that gained momentum following the passage of 1954's *Brown v. Board of Education*, African American parents and the wider African American community were keenly disappointed by the dismal failure of even the most sincere efforts to integrate the public schools in urban neighborhoods (see Cronin 1973; Maynard 1970; New York CLU 1969; Stein 1970). With the passage of the Civil Rights Act in 1964, the federal government actively pressed for desegregation first in the South, then in northern cities (Watras 1997). However, by 1967, more than half of the African American and Puerto Rican children in New York City were attending completely segregated schools, most located in low-income neighborhoods (Stein 1970: 21).[3]

With the failure of integration, many black leaders and black parents recognized the need to reconceptualize how to improve the quality of education for African American children in urban neighborhoods (see Watras 1997). While Black Power movement activists articulated a radical vision of "black self-determination," liberal organizations like the National Association for the Advancement of Colored People (NAACP) and the Urban League supported a more circumscribed version of community control. The NAACP and the Urban League both passed a resolution supporting community control of schools in 1969; however, their understanding was more in keeping with liberal reform than radical separatism. When the struggle for community control erupted in New York City, liberal black organizations like the NAACP were reported to support "community control so long as it did not prevent integration" (Ornstein 1974: 244). According to educational analyst Allan Ornstein, this left these groups and their leaders "without a practical strategy and they eventually fell into the background." In addition, Ornstein reports, "A. Philip Randolph and Bayard Rustin and a large group of trade unionists publicly denounced community control" (244).[4]

African American leadership in urban communities recognized "that white America is much more likely (though still not very) to concede a large measure of ghetto self-determination than to accept large numbers of blacks into its neighborhoods" (Altshuler 1970: 24). Altshuler views black residents' call for community control as a pragmatic response to white resistance to integration. In the context of growing tensions, riots erupting in minority urban neighborhoods across the United States, and apparently insurmountable difficulties in achieving integration, it is not surprising that school and city officials began to see the benefits of community control. After all, as Diane Ravitch (1974: 305) writes: "If the parents assumed control, they would have only themselves and their appointees to blame for failure."

Mayor Robert Wagner became interested in decentralization when he recognized the fiscal benefits that could accrue to New York City as a result. He did not frame his support for decentralization as a way to encourage democratic participation of local communities in the management of public schools (Zimet 1973). During his administration, a temporary commission was established to evaluate city finances. It concluded the city would benefit financially if the school system were reorganized into five separate school districts. When John Lindsay became mayor in 1966, he latched onto this idea as a way to bring more state money into the city (Zimet 1973: 9). In addition, these arguments drew on the discursive theme of increasing "competition" through enhancing parental choice. Contrasting the monopolistic approach of large centralized bureaucracies with more decentralized strategies, Anthony Downs of the Real Estate Research Corporation (1970: 219) argues: "Since consumers can shift their trade from suppliers who do not please them, suppliers have a strong incentive to provide what the consumers want.... Clearly, if greater competition causes these results in general, it might produce some tremendous improvements in big-city school systems."

In contrast to the administrative, fiscal, and consumerist construction of decentralization, interest in community control originated in the liberal reform efforts of social scientists like Lloyd Ohlin and Richard Cloward, Ford

Foundation social planners (notably Paul Ylvisaker), and progressive federal officials like David Hackett and other White House staff of President John F. Kennedy (Altshuler 1970). With the passage of the Economic Opportunity Act of 1964, the state formally incorporated a feature that emphasized *maximum feasible participation* of residents in poor neighborhoods, thus linking the struggle for community control with state-funded community action centers. The 1965 Elementary and Secondary Education Act also included the establishment of citizen advisory councils to assess local education policies (Gittell 1970: 248). The state's support for community activism and community decision making was short-lived; for example, by 1971 most community action programs were circumscribed by narrow definitions of service delivery that undercut the enactment of maximum feasible participation (see Naples 1998b). Nevertheless, local residents (a disproportionate number of whom were women of color) seized this window of opportunity to support their struggle to improve the services and quality of life in their neighborhoods. The schools became a central focus on their efforts.

The call for community control of schools was made in the context of a variety of competing political goals and discursive themes. Some actors supported community control as a pragmatic response to institutional racism. Others based their call for community control on a liberal construction of social reform. A third group drew on a radical construction of community control to articulate separatist claims as in the Black Power movement. Another set of actors drew on the discursive theme of enhancing competition between school districts. City officials drew on the discursive theme of administrative efficiency to construct the fiscal and political advantage of decentralization in contrast to political decentralization. In addition to these competing discursive themes, other observers point to the racist subtext of white support for community control. Diane Ravitch (1974: 305) writes that community control for "black schools appealed to a surprising cross-section of whites" for "black control of black schools implied white control of white schools, which they could comfortably support, for it guaranteed that black problems, black dissidence, and black pupils would be safely contained within the ghetto." Whereas the fact that community control could be abstracted from the particular political, racial, and economic context and applied to other communities and other populations makes the concept appealing to a broader constituency, it also reveals how it could be appropriated and wielded by groups for racist and other reactionary goals (also see Tarrow 1992).

Surprisingly, given the diversity of perspectives on community control, few participants in the controversy and subsequent legislative initiatives addressed class and the economic constraints that inhibit the delivery of quality education in poor communities. Also missing in the discursive themes of the community control controversy was recognition of women's essential role in producing the public school itself. In fact, the daily practices of teachers and administrators contain often unspoken expectations that much of the learning process depends on parents, particularly mothers. Mothers are expected to provide labor in the homes (e.g., supervising homework, assisting in school projects), in the schools (e.g., as volunteers in the classroom or for school trips), and in the community (e.g., fund-raising and organizing school-community events) (Griffith and Smith 1990). Furthermore, mothers have consistently formed the constituents for political action designed to improve the quality of education for their children and other community members (e.g., Stern 1998).

For mothers of children in low-income and minority communities, activism is an essential part of mother work (see Naples 1998a). Because mothers often negotiated with the schools on their children's behalf, they were in the forefront of the battles for community control of schools. For example, Paula Sands became active in her Harlem community when she enrolled her child in an overcrowded public school in the late 1960s (also see Naples 1998c: 327). She was appalled by the conditions she witnessed in the school. She found administrators and teachers insulting and unsympathetic when she complained. Her early activism against the racist and irresponsible school district led her into other struggles, against absentee landlords and police harassment, for welfare rights and bilingual education, and to increase voter registration of low-income residents and expand library services. Through her activism, Sands developed a complex analysis of how power dynamics and relations of ruling in education and other spheres served to reproduce gender, race, and class inequality. Thus, by shifting to the perspective of low-income women living and working in poor communities who were active in the struggle for community control of school, the gender and class relations missing from dominant discourse and recorded history become visible. This feminist materialist perspective highlights the intersection of race, class, and gender in the struggle for community control of schools and provides the basis for explicating the cooptation of the frame for conservative, racist, sexist, and homophobic political goals.

The People's Board of Education

Community control of schools' activist Sukie Ports (1970: 65) explains that attempts to integrate the New York City public schools began in 1962 "when local school boards were asked to submit ideas for achieving integration within their own boundaries." Since her Harlem district was totally segregated at the time, no plan reliant on internal strategies could effectively integrate the neighborhood schools. Local parents also recognized many problems with the "open enrollment" and "free transfer" plans that permitted students to register for schools outside their district (e.g., the "creaming" of the better prepared students from the local schools). Their district (District 10–11) was the first to defy the Board of Education's "desegregation" policy and to demonstrate that the "policy could not be handed down city-wide and implemented systematically or effectively without the participation of the local staff and parents involved" (68).

In the beginning of the 1965 school year, the Board of Education redrew the boundaries between districts, breaking up Harlem District 10–11 and consequently disqualifying several members of the oppositional school board from membership on the board. The redistricting also removed virtually all of the white and middle-income children in East Harlem (Ports 1970). Part of the justification for the redistricting plan was to merge the predominantly African American area with the adjacent community that was predominantly Puerto Rican, thus achieving "integration" by serving African American and Puerto Rican children without devising a plan that would incorporate white students as well (Cronin 1973; Ports 1970). Along with the redistricting plan came the announcement that a new junior high school (Intermediate School [IS] 201) would be established in the redrawn district to be located at 127th Street and Madison Avenue in Harlem. As the beginning of the new school year drew near, parents and other local activists decided to shift their focus from integration of the school to the establishment of a quality segregated school under the leadership of a black principal and with local community control of staffing and other decisions.

When the Board of Education proposed opening IS 201 in East Harlem, a group of local leaders and parents formed an ad hoc parent council to oppose the board's plan. A central actor was Preston R. Wilcox, then the director of the East Harlem Project, the community action program linked to two settlement houses. When the Economic Opportunity Act was passed in 1964, Wilcox, now professor at Columbia University School of Social Work, wrote a proposal for a coalition of East Harlem community organizations to establish a community action agency in East Harlem called MEND (Massive Economic Neighborhood Development). He followed the approach developed by Richard Cloward, a fellow professor at Columbia, "which held that powerlessness was itself a major cause of poverty" and "that the process of organizing and participation would help to overcome the neighborhood's sense of powerlessness" (Ravitch 1974: 294). Wilcox circulated a paper he titled "To Be Black and To Be Successful" proposing that IS 201 be designed as an experiment in community control. At a community meeting with Mayor Lindsay and School Superintendent Donovan in March 1966, Wilcox argued that "if the school system can do no more than it is already doing, then the communities of the poor must be prepared to act for themselves . . . just as they must become involved in the direction of all programs set up to serve their needs" (quoted in Ravitch 1974: 296).

On the first day of the 1966 school year, parents in Harlem boycotted IS 201. Boycotts against other public schools erupted across the city, "and the concept of community control spread with them" (Berube and Gittell 1969: 13). In December 1966, the 201 protest group joined with other parent activists and their allies in a three-day sit-in at the Board of Education, declaring themselves the People's Board of Education. These events forced the school superintendent to meet with teacher union representatives, community leaders, and Ford Foundation staff to develop a plan that would give parents of public school children a role in educational policy making (Ravitch 1974).

A key organization that helped to coordinate parents' efforts to reform their children's schools was Bronx Parents United.[5] Bronx Parents United originated when parents in a Bronx elementary school joined to protest their children's expulsion from kindergarten. Jewish community worker and parent advocate Teresa Fraser, an active member of Bronx Parents United, explained that the children were "suspended from kindergarten for some very silly, minor infraction." Bronx Parents United then became the vehicle for expanded parent organizing following the People's Board of Education. Fraser described how the People's Board of Education developed spontaneously from the dismissive behavior of formal board members.

> There was a finance hearing at the Board of Education and it was one of these typical things where nothing—I know because I was really involved in it—nothing special was planned. . . . We went down and carried on about where the money was going. Some lady from Brownsville asked if she could speak earlier than her time because she had to go pick up her kids, and they said: "No." And the person who was at the microphone, whoever's turn it was, said: "She can have my time." . . . And whoever it was running the meeting said: "No way!" And people got pissed and said: "Let her talk!" And I'm telling you, I swear to God this was not a planned thing. And they got up and recessed. And people were just furious. And they came back and they called off the hearing on the Board of Education budget because some lady from Brownsville wanted to speak so she could go pick up her children. And . . . a couple of other people were in the audience, said if they're not going to listen, we will listen. And that became the People's Board of Education.

The parents and their allies stayed in the building for three days and three nights. Fraser recalled with amazement that the Board of Education officials "tried to freeze" the parents out of the building by turning on the air blowers.

After three days, the members of the People's Board of Education were arrested. Their arrest was followed by the Board of Education's release of reading scores for each school in the city, which revealed that 20 percent of the city's schoolchildren were falling two years behind their grade level. Not surprisingly, poor neighborhoods had the lowest reported reading scores, while "well-to-do neighborhoods" had the highest scores (Ravitch 1974: 309). With these data, advocates of community control had empirical evidence that the public school system systematically failed to educate low-income and minority children. Parent advocates viewed gaining access to the reading scores as one of their most important and successful achievements. Once parents realized the collective nature of the reading problem, they were in a much better position to push for changes in the school system (also see Stern 1998).

Decentralization Versus Community Control

In 1967, Mayor Lindsay appointed Ford Foundation President McGeorge Bundy to chair the Advisory Panel on Decentralization.[6] Their report asserted that local public schools should become community institutions "that will liberate the talents, energies and interests of parents, students, teachers, and others to make common cause toward the goal of educational excellence" (Mayor's Advisory Panel on Decentralization of the New York City Schools 1967: 119). In this way, the schools would become "responsive to the needs and sensitive to the desires of groups that are in a minority in a particular locality" (119). The advisory panel believed that the decentralization of the schools would "couple the advantages of urban bigness with the intimacy, flexibility, and accessibility associated with innovative suburban school systems" (120).

The report recommended "the creation of a Community School System, to consist of a federation of largely autonomous school districts and a central education agency" (120). They envisioned the community school districts as "governed by boards of by residents chosen jointly by the Mayor (on the advice of the central education agency), and by parents of children attending district schools" (120). According to Ravitch (1974: 334), "all the major organizations of education professionals in the system attacked the report." The Combined Action Committee, a joint committee of the Council of Supervisory Associations of the Public Schools of New York City and the United Federation of Teachers, argued against the report, fearing that it established "'community control' as a new civil liberty" (Stone 1969: 353). Parent advocates and many community organizations saw it as offering local communities less autonomy and power than they desired.

In the midst of heated arguments between and among proponents and opponents of community control, the State Board of Regents cosponsored another decentralization bill with the New York State Commissioner of Education. The Regents' bill emerged as the preferred form of decentralization legislation even as other groups were promoting alternative visions of community control. But as the Regents' bill was gaining support, tensions erupted in Ocean Hill–Brownsville. These events caused the legislators to be more cautious in their attitudes toward decentralization (Ravitch 1974: 360). They passed a bill that added another year to the deliberation process. Among other features, this Marchi Bill "empowered the Board of Education to delegate to local school boards 'any or all of its functions, powers, obligations and duties' and recognized the three demonstration districts as equivalent to regular local school boards" (360). After heated discussion, legislators passed a law that emphasized administrative decentralization rather than community control (Zimet 1973).

Evaluation of the law reveals, at best, only modest achievements. Many critics, as well as allies, saw little improvement in the quality of education for the children in low-income and minority urban neighborhoods in New York City. Furthermore, resident participation in school board elections declined greatly from a disappointing high of 15 percent in the first elections in 1970.[7] Fewer eligible voters participated in the second elections in 1973. By 1986, only 7.5 percent of the eligible voters participated in the triennial school board elections. The composition of the school boards also became less representative of the local community over time. By 1988, "employees of the school system, including 27 members of the teachers' union, filled 70 of the 288 seats on local boards" (Buder 1988: E6). *New York Times* reporter Leonard Buder pointed out that "in one Brooklyn district where 85 percent of the pupils are black or Hispanic, eight of the nine school board members are white" (E6).

A number of factors contributed to the difficulties faced in implementing the decentralization plan in the low-income neighborhoods. Those living in poverty are hard pressed to find the time and resources (such as money for transportation and child care) required of community board members (Gittell 1970). Many do not have jobs that permit them to take time off, nor can working mothers afford to take time away from their families after work without alternative child care or household help (Zimet 1973: 34).[8] Time constraints and financial difficulties, coupled with organized campaigns by groups like the teachers' union and the Catholic church, placed low-income parents in a relatively weak position in vying for seats on the school boards and participating in school board politics over time. However, participation in the struggle for community control of schools did encourage many mothers to broaden their activism on behalf of their children and communities.

Limits and Unintended Consequences of the Community Control Frame

For some movement participants, "'community control' came to symbolize the struggle for democratic power just as 'no taxation without representation' symbolized a similar struggle by the founders of the American republic" (New York CLU 1969: 340). According to Frank Lutz and Carol Merz (1992: 33), "The *local* governance of public education has its roots in the basic idea of American democracy." Citing de Tocqueville, they argue that "school boards are the 'grassroots of American democracy'" where people gain "hands-on experience in the political process. . . . This is what grassroots democracy is about and why local school governance is democratic in the unique sense of American democracy" (Lutz and Merz 1992: 63). Whereas many of the women I interviewed drew on this discursive theme in their discussion of the community control of schools movement, they also emphasized that community control was necessary to ensure the survival of their communities and to promote the empowerment of community members. Their narratives contained a complex analysis of the intersection of race, class, and gender, as well as emphasizing the significance of participatory democracy for social justice. My materialist feminist analysis of this discourse reveals a "critical praxis" (Lemke 1995: 131) that stressed the dialectical relation between activism and democratic theory, between experience and reflection. The community workers did not separate their politics from their social locations and personal commitment to improve the conditions of neighborhood schools and other community-based institutions. Furthermore, they explained, their participation in the movement changed them and changed how they viewed the role of American institutions in poor urban neighborhoods.

Mario Fantini (1969: 335), who helped write the advisory panel's report on decentralization, observed that East Harlem parents "became more engaged in the education process" through the process of participation in the community control of school movement, and, as a result, the call for "'Quality education' replaced 'Black Power' as the slogan for the movement." His findings seem to support the fear expressed by some critics that decentralization and community control channel social protest into less radical challenges to the status quo. Seymour Martin Lipset (1970: 32) argues, for example, that "local control can be a very conservatizing influence," diverting attention from the issue of class inequality, which is at the core of the problems faced by inner-city residents. He contends that "to encourage those in the lower class to believe the problem is largely one of community control rather than of class structure must simply lead to a further sense of defeat, will reinforce the basic inferiority feelings which class-linked values impose on those at the bottom" (also see Piven and Cloward 1979). The women I interviewed also recognized the limits of community control for communities with few financial resources and for children whose families are grappling with a host of problems related to poverty, poor housing and health care, and drug addiction. Yet they remained convinced that those educators who do not live in the community "don't have a stake in making the school good." So while community control may not be the answer to the educational problems of poor neighborhoods, it is a necessary foundation for improving the quality of education for minority and low-income students.

Community control can contribute to empowerment of local residents as well as provide the grounds for local interests to wield power over others in the community. In fact, most participants in the debate, passionate supporters as well as ardent critics, treated the content of the "community" as a given. Few advocates or opponents discussed who comprised the "community" or pointed to the fluidity of its construction over time. Whereas there were heated deliberations on how to draw geographic boundaries to define community districts, how to achieve local control of schools, and what mechanisms would contribute to effective community representation on local school boards, none of the written accounts or oral narratives I gathered mentioned the instability of the construct "community." In contrast to this view of "community," a materialist feminist perspective emphasizes the diversity of perspectives and needs, as well as inequalities of power and resources within different locales. Relations of ruling are woven into local interactions in ways that privilege some residents, some members of the defined polity, over others. Inequalities among community members grow from age, race, gender, class, length of time in the locale, marital status, caretaking responsibilities, language facility, level of literacy, type of occupation, religion, cultural background, and immigrant status, among others features too numerous to list. Furthermore, many who might be physical and legal members of a certain locale may not feel part of the "community" in which they live and work and therefore will not make claims on the polity (Naples 1996). I turn now to the contemporary context in which the call for community control has been mobilized to reveal the complex relations of ruling embedded in the frame.

Community Control in Contemporary Perspective

Following the death of United Federation of Teachers President Albert Shanker, Nathan Glazer (1997: 25) revisited the community control of school movement in New York City in his *New Republic* column. He noted that the system of local community control initiated in 1968 ended just before Shanker died (also see Berger 1989). He points out that in contrast to the community control struggles of the late 1960s, the contemporary "attack on school bureaucracies comes from the right." Glazer sees many parallels between the community control of school movement and conservative support for charter schools. Charter schools are "funded by the government," "free of local bureaucratic controls," and can be run by private entrepreneurs as well as public and not-for-profit entities. Conservative policy analysts, as well as corporate interests, argue that charter schools will "improve the achievement of minority and low-income students" (25). In addition to a number of similarities in the discursive support for community control and for charter school movements, Glazer also sees a parallel in the nature of concerns raised against both policy initiatives, particularly whether local boards can "run schools independent of centralized bureaucracies" (25). Glazer's defense of charter schools includes many of the discursive themes evident in the earlier community control movement. He argues that charter schools will increase competition between schools by enhancing parental choice and, as a result will improve the quality of education; even if educational quality does not improve, he contends, charter schools can produce informed parents better prepared to advocate for their children's education.

The community control of schools movement did focus on who had the legitimate right to teach minority children (white teachers were often criticized for not understanding the needs of minority children), yet contemporary attacks on public schools by parents and religious groups go further. They also include protests against sex education; evolutionary biology curricula; readings such as *Of Mice and Men* by John Steinbeck, *Catcher in the Rye* by J. D. Salinger, and *The Color Purple* by Alice Walker; gay and lesbian student clubs, and even self-esteem programs (e.g., Jackson 1992; Katz 2000; Warren 1991).[9] Conservative parents active in these struggles complain that "schools are subverting the values that children learn at home" (Boyer 1984: 14). Resistance to textbooks said to promote "secular humanism" has received support from conservative judges like Alabama District Court Judge W. Brevard Hand, a Nixon appointee, who banned over forty textbooks from Alabama public schools in 1987 (Vobejda 1987). In explaining his decision, Hand said "that the books ignored the history of the Puritans and presented colonial missionaries as oppressors of native Americans" (A19). The "conflict over parents' rights to restrict what their children hear" includes parents' demands "to allow students to 'opt out' of being subjected to material that offends their parents' religious beliefs" (Thomas 1987: 16).

These challenges come from progressive as well as conservative corners. For example, Fred Hechinger (1986: C1,14) reports that an Arizona chapter of the NAACP "objected to Harper Lee's novel *To Kill a Mockingbird* because it contained 'derogatory terms for blacks.'" However, People for the American Way, a Washington-based group concerned with the separation of church and state among other constitutional issues, found that only "5% of the protests were launched by liberal groups seeking to ban material they deemed politically incorrect" (Warren 1991: A3). Many of the protests waged under the banner of local control are fueled by conservative organizations located far from the local scene, like Reverend Pat Robertson's National Legal Foundation, Beverly LaHaye's Concerned Women for America, National Association of Christian Educators, and Phyllis Schlafly's Eagle Forum (e.g., Hechinger 1986).

The religious right formulates the struggle in terms of parental control over their students' education, which parallels a central discursive theme of the 1960s debates over community control of schools. Representatives of two organizations promoting "censorship" of certain reading materials in California schools, for example, argue "that they are merely exercising their right to have a hand in what their children learn" (Warren 1991: A3). Not surprisingly, there is a fundamental difference in their interpretation of who has "superior vested interest in the future of the children" (A30). The issues in the forefront of these battles include attacks against gays and lesbians, ethnic diversity, and sexual activity. When students in an Orange County school started a Gay-Straight Club in 1999, the school district voted to prohibit all student clubs rather than allow this club to continue. Parents and other "anti-gay protesters . . . traveled from Kansas to picket the school" (Kate 2000: B12). In settling a federal lawsuit initiated by students and parents who supported the club, school district trustees voted to allow the club to meet on school grounds but ruled that "no student clubs may use meetings to talk about sexual activity, defined as 'explicit discussion of sex acts or sexual organs'" (ibid.).

Conservative parents and religious groups wage war against any curriculum that they believe "promotes homosexuality and teen-age sexual activity" (Trombley 1992: A3). Their emphasis on the "family ethic" (Abramovitz 1988) reveals the invisible heteronormative dimensions of "community control" that did not find direct expression in the 1960s. At that time, given the historical and political context, race was in the forefront of the discursive staging for the community control of schools movement. The dimensions of class and gender were close to the surface and were revealed from the standpoint of women who were active in the movement. However, as activists mobilized the frame in different contexts and under different historical conditions, the taken-for-granted heteronormativity of the "community" meant that the community control frame could be used for the social regulation of individuals and groups who do not fit into the normative "American" family.

Bitter fights have erupted across the country against course materials that include discussion of alternative family forms and gay and lesbian issues, like the "Rainbow Curriculum" designed for New York City public schools. Not surprisingly, the challengers do not always represent "community" concerns. For example, in 1997 Seattle Councilwoman Tina Podlodowski and her lesbian partner Chelle Mileur, a vice president for the gay and lesbian Internet service PlanetOut, gave $6,000 to support the Seattle Public Schools' purchase of children's books about gay families (*New York Times* 1997: N20). A *New York Times* article noted that "purchases were approved by most city schools through committees that included parents" (N20). In this case, the majority of parents did not oppose the purchase of such books as *Heather Has Two Mommies* and *Daddy's Roommate*. Instead, resistance came from organized conservative and religious groups. The instability of the term "community" allows diverse group of individuals to claim that they are speaking on behalf of the community.

Ironically, in discussing her objection to Seattle's public schools' decision to purchase the books, Linda Jordan, president of Parents and Teachers for Responsible Schools, stated that her group was preparing a "parental-rights form" as part of a campaign to mobilize parents against the school system. She feared that "the school district was not going to respect the diversity within their district and was not going to let parents be the moral authority" (*New York Times* 1997: N20). This notion of diversity is a far cry from that described by the Puerto Rican and African American parents who felt that the white-dominated school system did not understand and respond to their children's differential needs. The discourse of community control is, in many ways, "anti-diversity," even as it appropriates the discourse of diversity.

Despite the numerous criticisms leveled against decentralization, decentralized institutional strategies did open up avenues of participation for the community workers I interviewed that increased their political efficacy, as well as their politicization, at least in the short run. Concern for their children's education and the activism they undertook on their children's behalf led them into other avenues of protest and enhanced their understanding of how relations of domination circumscribed the lives of the poor. For a number of years, parents were successful in gaining some control of the school system, in hiring African American and bilingual teachers, and in establishing local school boards that were, at one point in time, community-led and community-controlled. However, as with other community-based struggles to gain control of local institutions, changes within the wider political economy and backlash from powerful interest groups quickly coopted these efforts. As I note elsewhere, "demands for decentralization in the name of democracy and to move social services closer to local communities opened spaces for 'off loading' of the fiscal problems of the other levels of government. This 'off loading' process also entails shifting the provision of services like child care and health from state-run to private, for-profit institutions" (Naples 1998c: 57). Supporters of state-sponsored educational vouchers justify their support for this strategy through a rhetoric of parental choice, an individualistic variant of community control.

We have come to an interesting historical moment when the interests of many minority parents and conservative groups are converging to support vouchers as a way to provide "parental choice" and to ensure a better education for minority children. First school integration and then "community control" of public schools failed to improve the quality of education offered to low-income students of color. Now, frustrated minority parents are joining conservative groups in advocating a system of charter schools and educational vouchers that would enable them to use state money for different educational options. These options include the Milwaukee Parental Choice Program, featured on CNN's *Democracy in America*, which was first funded by the state of Wisconsin in 1990 and expanded in 1995 to include religious schools among the educational choices. The Wisconsin Supreme Court upheld the state's decision to include religious schools in the program in 1998. As of fall 2000, sixty-three of the ninety-one schools in Milwaukee that participate in the choice program are religious schools, most of which are Catholic (CNN 2000).

Annette Williams, the African American state legislator who promoted this program, saw it as a way to give low-income parents access to private schools that offered a better education than the Milwaukee public schools. She argued that "if the state was going to pay for the miseducation of children in the public schools, surely they would not object to paying a small portion to allow parents then to pick a school outside of the public schools" (CNN 2000). Ten years later, she is involved in a battle to restrict the program to the low-income constituency for which it was designed. Drawing on the democratic frame of "freedom of choice," parents and conservative groups insist that the program should be expanded so that all parents can take advantage of it regardless of income. In explaining his support for educational vouchers, Clint Bolick, legislative director for the Institute of Justice, writes: "The same Constitution that guarantees an equal educational opportunity to every child— black, white, rich or poor—will not be subverted to deny children that very opportunity" (CNN 2000).

In producing specific frames, social movement actors draw on already existing popular constructions of social justice, democracy, or other discursive formulations that will have resonance for potential constituents (also see Tarrow 1992). In this way, frames like community control of schools are infused with "a repertoire of interpretations" (Mooney and Hunt 1994) that leave open the possibility that actors with diverse political views can mobilize the frame for different goals within particular relations of ruling. Furthermore, as frames are incorporated into practice, they "descend to a lesser level of generality" (Fraser 1989: 164), where the contradictions embedded in the frame become more visible and we can see the extent to which certain interpretations "are skewed in favor of the self-interpretations and interests of dominant social groups" (ibid.: 154; also see Naples 1997b).

Conclusion

I have emphasized throughout this analysis that discourse is not the property of individual actors or social movement organizations; it is "a practice, it is structured, and it has real effects" (Ferguson 1994: 18; also see Loseke 1992). The materialist feminist approach situates the construction and interpretation of frames within the broader discursive and institutional context of mobilization and attends to relations of ruling and structural inequalities within the framing process. Furthermore, a materialist feminist analysis of discourse focuses on historical and structural patterns of domination and resistance to render visible unspoken or unrepresented features of everyday life in discursive frames.

Discourse has material consequences for social movement actors. For movement frames to gain wide acceptance, they need to resonate with prevailing cultural constructions. Because master frames frequently draw on recognizable symbols and values to mobilize and effect social change, they can be incorporated into the wider political environment in ways that their originators might not have intended. A materialist feminist analysis explores the processes by which movement organizations and movement actors are constrained in constructing their frames and political identities and suggests that, even when movements do successfully produce oppositional frames, other groups can take up these frames and use them for different ends. Furthermore, social relations within movement organizations, and the structure and material practices of the institutions and communities in which these organizations are embedded, shape how movement frames are produced, circulated, and taken up by potential allies as well as opponents.

The movement for community control of schools illustrates the structural and material social relations that infuse the discursive fields that shape the framing process. Movement frames both contest and reinforce relations of ruling. The community control of schools frame was produced in the context of a heightened awareness of racial inequality, as well as organized resistance to integration. It was mobilized within an environment that privileged administrative decentralization over political decentralization and therefore contributed to deradicalization of the movement for local control. Different political and social actors brought contrasting visions of community control into their negotiations, and those who held greater power in the process of implementation successfully gained control over the interpretation of the frame and the decentralization plan. A materialist feminist approach offers a powerful tool for social movement research, as well as critical praxis, because it offers an epistemology for examining how race, class, gender, and other dimensions of social inequalities are inevitably woven into even the most radical political projects. With this heightened analytic sensitivity to the dynamics of power within social movement organizations and across different arenas of social activism, movement actors may become more effective in resisting the depoliticization and co-optation of movement frames.

NOTES

My thanks to Mary Bernstein and Val Jenness for their invaluable comments on earlier drafts and to David Meyer and Nancy Whittier for their editorial suggestions.

   1. My materialist feminist use of the term "discourse" contrasts with David Snow and Robert Benford's (1992: 136) conceptualization of "collective action frames," "framing," and "master frames" as follows: (1) "Collective action frames" refer to how social movement organizations produce and maintain meaning "for constituents, antagonists, and bystanders or observers." In contrast, my case study explores how "discursive frames" limit what can be discussed or heard in a political context and are not tied necessarily to particular organizations. (2) Snow and Benford view the process of "framing" as "an active, process-derived phenomenon that implies agency and contention at the level of reality construction." In my understanding, framing or the conscious use of certain discursive frames is a process bounded by the discursive field itself. (3) Snow and Benford view "master frames" as successful to the extent they mobilize constituents to engage in collective action. In my analysis, framing necessarily delimits action. One point of connection with my understanding of discursive frames relates to the issue of resonance; namely, certain statements within particular discursive frames achieve status and authority when tied to larger discourses that resonate with prevailing cultural constructions (Naples 1997a: 908).

   2. This forms part of a larger study of New York City and Philadelphia community workers in the War on Poverty (see Naples 1998a). For this chapter, I focus on a subsample of the women interviewed who lived in New York City and were active in the community control of schools movement. This sample includes sixteen women who were living in the low-income communities that were the target of the War on Poverty when they were hired by community action agencies and eleven who were not residing in these communities and consequently are defined as "nonresident" community workers. These communi-

ties include the Lower East Side of Manhattan, Harlem, the South Bronx, and Bedford-Stuyvesant.

3. In the mid-1960s, 25 percent of African Americans in urban areas lived in poverty, while only 10 percent of urban white residents lived at or below poverty. By the early 1970s, almost 50 percent of the parents of public school children in the ten major U.S. cities were living in poverty (Tyack 1974: 278). Not surprisingly, a disproportionate number of these parents were African American and Latino.

4. Michael Harrington also came out against community control in the context of the 1968 Ocean Hill–Brownsville struggle between the teachers' union and the local community leaders. Cronin reports that Harrington viewed this struggle "not a simple conflict of right and wrong, but an antagonism of two rights . . . effective community involvement in the educational process" and "academic freedom and due process when a professional is dismissed" (Cronin 1973: 193).

5. This discussion also appears in Naples 1998a: 133–34.

6. The Ford Foundation subsequently agreed to fund three experimental community control projects. The Board of Education, in consultation with the teachers' union, announced that the three projects would include East Harlem's IS 201 district, Ocean Hill–Brownsville district in Brooklyn, and the Two Bridges district in the Lower East Side of Manhattan.

7. This corresponds to the low voter turnout for the community action programs (Ornstein 1974; Yates 1973).

8. Discussions about financial support for community school board members led to compensation for members that did not take effect until July 1972. Not surprisingly, the law provided "compensation for the members of the central Board of Education, even though no such recommendation had been made" (Zimet 1973: 153).

9. The National Council of Teachers of English's Committee Against Censorship surveyed schools in 1977 and found that 34 percent "that responded to its questions had received challenges to materials in their libraries; by 1982, the figure had risen to 56 percent" (Hechinger 1986).

14

From the "Beloved Community" to "Family Values": Religious Language, Symbolic Repertoires, and Democratic Culture

RHYS H. WILLIAMS

One of Karl Marx's most frequently quoted observations is that "men make their own history, but they do not make it just as they please; they do not make it under circumstances chosen by themselves, but under circumstances directly found, given and transmitted from the past" (in Tucker 1978: 595). Presumably this calls attention to Marx's careful balancing of the fact that society is created by humans and through active human agency, yet any given set of historical actors is constrained powerfully by social settings that they did not create and cannot control completely.

As it is with history, so it is with "meaning." People construct the social world symbolically, but they do not do it de novo. Rather, they use symbolic tools handed down to them from previous generations—the "symbolic repertoire"—and these are bounded, at least to some extent, by the conventions established within a culture. Only by operating within boundaries recognizable to people in the extant culture can humans communicate and create meanings—and this is true even when those meanings are intended to foster innovation, creativity, or social change.

The relevance of this observation to a volume on social movements should be clear. An irony of social movements is that to achieve their aims of social change, movements *must* produce rhetorical packages that explain their claims within extant, culturally legitimate boundaries. I argue that this ironic fact of social movement rhetoric helps explain why so many social change movements in American political history have been based in religious communities or have used religious symbols and rhetoric prominently in their ideology, or both. Religion has offered movements of the Left and Right both the *organizational* and *cultural* resources that facilitate mobilization and help achieve at least some success (see Smith 1996; Williams 1994). Here, I focus on religion as a cultural resource for social movement ideology.

To ground my theoretical considerations in real-world rhetoric, I will draw on the claims made by two recent American sociopolitical movements, the 1960s civil rights movement and the 1980s New Right. Each movement was nurtured in and enormously influenced by religious organizations. Churches, the central organizational points for gathering movement members, provided meeting space, communication networks, and sometimes even direct financial support. Morris (1984), Robnett (1997), and others have documented this for the civil rights movement, whereas Wilcox (1992) and Rozell and Wilcox (1995) show this dynamic in the Christian Right.

These two movements also provide excellent examples of how religious language can serve as movement ideology, even in a nation that celebrates its institutional "separation of church and state" (see Williams and Demerath 1991). Martin Luther King Jr. offered a religious vision for a nonracist American society, a "beloved community," embracing and inclusive, reconciling former antagonists. The New Christian Right, through such visible leaders as Jerry Falwell, James Dobson, and Pat Robertson, has crystallized much social discontent by calling for a return to "family values," conceptualized as both a particular family structure and set of normative values.

Each of these symbols, the "beloved community" and "family values," has served as classic movement ideology. They have helped mobilize adherents and define the public debate about important social issues. Yet the content of the frames is different: one was dedicated to opening the cultural space for more widespread participation in society; the other was meant to close interpretive space by setting some social options outside the pale of legitimate values. These functions, too, are dimensions of the religious culture from which the rhetoric was drawn. That is, the opening and closing functions were part of the larger sets of meaning from which the movement ideologies emerged, and thus were partially "built in" to the claims themselves because they were part of the symbolic repertoire; those functions were not just a matter of the *intentions* of, or the *instrumental* use by, the activists themselves.

The cultural context from which these two movement ideologies were drawn can be described as a particularly American form of Protestantism. This is not to say that members of other religious communities were not present in the movements. Both Catholics and Jews played significant roles in the civil rights movement, and Orthodox Jews and conservative Catholics have been important supporters of parts of the "family values" agenda. However, the *public rhetoric* that formed the backbone of the movements' claims—the language with which movement leaders addressed the public sphere—has been drawn from the symbolic repertoire of American Protestantism. I make this claim in part out of conviction that Protestantism forms the basis for our nation's political culture (Williams 1999b). But I also intend to demonstrate that particular features of American Protestantism provide both of the seemingly contradictory readings that inform these movement discourses. That is, elements of the cultural context of American Protestant religion lend themselves both to opening and closing the public sphere.

Thus, thinking about religious language as social movement rhetoric serves two purposes here. First, it illuminates some classic theoretical dilemmas in the study of social movement culture; second, it serves as an example for a general claim as to how cultural contexts affect social movements. This chapter will connect the internal dynamics of movement framing with the external context of the public culture from which the rhetoric was drawn. I will consider religious language itself as a particular form of social movement ideology and also examine its contribution to the democratic culture of the contemporary public sphere.

Religion as Social Movement Language

There has been an explosion of scholarly literature attempting to elicidate the cultural and symbolic dimensions of social movements. The most frequent concepts used in this literature are "frames" and "framing" (see reviews and critiques in Benford 1997; Benford and Snow 2000; Jasper 1997; Williams and Benford 2000). From this literature a consensus on the functional character of collective action frames has emerged. For example, Snow and Benford (1988, 1992) note that effective social movement frames must provide "diagnostic," "prognostic," and "motivational" functions. That is, frames must tell movement participants what is wrong, what can be done to fix it, and why they should be involved. Similarly, Gamson (1992b) identifies three necessary components for a collective action frame: injustice, agency, and identity. People must have a sense of an unjust situation that must be corrected, a sense that they can have an effect in changing it, and an identification of who is responsible for the problem (an "us" and a "them").

Reviews of the framing literature make two common critiques: first, that movement elites' focus on framing shows a cognitive bias in understanding activism; and second, that the focus on activists' interpretive work in constructing frames slights the extent to which framing is culturally constrained (see Williams and Kubal 1999). Attention to religion as a social movement language can address these criticisms.

Cognitive Bias.   Several critics have noted (Benford 1997; Jasper 1997; Polletta 1998b) that in practice scholars have treated framing as a primarily cognitive and strategic challenge for activists. These arguments need not be repeated here. However, the core concepts in the framing idiom do not require that cognitive bias, and empirical attention to religion as a social movement discourse, reveals all the components necessary for social movement symbolization (see Hart 1996). Religion joins the cognitive, affective, and moral dimensions of movement action. It contains wholistic and often highly articulated belief systems, usually tied to history and traditions. It can give a fairly complete "explanation" as to why the world is the way it is and how it became that way. And this framework provides a moral universe in which concepts such as "injustice" have meaning. Finally, because religious organizations are intensely social settings, religion can integrate personal and social identity and provide the networks and rationale for action. Studying religion as an empirical case is a healthy antidote for overly cognitive approaches to movement culture and mobilization.

The Cultural Context.   The study of collective action frames has often ignored the relationship between those frames that social movements actually use and the larger cultural themes, worldviews, and ideologies from which they are drawn. Frames must come from somewhere; they cannot be conjured from whole cloth and still be convincing. Focusing on cultural innovation and actor agency in movement and activist rhetoric (as many interactionist accounts of framing do) runs the risk of ignoring the constraining dimensions of tradition and the structure of the extant culture. A social movement can do only so much to be innovative; it must try to articulate change from within a received set of categories and understandings. On the other hand, exploring the stability and structuring aspects of cultural traditions, codes, repertoires, and scripts (as structuralist approaches to culture often do) must confront the reality of social change—and the fact that movements' innovative agency is responsible for much of that change.

In large part, the dilemma for movements is an issue of intelligibility. At the least, movement claims must make sense to potential recruits, bystander publics, and target elites. But beyond this, if claims are to spark action, they must "resonate" with audiences (Snow and Benford 1988, 1992; Williams and Kubal 1999). Resonance implies alignment between movement claims and what audiences already know, feel, or have experienced. So movement ideology must cover familiar ground, even as it offers self-conscious innovations. Pulling the dual concerns of innovation and intelligibility into focus calls for the exploration of the larger culture from which collective action frames are drawn and back into which collective action frames are launched, once issues become public concerns.

The dilemma confronting movement symbolizations—to offer an innovative message within a legitimate cultural repertoire—shows why religion serves so effectively in movement cultures. The ultimate effectiveness of religion as a social movement force, as opposed to reliance on secular bases of organization and rhetoric, varies by historical circumstances and regional and social contexts. Not all successful movements in American history have been religiously based; indeed, movements such as those for gay and lesbian liberation, or aspects of the labor movement, have had to distance themselves from organized religion. Nonetheless, the sheer variety of religiously based movements in America clearly indicates its importance. Religion, particularly Protestantism in American society, has deep social legitimacy and cultural resonance. Beyond its institutional location and ubiquity, and beyond the fact that many Americans are personally religious, I argue that religion has a cultural resonance in U.S. society. It is deeply ingrained in our national stories and myths and helps form the cultural models with which we think about our national life.

Religion and Democratic Culture

Particularly significant to my argument here is that religion can be a progressive or conservative force, opening or closing public space. This reflects a crucial aspect of religious language in American culture: it is *democratically available*. Anyone may use religious language to frame diagnosis of societal problems and rely on its motivational capacities. As important, of course, is religion's explicit moral universe, which does not necessarily need to be invoked directly to produce an injustice frame based in that moral framework. But the United States has a religious culture that emphasizes the immanent and the experiential, thus opening religion well beyond clerical hierarchies and the theologically trained. Clergy do still enjoy a presumptive legitimacy that comes from their institutional location, but many others use religious language to express programs for or against social change.

Because religious language is both legitimate and democratically available, almost any group, especially those mobilized at the grassroots, can use religious symbols, metaphors, and authority to legitimate its public claims. A second characteristic of religious language is that religion, almost by its nature, does not take the world as it is as the ultimate value. Although religion as a social institution has often played an important role in reinforcing the status quo, religion as a rhetorical system includes critique as a constitutive component. This critique can be devastatingly effective because of its position as a morally legitimate, transcendently authoritative, but still democratically available discourse. By rooting ultimate authority in the transcendent, religion can make any worldly system accountable to a standard of judgment that lies outside that system itself. This can put a brake on any political ambition, including, ironically, that of religiously inspired political movements (Ackerman 1985). Religion can make all forms of established authority suspect, as long as there are grounds for separating that authority from its institutional moorings. A language available to many different people, justified on an experience set specifically outside the routine, thus becomes a wide-ranging, if sometimes undisciplined, tool for social change.

Thus, religion's contribution to democratic culture goes beyond Tocqueville's voluntary associations and the practical training they provide in self-government or the more current versions of Tocqueville's argument that focus on "social capital." I do not argue with those formulations. Rather, I claim that an element of potential democratic culture also inheres within the very nature of religious language and its near ubiquity as a symbolic repertoire.

Conversely, not all religious language is used to open a cultural or political system to more participation or alternative social arrangements. Religion often functions as an institutional and cultural prop for the status quo. Two different processes produce this outcome. First is a straightforward legitimation, in which the content of the religious message claims a direct connection between God's will and a particular political arrangement. In the United States this claim has usually taken the form of a "priestly" version of a civil religion, in which the nation is portrayed as uniquely blessed by God. Sometimes this is interpreted in direct political terms, as in the nineteenth century's "manifest destiny" concept, or Jerry Falwell's contention that American political institutions are "ordained by God" and described in the Bible (e.g., Falwell 1984: 121–22). But the less direct use of civil religion is the reliance on what Geertz (1973) calls the "borrowed authority" between the religious worldview and earthly social arrangements. What is real and manifest in this world is seen as verifying what is believed to be real in the unseen transcendent realm; and the transcendent cosmos provides moral justification for the tangible products of extant society. So both the sacred cosmos and the world as it is borrow legitimating authority from each other.

A second and subtler way in which religion supports the societal status quo is the extent to which religion facilitates political quiescence. Rather than legitimate extant political arrangements directly, religion offers succor to the dispossessed and assures them of otherworldly rewards, the ephemeral nature of worldly status, and the intractability of human injustice. This is Marx's "opiate of the masses"; it is not an opiate *for* the masses, produced and distributed by a hegemonic elite to keep lower classes pacified. Rather, religion is produced by the suffering of humans who seek relief; like opium, it offers real relief even if it is addictive and leaves societal conditions unchanged.

Ultimately, of course, by disconnecting religious legitimacy from direct support of any regime, political quiescence effectively reinforces the status quo. Even among those people who recognize the distance between the world that is and the world that "ought" to be, religion's transcendent reward system and worldly fatalism induce political passivity.

I turn now to the religious language used by the 1960s civil rights movement and the 1980s Christian Right. Through these examples, I highlight how religion has served as social movement ideology and discuss the connections between the legitimacy of the movements' ideology and themes in the larger context of American political and religious culture. Thus, I argue, religion holds a particular capacity to offer American social movements a legitimate and change-oriented language.

Religious Rhetoric in Two Movements

This chapter's title refers to two well-known sound bites from recent American politics. The "beloved community" was an image with which Martin Luther King Jr. led the civil rights movement and fought legal segregation and informal prejudice. It was a vision of the good society that the United States could become but, not surprisingly, one for which few details were presented or defended. Rather, it appeared as a lofty, moral goal—it had content, but that content was only hinted at. Nonetheless, the term "beloved community" became a well-known condensed symbol of the hopes of the civil rights movement in the 1960s.

"Family values" has been the more recent rallying cry for the Christian Right. With it, conservative religious activists and politicians have criticized post-60s American society as morally lax and ruinously out of control. The term has been particularly directed as a counterclaim toward those social movements that aim to reconfigure sex, gender, and family structure. The term originated specifically with conservative Protestant activists, but it has spread more widely among conservative political constituencies and now represents a number of different issues.

True, these two movements differ by more than just rhetoric. They arose during different historical and social contexts, and though they drew on a similar religious culture (Protestant Christianity), the core constituencies of the two movements derived from different traditions within that culture. The civil rights movement emerged to call for the racial opening of American society during a period of expanding economic opportunity when "mainline" Protestantism was itself relaxing some traditional social constraints. In contrast, the New Christian Right arose as economic opportunities were contracting, after a period of social experimentation. Further, the movement was a product of the increasing public visibility and national expansion of Southern white evangelical versions of Protestantism. Nonetheless, these historical contexts did not "determine" the shapes the movements assumed. The social and cultural contexts provided material with which movement actors worked—shaping the often pliable messages of Protestant Christianity to their own purposes. At the same time, the messages that movement leaders could craft were constrained and channeled by existing symbolic repertoires.

I am analyzing public social movement rhetoric, not making claims about the values and beliefs of rank-and-file members. Every movement must go through a translation process, in which the "formal ideology" of movement leaders becomes an "operative ideology" (Williams and Blackburn 1996) by particular people in particular circumstances; however, social movements in contemporary politics must engage the public sphere, usually through mass media. They need to produce a public discourse that defines their purposes in generally legitimate language. Thus, I draw on the publicly available texts produced by two sets of movement leaders. I make no claim as to how accurately this public language reflects social "reality."

Rather, I am interested in how each movement's public language connects to larger themes in American political and religious culture. Both the movement rhetoric and the larger cultural repertoire contain visions of the "good society" (Williams 1995, 1999b). Thus, I examine one particular public symbol that appears often in the discourse of each movement's leaders and show its connections to themes already extant in American religious culture.

Beloved Community

Martin Luther King Jr.'s rhetoric of integration and the "beloved community" was well positioned within the culture of American Christianity. King imagined an American society where a harmony of vision could produce both justice and peaceful coexistence among races. This vision would transcend the current worldly divisions of a racist society and thereby lead simultaneously to a harmonious future and restore the nation to the glory of its founding principles. The forward-looking aspects of King's rhetoric were most gloriously apparent in his "I have a dream" speech in Washington, D.C., in 1963:

> I have a dream that one day the state of Alabama, whose governor's lips are dripping with the words of interposition and nullification, will be transformed into a situation where little black boys and black girls will join hands with little white boys and white girls and walk together as sisters and brothers. I have a dream that one day every valley shall be exalted, every hill and mountain shall be made low, the rough places will be made plains, and the crooked places will be

made straight, and the glory of the Lord shall be revealed and all flesh shall see it together. . . .

We will be able to speed up that day when all of God's children, black men and white men, Jews and Gentiles, Protestants and Catholics, will be able to join together and sing in the words of the old Negro spiritual "Free at last, free at last, thank God Almighty, we are free at last!" (Quoted in Oates 1982: 255)

Though this imagery has become synonymous with a liberal integrationist position on race relations, it strikes me as much more subtle than that. It is a critique of existing societal arrangements and even of a particular political figure, all the while presenting an image of the good society and—with the clear reference to King's Ghandi-inspired nonviolence—how to get there. Existing social arrangements are boundaries between people that appear to be as natural as mountains and valleys. But they need not be; they are burdens to God's people and barriers to the full revelation of divine love—for individuals and for the nation as a whole.

However, this religious vision was not going to appear magically through the direct intervention of a divine hand or through platitudes about love and togetherness. It was the product of social struggle, a struggle that may divide the haters from the healers in the short term while it held the promise of long-term reconciliation:

> With this faith we will be able to transform the jangling discords of our nation into a beautiful symphony of brotherhood. With this faith we will be able to work together, pray together, struggle together, go to jail together, stand up for freedom together. . . . This will be the day when all of God's children will be able to sing with new meaning "My country 'tis of thee, sweet land of liberty." (Quoted in Oates 1982: 254)

> We are gravely mistaken if we think that religion protects us from the pain and agony of mortal existence. . . . I can hear God saying that it's time to rise up now and make it clear that the evils of the universe must be removed. (Quoted in Branch 1988: 696)

> Now we say in this nonviolent movement that you've got to love this white man. And God knows he needs our love. . . . And let me say to you that I'm not talking about emotional bosh when I talk about love. (Quoted in Branch 1988: 773)

> You love those that you don't like. You love those whose ways are distasteful to you. You love every man because God loves him. (Quoted in Branch 1988: 724)

Like much social movement language, King's words here do not portray his group's claims as narrow self-interest. He was making moral claims on the American body politic—citing both the injustice and the remedy for that injustice. But, beyond the moral tone, King was not presenting the civil rights movement's goals and vision as benefiting only black Americans. While he was explicit about recognizing and institutionalizing the rights of African Americans, his grounds were seldom group interest. His grounds were the common good of the nation and the eventual reconciling of the oppressor with the oppressed.

> One aspect of the civil-rights struggle that receives little attention is the contribution it makes to the whole society. The Negro in winning rights for himself produces substantial benefits for the nation . . . the revolution for human rights is opening up unhealthy areas in American life and permitting a new wholesome healing to take place. Eventually the civil-rights movement will have contributed infinitely more to the nation than the eradication of racial injustice. It will have enlarged the concept of brotherhood to a vision of total interrelatedness. On that day, Canon John Donne's doctrine, "no man is an islande," will find its truest application in the United States. (King 1964: 151–52)

> [The movement's struggles have enabled the African American] to transmute hatred into constructive energy, to seek not only to free himself but to free his oppressor from his sins. This transformation, in turn, had the marvelous effect of changing the face of the enemy. (King 1964: 38)

Thus, there was a universal call, and a universal appeal, in King's understanding of the movement's ultimate purposes. What was true and just was universally applicable and a standard for all society. Further, it included all people, as when King noted, "A nonviolent army has a magnificent universal quality" (King 1964: 38), and then described how the movement reached across age, physical ability, caste, social rank, and, above all, race. Human boundaries, either social or political, are not to stand against universal standards of justice and reconciliation—and each of those concepts means little without the other. King justified his work across the South in his famous "Letter from a Birmingham Jail":

> I am in Birmingham because injustice is here. Just as prophets of the eighth century B.C. left their villages and carried their "thus saith the Lord" far beyond the boundaries of their towns . . . and Apostle Paul

left his village . . . so I am compelled to carry the gospel of freedom beyond my own home town. Moreover, I am cognizant of the interrelatedness of communities and states. . . . Injustice anywhere is a threat to justice everywhere. We are caught in an inescapable network of mutuality, tied in a single garment of destiny. . . . Anyone who lives inside the United States can never be considered an outsider anywhere within its bounds. (King 1964: 77)

This vision of a beloved community—a universal moral community—was legitimated with King's construction of the American nation's founding ideals. He used such key value words as "freedom," "liberty," and "equality"; affirmed their civil religious pedigree while interpreting them prophetically (Williams and Alexander 1994); and called for the nation to move forward to recapture a golden (if mythical) past promise: "We will win our freedom because the *sacred heritage* of our nation and the eternal will of God are embodied in our echoing demands" (quoted in Branch 1988: 743; emphasis added).

In this way, King called upon both the Christian identity and the patriotism of black and white Americans. The concept of America as a nation both uniquely chosen (America as a "New Jerusalem") and also a universal example to other nations ("a light unto the world") fits neatly into this scheme. This distinctly American religious rhetoric it called upon Christian universalism, as well as on the national mythology of opportunity and a limitless future. After the march on Washington, James Baldwin remarked: "That day, for a moment, it almost seemed that we stood on a height and could see our inheritance; perhaps we could make the kingdom real, perhaps the beloved community would not forever remain that dream one dreamed in agony" (quoted in Oates 1982: 255).

King was both an innovative and resonant speaker. He could use core American symbols to appeal for a change in the condition of a previously disenfranchised population. In addition, he tied domestic concerns to international events and connected social and political change with economic issues. But, clearly, much of the resonance in both King's language and in its delivery was based in its firm roots in American Judeo-Christian content and forms. His call for a universal moral community spoke to a deep theme in our religious culture and helped the civil rights movement's message reach a wide set of constituencies.

Family Values

By now the term "family values" has become a well-understood symbol for a collection of political issues centering on sex, gender, and family relationships. Since the New Christian Right appeared in the late 1970s behind such spokesmen as Jerry Falwell, James Dobson, Tim and Beverly LaHaye, and Pat Robertson, family values issues have been a mainstay of conservative politics and attempts to mobilize often politically passive evangelical Protestants (and some Catholics and Orthodox Jews). The collection of issues that fall under the family values rubric usually includes gay marriage, out-of-wedlock sex and procreation, parental rights, and abortion. In the early 1970s, activists often mentioned defeating the Equal Rights Amendment and turning back the "feminist" challenge to the "traditional" family structure of a conjugal relationship with a working father and homemaking mother. By the 1980s, the "gay agenda" also assumed the position of primary foil. Jerry Falwell said, "It is now time to take a stand on certain moral issues, and we can only stand if we have leaders. We must stand against the Equal Rights Amendment, the feminist revolution and the homosexual revolution" (1984: 125). And Frances Schaeffer wrote, "[We] have gradually become disturbed over permissiveness, pornography, the public schools, the breakdown of the family, and finally abortion" (1984: 127).

These remarks will not surprise anyone who has followed contemporary politics. And many analysts have connected this particular list of issues to Victorian culture and its inhibitions about sex. Family values rhetoric is easily portrayed as a repressive, patriarchal reaction to a society slipping away from the cultural dominance of a specific social and religious group. These issues, with abortion at center stage, could represent what Gusfield (1986) called "symbolic politics"—a symbolic attempt by a group to control the public sphere, even as its material and political fortunes fade.

My claim here is slightly different. The family values agenda, and the vehemence with which it is embraced by those mobilized by the Christian Right, has an ideological coherence beyond the substantive issue of sex. Rather, there is an underlying concern with boundaries, their clarity, and the structure of meaning they provide for movement adherents as a way of interpreting society generally. Consider the following claims from Jerry Falwell:

> God Almighty created men and women biologically different and
> with differing needs and roles. . . . [The family is] the marriage of
> one man and one woman together for a lifetime with their biological
> or adopted children . . . in families and in nations where the Bible is
> believed and practiced . . . women receive more than equal
> rights. . . . God's plan is for men to be manly and spiritual in all
> areas of Christian leadership. . . . Women are to be feminine and to
> manifest the ornament of a meek and quiet spirit. . . . In the Chris-
> tian home the woman is to be submissive. (Quoted in Kater 1982:
> 82–84)

The core of this rhetorical claim is the danger of blurring what were intended to be clear boundaries. Further, these boundaries, and the societal arrangements they structure, are perceived as God-given and absolute. When Pat Robertson was making the announcement that he would seek the presidency in 1988, he stated: "Instead of absolutes, our youth have been given situational ethics and the life-centered curriculum. Instead of a clear knowledge of right and wrong, they have been told 'if it feels good do it.' Instead of self-restraint they are often taught self-gratification and hedonism" (quoted in Hertzke 1993: 86).

The importance of maintaining moral boundaries provides the resonance of this movement language with a major theme in American religious culture. It is not just that the feminist and gay movements want to open public and private space to disenfranchised and often despised populations. Their demands seem to impinge on a created order that is moral, transcendently justified, and supposedly immutable. This aspect of God's creation is the foundation of social order and that order's alignment with a sacred cosmos. The order cannot be trifled with without risking an entire social collapse: "Male leadership in our families is affecting male leadership in our churches, and it is affecting male leadership in our society" (Falwell 1984: 123). Furthermore, "much of the conflict in the modern family is caused either by misunderstanding of or by the refusal to accept the role each member was designed by God to fulfill" (LaHaye 1982: 210).

According to this understanding, the divinely ordained order is structured into recognizable roles with clear boundaries. These boundaries, and the clear and complementary roles they protect, must not be tampered with, lest social order and moral health disintegrate. Rosaline Bush of Concerned Women of America explained: "At Creation, God designed the family as the foundation of civilization. And for those who followed His directions, He provided a guarantee against structural damage and collapse" (quoted in Diamond 1999: 126).

In a similar manner, Charles Colson refers to the "traditional" family as the "fundamental social institution," and an "objective moral order." To alter it—for example, by legitimating gay marriage—"assumes that the universe is malleable and that individuals create their own truths, their own values. . . . Family structure is as pliable as Play-Doh, and virtually any form is acceptable" (Colson 1996: 104).

Social arrangements predicated on a lack of distinction and difference are a social problem, because they are a moral problem; the symbolic boundaries, especially regarding gender and the family, are morally necessary. James Dobson, the founder of Focus on the Family, argues:

> Taking that concept to its illogical conclusion, the radicals want to dissolve the traditional roles of mothers and fathers. They also hope

to eliminate such terms as *wife, husband, son, daughter, sister, brother . . . masculine* and *feminine*. These references to sexual identity are being replaced with gender-neutral terms, such as *parent, spouse, child* and *sibling*. (Quoted in Diamond 1999: 126)

Further, Dobson notes, "The heated dispute over values . . . is simply a continuation of the age-old struggle between the principles of righteousness and the kingdom of darkness" (Dobson 1995: 28). This Manichean rhetoric, where one side represents total good versus another of pure evil, emphasizes the identification and preservation of the boundaries between the sides. And, clearly, those falling "beyond the pale," on the side of moral corruption and social disorder, are to be chastised, controlled, and kept at some distance.

In this way, the family values rhetoric of the Christian Right is about power and the ability to regulate human behavior in society. But many of its supporters do not think the social issues involved here involve the expression of power. Instead, the complementarity of God-given roles is their key concern. Although the public sphere must not recognize, and hence legitimate, immoral behaviors, there is also a great wariness about too much governmental intervention in the family sphere. Parental rights, rather than governmental dictates, are the way to assure a moral society. In part, the Right's reluctance to legitimate worldly power may be a response to the modern political culture of egalitarian rights. That is, conservatives may calculate that any solution that seems too hierarchical and authoritarian will meet resistance. However, their suspicion is also consistent with the individualist assumptions in evangelical Protestantism, in which the institutions of government must be kept separate from the moral sphere of religion, especially the family.

Similar concerns animate more recent movement attempts at solidifying the traditional family; one notable example is the all-male group known as the Promise Keepers (Diamond 1999; Donovan 1998). Promise Keepers has made headlines by holding large rallies in athletic stadiums and, in 1997, in Washington, D.C. Though its public visibility has diminished recently, Promise Keepers still has an impact on men and families through its small groups based in religious congregations. One would be wrong to think that all men who attend Promise Keepers rallies are motivated by patriarchal intent, or that the group itself is nothing but a simple tool of the politicized Christian Right (see Williams forthcoming). However, the dominant Promise Keepers messages promise a redemptive return to a God-ordained order. Allegedly, re-structuring the now broken relationship between men and women within the family is the key to personal, social, and societal harmony, success, and happiness. Interestingly, Promise Keepers' leadership also preaches a version of racial reconciliation that has the individual, universal, and integrationist themes now claimed as the legacy of Martin Luther King. That set of frames has not, however, resonated with movement adherents as strongly as have the boundary-clarifying messages about gender roles.

Resonant Themes in American Religious Culture

The different rhetorics of these two movements, then, illustrate that religion as a cultural system, at least in American culture, has the capacity to open or to close the space for democratic participation. The structure of the Christian message in the United States supports this capability. Other religions may have the potential to function culturally as Christianity does; Islam, specifically, has structural similarities. However, religious traditions such as Hinduism and Judaism may have more trouble functioning in the ways I describe later, primarily due to certain assumptions in their theologies.[1]

The historical and cultural shape of Christianity, particularly Protestantism, in the United States offers two important themes for addressing the nature of our society. I used the rhetoric of the beloved community and family values to demonstrate how social movement claims open or close space in American political culture. These rhetorics, and their functions, resonate with two themes in American religious culture: universalism and symbolic boundary maintenance.

Universalism.   American Christianity has a deep strain of universalism in its theology and social ethics. That is, deep in Christian thought and practice is the idea that all people can—and should—accept its religious truth. This has been interpreted by many Christians as a call for evangelism—that is, spreading the truth of the gospel. But it has also been interpreted as a criticism of worldly borders and boundaries. The divisions between different nations and peoples are often traced to God's displeasure at the Tower of Babel, and thus social differences are a punishment to be transcended when the Kingdom of God is achieved. Jesus in the Gospels, and Paul in his epistles, provided language that can reinforce this interpretation. By claiming that in Christ there is no Jew or Greek, or male or female, this version of the Christian message calls believers to go beyond worldly boundaries and anoints a de-racinated identity as a godly achievement. In this regard, recall King's justification for the SCLC's integrationist campaign that moved from one community to another.

In Western traditions, this universalism has often been interpreted as a critique of hierarchical differences as well as horizontal social distinctions. Thus, Matthew's "the last shall be first" can be a call for quiescence and patient forbearance with the ills of this world, or it can be read as a show of

God's siding with the poor and oppressed. Further, recognizing the total sovereignty of the divine also offers a law that controls political and social elites as well as commoners (Williams 1999a). Even the idea that no person is above the law is ultimately a product of secular Enlightenment thinking; it certainly resonates with Protestant conceptions of the complete "otherness" of the divine and the requirement that all worldly institutions be subject to God's will and justice (see Bendix 1978; Walzer 1965). Such incipient egalitarianism, combined with wide access to religious truth—democratic availability—renders many forms of American religion as potentially powerful ideological tools for societal leveling.

In sum, religious language can open cultural space for democratic participation and serve as a prophetic voice for social change. Of course, religious language can close cultural space as well. Several of its properties reinforce this capacity; I next turn more attention to the boundary maintenance function of religious distinctions.

Boundary Maintenance.   Many aspects of liberal democratic culture are at odds with the characteristic nature of religious truth used to support political and policy preferences. Jasper (1992) analyzes political discourse by drawing on Kenneth Burke's idea of "god terms"—political terms meant to shut down debate by offering a final irrefutable authority. Rather than generalizing the capacity to participate in dialogue (i.e., opening cultural space), god terms are meant to reserve and preserve authority; they are inherently not open-ended. Burke and Jasper both note that other languages share this characteristic with religious language; Jasper focuses much of his research on how scientific authority functions in practice as a source of god terms.

Similarly, Jelen (in Segers and Jelen 1998) argues that liberal democracy requires public claims in a "neutral" language. Neutral language is equally accessible to all people and can be debated, refuted, and modified in the course of public debate. With this criterion, many religious claims would not be admissible in public discourse, as they are, in principle, not debatable or refutable. As Jelen points out, however, not all claims must be subject to examination based on empirical evidence. He illuminates a space between pure value and belief statements (that are beyond the realm of objective assessment) and statements subject to tests of empirical validity (such as scientific "facts"). He calls these intermediate areas the realm of "judgments" where issues of collective values can be debated, but where the grounds and warrants of debate must remain within the domain of collective examination rather than subjective belief. Religious claims find access to public discourse here.

Religion plays a powerful role in creating, sustaining, and providing meaning to social boundaries and divisions. It is reasonably argued that the creation of symbolic boundaries is an inherent and necessary human capacity. We know what things are by knowing what they are not; purity makes sense only when contrasted with pollution, the sacred when contrasted with the profane (Douglas 1966). Recent social theory has focused on how symbolic boundaries work in the creation and reinforcement of inequality, along racial, class, gender, or cultural lines (Lamont 1999).

Religion gives these boundaries *moralized* meanings. If other types of material and ideal interests are responsible for the creation of boundaries, religious systems can place their significance in a sacred cosmos and connect that to earthly divisions. Thus, to put a different spin on the Tower of Babel example offered earlier, one could argue that God's actions separated the races, and He intended them to live apart. In this interpretation, divisions between peoples are God-given and should be preserved. Any attempt to change the world as it has been created by God is both doomed to failure and an act of secular hubris.

Though the creation and maintenance of social boundaries by religion is hardly unique to the United States or even to Europe (e.g., India's caste system), themes in American Protestantism continue to reinforce and justify the symbolic boundaries that keep the political culture closed. The central distinction is between the saved and damned, the elect and the nonelect. Particularly in early Calvinist versions of Protestantism (those Weber highlighted in his study of the Protestant ethic), this division is God-ordained and immutable. Humans were predestined for heaven or hell and had no ability to influence that election—only to manifest appropriately godly lives. The predestination of early Calvinism was not sustained over generations but rather was transformed into a more voluntary division between the elect and those outside. That is, an individual act of conversion and transformation was required to achieve the status of a member of the religious community (being "born again"). While volitional, the boundaries between those within the community and those without remained sharp. God's church was not, in fact, open to any and all.

Over time, the voluntary and individual quality of belonging became attached to ideas of moral worthiness—those who had experienced the transformation were elect; those who had not were not entitled to membership and, in fact, were subject to the legitimate control of the moral community. Two aspects of this heritage remain in the culture of American Protestantism, particularly in its more conservative forms. First is the significant attention paid to issues of boundaries, membership, inclusion, and exclusion (see Williams 1994). Second is moral valuation of these boundaries as those between the "deserving" and the "undeserving." This notion emerges in the general culture in terms such as the "deserving poor" (see Gans 1995) and is particularly salient in any social issue that involves moral assessments. The boundaries of the moral must be protected from the pollution of the nonelect, now understood as the undeserving.

The connection between this theme and the family values language presented earlier should be clear. A syllogism runs from the God-given structure of social order and family roles, to the moral boundaries that must be protected from dangerous tampering, to the closing of the cultural and political space to those whose behaviors would jeopardize social and moral order. If the nonelect must be cast out in order to protect the moral health of the community, that may be the cost of their actions and an "objective moral order."

Thus, recent social movement rhetoric highlights two themes in American religious and political cultures. One is an assumption of universalism that aims to spread its truth and privileges to all persons, transcending the divisions among them. The other is an intense concern with boundaries and divisions, with the attendant assumption that maintaining such boundaries is essential for the moral health and material prosperity of the community. These themes undergird the language and the political implications of the civil rights movement and the more recent Christian Right.

Conclusion

I have considered two different religiously based rhetorics used by two recent social movements. The rhetorics are classic movement ideologies. They galvanize movement participants, persuade many noncommitted bystanders of the moral value of the movements' agenda, and neutralize the moral legitimacy of movement opponents. Each rhetoric came out of a particular sociocultural group, African Americans or white evangelical Protestants, yet has reached well beyond the members of that group to become part of the public discourse. That is, each discourse has had an artful ambiguity that has helped it bind the coalitions of social groups that form the movement.

Each rhetoric connected aspects of the internal movement culture to external dimensions in the larger culture, in this case, American religious culture. Each played on the collective identity among movement participants, in that the rhetoric articulated participants' interests and validated their sense of injustice and moral mission. But each ideology did so by resonating with a deep theme in American religious culture. Without such "cultural resonance" (Williams and Kubal 1999), rhetoric cannot reach beyond its immediate beneficiaries, either to pull in other populations or to convince bystanders of the moral validity of movement claims.

To return my original theoretical point, social movement discourse, at least the public part of that discourse, must be simultaneously innovative and familiar. To be effective in a call for change, a movement must couch its innovative meanings within a symbolic repertoire that is both familiar and legitimate to those hearing the messages. The cultural context shapes the meanings that movements can successfully generate. It acts as a constraint and as a channel, making some symbols and language difficult to use successfully and shaping the meanings that actors interpret. Of course, I am not making a case for cultural determinism. As demonstrated by these two movement rhetorics, drawn largely from American Protestantism, a legitimate cultural context can have multiple uses and interpretations. Actors must transform received symbolic repertoires into active movement messages. But that agency operates within the boundaries of the extant culture.

That the public discourse of the civil rights movement and the family values agenda of the New Right both were rooted in American religion is not accidental, and it goes beyond the importance of religion and belief in the minds and personal identities of movement adherents. Rather, the religious characteristics of their claims placed the movements within a legitimate social landscape and gave each movement a moral purpose difficult for opponents to debunk. Both the beloved community and family values share an important "restorationist" emphasis—that is, they embody a call to return the moral community, and by extension the nation, to a purer state. Hughes and Allen (1988) call this American religion's tendency toward "first times." As such, both sets of rhetorical claims call for change that restores a godly society. Religious themes of the universal transcendence of worldly divisions, or of the moral validation of social boundaries, were both available to distinctly different American social movements. Both themes helped structure the social movements' places in the public sphere, as the movements, in turn, used the rhetoric to try to shape that public sphere.

NOTES

Thanks to Paul Lichterman, David Meyer, Belinda Robnett, and Nancy Whittier for comments on an earlier draft.

1. Whether, in adapting to the American context, Islam, Hinduism, and Buddhism will become more like Christianity in their political impact is an unanswered empirical question.

External Political Change, Collective Identities, and Participation in Social Movement Organizations

BELINDA ROBNETT

After '65 I don't know what happened. Before '65 it [the Student Nonviolent Coordinating Committee] was very loosely structured, very egalitarian, an organization with easy entry and easy acceptance, and a lot of respect for whoever was there.

—Jean Wheeler Smith Young

Between 1964 and 1966 the Student Nonviolent Coordinating Committee (SNCC) transformed from an organization that cultivated a nonviolent civil rights collective identity to one that imposed a black nationalist perspective. What accounts for this substantial change? This chapter answers that question with a relational approach to the study of collective identity, arguing that this transformation directly resulted from the interaction of external (political) and internal (cultural and organizational) change. Although historical and biographical accounts of the demise of the SNCC highlight both external and internal causes, most theoretical treatments of social movements do not analyze these factors as they interact with collective identity sustenance in social movement organizations (Carson 1981; Forman 1985; King 1987; Sellers and Terell 1990). Equally troubling is the lack of substantial comment on the race/class/gender mix of these interactions. Scholars often address internal and external factors as though they were unsignified; therefore, we rarely come to understand the complexities of race, class, and gender in the formation of collective identities.

In the case of the SNCC, the shift from a nonviolent, interracial, participatory democracy to a violent, black separatist, hierarchical organization was precipitated by political changes outside of the movement organization. The

1964 Mississippi Freedom Democratic Party's (MFPD) unsuccessful challenge to illegally elected white officials at the Democratic National Convention contributed to SNCC members' growing disillusionment with the status quo, as scholars have recognized (McAdam 1988a; Evans 1979). In addition, however, state concessions, in the form of the 1964 Civil Rights Act, also negatively affected collective identity sustenance. Quite rightly, previous work argues that the Freedom Summer Project, in which middle-class white students were recruited en masse to work in Mississippi, exacerbated racial tensions and undermined adherence to principles of nonviolence. Yet these internal changes were preceded and followed by equally important political concessions.

A relational approach to the study of collective identity analyzes the dialectical interplay between external political events and internal collective identity sustenance and change. I argue that (1) external changes and pressures were under way prior to significant internal changes (namely, the Freedom Summer Project) in SNCC; (2) an interplay between internal and external factors produced changes in collective identity and commitment; and (3) race, class, and gender relations, manifested through internal and external factors, significantly affected the final outcome. In the case of SNCC, as the political climate shifted with the passage of the 1964 Civil Rights Act and the events at the Democratic National Convention in Atlantic City, so did the meaning of SNCC's collective identity. Moreover, these political events operated within the context of race, class, and gender relations in the United States. In effect, the passage of the Civil Rights Act and the failure to seat the MFDP delegation at the convention demonstrated that mainstream politics might be slightly open to conventional participation, bargaining, and advantages for the black middle-class, but remained closed to poor blacks. As SNCC's internal debates and struggles about politics and identity took place in this context, SNCC became more rigid, more confrontational, and ultimately more marginal.

A Relational Approach to Collective Identity

Numerous scholars have documented the centrality of collective identity for movement participation (Castells 1997; Cerulo 1997; Friedman and McAdam 1992; Hunt and Benford 1994; Jasper and Polletta 2000; Melucci 1985a, 1989; Snow 2001; Snow and Anderson 1987; Snow and McAdam 2000; Taylor and Whittier, 1992). Collective identity is made up of shared "cultural capital" that members acquire through the deployment of knowledge within the movement and use to constitute themselves in their own terms. Through collective identity processes, movement actors develop a shared cultural toolkit (a repertoire of protest methods including nonviolent tactics).

If collective identity does not resonate with either potential recruits or adherents, they will choose not to join or will leave a movement.

Collective identities form within social movement communities but are shaped by both internal and external factors. The internal day-to-day practices of the organization construct and deconstruct the boundaries between its members and between a challenging group and dominant groups (Gamson 1997; Taylor and Whittier 1992). Resources, political opportunities, and organizational strength are important determinants in creating a social movement culture that in turn creates collective identities. External events and structures can shape internal collective identity negotiations and its subsequent formation in a social movement organization. Yet scant theoretical attention has focused on the impact of external events on collective identity.

I suggest two main effects of external events on collective identity and, in turn, the sustenance of participation. First, external events and institutions directly affect how participants see their position, the possibilities and limits of change, and the dilemmas they face. Internal attempts to confront such events shape changing collective identities. Second, cultural capital—the knowledge and information important to participating in a movement—is dispensed and controlled in the context of relations of power. Whoever controls the deployment of cultural capital, the field of power, and the organizational context in which it is deployed affects participants' decisions to remain or leave a social movement organization. U.S. society is hierarchically aligned by the intersections of race, class, and gender. Therefore, access to cultural capital, within and outside movement contexts, depends on one's position in society.

A historically specific and dynamic relational approach to the study of social movements provides a way to grasp the complex interplay between internal and external influences on collective identity. Factors internal as well as external to social movements are not stable. Rather, political opportunities, actors, recruitment patterns, resources, and ideologies shift over time. These factors do not operate singularly in a linear causal model. Instead, they interact in a dialectical fashion to produce historically specific outcomes.

Recently, scholars have moved closer to a relational approach in their research. Whittier (1997) has examined the different collective identities of movement cohorts as a result of the external contexts and internal conditions of the movement at the time they enter. Sawyers and Meyer (1999) examine how political changes may shape a social movement organization's strategies; Taylor and Raeburn (1995) and Bernstein (1997) have documented the strategic uses of collective identities. Building on these studies, this chapter argues for a relational approach to the study of collective identities in social movements, which captures the interactions of challengers and authorities. After discussing methods, I trace the changes in collective identity and sustenance of participation in SNCC, first describing the collective identity before 1964, then showing how the 1964 Civil Rights Act, the events surrounding the MFDP, and the entry of white volunteers through Freedom Summer affected collective identity. I then describe how the rise of a Black Power collective identity constricted access to cultural capital within the movement and diminished commitment and participation.

The Study

The Student Nonviolent Coordinating Committee, a 1960s civil rights movement organization, provides an excellent example of how race/class/gender changes inside and outside movements converge to shape collective identities within a social movement organization. Historians and other scholars have documented the internal and external changes after 1964/1965 that shifted SNCC from a civil rights movement organization to a Black Power movement organization, but the theoretical implications of these changes have been neglected (Carson 1981; Evans 1979; McAdam 1988; Robnett 1997).

This study used a number of qualitative data sources: life histories, archival materials, secondary sources, and personal interviews with a snowball sample of female leaders in the civil rights movement (see Robnett 1997). I used data from a subset of twenty-five telephone interviews with respondents who discussed SNCC's shift in orientation.[1] Archival research in several locations (the Martin Luther King Jr. Center for Non-Violence in Atlanta, the Civil Rights Documentation Project at the Moorland Spingarn Research Center at Howard University, and the Dr. Martin Luther King Jr. papers at Boston University) supplied detailed information regarding women's activities in SNCC.

Collective Identity before the Passage of the 1964 Civil Rights Act

In fact, SNCC not only provided collective identities that redefined the message of the movement and reinterpreted shared experiences; its collective identity also redefined leadership and power (see Carson 1981; McAdam 1988; Robnett 1997). And SNCC's collective identity moved beyond ideological rhetoric to attack the daily practices of institutions, beginning with its own. Seasoned activist, Ella Baker, who helped to create SNCC, did not believe that leaders should define a movement and often stated that "strong movements don't need strong leaders." Instead, SNCC focused on the development of community leadership and grassroots mobilization (Dallard 1990: 32).

Baker's anti-hierarchical, decentralized view of power became central to the operation of SNCC. The group used rotating chairs and an executive committee and emphasized group-centered leadership that required decision making through mutual understanding. This weakened internal boundaries, creating a more equitable exchange of cultural capital, because important knowledge could be widely distributed.

This distribution of power had unintended consequences that sustained commitment and broad participation. It allowed individuals to develop their own identities and gave organizational power to those who would not normally have such access, including those with little schooling and women. In other words, although scholars have talked about the structural consequences of decentralization of power in SNCC, they have not paid close enough attention to how this organizational form shaped collective identity. Activist Mary King explains:

> The cultural diversity of SNCC's staff . . . included individuals who were first-generation college-educated southern blacks, rural local blacks, northern middle-class blacks, upper-class southern elite blacks, middle-class Christian whites, privileged whites, New England Quakers, Jews, white ethnics, members of the Left, and southern conservative whites. The divisions inherent in such variation in background and perspective were overcome. . . . Our heterogeneity— a strength . . . made ours an imperfect but sincere attempt at a society free of race, class, and gender discrimination. (1987: 522)

In effect, SNCC deconstructed and reconstructed the meaning of power. Bernice Johnson Reagon, an active participant in SNCC, said, "my whole world was expanded in terms of what I could do as a person . . . unleashing my potential as an empowered human being . . . searching within myself to see if I had the courage to do what came up in my mind." This statement provides an insightful summary of the process of collective self-identification in SNCC's early years. The deconstruction of boundaries within the organization and Reagon's access to empowering cultural tool kits increased her feelings of efficacy; she says that she never "experienced being held back" and was "pushed in ways [she] had never experienced before" (Bernice Johnson Reagon interview, November 30, 1992).

"For Reagon and others, participation in the civil rights movement, in general, and in SNCC, in particular, created new identities, both personal and political. Reagon and others continually expressed their newly found self-empowerment derived from movement participation. They were challenged to transcend not only personal boundaries, but political and social ones as well. Nothing was sacred, neither their identities nor society's boundaries"

(Robnett 1997: 37). Participants' feelings of efficacy and empowerment during SNCC's early years developed out of a dialectical exchange or negotiation process, supported by a participatory democracy, between the organization's collective identity and individuals' efforts to align themselves with that identity (see Snow and Benford 1988). Identities were not created for the movement participants. Rather, participants interacted within the cultural context, gaining knowledge for self-empowerment (cultural capital) and collectively developing identities.

The Impact of the 1964 Civil Rights Act on Collective Identity

Although participants in social movements constantly negotiate collective identities, political change can dictate the content and direction of these negotiations in the absence of significant internal change. The Civil Rights Act raised new possibilities and concerns about the entry of middle-class blacks into the power structure, while the needs of poor blacks remained untouched. As former SNCC Chair, James Forman noted, "With the passage of the Civil Rights Bill, the entire character of this organization changed" (1985: 478). External events thrust SNCC into a collective identity crisis.

An examination of SNCC meetings prior to June 1964 highlights this point. Previously, scholars have argued that the large influx of whites into the organization following Freedom Summer precipitated its shift to Black Power (Carson 1981; McAdam 1988). Yet, even before the large influx of northern whites into SNCC's 1964 Freedom Summer Project, the discussion at the meetings shifted as a result of external political concessions in the form of the successful June 9 Senate cloture vote on the Civil Rights Act (Garrow 1986: 330). Anti-white sentiment, radical tactics, redefinitions of goals, anti-middle-class articulations, and discussions of the very meaning of "black" were all a part of the crisis in SNCC's collective identity *prior to* any significant internal changes in membership. Such discussions were not central before June 1964 when the Civil Rights Act effectively passed into law.

Identity Crisis Begins

By June 1964, prior to Freedom Summer, SNCC had already begun to redefine its identity. Therefore, clearly its internal crisis was not precipitated by internal shifts alone. At a June 9–11, 1964, meeting, the ideological underpinnings and identity of SNCC took center stage. The discussions were precipitated by the growing awareness that political inclusion would not substantially change the lives of most African Americans. Many SNCC par-

ticipants were decisively middle-class; while changes would be gradual, opportunities would become available to them. Yet, for the masses of African
Americans, particularly those in poor urban and rural communities, little
would change. For many, this unexpected realization created a collective
identity crisis for an organization committed to grassroots empowerment and
equality for all.

This understanding led to discussions of direction, with some advocating
a more militant stance. Ruby Doris Smith Robinson, who would later chair
SNCC, suggested that the executive committee needed to give more direction to the projects and to redefine SNCC's principles. Underpinning her
argument is the articulation of her awareness of continued inequality for most
blacks. She argued:

> We could begin with discussion of whether we're working to make
> basic changes within existing political and economic structure (i.e.,
> the system). For example, the Freedom Democratic Party and Freedom
> Vote campaign are radical programs. What would the seating of the
> delegation mean besides having Negroes in the National Democratic
> Party?[2]

Smith is grappling with the irony of marginal inclusion and the tension
between "selling out" and participating in a system of inequality. Similarly,
Jim Forman, in struggling with SNCC's identity and the growing awareness
of the futility of marginal inclusion, said:

> SNCC's role is to agitate. To end racial discrimination in all forms.
> We use the tool of voter registration. We agitate for dignity. Voter
> registration can be used toward that end. We must agitate to force
> changes. Agitation to eliminate racial discrimination is just one
> element. Dignity is an umbrella concept, e.g., a man without a job
> has no dignity.

Though the concept of dignity and the use of voter registration were not
new to SNCC, the notion of agitation was a major shift. Others began to
expand on the meaning of agitation and dignity and to carry these concepts
toward a more militant set of strategies and goals. This preceded the later
takeover by the more militant wing that shifted SNCC's identity to one of
Black Power and armed resistance. Jim Jones asked, "At what level should
SNCC agitate? Problems are created by those who are considered liberals and
moderates. SNCC's program is limited to desegregating facilities and voter
registration." Jim Forman replied, "There are higher levels of agitation. We
have been successful with the Mississippi Project in that people are begin-

ning to be aware of the Mississippi situation." Ruby Doris Smith added, "Agitation demonstrates and exposes this country internationally. We expose the institutions and the government. We could employ radical action such as asking for political asylum."

They continued by discussing the possibility of protesting at the UN, viewing this as a radical step and a means of embarrassing the United States. Ivanhoe Donaldson called for even more radical thinking:

Picketing is radical. Knowing who holds the dollars in the country because what do we do once we know? Is it important to run a Mrs. Hamer in the political structure just to be part of the political machine? If we are working in a program which is completely controlled by those working against us what is the point of working within the Democratic Party? It is not a radical tool.

Others disagreed, but the conversation moved to a discussion of the loyalty of those blacks who would take office. Class became central to their discussion, with many articulating a belief that middle-class blacks would sell out to the status quo. Ruby Doris Smith, for example, stated: "The candidacy of Mrs. Hamer has value in that she is able to articulate the grievances of Mississippi Negroes. This isn't necessarily true of Mrs. Boynton" (a middle-class candidate).

Although SNCC members were concerned with SNCC's structure and strategies, its lack of identity was the central problematic. Discussion centered on the usefulness of becoming a part of a system likely to co-opt the middle class and represent those values. Jim Forman provided an insightful summary of the concerns of SNCC members:

There are certain middle-class values in our society which emphasize social mobility which is not in conformity with dignity. What will we emphasize concerning American society—perhaps our criterion for achievement should be the amount of work done not the amount of money gained. Once we have obtained certain rights, the vote, employment, etc., we may have to address ourselves to conditions created under the new situation—the situation of middle-class life. It is true that once we have our rights they may be betrayed—we will always have this struggle.

The SNCC members were beginning to confront the meaning of marginal acceptance and the possibility of their own cooptation. Class became significant in that it stood to split the black constituency, leaving the poor and working class behind. Mainstream liberal tactics would no longer suffice in a system with cleavages beyond the racial divide. Already the members were moving toward a more radical political stance in response to the possibility that some—not all—blacks would benefit from inclusion.

A Shift from Nonviolence

In response to the passage of the Civil Rights Act and the possibility of political inclusion, SNCC needed to redefine itself. This redefinition included a more radical posture that rejected inclusion based on the acceptance of "white" middle-class values. Even more fundamental, members began to question SNCC's nonviolent identity. For example, Hollis Watkins noted "a change since he was working in Mississippi. People had guns in their houses then too; they were protecting their homes. Things have changed, however. There was a nonviolent attitude then." Ruby Doris Smith responded: "In 1961 people had arms, but nothing was made of it. The objective conditions have been changed since then. We are asking people to expose themselves to more and more. In Cambridge, Md. we have taken people onto the streets, stirred them up, and then turned them back with talk of non-violence." Along these lines, Mike Sayer made a strong case against nonviolence: "In Monroe, N. Carolina men defend their homes with guns. The Klan drove through and were shot at and they didn't come back. *Defending your home is dignity*" [author's emphasis].

Eventually, they came to a consensus as stated by Charlie Cobb: "SNCC had indicated it stands behind the position that a man has the right to defend himself and will stand behind persons put in that position."

This transition to tolerance for violence, and a redefinition of defending one's home with arms as "dignity," is significant. The fact that all of this took place before the large influx of white volunteers into SNCC suggests that internal factors were not the main contributor to SNCC's redefinition. Though SNCC had begun to experience growth and difficulties with structure, these changes cannot fully explain the collective identity shifts. Instead, the changes grew from participants' attempts to deal with their changing political context.

The Beginning of Black Separatist Discussion

As participants anticipated the upcoming Freedom Summer project, they discussed the issue of whites coming into the movement en masse. Hollis Watkins summed up the dilemma:

> We don't know what will happen with whites coming into the State. Neither do we know our own feelings and hatred of whites. When Travis was shot in Greenwood there weren't whites there. The whites

that came into Greenwood weren't shot, though we thought they would be. We must go back over events and check our interpretation and deal with our own hates.

Grappling with their feelings toward whites became a central concern for the movement participants, with MacLaurin concluding, "Whites should develop within the white, not Negro community."

A discussion ensued about the feasibility of sending the summer volunteers into white communities, with Jack Minnis concluding that SNCC was not equipped to supervise such an effort:

Sending summer people into the white community; the people we recruited for the summer were recruited on the basis of their commitment to civil rights. It takes more political sophistication to understand the problems of politics and economics for the poor whites who don't have the white man to focus on as the cause of their troubles, nor do they have the Negro to focus on. Working in the white community requires preparation that we have not done.

Even before the actual conflicts that coincided with Freedom Summer, then, redirecting whites to work outside the black community was already a part of the discussion that would eventually lead to their expulsion from the SNCC. In the meantime, members grappled with their feelings toward not only the race issue but class as well. Don Harris explained: "We should know that when whites come into a project [the] egos of the Negroes will be destroyed. Negroes in the community haven't associated with whites on an equal basis and it will difficult to deal with." In response, Guyot asked: "Is it really the racial aspect of the black/white issue that bothers people or is the issue really that of skilled vs. unskilled people? Are we concerned that whites are taking over SNCC or would take over SNCC? Is the real fear one of lack of trust?" Ella Baker responded: "The conversations sound as though this is the first discussion of white involvement. We can't grow without examining our own reactions to prejudice. We feel inferior because whites who come down from the North have glib [transcription unclear], etc. We must show that we have something to give and not crow when they are wrong." Dona Moses replied: "We began these discussions in Greenville in November, but the talk was cut off. We didn't really grapple with the problems because people were ashamed of admitting their feelings."

These discussions show that the struggle to maintain power and control of SNCC was explicitly racial and classist. Elsewhere, I have shown that it was also gender-related, gendered, as black males dominated the more visible tier of leadership, with women assuming the position of bridge leaders or those who provided the day-to-day activities of connecting the masses to the movement, and with black and white women occupying different positions within the organization (Robnett 1997).

Even before a large number of educated whites entered the organization, SNCC's collective identity was at stake. How would it define itself and, more important, who would have the power to define SNCC's collective identity? How could the current staff, which consisted of a small number of long-term white participants and a majority of black male leaders, maintain control? These feelings, and the discussions of them, were clearly exacerbated by the limited concessions made by the state.

The Mississippi Freedom Democratic Party Challenge

Much of SNCC's programming was centered on the development of the Mississippi Freedom Democratic Party and the attempt to unseat illegally elected white officials in the South. The MFDP formed in 1964 to counter the racist Southerners who continued to prevent blacks from voting. Despite increasingly violent reprisals, the MFDP succeeded in challenging the Southern order by holding alternative elections. With sixty-eight delegates and elected representatives, they later went to the National Democratic Party Convention in Atlantic City. Despite the success in organizing the MFDP, some were concerned that this appeared to be SNCC's only program, pulling the organization too far into a model of political access. For example, Stokely Carmichael commented, "People came to SNCC because of radical programs. The Voting Bill will squash a lot of SNCC work. What then?"

However, SNCC's work was effectively squashed by the events at the Democratic National Convention in Atlantic City. When the MFDP delegation challenged the seats of the illegally elected officials at the 1964 Democratic National Convention in Atlantic City, the black middle-class leadership accepted a compromise, ignoring the wishes of the delegation that largely consisted of unlettered rural women. Here, SNCC's concerns that the middle class would capitulate to the status quo were born out, exacerbating race, class, and gender tensions.

In his autobiography, longtime SNCC activist Cleve Sellers describes the event:

> The national Democratic party's rejection of the MFDP at the 1964 convention was to the civil rights movement what the Civil War was to American history: afterward, things could never be the same. Never again were we lulled into believing that our task was exposing

injustices so that the "good" people of America could eliminate them. We left Atlantic City with the knowledge that the movement had turned into something else. After Atlantic City, our struggle was not for civil rights, but for liberation. (1990: 111)

Dottie Zellner, a white SNCC participant, agreed:

People felt they had been close and that the doors had been slammed on them again. They felt that the people that they had traditionally relied on, the white liberals, had betrayed them, which they had. It was time for something new. How could they just keep on register-ing people to vote for . . . who? Lyndon Johnson. You know? I mean, some very serious, profound questions and at the same time and maybe not so coincidentally, the racial issue became much more severe. (Dottie Zellner interview, July 27, 1992)

In response, there was a dramatic change from the collective identity and cultural context within SNCC to that of the Black Power Movement. Much as Jim Miller (1987) documents, the state's concessions coopted those who could get through the "gate," or those with an education and middle-class status. While these fissures always existed among black Americans, the con-cessions served to further stratify movement participants, creating an increased imbalance of power. The Black Power movement sought to reclaim the move-ment on behalf of the urban poor, thus wresting momentum away from edu-cated Southern leaders. This shift led to a weakened collective identity and the loss of participants.

Internal Changes

Even though internal changes were significant to SNCC's demise, as already indicated, careful scrutiny of SNCC's minutes prior to the summer of 1964 suggests that the external political context played an even greater role in SNCC's shift from a nonviolent inclusion-oriented organization to one ad-vocating separatism and the use of "any means necessary" for survival.

Although the Freedom Summer project, in which volunteers, mostly middle-class northern whites, spent time in the South and assisted with voter registration and the Freedom School, dramatically increased the number of SNCC workers, this is not what seems to have precipitated the crisis in SNCC. Admittedly, Freedom Summer created two distinct internal difficulties in SNCC. Structurally, because of the large influx of volunteers, the organization could not maintain its participatory democracy process that was central to the collective identity of the group. Second, the influx of largely white educated volunteers exacerbated racial tensions. Scholars (Carson 1981; McAdam 1988) have elaborated these changes, yet the theoretical implications of their interface with external political changes have not been discussed in connection to collective identity sustenance.

In particular, the different treatment of black and white volunteers by the media highlighted the preexisting concerns within SNCC about poor blacks' continuing marginalization. As activist Mary King noted, "In addition to rapid growth in 1964, reverberations from the society at large must be considered" (1987: 520–21). King explained:

> The difference in the responses accorded to the black and white deaths in Neshoba County and at Selma was an essential element in the deterioration of SNCC. Not only the White House but reporters and television crews—and therefore the nation—emphasized, in ways that SNCC's own egalitarian ethos was powerless to contradict, a simple but stunningly clear message: White people were still of more consequence than blacks, and white lives were still more important than black lives. (1987: 523)

This was exacerbated by the fact that the white volunteers were predominantly nonworking-class students from elite universities. Often they "took over" because they possessed better skills than those in the rural areas did. This, coupled with the expansion of SNCC from about 80 staff members to 160 after many of the Freedom Summer volunteers chose to remain, strained the structure and increased racial tensions. Thus, SNCC was not equipped to oversee the activities of all its new volunteers within a participatory democracy. These internal changes, preceded and followed by external political events, cemented SNCC's collective identity crisis.

Collective Identity, Sustained Participation, and the Shift to Black Power

State concessions shift the internal balance of power in social movement organizations (Freeman 1975; Matthews 1994). The events at the Democratic National Convention had illustrated the divide between the black middle class, willing to accept concessions, and those below. The limitations of the strategies and tactics of the civil rights movement had been made apparent to much of SNCC's membership. While organizations like the NAACP and the Southern Christian Leadership Conference worked within the system, power within the movement shifted from the educated Southern leadership to the young black middle-class male leaders of the Black Power movement. While the civil rights movement sought inclusion, the Black Power movement recognized the futility of seeking mainstream inclusion into white society. Instead, collective identity transformation became a central goal of the movement, since transcending racism through upward mobility was impossible for most blacks, particularly the uneducated.

The Narrowing of Collective Identity

The convergence of the race/class/gender political changes and internal shifts led to the narrowing of collective identity in SNCC, as well as a shift in organizational structure. Ironically, these changes precipitated a loss in access to cultural capital on the part of the unlettered, women, and whites. While certainly information was still available, such as black history as controlled by blacks, an equally important form of cultural capital was lost, namely, the ability to define oneself that had been crucial in SNCC's earlier period.

The collective identity of SNCC shifted in several ways. Collective identity is embedded in and shaped by organizational structure and practices that, in turn, are embedded in and shaped by collective identity. As the collective identity ceased to be nonviolent, consensus-seeking, and egalitarian-oriented, and as the black male leadership lost feelings of efficacy, a hierarchy was put into place to maintain control of the organization. The faction known as the "Hardliners" vehemently opposed retaining participatory democracy, advocated by the "Floaters." As activist Cleve Sellers stated:

> Those who supported the faction to which I belonged were known as "Hardliners." They were primarily black. We were moving in a Black Nationalist direction. The Hardliner-Floater schism probably wouldn't have become important had it not been for three things: (1) the attacks being made against SNCC by various government officials; (2) the passage of civil rights legislation by the federal government . . . , and (3) our continuing confusion about who we were and what we should be doing. (1973: 132)

SNCC's new hierarchical structure would, in turn, construct and maintain more narrowly bounded collective identities. The hierarchy effectively stifled the dialectical exchange among participants and between participants and leaders, thus hampering the formation of individual identity, the exchange of cultural capital, and the construction of empowering tactical tool kits. In other words, hierarchical structure weakened collective identity processes and led to the loss of feelings of empowerment and efficacy for those who were not among the black male leadership or in their innercircle. Jean Wheeler Smith Young, who participated in SNCC between 1963 and 1968, explained the changes:

> I stayed in one capacity or other after '64. I finally left Mississippi in '68. After '66 there came the big division about who's in and who's out because of the developing interests in black power. Well, the leadership changed after '65 and on into '66 and then it became much less of an open organization. In the beginning, if you were there, you were part of the staff. After about '66 the central organizational part of the organization wanted to make it more defined toward more limited goals and so then they got into who's in and who's out. Now I do see a difference in SNCC before '65 and after '65. After '65 I don't know what happened. Before '65 it was very loosely structured, very egalitarian, an organization with easy entry and easy acceptance and a lot of respect for whoever was there. Then after '65 it became more of a big organization with its own machine. I left SNCC in '68 and came back to Washington, basically because there wasn't anything more to do. I stopped going to SNCC meetings in about '66. (Jean Wheeler Smith Young interview, August 1992)

She stopped participating in SNCC because she "didn't like the leadership and its direction" (interview, August 9, 1992). Its collective identity shifted from a nonviolent stance to "equality by any means necessary."

As discussed earlier, SNCC had contemplated its position on nonviolence prior to any significant internal changes. By summer 1965, as former SNCC chair John Lewis noted:

> Black Panther political parties began popping up everywhere. The Lowndes County Black Panther Party members, some of them SNCC staffers, began openly carrying weapons that summer, prompting Rowland Evans and Robert Novak, the conservative syndicated columnists, to call SNCC the "Nonstudent Violent Coordinating Committee." I didn't know any of this was coming—the creation of the Black Panther Party, the use of weapons—until it happened. And the fact that some of them carried weapons violated our most basic tenets of nonviolent action. But we had no means of enforcing those tenets. We never had. SNCC wasn't built that way. (1998: 353)

Later, many of SNCC's members would form an alliance with the Black Panther Party (see Forman 1985). Other significant changes would occur, including a shift from an emphasis on individualism to narrower racial, gender, and class boundaries.

Racial Boundaries.   As former SNCC participant and sociologist Joyce Ladner noted: "'Black consciousness' refers to a set of ideas and behavior patterns affirming the beauty of blackness and dispelling any negative images that black people may have incorporated about blackness" (1970: 139).

Embracing these new definitions of blackness and shifting the meaning and symbols of black were to have far-reaching consequences. The new definition was to become a positive base for black identity, race pride, and self-respect. However, this change in collective identity brought the development of more boundaries. The meaning of "black" became strictly bounded as a response to the state's minimal inclusion of the black middle-class and the participation and concessions privileged blacks maintained. The definition of "black" came to be defined as "not-white" (anti–middle class values, anti–status quo).

Many objected to these narrowly bounded definitions of race. Muriel Tillinghast, another SNCC activist, believed that the organization began to change when Stokely Carmichael become chair: "I don't have any problem with us through self-recognition [a term used by Black Power advocates to acknowledge the capacity for self-determination and leadership], but you have to keep that on a continuum where we all link up [meaning including whites] (Muriel Tillinghast interview, July 19, 1992).

And on the expulsion of whites from SNCC, Muriel Tillinghast expressed the view of many of my interviewees. Of Bill Hanson, a longtime white SNCC activist who had put his life on the line for civil rights and was expelled from the organization, Tillinghast remarked:

> Bill Hanson was in the South for years, in fact Bill was [disowned] by his family. I was talking to him last weekend and he has not seen his parents since he was about nineteen. He is the person that lost literally everything and the one group of people that he had bargained with were now throwing him to the bulls because of philosophy. What kind of philosophy is this? And white people can't understand or advocate black power? (Interview, July 19, 1992)

Tillinghast left SNCC in 1966. Narrower definitions of race, established within a hierarchical structure, led to a loss of participation when individuals could not reconcile them with their own identities.

Gender Boundaries.   As SNCC came to embrace Black Power, some came to accept black cultural nationalism as well. These teachings included Imamu Amiri

Baraka's belief that "nature . . . made woman submissive, she must submit to man's creation in order for it to exist," and Ron Karenga's adherence to the idea that "what makes a woman appealing is femininity and she can't be feminine without being submissive" (Giddings 1984: 318). This confrontation with newly defined roles for women prompted longtime SNCC leader Prathia Wynn Hall to become frustrated with "all of the black macho rhetoric and 'the best thing women can do for the movement is have babies,' and all the women walking—I've forgotten how many steps behind." Female activists Angela Davis (1981) and Elaine Brown (1992) have documented their struggles against male chauvinism in the Black Nationalist movement. Of course, this shift meant that women's experiences in SNCC changed markedly after 1965.

Some female leaders remained in SNCC because at some level they embraced the newly defined collective identity. Longtime leader Ruby Doris Smith Robinson "argued that even though African-American women were uniquely assertive and had been effective leaders in the civil rights struggle so far, black men should be given even more leadership responsibility than they had already assumed. She went on to suggest that the crusade for racial justice was really men's work after all" (Fleming 1998: 166). Many others, such as Prathia Wynn Hall and Jean Wheeler Smith Young, left SNCC because of how its new collective identity changed the position of African American women within the organization. Previously many of these women had served as leaders; now they were receiving explicit messages that women were unsuited to leadership. Again, the narrowing of collective identity decreased participation.

Class Boundaries.   Even those who remained in SNCC were critical of its failure to mobilize black communities at the grass roots, including founder Ella Baker, who stated: "It has not been successful in developing basic leadership in Mississippi, Alabama, Southwest Georgia. Its greatest difficulty has been in reconciling its genius for individual expression with the political necessity for organizational discipline" (Stoper 1989: 272). And historian Clay Carson notes that SNCC was "no longer the catalyst for sustained local struggles. Rather than encouraging local leaders to develop their own ideas, SNCC was becoming merely one of the many organizations seeking to speak on behalf of black communities. Instead of immersing themselves in protest activity and deriving their insights from an ongoing mass struggle, SNCC workers in 1966 stressed the need to inculcate among urban blacks a new racial consciousness as a foundation for future struggles" (Carson 1981: 234–35).

In short, while SNCC's new rhetoric centered on a collective identity for the masses, it failed to develop programs to meet the needs of the poor and unlettered. In this way, its early grassroots empowerment approach, which offered cultural capital to those who otherwise lacked access to such resources and knowledge, was supplanted by a hierarchical model that effectively restricted access to those SNCC purported to represent.

The Loss of Cultural Capital

Purportedly, SNCC was committed to the notion of self-empowerment. Members' collective identity developed out of access to cultural capital, particularly knowledge. For example, SNCC provided information about African and African American history, the inner workings of government, individual and group rights, and methods of protest. Before the 1960s era, little African American history was a part of the school curriculum. Most conceptions of African history rested on the Eurocentric conception of the "savage other." Thus, acquisition of alternative understandings of African American heritage was empowering for most SNCC participants. The deployment of knowledge was central to the development of a collective identity in SNCC and provided the underpinnings of shared protest in the form of nonviolent civil disobedience.

The organizational relations of power are critical to the deployment of cultural capital. Race/class/gender power relations determine inequalities in access to knowledge and cultural resources (Bourdieu 1984; Foucault 1977, 1983). Yet, as mentioned, the acquisition of cultural capital is not a zero-sum game. Previously, elite whites dominated African American knowledge; now it was controlled by the black male middle-class. In SNCC's early days, this had little effect on the acquisition of cultural capital because SNCC was committed to a participatory democracy in which everyone was expected to participate. Also, SNCC's adherence to broad participation embodied belief in a relatively unbounded collective identity, where individualism was highly valued. This gave participants a great deal of latitude because they were not required to adhere to a narrow definition of identity. They processed the information (or cultural capital) individually. A part of SNCC's collective identity was embodied in its participatory democracy process, in which individuals were encouraged to challenge existing beliefs. This facility with debate and participation in collective identity construction is a form of cultural capital in itself. As external events increased access to mainstream politics, SNCC's organizational process changed to a more authoritarian model, thus restricting access to cultural capital. And this restriction limited women, the poor, and whites.

Race, class, and gender tensions heightened as the black male middle-class leadership gained mainstream access as a result of political change. Yet the elevation of this group remained severely limited. Ironically, this highly marginal entrance into mainstream politics created a gender/class/race backlash within SNCC. Many young middle-class black men, feeling that their nonviolent efforts to gain white male entitlements had been severely curtailed and limited, sought increasingly radical approaches to change. Their efforts were decisively *gender-oriented*, with the infusion of male hierarchical models and specific ideas about the roles of men and women; *race-related*, with the expulsion of whites from SNCC and a new definition of black; and *class-ordered*, with the development of an anti-middle-class discourse (albeit one that maintained the leadership's class privilege within the hierarchy of the movement). Not only did a new collective identity emerge in SNCC but the hierarchical organizational structure also precluded the open discussion and acquisition of cultural capital that had previously been available to all participants. These changes, precipitated by external political events, led many to leave SNCC.

Conclusion

With the rise of the Black Power movement came a shift in SNCC's collective identity and cultural context. The extent to which a social movement organization allows for self-labeling and re-labeling is crucial to recruitment and to sustaining commitment. Redefined movement collective identities must resonate with participants' own identities. As leaders constrict group representations into narrower, more specific collective identities, members are less likely to remain in the organization (contrary to Friedman and McAdam 1992).

Collective identity change affects movements differently, depending on organizational and contextual factors. When new recruits have "shared fundamental ideological and strategic commitments" and collective identity changes are shaped by internal as well as external factors, movement continuity can be strengthened (Whittier 1997). Conversely, the rapid influx of new members into decentralized and nonhierarchical organizations can lead to a loss of control by long-term members (Staggenborg 1989). In SNCC, a large influx of new recruits were predominantly white; rather than taking control of the organization, they were expelled and collective identity boundaries were tightened.

This highlights the importance of viewing movements in relational ways. A relational approach to the study of collective identities provides a critical starting point for studying participant sustenance. Collective identities are shaped by the dialectical relationship of race/class/gender internal and external factors. In this case, collective identity changed as a result of the large influx of educated whites into SNCC (an internal factor), the passage of the 1964 Civil Rights Act (an external factor), and the defeat at the 1964 Democratic National Convention (an external factor).

Whereas recruitment shifted the cultural context of SNCC, it did not do so in ways previous scholars would have predicted. Rather than new recruits taking over the decentralized, anti-hierarchical organization, the internal changes converged with external changes to produce collective identity shifts among a portion of the existing cohort of participants. Political changes converge with internal processes to form new identities. Whether these become collective identities, adopted by the organization, depends on the processes of developing collective identities that are open to negotiation and organizational structure that facilitates or discourages the participation of those who would otherwise be excluded.

NOTES

I thank David Meyer and Nancy Whittier for their constructive comments and helpful suggestions.

1. Because the original project focused primarily on women's leadership, I did not probe the interviewees for information about SNCC's shift in orientation. Included respondents addressed the issue in the open-ended questions. This, of course, means that those who felt more strongly about the issue may have been more likely to offer this information. Still, these interviewees provide insight into the feelings participants experience when collective identities shift as a result of the organization's response to the convergence of internal and external change.

2. SNCC Staff Meeting Minutes, June 9–11, 1964. Box A 7 #1 7 of 14. Subsequent quotations from that meeting come from the same source.

Part Five

CONCLUSION

Meaning and Structure in Social Movements

NANCY WHITTIER

The chapters in this book outline a new theoretical approach to social movements, which, in this view, are not self-contained. State structures, dominant cultures, and civil society shape movements, and, in turn, movements can reshape the states, policies, civil societies, and cultures within which they operate. Social movements are neither fixed nor narrowly bounded in space, time, or membership. Instead, they are made up of shifting clusters of organizations, networks, communities, and activist individuals, connected by participation in challenges and collective identities through which participants define the boundaries and significance of their group. Like movements, states and institutions also have structure, engage in action, and construct meaning. Like movements, states are not unified actors but are composed of specific organizations, campaigns, ideologies, factions, and individuals. These are grounded in particular organizational contexts and relationships, alliances, chains of command, and power struggles, and in legitimizing discourses and collective identities. This multilayered view of social movements highlights the interplay between collective identities, political opportunities, and culture and gives us a complex view of movements and their impact. In this chapter, I will lay out such an approach, outlining four basic assumptions. I will then move to a discussion of the state of knowledge about how meaning, structure, and internal and external dynamics interact to shape movement structure, strategies, and meanings.

It is by now a well-worn critique that political process and new social movement or collective identity paradigms need to be integrated (see, e.g., Ferree 1992; Johnston and Klandermans 1995; Meyer 1999; Morris and Mueller 1992; Polletta 1999). For some time now, in fact, the conventional theoretical distinctions in the field—between political process, resource mobilization, and new social movements theories—have been breaking down.

Textbooks and literature reviews still invoke these approaches in their theoretical taxonomies, but far more often than scholars actually employ them in distinguishable form. Recent work by scholars identified with a political process perspective has moved to incorporate a consideration of meaning (McAdam, McCarthy, and Zald 1996; McAdam, Tarrow, and Tilly 1996; Tarrow 1998). Collaborations across the other infamous theoretical divide between scholars in the United States and Europe have only intensified this trend (see, e.g., Giugni, McAdam, and Tilly 1999; Jenkins and Klandermans 1995; Laraña, Johnston, and Gusfield 1994). Some of this work has been criticized (often justifiably) for employing a simplistic conception of meaning, usually as a relatively straightforward "frame" (Benford 1997; Goodwin and Jasper 1999; Steinberg 1999b, this volume); nevertheless, it represents an important theoretical shift. Despite such promising changes, however, considerable work remains to combine the sophisticated advances in theories of discourse, collective identity, and other meaning processes with a similarly complex understanding of states and political processes.

This work also entails bringing together the rich studies of movements' internal dynamics (both their structure and their culture) with those of movements' external contexts. Theorists who focus primarily on movements' internal workings acknowledge that external political and cultural institutions shape what happens inside movements; those who analyze political processes agree. Analysis of the relationship between movements' internal dynamics and external contexts has been growing within the field (Bernstein 1997; Banaszak 1996; Buechler 1990; Matthews 1994; Polletta 1999; Ray 1998; Rochon and Meyer 1997; Taylor 1996). Even so, there has been relatively little complex analysis of how, exactly, movements' particular internal processes interact with external political opportunities, and even less analysis of the interaction with dominant cultural contexts. The contributors to this volume have taken on these tasks.

Taking such an approach means serious consideration of *structure* (movement organizations, communities, and fields), *strategies and collective action* (challenges, protest events), and *meaning* (collective identities and discourse). Interactions between movements and external contexts shape the content, type, and relative intensity of movement organization, collective action, collective identity, and discourse within different movements. Some movements, like the women's or lesbian and gay movement, want to construct new collective identities that challenge subservient definitions of the group, whereas others, like the peace or environmental movement, construct new identities as a means of promoting mobilization rather than as a goal in themselves. Some movements, at some points in time, may emphasize policy change, or cultural change, or the construction of alternative institutions. These variations depend on a host of both internal and external factors. At their peak, movements may have highly developed, thriving formal organizations, rich movement communities, frequent and visible collective actions and protests, intense collective identities, and elaborated discourses.

At lower levels of mobilization, one of these elements may dominate: the survival of a formal, professionalized organization as mass mobilization declines, for example, or the diffusion of an oppositional collective identity into daily life in the absence of collective action, as Suzanne Staggenborg points out in her chapter.[1] It makes a difference whether movements shift to professionalized organizations or to submerged cultural networks during downtimes, whether they resurge through visible cultural confrontations (like ACT-UP) or revitalized centralized organizations (like the AFL-CIO's Organizing Institute). The paths movements take are shaped by both *internal* identities, discourses, "traditions," and organizational infrastructure, as well as *external* political opportunities and dominant cultural possibilities and constraints. In short, the interpretative processes by which groups construct collective identities and other oppositional meanings are inextricable from public confrontations with authorities. These interpretive processes, and the particulars of how collective identities acquire oppositional meaning, distinguish movement identities and associations from those not oriented toward social change. Further, movements include not only public challenges oriented toward the state but also the vast array of actions undertaken by individuals and small groups in everyday life as part of a struggle for social change. This is particularly important for women, people of color, and gays and lesbians, for whom structural inequality—requiring policy change—and symbolic degradation—requiring change in culture and daily life—are both critical.

The forms of collective action that activists undertake are varied, as are the ways that activists are linked together. Those links include public collective action, formal organizations, and collective identities—a sense of being part of a struggle for change that shapes the actions that people undertake, both in their daily life and in participation in campaigns. The processes at work within the battles that movements wage over meaning, constructing oppositional meanings out of their own experiences, ideologies, and fragments of dominant meanings, then deploying those meanings publicly and privately, are complex. These processes do not necessarily vary according to the same factors that shape movements' attempts to gain access to power holders. For example, policy concessions on gay rights and shifts in dominant understandings about sexuality do not necessarily follow the same causal processes, yet both are central to the gay and lesbian movement and to the larger question of social change around sexuality. The intersections among oppositional collective identities, movement cultures, movement organizations, networks of supporters and participants, power holders, dominant institutions, demonstrations, meetings, and even "private" conversations about movement goals or beliefs are indispensable to understanding how collectivities work to make social change.

The chapters in this book analyze segments of the phenomena that make up social movements, but they share an attention to their intersection, examining how visible challenges, for example, are shaped by internal strategizing (Barker and Lavalette) or hegemonic and collective identities (Moodie), or how the demands of movement organizations' political contexts shape their structure and, in turn, their collective identities (Reger, Schwartz) or forms of collective action (Boudreau, Moodie). They share an attention to how discourses and collective identities emerge in particular contexts and acquire particular implications, depending on interpretive processes and material interests (Bernstein, Steinberg, Naples, Williams). By explicitly analyzing the intersections between collective identities, movement organizations and communities, dominant culture, and political opportunities, this book moves beyond ontological statements about the nature of movements and toward a synthetic approach that allows us to analyze the range of phenomena important to movements. After discussing the assumptions of a synthetic theoretical approach, I will discuss the state of knowledge about how meaning and structure and internal and external dynamics interact to shape movement *structure*, *strategies*, and *meanings*.

Four interrelated assumptions emerge from this book. *First, both meaning and structure are important for understanding movements' internal dynamics, their external contexts, and the interaction between the two.* Structural elements include state structures and political opportunities and social movement organizations and communities. Meanings include the cultural context in which movements operate, that is, the dominant culture, discourse, and collective identities that explain and justify existing hierarchies, practices, and distinctions among groups. These understandings are embedded in the state and public policy, other institutions, mass media, and "common sense" (Moodie). Movement organizations and communities are also the site for construction, interpretation, and deployment of their own cultures, discourses, and collective identities. In addition, as Rebecca Klatch points out, individuals' identities and consciousness are a central part of how understandings of the world shape movements' trajectories.[2] Table 16.1 maps some of the components of structure and meaning internal to movements and in their external contexts.

Second, meaning and structure are mutually constituted and cannot be understood separately. Both state and movement structures are constructed around ideological and symbolic imperatives, as well as those of power, resources, and efficiency; conversely, states and movements produce meanings—identities, discourses, representations—within structural contexts. It is difficult to separate the cultural and material dimensions of policy on gays in the

TABLE 16.1 Components of Meaning and Structure in Movements'
Internal and External Contexts

	Structure	Meaning
Internal	SMO, SMC networks	Movement culture, collective identity, discourse; individual identities and consciousness; emotion (collective and individual)
External	POS, state, institutions; resources; other SMs, social movement sector	Hegemonic culture: discourse, identities; oppositional discourse and collective identities from other social movements (social movement meanings); emotion cultures and norms

military, for example, which is defined through the military chain of command and procedures for questioning and expelling gay or lesbian servicemen and -women (structure), as well as through definitions of what constitutes homosexuality and beliefs about the relationship between claiming an identity ("coming out" as lesbian or gay) and engaging in same-sex sex (meaning). The elimination of welfare in the United States simultaneously perpetuates material inequalities and reinforces a symbolic system of meanings about race, gender, and class. Likewise, movement participants construct and evaluate organizations according to their beliefs. They establish networks and coalitions with those they see as similar to themselves, in terms of their interests and goals, the identities they claim, and their daily practices or styles (see Lichterman 1996). Movement institutions, such as feminist bookstores, stand as a challenge to the structural domination of the state and capital as they promote new definitions of gender and demonstrate a different logic for business, based in oppositional rather than dominant meanings. When activists operate by consensus, they implement a certain organizational structure, to be sure, but they also attempt to enact particular ideologies and collective identities, a sense of themselves as valuing everyone's perspective rather than imposing the will of leaders—or even majorities.

Third, movements' internal dynamics interact with their external contexts. The processes through which movements and their contexts shape each other are complicated because influence flows in both directions. Movements' interactions with external contexts are clearly about structure: the control of power and resources, opportunities for movements to gain access or exploit disputes among power holders, states' ability to compel, repress, or co-opt movements' organization or action. Movement organizations may adopt structures that mirror those of their targets or may deliberately differentiate themselves, elevating collectivism over bureaucracy, for example. Similarly, the structure of the state can change as it responds to movement demands to develop new programs or policies, or as new constituencies gain access, as Kenneth Andrews shows in his chapter.

But movements' interactions with external contexts are also about meaning. Both movements and the state construct discourses, collective identities, and representations. And movements, institutions, and the state incorporate and reformulate each others' meanings even as they challenge them. The explanations and justifications of the status quo that the state promulgates form a powerful part of the external context that movements must operate within; just as movements are shaped by—and try to exploit—political openings, so too do activists move in directions where there are cultural openings. Hegemonic culture constrains and influences movements, in other words, and activists simultaneously incorporate and challenge dominant definitions of their group and discourses about their issue. At the same time, movement participants produce new discourses, collective identities, and frames that can make their way into the state and dominant institutions, sometimes carried by entering movement veterans (Katzenstein 1998; Klatch 1999; McAdam 1989; Whalen and Flacks 1989; Whittier 1995), sometimes by attempts to respond to changing public opinion (Burstein et al. 1995). Activists, their opponents, and authorities all strategize about these interactions and modify their structure, discourse, and collective identities over time in response to each other.

The interaction between movements and external institutions is also obviously never a simple two-party relationship in which Movement A addresses Arm-of-the State B. Instead, these interactions take place in a complex set of relationships among participants in multiple movements, branches of the state, other institutions, political parties and factions within them, interest groups, and so forth, in what Raka Ray (1998) calls a political field. How activists frame issues, the strategies they choose, their central goals, and their discourse are shaped by other movements operating in their protest field and by alliances with other institutions, as well as by the state (Katzenstein 1990; Klandermans 1992; Meyer and Staggenborg 1998; Meyer and Whittier 1995; Ray 1998).

In fact, the boundary between "movement" and "context" can be quite blurred. This is less a product of problematic scholarly definitions than it is a reflection of the interpenetration of institutional and extra-institutional agents of social change. Consider a state agency, for example, headed by a movement veteran, that exists because of movement pressure, and disseminates funds according to both movement goals and state imperatives, such as the Violence Against Women Office within the U.S. Justice Department. Clearly such an agency is part of the state, but it is also an outcome of the movement and may be a channel through which movement goals, and movement members still outside the state, may influence other—less receptive—

arms of the state. How do we understand social movements that are also political parties—either marginal ones in two-party systems (e.g., the Green Party in the United States), or parties within parliamentary systems that operate both within and outside the government (what Mildred Schwartz calls "party movements"), or the pressure and interest groups that operate (with varied success) within larger parties that do not always reflect their goals (in the United States, for example, abortion rights activists within the Republican Party)? Such examples underline the importance of examining the complicated forms of interaction between the internal and external dynamics of movements.

Fourth, systemic inequalities of gender, race, class, and sexuality shape both movements and the institutions they confront. Increasing recognition of the ways that movements are shaped by race, class, gender, and sexuality is one of the most important new strands in considering the connections between movements and the societies in which they organize and provides a theoretical model for conceptualizing intersections of structure and meaning more broadly. Recently, numerous scholars have begun to examine how movements are gendered in their organizational structures, recruitment and mobilization processes, emotions, collective identities, frames, and political opportunities (Abdulhadi 1998; Einwohner 1999a; Schmitt and Martin 1999; Staggenborg 1998b; Taylor 1996, 1999). Likewise, the intersections among race, class, and gender shape movements, although less work has sorted out these processes to date (but see Einwohner 1999; Morris 1992; Robnett 1997; White 1999). In this volume, Belinda Robnett shows that collective identity formation is racialized, gendered, and classed, shaped by the relative power and meanings held by members of different constituencies within movements and by the access movements have to racialized, classed, and gendered institutions. Dunbar Moodie shows how specific definitions of masculinity and ethnicity helped maintain South African mine workers' subordination for a time, whereas Nancy Naples shows how racialized, classed, and gendered social locations affect the meaning and implications of a "community control" frame. These writers exemplify several different approaches that show how movements are fundamentally shaped by the intersections of race, class, and gender.

Such work is grounded in theories of the intersectionality of race, class, and gender that highlight the links between meaning and structure. These systems of inequality are maintained and justified through institutionalized inequalities in power and resources, discourses about dominant and subordinate groups' nature and worthiness, and symbolic and interpretive processes that enact inequalities in institutionalized practice and daily life. This perspective has gained currency in social theory from various angles, including black feminism (Hill Collins 1990), materialist feminist discourse analysis

(Naples, this volume; Smith 1987), and poststructuralism and postmodernism (Butler 1990, 1997). Understanding how movements are shaped by the intersections of internal and external processes, and by meaning and structure, requires an analysis of how the racialized, gendered, and classed nature of both movements and dominant institutions shapes mobilization and outcomes.

So, how do we get at such complex overlapping factors? Most of the contributors to this volume begin at the meso level and working out toward both micro and macro levels. There are several promising directions for analysis that gets at the intersections between micro, meso, and macro, between meaning and structure, and between movements' internal worlds and their external contexts. In this vein, I will focus next on the construction of movement *organization*, *strategies*, and *meanings*, drawing on the work of authors in this book, as well as my own work on women's movements and movements against child sexual abuse in the United States.[3] Movement organizations, strategies, and meanings are shaped by factors both internal and external to movements, by meanings as well as structures, and they are imbued with gender, race, class, and sexuality.

Constructing Movement Structures

If movements are networks of organizations, communities, sites for the production of oppositional discourses, collective identities, unaffiliated individuals, and collective actions, then their structure represents links among these different components and external institutions. Questions about the structure of the social movement as a whole and its place in larger organizational and political fields are distinct from questions of organizational structure. The latter set of questions includes whether an organization is bureaucratic or collectivist, whether its structure is formal or informal, federated or not, and whether its decision making and power are centralized and hierarchical or organized around consensus, or some hybrid form. Considering movement structure in both senses helps us to see how internal discourses and collective identities as well as external structures and meanings shape movement structure.

First, collective identity and ideology affect a movement's organizational structure. Participants' ideology can promote collective or bureaucratic structure or consensus or efficiency in decision making (Downey 1986; Rothschild-Whitt 1979; Thomas 1999). In this volume, for example, Jo Reger shows that one faction of a movement organization defined feminism as requiring collective structure because of opposition to hierarchy, whereas another, which valued efficiency and instrumental change more highly, saw bureaucratic structure as preferable. Such choices are bound to participants' perspectives on the world and their sense of who they are, both as individuals and collectively. Considerable scholarship documents attempts by the civil rights, peace, and feminist movements to put their worldview into practice in their organizational structure and relations (Epstein 1991; Polletta 1997; Robnett 1997; Whittier 1995). This form of prefigurative politics (Breines 1982) is an important way that the internal culture of movements influences their structure.

But movement identities and discourses also affect—and are produced within—an organization's structure in other ways. For example, Reger shows how structural segmentation in one organization accommodates multiple collective identities, one that promotes recruitment and another that contributes to the survival of the organization. These multiple identities and their structural accommodation arose both because of internal considerations—the existence of experiences and interpretations within the constituency and the need to provide face-to-face consciousness raising for recruitment to the women's movement—and because of external forces—a highly competitive social movement sector and political field, in which both efficient organizational maintenance and effective recruitment were essential for a long-lived organization. Similarly, Mildred Schwartz shows how multiple, sometimes contradictory ideologies lead to factionalization, which can promote organizational change and, ironically, survival. In both cases, the divisions within organizations were shaped by meaning (ideological conflict in the case of Schwartz, collective identity difference in Reger's case), strategizing (disagreements about how best to achieve influence), and the external environment (resource requirements, relationships with political allies and opponents).

Beyond the structure of individual movement organizations, structural features of the larger social movement and its position in a political field also interact with movement meanings. Social movements vary in size and diversity, both in terms of structure (organizations, movement communities, unaffiliated individuals) and in terms of discourse and identities. Many different organizations in a social movement, combined with weak coordination among them, can promote diversity in collective identities and discourse. For example, the social movement against child sexual abuse consists of a large number of organizations, mostly small, with fairly minimal connections among them. Although most of these organizations, communities, and affiliated individuals claim identity as "survivor" of child sexual abuse, they define that identity and their discourse about child sexual abuse differently. How is it possible for organizations that believe that the solution to preventing child sexual abuse is to shore up the traditional nuclear family to coexist and cooperate with those who identify the traditional nuclear family—and the sexism, homophobia, and adult privilege that it represents—as the source of the problem? How is it possible for law-and-order conservatives, advocating stricter mandatory minimum sentencing and offender registration, to be part of the same movement with advocates of sex offender treatment, critics of the prison system, and opponents of the state in general?

Although these divisions are sometimes contentious, coalitions and participation in shared community events are surprisingly common because a strong movement value on being supportive, respecting individual experiences, and "claiming one's own voice" mitigates against fierce conflict. In addition, however, these diverse meanings survive within a movement structure in which local or issue-focused organizations coexist with national organizations that are relatively "nonpartisan" on these cleavages. Organization members and unaffiliated participants come together at periodic conferences (usually sponsored by the national organizations), are connected by reading movement newsletters and websites, and see themselves as part of a larger social movement community. The loose structure makes the coexistence of varied discourses and identities possible.

The nature of movements' connections to the state are also central in shaping internal organizational and identity composition. Boudreau shows how the type of movement organization varies comparatively, depending on the type of repression directed against revolutionary movements. Where repression focuses on wiping out movement organization, only episodic protest can survive, relatively uncoordinated or unchannelled, with loose links to past resistance history. Where repression focuses, instead, on reprisals against public demonstrations or other protests, organizations can survive better underground, where they can provide a basis for a later resurgence. Similarly, Dunbar Moodie shows that repression in the South African mines meant that organizing occurred through informal networks until legal and political changes opened possibilities for formal organizations.

Under less repressive conditions, access and opportunities certainly shape the connections a movement has with the state and external institutions. But activists also make choices about allegiances to pursue, based on their beliefs and identities. Of course, the opportunities and consequences of moving within the state or working with particular allies also shape internal ideological debates and collective identity. Debates among activists over "selling out" versus "ideological purity" carry a charge precisely because they involve collective identities—questions of "What kind of people are we?"

In sum, activists construct collective identities and discourses within particular organizational and contextual locations, which permit more or less diversity and favor some meanings over others. In turn, movements' collective identities and understandings of the world shape how they structure their organizations and form coalitions and alliances with others. In the next section, I turn to the factors that shape movement actions, primarily through questions of strategizing.

Strategizing and Movement Actions

The forms of collective action that activists engage in, how they frame their issues for public consumption, and the targets and goals they address emerge from the intersection of structures and meanings, both within and outside movements. Strategizing is the process of interpreting political opportunities, cultural acceptability, goals, and the tactics likely to promote change. When they strategize, movement participants debate how to balance their beliefs about what is possible with their views on what matters, what compromises are acceptable, and who they are (their collective identity). In other words, strategies are a result of both external contexts and internal movement dynamics. For example, Barker and Lavalette show that striking dock workers continually adapted their actions over the course of the campaign, based on their assessment of company response. These strategic shifts are less the result of objective external circumstances than of how participants interpret those circumstances. These interpretations grow from interaction within movement contexts, the ongoing conversations and relationships within the movement that constitute collective identity definitions, ideologies, and oppositional discourses. Whether a wildcat strike grows and sustains itself or quickly burns out depends not only on the repression that greets it but on the cultural context that it grows from, as Barker and Lavalette show (see also Fantasia 1988).

Collective action and movement organization influence each other, as Kenneth Andrews and Suzanne Staggenborg both show. Andrews suggests the importance of movement organization in providing a base for collective action and in coordinating the implementation of social change, either when organizations establish new programs themselves, or when they facilitate the implementation of policy changes. Staggenborg further argues that activists' perception of political opportunities and threats is crucial to the strategies they pursue and, indeed, to the outcomes of the movement, pointing to several ways that movement structures affect activists' perceptions. Activists who are immersed in a thriving social movement community, for example, may be inspired by their interactions with like-minded people, even in the face of limited external opportunities. In addition, when social movement communities are linked, different movements can share information and strategize about overlapping campaigns. Such campaigns, which Staggenborg suggests are especially likely to draw participants from several movements during

downturns in the cycle of protest, are crucial both to maintaining a movement and to helping to change external contexts.

Outcomes and how activists interpret them can also shape subsequent
strategies. Barker and Lavalette show that failing to win one campaign can
leave activists pessimistic about waging another. Conversely, Staggenborg
suggests that even apparently futile attacks on hostile authorities can inspire
activists to try to change their political opportunities by electing more sympathetic officials. Belinda Robnett shows, however, that winning some gains
can polarize a movement between activists who can benefit from access to
the state and those who cannot. These distinctions, of course, rest largely on
inequalities of education, class, gender, and race. Those who are excluded
from conventional means of power may become disillusioned by gains in
mainstream political access. Some activists' perceptions that such gains did
not serve them produced a strategic move within the civil rights movement
away from assimilation and integration.

In a contrasting case, Mary Bernstein suggests that the openness of the
polity, along with internal movement dynamics, shapes how activists strategically present their collective identity. Lesbians and gay men in Vermont
constructed an identity that highlighted sexuality over gender because feminist groups, under pressure from opponents, distanced themselves from lesbians, severing ties between the two movements and undermining potential
for a feminist-based lesbian identity. At the same time, an unusually open
polity encouraged lesbian and gay activists to pursue recognition as a mixed-
gender minority group. Nevertheless, the community and campaigns did not
adopt a straightforward essentialist identity, rather remaining diverse in identity and presentation of self within community contexts, even as they highlighted particular versions of identity at legislative hearings for strategic
reasons. Bernstein suggests that lesbian and gay collective identity, rather
than being based on fundamental beliefs about the nature of sexual orientation, emerges strategically in response to a particular constellation of
external factors.

The intersection of internal and external forces in movement strategies,
then, is far from straightforward. The view that participants simply act on
external opportunities would suggest, for example, that movements are more
likely to target external institutions, adopt militant tactics and sweeping demands, and expand tactical repertoires through movement spillover during
periods of high mobilization across the social movement sector. But these
trends are also apparent during periods of low mobilization (see Gamson and
Meyer 1996). Consider, for example, the Revolutionary Communist Party
in the United States during the conservative 1980s, a visible sectarian organization that declared itself to be "the only political organization going for
revolution in the '80s!" (a slogan later changed to "the only political organi-

zation going for revolution by the year 2000!"). It took this approach not because of an objective assessment of its quite dismal political opportunities but because increasing external conservatism fit into the group's Marxist ideology, suggesting that grim conditions would encourage the working class to rise up. Participants, heirs to the cultural legacy of millennial strands from the sectarian late New Left, believed that revolution was near.

During the same period, the women's movement focused on constructing a feminist oppositional culture because of both opportunities and internal dynamics: maintaining mobilization was increasingly untenable given the loss of resources, political hostility, and decline of the Left social movement sector more broadly (Whittier 1995). In addition, however, a variety of forces favored some collective identities over others. Both movement and mainstream culture valorized women's traditional characteristics such as nurturing or peace making (Taylor and Whittier 1992), and spillover from racial and ethnic movements legitimized separatism and the celebration of identity distinctions. Internal structure and preexisting collective identities mattered too. The women's movement already had a strong, rich culture, a collective identity that linked the personal and the political, and a base of autonomous organizations.

Thus, the response of a movement to a set of external circumstances is shaped not only by those circumstances but by activists' perceptions, which, in turn, are a function of the organizational structure, history, and collective identity of the movement. Different movements, and different factions within the same movement, therefore adopt different strategies under similar external circumstances. Theorizing activists' perceptions leads next to questions of meanings within social movements.

Constructing Movement Meanings:
Discourses and Collective Identities

Meanings constructed within movements emerge from interaction between the challenges to dominant culture that activists produce (which are continually shifting and multiple even at any given time) and equally contradictory and changeable external political and cultural systems. Much work has documented how movements construct *frames* that draw on both oppositional and dominant beliefs, in dialogue with the larger culture and institutional contexts in which the movement makes its claims (Benford 1997; Snow and Benford 1992; Snow et al. 1986). The chapters in this book have added a focus on how *collective identity* and *movement discourse* develop in interaction with external contexts. Here, I focus on the interactions and contradictions between the discourses and collective identities that movements construct and views of an issue in the larger culture and policy arenas. Theoretical work on discourse and collective identity gives us a basis from which to analyze how movements transform the meanings inherent in dominant culture, the state, and institutions. Theory about collective identity and discourse has developed largely separately, both within social movement theory and in the broader discipline, and each provides its own useful perspective on the intersections between internal and external forces in movements.

Collective identity emerges from interaction within movement contexts as participants transform their sense of themselves. It entails the definition of a constituency as a meaningful group and the redefinition of that group's characteristics in opposition to dominant culture's definition of the group (Melucci 1989; Taylor and Whittier 1992). Collective identity is grounded in the group's social location, that is, its structural position, its common experiences, and dominant definitions of the group. It thus is shaped by forces external to the movement, but it is never a straightforward result of a shared social location. Many movements construct collective identities that bring together individuals from different social locations, such as the peace or environmental movements (see David Meyer's introduction to this volume). Even movements that organize around collectivities that are recognized and legitimized by the dominant culture, such as gender, race, or sexuality, must nevertheless construct collective identities. Collective identity, thus, is an *interpretation* of a group's collective experience: who members of the group are, what their attributes are, what they have in common, how they are different from other groups, and what the political significance of all this is.

One especially useful approach to conceptualizing the links between political and cultural context and collective identity is Mannheim's generational perspective, outlined in Rebecca Klatch's chapter (see also Klatch 1999; Schneider 1988; Whittier 1997). Picked up by scholars of social movements, this perspective suggests that generation units—that is, groups who share a temporal location and who interact with each other—"work up" or interpret their experiences in particular ways. Shared social location and experiences certainly influence these interpretations, but they really take shape through interaction within movement contexts.

Discursive approaches approach the question from a different direction but also bridge meaning and structure, the idealist and the materialist. Discourses are systems of meaning that provide a way of seeing and interpreting information, categorize individuals and events, and justify power relations. As Janice Irvine (forthcoming) writes, "Because meanings, identities, knowledges, and emotions—indeed, social reality—are constituted through discourses, the discursive field is a key site for contests among collective actors." An examination of discourse entails looking at explicit conceptual frameworks but also at more subtle cultural codes, linguistic practices, and how interpretive processes produce particular identities and power relations (Lehring forthcoming). Institutions and relations of power simultaneously produce discourses and rely on those discourses for legitimation. Discursive change entails telling new stories about the operation of institutions, challenging the legitimation of power and the production of identities that are part of the dominant discourse (Katzenstein 1998).

Discourse theory, like collective identity theory, conceptualizes the influence of the external in terms of power and structure and meaning. Thus, dominant discourses are produced within specific institutional settings, structured by power relations, and reproduce those power relations. But discourses operate at the level of meaning, shaping what is thinkable, possible, comprehensible. Discourse theory grows largely out of the effort to understand how the powerful control meanings, even as there are openings for dissent and opposition. The state and other powerful institutions construct particular discourses, but movements and others dispute them. Discursive change is an important goal for movements.

However, external constraints and opportunities, both cultural and structural, influence movement identities and discourses. For example, groups organized around gender, race, or sexuality operate within a dominant culture that recognizes the group, polices its boundaries, constructs a collective identity (often defining it in essentialist terms), and develops discourse legitimating both the group's distinctiveness and its subordination. That is, because the state constructs the category "race" and uses it to differentiate and stratify individuals, race is a salient category for potential recruits. Yet mobilization requires constructing an oppositional collective identity and discourse that dispute dominant understandings of race and that link group membership to political action. As those who write about lesbian/gay or queer organizing point out, mobilizing a constituency around an identity that the dominant system has made salient can shore up the distinctions the movement is trying to undermine (Butler 1990; Gamson 1995; Lehring forthcoming). Similarly, organizing around the category "woman" can gain strength by drawing on characteristics conventionally attributed to women, such as nurturance or motherhood, but doing so simultaneously reinforces hegemonic definitions of gender that maintain inequality (Taylor 1996). In addition, because racism and sexism are pervasive, organizing around gender has tended to mean constructing a collective identity based on the gendered experiences of white women (Hill Collins 1990; Smith 1998). To construct a collective identity that binds women of different races, classes, cultures, and sexualities is a far harder task because the dominant culture provides less basis for such an identity.

Nevertheless, how activists define their group is by no means dictated by the dominant society. Movements transform hegemonic collective identities and discourses when they organize, and they continue to debate and redefine those group meanings as time passes. Groups rarely mobilize, however, by rejecting dominant discourses and collective identities wholesale. For example, Dunbar Moodie shows that dominant culture makes its way into daily practices through "common sense." Emphasizing the way that South African mineworkers' common sense commitments to rural masculinity initially maintained their cooperation with the status quo, Moodie also shows how organizers drew on elements of those same commitments. When shifting external events brought new workers—without the same commitment to rural masculinity—into the mines, organizers were able to draw on the commitment to dignity and respect that all the workers shared to build loyalty to the union. As Moodie stresses, external conditions by no means determined these transformations, which were contingent on leaders' actions and the relationships between leaders and followers.

Similarly, Rhys Williams argues that movements can draw on the same cultural resource—in his case, religion—for quite different ends. This is possible because Christianity in the United States contains multiple strands, permitting movements to use it to legitimate an opening of political and cultural space to excluded groups or to narrow the range of acceptable groups, beliefs, and behaviors. The meaning and deployment of cultural systems in movements, then, are contingent and multiple. In addition, as Steinberg points out, listeners do not simply receive discourses and absorb them whole, but interpret them according to the listener's own frameworks and contexts. As Nancy Naples shows, discourses and their interpretation acquire meaning in particular contexts, so the same phrase or attribution of blame for a problem can acquire quite different meanings and policy implications within dominant or oppositional contexts, or where the opposition has more or less structural influence.

Change in the collective identity and discourse of feminist identity provides an example of the influences of both internal processes and external opportunities and culture. For feminists who came of age during the 1970s and 1980s, being a feminist meant listening to "womyn's" music (spelled to omit "man"), celebrating universal sisterhood, building alternative feminist institutions, and wearing Birkenstocks (among other arguably more significant political views) (Staggenborg 1998a; Taylor and Whittier 1992; Whittier 1995). Feminism was distinguished by its priority on women's needs and experiences. Now, to women coming of political age in the late 1990s and early 2000s, feminism is distinguished by its self-conscious focus on the intersections of gender with race and class and its unwillingness to generalize about women's experiences (Baumgardner and Richards 2000; Findlen 1995; Walker 1995). It builds on a model of gender and sexuality as quite fluid and often perceives transgender issues as central to a larger project of ending gender (rather than simply ending gender oppression) (Wilchins 1997). Being a feminist can be displayed bodily through multiple piercings, practicing sex radicalism (witness a student who turned in a pornographic video of herself and her dormmates as a final project in her women's studies class), or eating fire as a demonstration of women's power and fearlessness. Yet young feminists serve in internships at the Justice Department and other state agencies.

Why did feminist collective identity and discourse change? First, they changed as a result of internal movement discussions, debates, writings, and cultural works. Second, changes in the larger cultural and political context emerged: more liberal attitudes toward women's sexuality (partly as a result of earlier waves of the women's movement), shifting mainstream style (piercings are not fashionable only among feminists, although pierced feminists assign them a politicized meaning), and greater access to the state for feminist policy makers (allowing the internships). Third, economic opportunities and constraints changed. In the 1970s and 1980s "women's culture" flourished in feminist institutions like bookstores and festivals, partly as a way to survive loss of resources brought about by cutbacks in funds to social change efforts. By the 1990s, corporate expansion brought resources to feminist cultural production but ironically threatened feminist cultural institutions. Superstores drove women's bookstores out of business by featuring large women's studies sections at considerable discount, and as major recording labels added feminist musicians, the small feminist labels suffered.[4] In short, we cannot understand the changes in feminist identity outside the contexts of the expansion and transformation of monopoly capitalism, the effects of earlier feminist activism and other social movements on the state and corporations, and changes in mainstream culture.

In addition, the specific meanings that the state and dominant culture support can shape the discourses and collective identities that dominate within a movement. This happens not because the state dictates movement meanings but because hegemonic meanings can strengthen one discursive or identity faction of a movement over others. In the movement against child sexual abuse, for example, the external climate is more conducive to law enforcement than to other kinds of social change, so the wings of the movement that work within that framework have been more successful. The climate is more conducive, both because of access to institutions and power holders and because of receptivity in the dominant culture. Dominant discourse understands child sexual abuse as a criminal pathology, with prison as the remedy. When a movement organization asks a state attorney general to be a keynote speaker at a conference, it solidifies its alliance with the state and makes the organization look stronger. It also reproduces the discourse that defines sexual abuse in criminal and medical terms and sees legal enforcement as the solution to child sexual abuse. As a result, it strengthens the faction of the movement that understands abuse in these terms, while other discourses about child sexual abuse are left to survive within alternative institutions and communities (Whittier 2000).

In sum, the connections between the meanings that movements construct and those offered by the dominant culture are far from straightforward. Movements draw on hegemonic discourses and categories to construct discourses that are both transformative yet constrained by the hegemonic meanings they wish to challenge. If we overlook collective identity and discourse, we miss many of the ways that political opportunities and cultural shifts affect movements and the ways that movements' construction of oppositional identities can reshape institutions.

Conclusions

The work assembled here represents a new generation of social movement theory. No longer arguing for the need for a synthetic model, these authors have proceeded to develop a synthesis. Their approaches take diverse forms, are influenced by various preexisting theoretical threads, and address an impressive range of substantive issues in the study of social movements. This new generation of theory ought to change our view of movements in several ways. Movements are significant simultaneously at individual, cultural, and structural levels. Meaning, consciousness, interaction, organization, cultural contexts, and political opportunities are all important to understanding how people work to change the world. Movements are not reified or static. Instead, they contain multiple, shifting, sometimes contradictory collective identities, and they contain and give rise to multiple meanings and discourses. The organizations and networks associated with a movement are not fixed; participants come and go in changing relationship to mobilizing structures.

Paradoxically, social movements are simultaneously the dramatic demonstration of human agency—that is, they determine their own course, and we must take their internal dynamics seriously—and they are inextricable from their contexts, shaped by encounters with and structures of the state, dominant culture, and other social movements. If we see multiple levels of analysis as linked and eschew a linear causal model in which political and economic forces structure movement organizations, which in turn shape collective identities, then the transformation of each level must be linked to that of the others. Internal dynamics of movements are not simply determined by external contexts. External structures and cultures, in turn, are shaped by the oppositional identities, cultures, organizations, and strategies of social movements. Individual, cultural, and structural transformation, then, are inseparable.

Gloria Anzaldua, the Latina feminist poet and essayist, suggests in her book *Borderlands* that borders—between identities, between conceptual fields, between cultures and categories—are where the interesting and challenging and troubling questions lie, those questions without clear answers. Anzaldua challenges us to focus our attention on the borderlands within our work—the borders between the individual and the movement, between the movement and the state, between movement culture and hegemonic culture. How do those on both sides negotiate these borders and influence each other across them? We can learn from the debates and connections in interdisciplinary studies, particularly queer studies, women's studies, and ethnic studies, which contribute important conceptualizations of the links between meanings and structure in the perpetuation of and challenge to domination. Social movement theory at such borders is important and rewarding, both for understanding social movements and for the larger task of understanding and promoting social change.

NOTES

1. We can debate whether one or the other of these paradigmatic states actually constitutes a movement; the definitional question is secondary, however, since certainly the surviving organization or identity is related to the movement and within the realm of phenomena that we want to understand.

2. The content, nature, and logic of meanings and of structure vary across contexts and even within the same context: the ideological tenets of a movement organization may not be internally consistent, or may be advanced in one form in a mass-membership meeting, and in quite another in a leadership caucus. The policy goals put forth by the state may take one form in an agency's official mandate but be put into practice in a different form by the people who staff that organization.

3. This includes research on radical and grassroots feminism between the 1960s and the 1990s and research on activism against child sexual abuse in the United States between the 1960s and the present. The latter data include intensive interviews with forty-five activists, documents and newsletters from most major national organizations, and participant observation at several conferences and collective actions (see Whittier 2000 for full methodological discussion).

4. Such inclusion represents a gain of the women's movement, but it also means that the products are sold outside of a political context, and the market drives what will be produced and distributed.

References

Abdulhadi, Rahab. 1998. "The Palestinian Women's Autonomous Movement: Emergence, Dynamics, and Challenges." *Gender & Society* 12 (6): 649–73.

Abramovitz, Mimi. 1988. *Regulating the Lives of Women: Social Welfare Policy from Colonial Times to the Present*. Boston: South End Press.

Ackerman, Robert J. 1985. *Religion as Critique*. Amherst: University of Massachusetts Press.

Aho, James. 1990. *The Politics of Righteousness*. Seattle: University of Washington Press.

Alcoff, Linda. 1988. "Cultural Feminism versus Post-Structuralism: The Identity Crisis in Feminist Theory." *Signs: Journal of Women in Culture and Society* 13 (3): 405–36.

Alexander, Jeffrey C., et al., eds. 1987. *The Micro-Macro Link*. Berkeley: University of California Press.

Almeida, Paul, and Linda B. Stearns. 1998. "Political Opportunities and Local Grassroots Environmental Movements: The Case of Minamata." *Social Problems* 45 (1): 37–60.

Alt, James E. 1995. "Race and Voter Registration in the South." Pp. 313–32 in *Classifying by Race*, edited by P. E. Peterson. Princeton, NJ: Princeton University Press.

Altman, Dennis. 1982. "The Gay Movement Ten Years Later." *Nation* (Nov. 13): 494–96.

Altshuler, Alan A. 1970. *Community Control: The Black Demand for Participation in Large American Cities*. New York: Pegasus.

Amenta, Edwin. 1998. *Bold Relief*. Princeton, NJ: Princeton University Press.

Amenta, Edwin, Bruce Caruthers, and Yvonne Zylan. 1992. "A Hero for the Aged? The Townsend Movement, the Political Mediation Model, and U.S. Old Age Policy, 1934–1950." *American Journal of Sociology* 98: 308–39.

Amenta, Edwin, Kathleen Dunleavy, and Mary Bernstein. 1994. "Stolen Thunder? Huey Long's 'Share our Wealth,' Political Mediation, and the Second New Deal." *American Sociological Review* 56: 250–65.

Amenta, Edwin, and Michael Young. 1999a. "Democratic States and Social

Movements: Theoretical Arguments and Hypotheses." *Social Problems* 46 (2): 153–68.

———. 1999b. "Making an Impact." Pp. 22–40 in *How Social Movements Matter*, edited by M. Giugni, D. McAdam, and C. Tilly. Minneapolis: University of Minnesota Press.

An Account of the Proceedings of the Committees of the Journeymen Silk Weavers of Spitalfields; in the Legal Defence of the Acts of Parliament, Granted to their Trade, in the 13th, 32nd, and 51st Years of the Reign of his late Majesty, King George the Third. 1823. London: E. Justins.

Anderson, Terje. 1986. "Election Commentary." *Out in the Mountains* 1 (10): 1–2.

Andrew, John A. 1997. *The Other Side of the Sixties: Young Americans for Freedom and the Rise of Conservative Politics.* New Brunswick, NJ: Rutgers University Press.

Andrews, Kenneth T. 1997. "The Impacts of Social Movements on the Political Process: The Civil Rights Movement and Black Electoral Politics in Mississippi." *American Sociological Review* 62: 800–19.

———. 2000. "The Civil Rights Movement and Black Politics after the Voting Rights Act: Mobilization and Demobilization in Two Mississippi Communities." Paper presented at the American Sociological Association Meetings, August 12–15, Washington, DC.

———. 2001. "Social Movements and Policy Implementation: The Mississippi Civil Rights Movement and the War on Poverty, 1965–1971." *American Sociological Review* 66 (February): 71–95.

———. Forthcoming. *'Freedom Is a Constant Struggle': The Dynamics and Consequences of the Mississippi Civil Rights Movement.* Chicago: University of Chicago Press.

Anzaldua, Gloria. 1987. *Borderlands–La Frontera.* San Francisco: Aunt Lute Press.

Archer, Keith, and Alan Whitehorn. 1997. *Political Activists: The NDP in Convention.* Toronto: Oxford University Press.

Arnold, Gretchen. 1995. "Dilemmas of Feminist Coalitions: Collective Identity and Strategic Effectiveness in the Battered Women's Movement." Pp. 276–90 in *Feminist Organizations: Harvest of the New Women's Movement*, edited by M. M. Ferree and P. Y. Martin. Philadelphia: Temple University Press.

Aspinall, Edward. 1993. *Student Dissent in Indonesia in the 1980s.* Working Paper No. 79. Clayton, Victoria: Centre of Southeast Asian Studies, Monash University.

Aung, Gyi. 1998. *Personal Letter to General Ne Win, June 29th, 1988.* Unpublished. Wason Collection, Cornell University.

Avakumovic, Ivan. 1978. *Socialism in Canada: A Study of the CCF-NDP in Federal and Provincial Politics.* Toronto: McClelland and Stewart.

Babb, Sarah. 1996. "'A True American System of Finance': Frame Resonance in the U.S. Labor Movement, 1866 to 1886." *American Sociological Review* 61: 1033–52.

Bagguley, Paul. 1996. "The Moral Economy of Anti–Poll Tax Protest." In *To Make Another World: Studies in Protest and Collective Action*, edited by Colin Barker and Paul Kennedy. Aldershot: Avebury.

Bakhtin, Mikhail M. 1986. *Speech Genres and Other Late Essays*. Translated by Vern W. McGee. Edited by Caryl Emerson and Michael Holquist. Austin: University of Texas Press.

Baldridge, Cates. 1994. *The Dialogics of Dissent in the English Novel*. Hanover, NH: University of New England Press.

Banaszak, Lee Ann. 1996. *Why Movements Succeed or Fail: Opportunity, Culture, and the Struggle for Woman Suffrage*. Princeton, NJ: Princeton University Press.

Barkan, S. E. 1979. "Strategic, Tactical, and Organizational Dilemmas of the Protest Movement against Nuclear Power." *Social Problems* 27: 19–37.

Barker, Colin. 1997. "Notes on Strategy." Working Paper, Sociology Department, Manchester Metropolitan University.

Barker, Colin. 2001. "Fear, Laughter, and Collective Power: The Making of Solidarity at the Lenin Shipyard in Gdansk, Poland, August 1980." Pp. 175–94 in *Passionate Politics: Emotions and Social Movements*, edited by Jeff Goodwin, James M. Jasper, and Francesca Polletta. Chicago: University of Chicago Press.

Barker, Colin, and Gareth Dale. 1998. "Protest Waves in Western Europe: A Critique of 'New Social Movement' Theory." *Critical Sociology* 24 (1/2): 65–104.

Barker, Colin, Alan Johnson, and Michael Lavalette. Forthcoming. *Strategies and Identities in Popular Protest*.

Basu, Amrita. 1995. *The Challenge of Local Feminisms: Women's Movements in Global Perspective*. Boulder, CO: Westview Press.

Baumgardner, Jennifer, and Amy Richards. 2000. *Manifesta: Young Women, Feminism, and the Future*. New York: Farrar, Straus, and Giroux.

Baumgartner, Frank R., and Bryan D. Jones. 1993. *Agendas and Instability in American Politics*. Chicago: University of Chicago Press.

Bell, Michael Mayerfeld. 1998. "Culture as Dialogue." Pp. 49–62 in *Bakhtin and the Human Sciences: No Last Words*, edited by Michael Mayerfeld Bell and Michael Gardiner. London: Sage.

Bendix, Reinhart. 1978. *Kings or People: Power and the Mandate to Rule*. Berkeley: University of California Press.

Benford, Robert D. 1993a. "Frame Disputes within the Nuclear Disarmament Movement." *Social Forces* 71: 677–701.

———. 1993b. "'You Could Be the Hundredth Monkey': Collective Action Frames and Vocabularies of Motive within the Nuclear Disarmament Movement." *Sociological Quarterly* 34 (2): 195–216.

———. 1997. "An Insider's Critique of Social Movement Framing Perspective." *Sociological Inquiry* 67 (4): 409–30.

Benford, Robert D., and David A. Snow. 2000. "Framing Processes and Social Movements: An Overview and Assessment." *Annual Review of Sociology* 26: 611–39.

Berger, Joseph. 1989. "Community Control Goes Awry in a City School Board." *New York Times* 139 (Oct. 29): E5.

Berliner, David C. 1997. "Educational Psychology Meets the Christian Right: Differing Views of Children, Schooling, Teaching, and Learning." *Teachers College Record* 98: 3381–385.

Bernstein, Mary. 1994. "Countermovements and the Fate of Two Morality Policies: Consensual Sex Statutes and Lesbian and Gay Rights Ordinances." Paper presented at the New York University Seminar on Politics, Power, and Protest, December.

———. 1997. "Celebration and Suppression: The Strategic Uses of Identity by the Lesbian and Gay Movement." *American Journal of Sociology* 103 (3): 531–65.

Bernstein, Mary, and Renate Reimann, eds. 2001. *Queer Families, Queer Politics: Challenging Culture and the State.* New York: Columbia University Press.

Berube, Maurice, and Marilyn Gittell, eds. 1969. *Confrontation at Ocean Hill–Brownsville.* New York: Praeger.

Billig, Michael. 1991. *Ideology and Opinions: Studies in Rhetorical Psychology.* London: Sage.

Billig, Michael, Susan Condor, Derek Edwards, Mike Gane, David Middleton, and Alan Radley. 1988. *Ideological Dilemmas: A Social Psychology of Everyday Thinking.* London: Sage.

Blanchard, Dallas. 1994. *The Anti-Abortion Movement.* Boston: Twayne.

Bland, A. E., P. A. Brown, and R. H. Tawney, eds. 1919. *English Economic History: Select Documents.* New York: Macmillan.

Blee, Kathleen M. 1991. *Women of the Klan.* Berkeley: University of California.

———. 1996. "Becoming a Racist: Women in Contemporary Ku Klux Klan and Neo-Nazi Groups. *Gender & Society* 10 (December) 6: 680–702.

Bonner, Raymond. 1987. *Waltzing with a Dictator: The Marcoses and the Making of American Policy.* New York: Times Books, Random House, Inc.

Borchorst, Annette. 1999. "Feminist Thinking about the Welfare State." Pp. 99–127 in *Revisioning Gender,* edited by Myra Marx Ferree, Judith Lorber, and Beth Hess. Thousand Oaks, CA: Sage.

Boudreau, Vincent. 1996. "Northern Theory, Southern Protest: Opportunity Structure Analysis in Cross-National Perspective." *Mobilization: An International Journal* 1 (2): 175–89.

———. 1998. "State Attack and Social Protest: Comparative Lessons from Three Southeast Asian States." Paper presented at the Collective Behavior Conference, August 19–23, University of California, Davis.

Bourdieu, Pierre. 1984. *Distinction: A Social Critique of the Judgement of Taste.* Cambridge: Harvard University Press.

Bower, Lisa. 1997. "Queer Problems/Straight Solutions: The Limits of a Politics of 'Official Recognition.'" Pp. 267–91 in *Playing with Fire: Queer Politics, Queer Theories,* edited by Shane Phelan. New York: Routledge.

Boyer, Peter J. 1984. "'Secular Humanism' Stirs School Censorship Furor." *Los Angeles Times* 103, (Nov. 11): 1, 14–15.

Branch, Taylor. 1988. *Parting the Waters: America in the King Years, 1954–1963.* New York: Simon and Schuster.

Brandist, Craig. 1996. "Gramsci, Bakhtin, and the Semiotics of Hegemony." *New Left Review* 246: 94–109.

Breckenridge, K. 1998. "The Allure of Violence: Men, Race, and Masculinity on the South African Goldmines, 1900–1950." *Journal of Southern African Studies*, 24: 669–93.

Breines, Wini. 1982. *Community and Organization in the New Left, 1962–68.* New York: Praeger.

Brenner, Johanna. 2000. *Women and the Politics of Class.* New York: Monthly Review Press.

British Library. London: Francis Place Collection of Newspaper Clippings and Pamphlets.

Broadbent, Jeffrey. 1998. *Environmental Politics in Japan: Networks of Power and Protest.* Cambridge: Cambridge University Press.

Brock, Irving. 1817. *A Letter to the Inhabitants of Spital-Fields, on the Character and Views of Modern Reformers.* London: F. C. and J. Rivington.

Brockett, Charles. 1995. "A Protest-Cycle Resolution in the Repression/Popular Protest Paradox." Pp. 117–44 in *Repertoires and Cycles of Collective Action*, edited by M. Traugott. Durham, NC: Duke University Press.

Brodie, M. Janine. 1985. "From Waffles to Grits: A Decade in the Life of the New Democratic Party." Pp. 205–17 in *Party Politics in Canada*, edited by Hugh G. Thorburn. 5th ed. Scarborough: Prentice-Hall Canada.

Brown, Elaine. 1992. *A Taste of Power.* New York: Pantheon Books.

Brown, Lorne. 1981. "The Waffle." Pp. 92–100 in *Western Canadian Politics: The Radical Tradition*, edited by Donald C. Kerr. Edmonton, Alberta: NeWest Institute for Canadian Studies Inc.

Buder, Leonard. 1988. "Decentralization of Schools Provides Painful Lessons: The Elusive Goal of Community Control." *New York Times* 138, (Dec. 11): E6.

Buechler, Steven M. 1990. *Women's Movements in the United States.* New Brunswick, NJ: Rutgers University Press.

Bull, Chris, and John Gallagher. 1996. *Perfect Enemies: The Religious Right, the Gay Movement, and the Politics of the 1990s.* New York: Crown.

Bunnell, Fredrick (with assistance from Alice Bunnell). 1996. "Community Participation, Indigenous Ideology, Activist Politics: Indonesian NGOs in the 1990s." Pp. 180–201 in *Making Indonesia? Essays in Honor of George McT. Kahin*, edited by D. S. Lev and R. McVey. Ithaca, NY: Cornell Southeast Asia Program.

Burkitt, Ian. 1998. "The Death and Rebirth of the Author: The Bakhtin Circle and Bourdieu in Individuality, Language and Revolution." Pp. 163–80 in *Bakhtin and the Human Sciences: No Last Words*, edited by Michael Mayfield Bell and Michael Gardiner. London: Sage.

Burstein, Paul. 1985. *Discrimination, Jobs, and Politics.* Chicago: University of Chicago Press.

———. 1993. "Explaining State Action and The Expansion of Civil Rights; The Civil Rights Act of 1964." *Research in Political Sociology* 6: 117–37.

———. 1999. "Social Movements and Public Policy." Pp. 3–21 in *How Move-ments Matter*, edited by M. Giugni, D. McAdam, and C. Tilly. Minneapolis: University of Minnesota Press.

Burstein, Paul, R. Marie Bricher, and Rachel Einwohner. 1995. "Policy Alterna-tives and Political Change: Work, Family, and Gender on the Congressional Agenda." *American Sociological Review* 60: 67–83.

Burstein, Paul, Rachel Einwohner, and Jocellyn Hollander. 1995. "The Success of Social Movements: A Bargaining Perspective." Pp. 275–95 in *The Politics of Social Protest: Comparative Perspectives on States and Social Movements*, edited by J. C. Jenkins and B. Klandermans. Minneapolis: University of Minnesota Press.

Burstein, Paul, and William Freudenburg. 1978. "Changing Public Policy: The Impact of Public Opinion, Antiwar Demonstrations, and War Costs on Senate Voting on Vietnam War Motions." *American Journal of Sociology* 84: 99–122.

Butler, Judith. 1990. *Gender Trouble: Feminism and the Subversion of Identity*. New York: Routledge.

———. 1997. "Merely Cultural." *Social Text* 52/53, 15 (3–4): 265–77.

Button, James. 1989. *Blacks and Social Change*. Princeton, NJ: Princeton Univer-sity Press.

Calhoun, Craig. 1993. "'New Social Movements' of the Early 19th Century." *Social Science History* 17 (3): 385–427.

Carden, Maren Lockwood. 1974. *The New Feminist Movement*. New York: Russell Sage Foundation.

———. 1996. "Master Framing and Cross-Movement Networking in Contempo-rary Social Movements." *Sociological Quarterly* 37 (4): 601–25.

Carson, Clayborne. 1981. *In Struggle: SNCC and the Black Awakening of the 1960s*. Cambridge: Harvard University Press.

———. 1986. "Civil Rights Reform and the Black Freedom Struggle." Pp. 19–32 in *The Civil Rights Movement in America*, edited by Charles W. Eagles. Jackson: University Press of Mississippi.

Carty, R. Kenneth, William Cross, and Lisa Young. 2000. *Rebuilding Canadian Party Politics*. Vancouver: UBC Press.

Carty, R. Kenneth, and David Stewart. 1996. "Parties and Party Systems." Pp. 63–94 in *Provinces: Canadian Provincial Politics*, edited by Christopher Dunn. Peterborough, Ontario: Broadview Press.

Cassell, Joan. 1977. *A Group Called Women: Sisterhood and Symbolism in the Feminist Movement*. New York: David McKay.

Castells, M. 1997. *The Power of Identity*. Oxford: Blackwell Publishers.

Cerulo, K. A. 1997. "Identity Construction: New Issues, New Directions." *Annual Review of Sociology* 23: 385–409.

Chong, Dennis. 1991. *Collective Action and the Civil Rights Movement*. Chicago: University of Chicago Press.

Claeys, Gregory. 1989. *Citizens and Saints: Politics and Anti-Politics in Early British Socialism*. Cambridge: Cambridge University Press.

Clapham, J. H. 1916. "The Spitalfields Acts 1773–1824." *Economic Journal* 26: 459–71.

Clark, Anna. 1995. *The Struggle for the Breeches: The Making of the British Working Class, 1780–1850.* Berkeley: University of California Press.

Clegg, Sue. 1996. "From the Women's Movement to Feminisms." Pp. 45–67 in *To Make Another World: Studies in Protest and Collective Action,* edited by C. Barker and P. Kennedy. Aldershot: Avebury.

Clemens, Elisabeth S. 1996. "Organizational Form as Frame: Collective Identity and Political Strategy in the American Labor Movement." Pp. 205–26 in *Comparative Perspectives on Social Movements: Opportunities, Mobilizing Structures and Cultural Framings,* edited by Doug McAdam, John D. McCarthy, and Mayer Zald. Cambridge: Cambridge University Press.

———. 1997. *The People's Lobby: Organizational Innovation and the Rise of Interest Group Politics in the United States, 1890–1925.* Chicago: University of Chicago Press.

Cliff, Tony. 1970. *The Employers' Offensive: Productivity Deals and How to Fight Them.* London: Pluto.

———. 1979. "The Balance of Class Forces in Recent Years." *International Socialism* 6: 1–50.

CNN. 2000. "Private Schools/Public Money." *Democracy in America* (Sept. 17). URL: wysiwyg://2http://www.cnn.com/SPECIALS/2000/democracy/

Cobb, J. M. 1970. "Youth Authoritarians for Freedom." *Libertarian Connection,* February.

Cohen, Jean L. 1985. "Strategy or Identity: New Theoretical Paradigms and Contemporary Social Movements." *Social Research* 52 (4): 663–716.

Colby, Charlotte Dennett. 1986. "ERA—The Real Issues." *Out in the Mountains* 1 (9): 4.

Colby, David. 1985. "Black Power, White Resistance, and Public Policy: Political Power and Poverty Program Grants in Mississippi." *Journal of Politics* 47: 579–95.

Coleman, James S. 1990. *Foundations of Social Theory.* Cambridge: Harvard University Press.

Collins, Chik. 1996. "To Concede or to Contest? Language and Class Struggle." Pp. 69–91 in *To Make Another World: Studies in Protest and Collective Action,* edited by Colin Barker and Paul Kennedy. Aldershot: Avebury.

Collins, Randall. 1981. "On the Micro-foundations of Macro-sociology." *American Journal of Sociology* 86: 984–1014.

Colson, Charles. 1996. "Why Not Gay Marriage." *Christianity Today* October 28.

Comaroff, J., and J. Comaroff. 1992. *Ethnography and the Historical Imagination.* Boulder, CO: Westview.

Costain, Anne N. 1992. *Inviting Women's Rebellion.* Baltimore: Johns Hopkins University Press.

"Coventry Freeman." 1824. *Animadversions on the Repeal of the Act for Regulating the Wages of Labour among the Spitalfields Weavers; and in the Combination Law.* London: R. Brown.

Cronin, James. 1979. *Industrial Conflict in Britain*. London: Croom Helm.

Cronin, Joseph M. 1973. *The Control of Urban Schools: Perspective on the Power of Educational Reformers*. New York: Free Press.

Crossley, Nick. 1999. "Habitus, Capital, and Repertoires of Contention in Recent Mental Health Processes." Paper presented at the Fifth International Conference on Alternative Futures and Popular Protest, Manchester Metropolitan University, March 31.

Crush, J., A. Jeeves, and D. Yudelman. 1991. *South Africa's Labor Empire*. Boulder, CO: Westview.

Currah, Paisley. 1997. "Politics, Practices, Publics: Identity and Queer Rights." Pp. 231–66 in *Playing With Fire: Queer Politics, Queer Theories*, edited by Shane Phelan. New York: Routledge.

Curtis, Russell L., and Louis A. Zurcher. 1973. "Stable Resources of Protest Movements: The Multi-Organizational Field." *Social Forces* 54: 53–61.

Dallard, Shyrlee. 1990. *Ella Baker: A Leader Behind the Scenes*. New Jersey: Silver Burdett Press.

Datar, Chhaya. 1998. *Nurturing Nature: Women at the Centre of Natural and Social Regeneration*. Bombay, India: Earthcare Books.

Datta, Bishakha, ed. 1995. *And Who Will Make the Chappatis? All Women Panchayats in Maharashtra*. Pune, India: Alochana, Centre For Documentation and Research on Women.

Davis, Angela. 1981. *Women, Race, and Class*. New York: Random House.

Davis, Flora. 1991. *Moving the Mountain: The Women's Movement in America since 1960*. New York: Simon & Schuster.

della Porta, Donatella. 1995. *Social Movements, Political Violence, and the State: A Comparative Analysis of Italy and Germany*. Cambridge: Cambridge University Press.

della Porta, Donatella, and Dieter Rucht. 1995. "Left-Libertarian Movements in Context: A Comparison of Italy and West Germany, 1965–1990." Pp. 229–72 in *The Politics of Social Protest: Comparative Perspectives on States and Social Movements*, edited by J. Craig Jenkins and Bert Klandermans. Minneapolis: University of Minnesota Press.

della Porta, Donatella, and Herbert Reiter, eds. 1998. *Policing Protest: The Control of Mass Demonstrations in Western Democracies*. Minneapolis: University of Minnesota Press.

DeMartini, Joseph. 1983. "Social Movement Participation: Political Socialization, Generational Consciousness, and Lasting Effects." *Youth and Society* 15: 195–223.

de Peuter, Jennifer. 1998. "The Dialogics of Narrative Identity." Pp. 30–48 in *Bakhtin and the Human Sciences: No Last Words*, edited by Michael Mayfield Bell and Michael Gardiner. London: Sage.

Desai, Manisha. 1996. "From Vienna to Beijing: Women's Human Rights Activism and the Human Rights Community." *New Political Science* 35: 107–19.

———. 2001. "India: Women's Movements From Nationalism to Sustainable Development." Pp. 99–112 in *Women's Rights: A Global View*, edited by Lynn Walter. Westport, CT: Greenwood Publishers.

Desai, Neera. 1997. "Negotiating Political Space: Indian Women's Movement and Political Participation." Pp. 46–60 in *Women, Empowerment and Political Participation*, edited by Veena Poonacha. Bombay, India: Research Centre for Women's Studies, S.N.D.T. Women's University.

Diamond, Sara. 1999. *Not by Politics Along: The Enduring Impact of the Christian Right*. New York: Guilford Press.

Diani, Mario. 1997. "Social Movements and Social Capital." *Mobilization* 2: 129–47.

Dittmer, John. 1994. *Local People: The Struggle for Civil Rights in Mississippi*. Urbana: University of Illinois Press.

Dobson, James. 1995. "Why I Use 'Fighting Words.'" *Christianity Today* June 19.

Donati, Paolo R. 1992. "Political Discourse Analysis." Pp. 136–67 in *Studying Collective Action*, edited by Mario Diani and Ron Eyerman. London: Sage.

Donovan, Brian. 1998. "Political Consequences of Private Authority: Promise Keepers and the Transformation of Hegemonic Masculinity." *Theory and Society* 27: 817–43.

Downey, Gary L. 1986. "Ideology and the Clamshell Identity: Organizational Dilemmas in the Anti-Nuclear Power Movement." *Social Problems* 33 (5): 357–73.

Downs, Anthony. 1970. "Competition and Community Schools." Pp. 219–49 in *Community Control of Schools*, edited by Henry M. Levin. Washington, DC: The Brookings Institution.

Dropkin, Greg. 1998. "Interviews with Sacked Liverpool dockers." URL: www.labournet.org.uk.

Duyvendak, Jan Willem, and Marco G. Giugni. 1995. "Social Movement Types and Policy Domains." Pp. 82–110 in *New Social Movements in Western Europe: A Comparative Analysis*, edited by Hanspeter Kriesi, Ruud Koopmans, Jan Willem Duyvendak, and Marco G. Giugni. Minneapolis: University of Minnesota Press.

Eager, Evelyn. 1963. "The Paradox of Power in the Saskatchewan C.C.F., 1944–1961." Pp. 118–35 in *The Political Process in Canada: Essays in Honour of R. MacGregor Dawson*, edited by J. H. Aitchison. Toronto: University of Toronto Press.

Edelman, Murray. 1971. *Politics as Symbolic Action*. Chicago: Markham.

Edsall, Thomas Byrne, and Mary D. Edsall. 1991. *Chain Reaction: The Impact of Race, Rights, and Taxes on American Politics*. New York: W. W. Norton.

Einwohner, Rachel L. 1999a. "Gender, Class, and Social Movement Outcomes: Identity and Effectiveness in Two Animal Rights Campaigns." *Gender & Society* 13 (1): 56–76.

Eisenstein, Zillah. 1983. "The State, the Patriarchal Family, and Working Mothers." Pp. 41–58 in *Families, Politics and Public Policy*, edited by Irene Diamond. New York: Longman.

Epstein, Barbara. 1991. *Political Protest and Cultural Revolution*. Berkeley: University of California.

Epstein, Steven. 1987. "Gay Politics, Ethnic Identity: The Limits of Social Constructionism." *Socialist Review* 93/94: 9–56.

Escobar, Arturo. 1995. *Encountering Development: The Making and Unmaking of the Third World.* Princeton, NJ: Princeton University Press.

Escobar, Arturo, and Sonia Alvarez. 1992. *The Making of Social Movements in Latin America: Identity, Strategy, and Democracy.* Boulder, CO: Westview.

Escoffier, Jeffrey. 1985. "Sexual Revolution and the Politics of Gay Identity." *Socialist Review* 81/82: 119–54.

Evans, Sara. 1979. *Personal Politics: The Roots of Women's Liberation in the Civil Rights Movement and New Left.* New York: Alfred Knopf.

Faludi, Susan. 1991. *Backlash.* New York: Crown Publishers.

Falwell, Jerry. 1984. "Listen, America." Pp. 117–27 in *American Political Theology,* edited by C. Dunn. New York: Praeger.

Fantasia, Rick. 1988. *Cultures of Solidarity: Consciousness, Action, and Contemporary American Workers.* Berkeley: University of California Press.

Fantini, Mario. 1969. "Community Participation." Pp. 323–37 in *The Politics of Urban Education,* edited by Marilyn Gittell and Alan G. Hevesi. New York: Frederick A. Praeger.

Fendrich, James M. 1974. "Activists Ten Years Later: A Test of Generational Unit Continuity." *Journal of Social Issues* 30: 95–118.

Fendrich, James, and Kenneth L. Lovoy. 1988. "Back to the Future: Adult Political Behavior of Former Student Activists." *American Sociological Review* 53: 780–84.

Fendrich, James Max, and Robert Turner. 1989. "The Transition from Student to Adult Politics." *Sociological Forces* 67: 1049–57.

Ferguson, James. 1994. *The Anti-politics Machine: "Development," Depolitization, and Bureaucratic Power in Lesotho.* Minneapolis: University of Minnesota.

Ferree, Myra Marx. 1992. "The Political Context of Rationality: Rational Choice Theory and Resource Mobilization." Pp. 29–52 in *Frontiers of Social Movement Theory,* edited by A. D. Morris and C. McClurg Mueller. New Haven, CT: Yale University Press.

Ferree, Myra Marx, and Beth B. Hess. 1985/1995. *Controversy and Coalition: The New Feminist Movement.* Boston: Twayne.

Ferree, Myra Marx, and Patricia Yancey Martin. 1995. *Feminist Organizations: Harvest of the New Women's Movement.* Philadelphia: Temple University Press.

Findlen, Barbara. 1995. *Listen Up: Voices from the Next Feminist Generation.* Seattle: Seal Press.

Fine, Gary Alan. 1995. "Public Narration and Group Culture: Discerning Discourse in Social Movments." Pp. 127–43 in *Social Movements and Culture,* edited by Hank Johnston and Bert Klandermans. Minneapolis: University of Minnesota Press.

Fleming, Cynthia Griggs. 1998. *Soon We Will Not Cry.* Maryland: Rowman and Littlefield Publishers.

Fording, Richard. 1997. "The Conditional Effect of Violence as a Political Tactic: Mass Insurgency, Welfare Generosity, and Electoral Context in the American States." *American Journal of Political Science* 41: 1–29.

Forman, James. 1985. *The Making of Black Revolutionaries*. Washington, DC: Open Hand Publishing.

Foucault, Michel. 1972. *The Archaeology of Knowledge and the Discourse of Language*. New York: Harper and Row.

———. 1977. *Discipline and Punish*. New York: Vintage.

———. 1983. "Afterword: The Subject and Power." In *Michel Foucault: Beyond Structuralism and Hermeneutics*, edited by Herbert Dreyfus and Paul Rabinow. Chicago: Univeristy of Chicago Press.

———. 1984. "Nietzsche, Genealogy, History." Pp. 369–91 in *Aesthetics, Method and Epistemology*, edited by J. D. Faubion. New York: New Press.

Frankel, Francine. 1977. *India's Political Economy, 1947–1977: The Gradual Revolution*. Princeton, NJ: Princeton University Press.

Fraser, Nancy. 1989. *Unruly Practices: Power, Discourse and Gender in Contemporary Social Theory*. Minneapolis: University of Minnesota Press.

Freeman, Jo. 1972/1973. "The Tyranny of Structurelessness." *Berkeley Journal of Sociology* 17: 151–64.

———. 1973. "The Origins of the Women's Liberation Movement." *American Journal of Sociology* 78: 792–811.

———. 1975. *The Politics of Women's Liberation*. New York: David McKay.

Friedan, Betty. 1977. *It Changed My Life: Writings on the Women's Movement*. New York: Dell.

Friedman, Debra, and Doug McAdam. 1992. "Collective Identity and Activism: Networks, Choices and the Life of a Social Movement." Pp. 156–73 in *Frontiers in Social Movement Theory*, edited by Aldon D. Morris and Carol Mueller. New Haven, CT: Yale University Press.

Friedman, S. 1987. *Building Tomorrow Today: African Workers in Trade Unions. 1970–1984*. Johannesburg: Ravan.

Gamson, Joshua. 1995. "Must Identity Movements Self Destruct: A Queer Dilemma." *Social Problems* 42 (3): 390–407.

———. 1997. "Messages of Exclusion: Gender, Movements, and Symbolic Boundaries." *Gender and Society* 11 (2): 178–99.

Gamson, William. A. 1988. "Political Discourse and Collective Action." Pp. 219–44 (vol. 1) in *International Social Movement Research*, edited by Bert Klandermans, Hanspeter Kriesi, and Sidney Tarrow. Greenwich, CT: JAI Press.

———. 1990 (1975). *The Strategy of Social Protest*. Belmont: Wadsworth.

———. 1992a. "The Social Psychology of Collective Action." Pp. 53–76 in *Frontiers in Social Movement Theory*, edited by Aldon D. Morris and Carol M. Mueller. New Haven, CT: Yale University Press.

———. 1992b. *Talking Politics*. New York: Cambridge University Press.

———. 1995. "Constructing Social Protest." Pp. 85–106 in *Social Movements and Culture*, edited by Hank Johnston and Bert Klandermans. Minneapolis: University of Minnesota Press.

————. 1998. "Social Movements and Cultural Change." Pp. 57–77 in *From Contention to Democracy*, edited by Marco G. Giugni, Doug McAdam, and Charles Tilly. Lanham, MD: Rowman & Littlefield.

Gamson, William A., and David S. Meyer. 1996. "Framing Political Opportunity." Pp. 275–90 in *Comparative Perspectives on Social Movements: Political Opportunities, Mobilizing Structures and Cultural Framings*, edited by Doug McAdam, John D. McCarthy, and Mayer Zald. Cambridge: Cambridge University Press.

Gamson, William A., and Emilie Schmeidler. 1984. "Organizing the Poor." *Theory and Society* 13: 587–99.

Gandhi, Nandita, and Nandita Shah. 1992. *Issues at Stake: Theory and Practice in the Contemporary Women's Movement in India*. New Delhi: Kali.

Gans, Herbert. 1995. *The War Against the Poor*. New York: Vantage.

Ganz, Marshall. 2000. "Resources and Resourcefulness: Strategic Capacity in the Unionization of Californian Agriculture." *American Journal of Sociology* 105 (4): 1003–62.

Gardiner, Michael. 1992. *The Dialogics of Critique: M. M. Bakhtin and the Theory of Ideology*. London: Routledge.

Garrow, David. 1978. *Protest at Selma: Martin Luther King, Jr. and the Voting Rights Act of 1965*. New Haven, CT: Yale University Press.

————. 1986. *Bearing the Cross*. New York: First Vintage Books.

Gaventa, John. 1980. *Power and Powerlessness: Quiescence and Rebellion in an Appalachian Valley*. Urbana: University of Illinois Press.

Geertz, Clifford. 1973. *The Interpretation of Cultures*. New York: Basic Books.

Gelb, Joyce. 1987. "Social Movement 'Success': A Comparative Analysis of Feminism in the United States and the United Kingdom." Pp. 267–89 in *The Women's Movements of the United States and Western Europe*, edited by M. F. Katzenstein and C. M. Mueller. Philadelphia: Temple University Press.

————. 1995. "Feminist Organization Success and the Politics of Engagement." Pp. 128–36, 290 in *Feminist Organizations: Harvest of the New Women's Movement*, edited by M. M. Ferree and P. Y. Martin. Philadelphia: Temple University Press.

George, M. Dorothy. 1925. *London Life in the Eighteenth Century*. London: K. Paul, Trench & Trubner.

Gerhards, Jurgen, and Dieter Rucht. 1992. "Mesomobilization: Organizing and Framing in Two Protest Campaigns in West Germany." *American Journal of Sociology* 98 (3): 555–95.

Giddings, Paula. 1984. *When and Where I Enter: The Impact of Black Women on Race and Sex in America*. New York: Bantam Books.

Gitlin, Todd. 1980. *The Whole World Is Watching: Mass Media in the Making and Unmaking of the New Left*. Berkeley: University of California Press.

————. 1987. *The Sixties: Years of Hope, Days of Rage*. New York: Bantam.

————. 1994. "From Universality to Difference: Notes on the Fragmentation of the Idea of the Left." Pp. 150–74 in *Social Theory and the Politics of Identity*, edited by in Craig Calhoun. Cambridge, MA: Blackwell.

———. 1995. *The Twilight of Common Dreams: Why America Is Wracked by Culture Wars*. New York: Metropolitan Books.

———. 1970. "The Balance of Power and the Community School." Pp. 115–37 in *Community Control of Schools*, edited by Henry M. Levin. Washington, DC: The Brookings Institution.

Giugni, Marco. 1998. "Was It Worth the Effort? The Outcomes and Consequences of Social Movements." *Annual Review of Sociology* 24: 371–93.

Giugni, Marco, Doug McAdam, and Charles Tilly. 1999. *How Social Movements Matter*. Minneapolis: University of Minnesota Press.

Glazer, Nathan. 1997. "Homegrown: Charter Schools (The Hard Questions)." *New Republic* 216 (19) (May 12): 25.

Goldstone, J. 1988. *Revolution and Rebellion in the Early Modern World*. Berkeley: University of California Press.

Goodwin, Jeff, and James M. Jasper. 1999. "Caught in a Winding, Snarling Vine: The Structural Bias of Political Process Theory." *Sociological Forum* 14 (1): 27–54.

Goodwyn, Lawrence. 1991. *Breaking the Barrier: The Rise of Solidarity in Poland*. New York: Oxford University Press.

Gordon, Barry. 1979. *Economic Doctrine and Tory Liberalism 1824–1830*. London: Macmillan.

Gordon, Dave, and Mel Watkins. 1970. *Gordon to Watkins to You*. Toronto: New Press.

Gould, R. 1991. "Multiple Networks and Mobilization in the Paris Commune. 1871." *American Sociological Review* 56: 716–29.

Gramsci, A. 1971. *Selections from the Prison Notebooks*. New York: International.

Greenberg, Polly. 1969. *The Devil Has Slippery Shoes: A Biased Biography of the Child Development Group in Mississippi*. London: Macmillan.

Griffith, Alison I., and Dorothy E. Smith. 1990. "What Did You Do in School Today?: Mothering, Schooling, and Social Class." Pp. 3–24 in *Perspectives on Social Problems*, Vol. 2, edited G. Miller and J. A. Hostein. Greenwich, CT: JAI Press.

Gusfield, Joseph. 1986. *Symbolic Crusade*. 2nd Edition. Urbana: University of Illinois Press.

Hage, Jerald. 1980. *Theories of Organizations*. New York: John Wiley and Sons.

Haines, Herbert H. 1984. "Black Radicalization and the Funding of Civil Rights: 1957–1970." *Social Problems* 32: 31–43.

Halcli, Abigail, and Jo Reger. 1996. "Strangers in a Strange Land: The Gendered Experiences of Women Politicians in Britain and the United States." Pp. 457–71 in *Feminist Frontiers*, edited by N. Whittier, V. Taylor, and L. Richardson. 4th ed. New York: McGraw Hill.

Hale, William. 1822. *An Appeal to the Public, in Defence of the Spitalfields Act: with Remarks on the Causes Which Have Led to the Miseries and Moral Deterioration of the Poor*. London: E. Justins.

Hall, S. 1997. "Subjects in History: Making Diasporic Identities." Pp. 289–99 in *The House that Race Built: Black Americans, US Terrain*, edited by W. Lubiano. New York: Pantheon.

Halle, Randall. 2001. "Political Organizing and the Limits of Civil Rights: Gay
    Marriage and Queer Families." Forthcoming in *Queer Families, Queer Politics:
    Challenging Culture and the State*, edited by M. Bernstein and R. Reimann.
    New York: Columbia University Press.

Hallman, Howard W. 1969. *Community Control: A Study of Community
    Corporation and Neighborhood Boards*. Washington, DC: Washington Center
    for Metropolitan Studies.

Hammond, J. L., and Barbara Hammond. 1967 (1919). *The Skilled Labourer,
    1780–1832*. New York: August M. Kelley.

Hansards Parliamentary Debates. New Series.

Harman, Chris. 1988. *The Fire Last Time: 1968 and After*. London: Bookmarks.

Hart, Stephen. 1996. "The Cultural Dimension of Social Movements: A Theoreti-
    cal Reassessment and Literature Review." *Sociology of Religion* 57: 87–100.

Hartmann, Heidi. 1981. "The Unhappy Marriage Between Marxism and Femi-
    nism." Pp. 1–41 in *Women and Revolution*, edited by Lydia Sargent. Boston:
    South End.

Hartstock, Nancy. 1983. *Money, Sex, and Power: Toward a Feminist Historical
    Materialism*. New York: Longman.

Haynes, M. J. 1985. "Strikes." Pp. 89–131 in *The Working Class in England
    1875–1914*, edited by John Benson. London: Croom Helm.

Hechinger, Fred M. 1986. "Censorship Found on the Increase." *New York Times*
    (Sept. 16): C1, 14–15.

Hennessy, Rosemary, and Chrys Ingraham, eds. 1997. *Materialist Feminism: A
    Reader in Class, Difference, and Women's Lives*. New York: Routledge.

Herek, Gregory M. 1991. "Myths about Sexual Orientation: A Lawyer's Guide to
    Social Science Research." *Law & Sexuality* 1: 133–72.

Hertzke, Allen D. 1993. *Echoes of Discontent: Jesse Jackson, Pat Robertson,
    and the Resurgence of Populism*. Washington, DC: Congressional Quarterly
    Press.

Hill Collins, Patricia. 1990. *Black Feminist Thought*. New York: Routledge.

Hilton, Boyd. 1977. *Corn, Cash, Commerce: The Economic Policies of the Tory
    Governments 1815–1830*. Oxford: Oxford University Press.

Hipsher, Patricia. 1998. "Democratic Transitions and Social Movement Out-
    comes: The Chilean Shantytown Dwellers' Movement in Comparative Perspec-
    tive." Pp. 149–68 in *From Contention to Democracy*, edited by M. Giugni, D.
    McAdam, and C. Tilly. Lanham, MD: Rowman and Littlefield.

Hirschman, Albert. 1991. *The Rhetoric of Reaction*. Cambridge: Harvard
    University Press.

Hlaing, Kyaw Yin. 1996. "The Mobilization Process in 'Four Eighths' Democratic
    Movement in Burma." Presented at the Association of Asian Studies Annual
    Meeting, April 14, Honolulu, Hawaii.

Hochstetler, Kathryn. 1995. *Social Movements in Institutional Politics: Organiz-
    ing about the Environment in Brazil and Venezuela*. Ph.D. dissertation,
    Department of Political Science, University of Minnesota.

Honneth, A. 1996. *The Struggle for Recognition*. Cambridge: MIT Press.

Horowitz, Gad. 1968. *Canadian Labour in Politics*. Toronto: University of Toronto Press.

Hoy, Mikita. 1992. "Bakhtin and Popular Culture." *New Literary History* 23: 765–82.

Huber, Joan, ed. 1991. *Macro-Micro Linkages in Sociology*. Newbury Park, CA: Sage.

Hughes, Richard T., and C. Leonard Allen. 1988. *Illusions of Innocence: Protestant Primitivism in America, 1630–1875*. Chicago: University of Chicago Press.

Hunt, Scott A., and Robert Benford. 1994. "Identity Talk in the Peace and Justice Movement." *Journal of Contemporary Ethnography* 22: 488–517.

Hunt, Scott A., Robert D. Benford, and David A. Snow. 1994. "Identity Fields: Framing Processes and the Social Construction of Movement Identities." Pp. 185–208 in *New Social Movements: From Ideology to Identity*, edited by Enrique Laraña, Hank Johnston, and Joseph R. Gusfield. Philadelphia: Temple University Press.

Huspek, Michael. 1993. "Dueling Structures: The Theory of Resistance in Discourse." *Communication Theory* 3 (1): 1–25.

IAWS (India Association of Women's Studies). 1995. *The State and the Women's Movement in India: A Report*. New Delhi: Systems Vision.

Irvine, Janice. Forthcoming. *Talk about Sex*. New York: Oxford University Press.

Jackson, Robert L. 1992. "Censorship Efforts in Schools Up 50% Last Year, Group Says." *Los Angeles Times* (Sept. 2): A16.

James, David R. 1988. "The Transformation of the Southern Racial State: Class and Race Determinants of Local-State Structures." *American Sociological Review* 53: 191–208.

Jasper, James M. 1992. "The Politics of Abstractions: Instrumental and Moralist Rhetorics in Public Debate." *Social Research* 59: 315–44.

———. 1997. *The Art of Moral Protest: Culture, Biography and Creativity in Social Movements*. Chicago: University of Chicago Press.

———. 1998. "The Emotions of Protest: Affective and Reactive Emotions In and Around Social Movements." *Sociological Forum* 13 (3): 397–424.

Jasper, James M., and Jeff Goodwin [as "Jaswin"]. 1999. "Trouble in Paradigms." *Sociological Forum* 14 (1): 107–26.

Jasper, J. M., and Francesca Polletta. 2001. "Collective Identity and Social Movements." *Annual Review of Sociology* 27: 283–305.

Jasper, James M., and Jane Poulsen. 1993. "Fighting Back: Vulnerabilities, Blunders, and Countermobilization by the Targets in Three Animal Rights Campaigns." *Sociological Forum* 8 (4): 639–57.

Jenkins, J. Craig, and Bert Klandermans. 1995. "The Politics of Protest." Pp. 3–13 in *The Politics of Protest: Comparative Perspectives on States and Social Movements*, edited by J. Craig Jenkins and Bert Klandermans. Minneapolis: University of Minnesota Press.

Jenkins, J. Craig, and Craig M. Eckert. 1986. "Channeling Black Insurgency: Elite Patronage and Professional Social Movement Organizations in the Development of the Black Movement." *American Sociological Review* 51: 812–29.

Jenness, Valerie, and Ryken Grattet. 1996. "The Criminalization of Hate: A Comparison of Structural and Polity Influences on the Passage of 'Bias-Crime' Legislation in the United States." *Sociological Perspectives* 39 (1): 129–54.

Jenson, Jane. 1982. "The Modern Women's Movement in Italy, France, and Great Britain: Differences in Life Cycles." *Comparative Social Research* 5: 341–75.

Johnson, Victoria. 1999. "The Strategic Determinants of a Countermovement: The Emergence and Impact of Operation Rescue Blockades." Pp. 241–66 in *Waves of Protest: Social Movements since the Sixties*, edited by J. Freeman and V. Johnson. Lanham, MD: Rowman & Littlefield.

Johnston, Hank. 1995. "A Methodology for Frame Analysis: From Discourse to Cognitive Schemata." Pp. 217–46 in *Social Movements and Culture*, edited by Hank Johnston and Bert Klandermans. Minneapolis: University of Minnesota Press.

Johnston, Hank, and Bert Klandermans, eds. 1995. *Social Movements and Culture*. Minneapolis: University of Minnesota Press.

Johnston, Hank, Enrique Laraña, and Joseph R. Gusfield. 1994. "Identities, Grievances, and New Social Movements." Pp. 3–35 in *New Social Movements: From Ideology to Identity*, edited by E. Laraña, H. Johnston, and J. R. Gusfield. Philadelphia: Temple University Press.

Jordan, W. M. 1931. *The Silk Industry in London, 1760–1830, with Special Reference to the Conditions of the Wage-Earners and the Policy of the Spitalfields Acts*. Unpublished Master's thesis in history, University of London.

Kater, J. L., Jr. 1982. *Christians on the Right*. New York: Seabury Press.

Katz, Alex. 2000. "Gay-Straight Club's Battle Is Won." *Los Angeles Times* Sept. 8: B1, B12.

Katz, Elihu, and S. N. Eisenstadt. 1960. "Some Sociological Observations on the Response of Israeli Organizations to New Immigrants." *Administrative Science Quarterly* 5: 113–33.

Katzenstein, Mary Fainsod. 1990. "Feminism Within American Institutions: Unobtrusive Mobilization in the 1980s." *Signs* 16 (1): 28–54.

———. 1998. *Faithful and Fearless: Moving Feminist Protest Inside the Church and Military*. Princeton, NJ: Princeton University Press.

Keiser, Richard A. 1997. *Subordination or Empowerment? African-American Political Leadership and the Struggle for Urban Political Power*. New York: Oxford University Press.

Kelkar, Govind, and Chetna Gala. 1990. "The Bodh Gaya Land Struggle." Pp. 82–110 in *A Space Within the Stuggle: Women's Participation in People's Movements*, edited by Ilina Sen. New Delhi: Kali For Women.

Kelly, John. 1998. *Rethinking Industrial Relations: Mobilization, Collectivism and Long Waves*. London: Routledge.

Kennedy, Jane, and Michael Lavalette. 1997. "Global Warfare: The Liverpool Dockers' International Campaign Against Mersey Docks and Harbour Company." In *Proceedings of the Third International Conference on "Alternative Futures and Popular Protest."* Manchester: Manchester Metropolitan University.

Kenniston, Kenneth. 1968. *Young Radicals*. New York: Harper and Brothers.

Kilmartin, Duncan. 1992. "Testimony." Testimony before the Vermont Senate hearing on S. 131. Courtesy of Susan Sussman.

Kimeldorf, Howard. 1988. *Reds or Rackets? The Making of Radical and Conservative Unions on the Waterfront*. Berkeley: University of California Press.

Kimmel, Michael S. 1993. "Sexual Balkanization: Gender and Sexuality and the New Ethnicities." *Social Research* 60 (3): 571–87.

King, Martin Luther, Jr. 1964. *Why We Can't Wait*. New York: Signet Books.

King, Mary. 1987. *Freedom Song*. New York: William Morrow.

Kingdon, John W. 1984. *Agendas, Alternatives, and Public Policies*. Boston: Little, Brown.

Kitschelt, Herbert P. 1986. "Political Opportunity Structures and Political Protest: Anti-Nuclear Movements in Four Democracies." *British Journal of Political Science* 16: 57–85.

Klandermans, Bert. 1989. *Organizing for Change: Social Movement Organizations Across Cultures*. Greenwich, CT: JAI.

———. 1992. "The Social Construction of Protest and Multiorganizational Fields." Pp. 77–103 in *Frontiers in Social Movement Theory*, edited by Aldon D. Morris and Carol McClung Mueller. New Haven, CT: Yale University Press.

———. 1997. *The Social Psychology of Protest*. Cambridge, MA: Blackwell.

———. 2000. "Must We Redefine Social Movements as Ideologically Structured Action?" *Mobilization* 5 (1): 25–30.

Klatch, Rebecca. 1987. *Women of the New Right*. Philadelphia: Temple University Press.

———. 1994. "The Counterculture, The New Left, and The New Right." *Qualitative Sociology* 17: 199–214.

———. 1999. *A Generation Divided: The New Left, the New Right, and the 1960s*. Berkeley: University of California Press.

———. 2000. "The Formation of Feminist Consciousness Among Left and Right-Wing Activists of the 1960s."

Kleidman, Robert. 1993. *Organizing for Peace: Neutrality, the Test Ban, and the Freeze*. Syracuse, NY: Syracuse University Press.

Klein, Ethel. 1984. *Gender Politics*. Cambridge: Harvard University Press.

Kniss, Fred. 1996. "Ideas and Symbols as Resoures in Intrareligious Conflict: The Case of American Mennonites." *Sociology of Religion* 57: 7–23.

Knoke, David. 1989. "Resources Acquisitions and Allocation in U.S. National Associations." Pp. 129–54 in *International Social Movement Research, Organizing for Change: Social Movement Organizations in Europe and the United States*, edited by B. Klandermans. Vol. 2. Greenwich, CT: JAI Press.

Knorr-Cetina, K., and A. V. Cicourel, eds. 1981. *Advances in Social Theory and Methodology: Toward an Integration of Micro- and Macro-Sociologies*. Boston: Routledge and Kegan Paul.

Kohli, Atul. 1990. *Democracy and Discontent: India's Growing Crisis of Governability*. New York: Cambridge University Press.

Koopmans, Ruud. 1995. *Democracy from Below: New Social Movements and the Political System in West Germany*. Boulder, CO: Westview Press.

———. 1999. "Political. Opportunity. Structure. Some Splitting to Balance the Lumping." *Sociological Forum* 14 (1): 93–106.

Kothari, Rajani. 1970. *Politics in India*. Boston: Little Brown.

Kriesi, H. 1996. "The Organizational Structure of New Social Movements in a Political Context." Pp. 152–84 in *Comparative Perspectives on Social Movements*, edited by D. McAdam, J. D. McCarthy, and M. Zald. New York: Cambridge University Press.

Kriesi, Hanspeter, and Marco G. Giugni. 1995. "Introduction." Pp. ix–xxvi in *New Social Movements in Western Europe: A Comparative Analysis*, edited by Hanspeter Kriesi, Ruud Koopmans, Jan Willem Duyvendak, and Marco G. Giugni. Minneapolis: University of Minnesota Press.

Kriesi, Hanspeter, Ruud Koopmans, Jan Willem Duyvendak, and Marco G. Giugni. 1995. *The Politics of New Social Movements*. Minneapolis: University of Minnesota Press.

———. 1995. *New Social Movements in Western Europe: A Comparative Analysis*. Minneapolis: University of Minnesota Press.

Krishnaraj, Maitreyi. 1995. *Remaking Society For Women: Visions—Past and Present*. New Delhi: Indian Association for Women's Studies.

Kumar, Radha. 1993. *A History of Doing: Women's Activism in India*. New Delhi: Kali.

Kurzman, Charles. 1994. "A Dynamic View of Resources: Evidence from the Iranian Revolution." *Research on Social Movements, Conflict, and Change* 17: 53–84.

———. 1996. "Structural Opportunity and Perceived Opportunity in Social-Movement Theory: The Iranian Revolution of 1979." *American Journal of Sociology* 61: 153–70.

Ladner, Joyce. 1970. "What Black Power Means to Negroes in Mississippi." Pp. 131–54 in *The Transformation of Activism*, edited by August Meier. Chicago: Aldine.

LaHaye, Tim. 1982. *The Battle for the Family*. Old Tappan, NJ: Fleming H. Revell.

Lamont, Michele, ed. 1999. *The Cultural Territories of Race: Black and White Boundaries*. Chicago: University of Chicago Press and Russell Sage Foundation.

Landry, Donna, and Gerald MacLean. 1993. *Materialist Feminisms*. Oxford: Blackwell.

Laraña E., Hank Johnston, and Joseph R. Gusfield. 1994. *New Social Movements: From Ideology to Identity*. Philadelphia: Temple University Press.

Laumann, Edward O., and David Knoke. 1987. *The Organizational State: Social Choice in National Policy Domains*. Madison: University of Wisconsin Press.

Lavalette, Michael, and Jane Kennedy. 1996a. "Casual Lives? The Social Costs of Work Casualization and the Lockout of the Liverpool Docks." *Critical Social Policy* 16 (3): 95–107.

————. 1996b. *Solidarity on the Waterfront: The Liverpool Lockout of 1995/96.* Liverpool: Liver Press.

Lehring, Gary. Forthcoming. *Officially Gay.* Philadelphia: Temple University Press.

Lemke, Jay L. 1995. *Textual Politics: Discourse and Social Dynamics.* London: Taylor and Francis.

Letters, Taken from Various Newspapers, Tending to Injure the Journeymen Silk Weavers of Spitalfields, with and Attack against the Acts of Parliament, Regulating the Prices of Their Work. Also, the Answers, by the Journeymen and Their Friends. 1818. London: E. Justins.

Lewis, John. 1998. *Walking with the Wind.* New York: Simon and Schuster.

Lichterman, Paul. 1996. *The Search for Political Community: American Activists Reinventing Commitment.* New York: Cambridge University Press.

Liddle, William R. 1995. "The Islamic Turn in Indonesia: A Political Explanation." *Journal of Asian Studies* 55 (3): 613–34.

Lintner, Bertil. 1990. *Outrage: Burma's Struggle for Democracy.* London: White Lotus.

Linz, Juan J., and Alfred Stepan. 1996. *Problems of Democratic Transition and Consolidation: Southern Europe, South America, and Post-communist Europe.* Baltimore, MD: Johns Hopkins University Press.

Lipset, Seymour Martin. 1968. *Agrarian Socialism: The Cooperative Commonwealth Federation of Saskatchewan.* Rev. ed. Garden City, NY: Doubleday Anchor.

————. 1970. "The Ideology of Local Control." Pp. 21–42 in *Education and Social Policy: Local Control of Education,* edited by C. A. Bowers, Ian Housego, and Doris Dyke. New York: Random House.

Lipsky, Michael. 1968. "Protest as a Political Resource." *American Political Science Review* 62: 1144–58.

————. 1970. *Protest in City Politics.* Chicago: Rand-McNally.

Livingston, Joy. 1986. "ERA Coalition Faces Controversy." *Out in the Mountains* 1 (5): 5.

Lofland, John. 1993. "Theory-Bashing and Answer-Improving in the Study of Social Movements." *American Sociologist* 24: 37–58.

Loseke, Donileen. 1992. *The Battered Woman and Shelters: The Social Construction of Wife Abuse.* Albany: State University of New York Press.

LSP 1823, (57) CLVI, Minutes of Evidence Taken Before the Lords Committees on The Bill, intitled, "An Act to repeal certain Acts of His late Majesty relating to the Wages of Persons employed in the Manufacture of Silk, and of Silk mixed with Other Materials, House of Lords Sessional Papers.

Lutz, Frank W., and Carol Merz, eds. 1992. *The Politics of School/Community Relations.* New York: Teachers College Press.

Manchee, W. H. 1913. "Memories of Spitalfields." *Proceedings of the Huguenot Society of London* 10: 298–34.

Mankoff, Milt, and Richard Flacks. 1971. "The Changing Social Base of the American Student Movement." *Annals of the American Academy of Political and Social Science* 395: 54–67.

Mannheim, Karl. 1952. "The Problem of Generations." In *Essays on the Sociology of Knowledge*, edited by Paul Kecskemeti. London: Routledge and Kegan Paul.

Mansbridge, Jane J. 1986. *Why We Lost the ERA*. Chicago: University of Chicago Press.

Markoff, John. 1996. *Waves of Democracy: Social Movements and Political Change*. Thousand Oaks, CA: Pine Forge Press.

———. 1997. "Peasants Help Destroy an Old Regime and Defy a New One: Some Lessons from (and for) the Study of Social Movements." *American Journal of Sociology* 102 (4): 1113–42.

Marotta, Toby. 1981. *The Politics of Homosexuality*. Boston: Houghton Mifflin.

Martin, Patricia Yancey. 1990. "Rethinking Feminist Organizations." *Gender and Society* 4: 182–206.

Matthews, Donald R., and James W. Protho. 1966. *Negroes and the New Southern Politics*. New York: Harcourt, Brace and World.

Matthews, Nancy. 1994. *Confronting Rape: The Feminist Anti-Rape Movement and the State*. London: Routledge.

Maynard, Robert C. 1970. "Black Nationalism and Community Schools." Pp. 100–11 in *Community Control of Schools*, edited by Henry M. Levin. Washington, DC: The Brookings Institution.

Mayor's Advisory Panel on Decentralization of the New York City Schools. 1969. "A Framework for Change [Reprinted from Reconnection for Learning: A Community School System for New York City, 1967]." Pp. 119–66 in *Citizen Participation in Urban Development Volume II—Cases and Programs*, edited by Hans Spiegel. Washington, DC: NTL Institute for Applied Behavioral Science.

McAdam, Doug. 1982. *Political Process and the Development of Black Insurgency*. Chicago: University of Chicago Press.

———. 1986. "Recruitment to High-Risk Activism: The Case of Freedom Summer." *American Journal of Sociology* 92: 64–90.

———. 1988a. *Freedom Summer*. New York: Oxford University Press.

———. 1988b. "Micromobilization Contexts and Recruitment to Activism." *International Social Movement Research* 1: 125–54.

———. 1989. "The Biographical Consequences of Activism." *American Sociological Review* 54: 744–60.

———. 1994. "Culture and Social Movements." Pp. 36–58 in *New Social Movements: From Ideology to Identity*, edited by Enrique Laraña, Hank Johnston and Joseph R. Gusfield. Philadelphia: Temple University Press.

———. 1996. "Political Opportunities: Conceptual Origins, Current Problems, Future Directions." Pp. 23–40 in *Comparative Perspectives on Social Movements: Political Opportunities, Mobilizing Structures, and Cultural Framings*, edited by D. McAdam, J. McCarthy, and M. N. Zald. Cambridge: Cambridge University Press.

———. 1999. Introduction to *Political Process and the Development of Black Insurgency, 1930–1970*. 2d ed. Chicago: University of Chicago Press.

McAdam, Doug, John D. McCarthy, and Mayer N. Zald. 1988. "Social Movements." Pp. 695–737 in *Handbook of Sociology*, edited by Neil J. Smelser. Newbury Park, CA: Sage.

————. 1996a. *Comparative Perspectives on Social Movements: Political Opportunities, Mobilizing Structures, and Cultural Framings.* Cambridge: Cambridge University Press.

————. 1996b. "Introduction: Opportunities, Mobilizing Structures, and Framing Processes—Toward a Synthetic, Comparative Perspective on Social Movements." Pp. 1–20 in *Comparative Perspectives on Social Movements: Political Opportunities, Mobilizing Structures and Cultural Framings*, edited by Doug McAdam, John D. McCarthy, and Mayer Zald. Cambridge: Cambridge University Press.

McAdam, Doug, Sidney Tarrow, and Charles Tilly. 2001. *Dynamics of Contention.* Cambridge: Cambridge University Press.

McAdam, Doug, Sidney Tarrow, and Charles Tilly. 1996. "To Map Contentious Politics." *Mobilization* 1: 17–34.

————. 1997. "Toward an Integrated Perspective on Social Movements and Revolution." Pp. 142–173 in *Comparative Politics: Rationality, Culture and Structure*, edited by Mark I. Lichbach and Alan S. Zuckerman. Cambridge: Cambridge University Press.

McCann, Phillip. 1977. "Popular Education, Socialization, and Social Control: Spitalfields 1812–1824." Pp. 1–40 in *Popular Education and Socialization in the Nineteenth Century*, edited by Phillip McCann. London: Methuen.

McCarthy, John D. 1994. "Activists, Authorities and the Media Framing of Drunk Driving." Pp. 133–67 in *New Social Movements: From Ideology to Identity*, edited by Enrique Laraña, Hank Johnston, and Joseph R. Gusfield. Philadelphia: Temple University Press.

————. 1996. "Constraints and Opportunities in Adopting, Adapting, and Inventing." Pp. 141–51 in *Comparative Perspectives on Social Movements*, edited by Doug McAdam, John D. McCarthy, and Mayer N. Zald. Cambridge: Cambridge University Press.

McCarthy, John, and D. W. Britt. 1989. "Adapting Social Movement Organizations to External Constraints in the Modern State: Tax Codes and Accreditation." In *Research in Social Movements, Conflict and Change*, edited by L. Kriesberg. Vol. 11. Greenwich, CT: JAI Press.

McCarthy, John, and Clark McPhail. 1998. "The Institutionalization of Protest in the United States." Pp. 83–110 in *The Social Movement Society*, edited by D. S. Meyer and S. Tarrow. Lanham, MD: Rowman & Littlefield.

McCarthy, John D., Clark McPhail, and Jackie Smith. 1996. "Images of Protest: Dimensions of Selection Bias in Media Coverage of Washington Demonstrations 1982 and 1991." *American Sociological Review* 61: 478–99.

McCarthy, John, and Mayer Zald. 1977. "Resource Mobilization and Social Movements: A Partial Theory." *American Journal of Sociology* 82: 1212–41.

————. 1987. "The Trend of Social Movements in America: Professionalization and Resource Mobilization." Pp. 337–91 in *Social Movements in an Organizational Society: Collected Essays*, edited by M. Zald and J. D. McCarthy. New Brunswick, NJ: Transaction Books.

McClellan, William. 1990. "The Dialogic Other: Bakhtin's Theory of Rhetoric." *Discours Social/Social Discourse* 3 (1/2): 232–49.

McHenry, Dean. 1950. *The Third Force in Canada: The Cooperative Commonwealth Federation 1932–1948.* Berkeley: University of California Press.

McMichael, Philip. 2000. *Development and Social Change: A Global Perspective.* 2nd ed. Thousand Oaks, CA: Pine Forge Press.

McNamara, J. K. 1985. "Black Worker Conflicts on South African Gold Mines. 1973–1982." Ph.D. dissertation, Department of Social Anthropology, University of the Witwatersrand, Johannesburg.

Mead, G. H. 1932. *The Philosophy of the Present.* Chicago: University of Chicago Press.

Melnyk, George. 1985. *The Search for Community: From Utopia to a Cooperative Society.* Montreal: Black Rose Books.

Melnyk, Olenka. 1989. *Remembering the CCF: No Bankers in Heaven.* Toronto: McGraw-Hill.

Melucci, Alberto. 1984. "An End to Social Movements?" *Social Science Information* 23 (4/5): 819–35.

———. 1985b. "The Symbolic Challenge of Contemporary Movements." *Social Research* 52: 789–816.

———. 1989. *Nomads of the President: Social Movements and Individual Needs in Contemporary Society.* Philadelphia: Temple University Press.

———. 1995. "The Process of Collective Identity." In *Social Movements and Culture,* edited by H. Johnston and B. Klandermans. Minneapolis: University of Minnesota Press.

———. 1996. *Challenging Codes: Collective Action in the Information Age.* New York: Cambridge University Press.

Melucci, Alberto, and Timo Lyyra. 1998. "Collective Action, Change, and Democracy." Pp. 203–28 in *From Contention to Democracy,* edited by M. Giugni, D. McAdam, and C. Tilly. Lanham, MD: Rowman and Littlefield.

Meyer, David S. 1990. *A Winter of Discontent: The Nuclear Freeze and American Politics.* New York: Praeger.

———. 1993. "Protest Cycles and Political Process." *Political Research Quarterly* 46: 451–79.

———. 1999. "Tending the Vineyard: Cultivating Political Process Research." *Sociological Forum* 14 (1): 79–92.

Meyer, David S., and Debra C. Minkoff. 1997. "Operationalizing Political Opportunity." Paper presented at the annual meeting of the American Sociological Association, Toronto, Ontario, August.

Meyer, David S., and Thomas R. Rochon. 1997. "Toward a Coalitional Theory of Social and Political Movements." Pp. 237–252 in *Coalitions and Political Movements: The Lessons of the Nuclear Freeze,* edited by T. Rochon and D. Meyer. Boulder, CO: Lynne Rienner.

Meyer, David S., and Suzanne Staggenborg. 1996. "Movements, Countermovements, and the Structure of Political Opportunity." *American Journal of Sociology* 101 (6): 1628–60.

————. 1998. "Countermovement Dynamics in Federal Systems: A Comparison of Abortion Politics in Canada and the United States." *Research in Political Sociology* 8: 209–40.

Meyer, David S., and Nancy Whittier. 1994. "Social Movement Spillover." *Social Problems* 41 (2): 277–98.

Miller, Jim. 1987. *Democracy in the Streets*. New York: Simon and Schuster.

Minkoff, Debra C. 1993. "The Organization of Survival: Women's and Racial-Ethnic Voluntarist and Activist Organizations, 1955–1985." *Social Forces* 71: 887–908.

————. 1997. "The Sequencing of Social Movements." *American Sociological Review* 62: 779–99.

Mitchell, Don. 1981. "The Waffle." Pp. 83–91 in *Western Canadian Politics: The Radical Tradition*, edited by Donald C. Kerr. Edmonton, Alberta: NeWest Institute for Canadian Studies.

Moodie. T. D. 1986. "The Moral Economy of the Black Miners' Strike of 1946." *Journal of Southern African Studies* 13: 1–25.

————. 1994. *Going for Gold: Men, Mines and Migration*. Berkeley: University of California Press.

Mooney, Patrick H., and Scott A. Hunt. 1996. "A Repertoire of Interpretations: Master Frames and Ideological Continuity in U.S. Agrarian Mobilization." *Sociological Quarterly* 37 (1): 177–97.

Moore, B. 1978. *Injustice: The Social Bases of Obedience and Revolt*. White Plains, NY: M. E. Sharpe.

More, Hannah. 1819a. *The Contented Spital-Fields Weaver; Jeremiah Nott, His Address to His Brother Artificers, Respecting the Smithfield Meeting, and Other Matters*. 8th ed. London: Howard.

————. 1819b. "The Delegate; with Some Account of Mr. James Dawson of Spitalfields." In Cheap Repository Tracts. London.

Morley, J. T. 1984. *Secular Socialists: The CCF/NDP in Ontario, A Biography*. Montreal: McGill-Queen's University Press.

Morris, Aldon D. 1984. *The Origins of the Civil Rights Movement: Black Communities Organizing for Change*. New York: Free Press.

————. 1992. "Political Consciousness and Collective Action." Pp. 351–373 in *Frontiers of Social Movement Theory*, edited by A. D. Morris and C. McClurg Mueller. New Haven, CT: Yale University Press.

————. 1993. "Birmingham Confrontation Reconsidered." *American Sociological Review* 58: 621–636.

Morris, Aldon D., and Carol McClurg Mueller, eds. 1992. *Frontiers of Social Movement Theory*. New Haven, CT: Yale University Press.

Morton, Desmond. 1986. *The New Democrats, 1961–1986*. Toronto: Copp Clark Pitman.

Mueller, C. M. 1994. "Conflict Networks and the Origins of Women's Liberation." Pp. 234–63 in *New Social Movements: From Ideology to Identity*, edited by E. Laraña, H. Johnston, and J. Gusfield. Philadelphia: Temple University Press.

Münch, Richard, and Neil J. Smelser. 1987. "Relating the Micro and the Macro." Pp. 356–87 in *The Micro-Macro Link*, edited by Jeffrey C. Alexander et al. Berkeley: University of California Press.

Murray, C. 1987. "Displaced Urbanization: South Africa's Rural Slums." *African Affairs* 86: 311–29.

Naples, Nancy A. 1996. "A Feminist Revisiting of the 'Insider/Outsider' Debate: The 'Outsider Phenomenon' in Rural Iowa." *Qualitative Sociology* 19 (1): 83–106.

———. 1997a. "Contested Needs: Shifting the Standpoint on Rural Economic Development." *Feminist Economics* 3 (2): 63–98.

———. 1997b. "The 'New Consensus' on the Gendered Social Contract: The 1987–1988 US Congressional Hearings on Welfare Reform." *Signs: Journal of Women in Culture and Society* 22 (4): 907–45.

———. 1998a. "From Maximum Feasible Participation to Disenfranchisement." *Social Justice* 25 (1): 47–66.

———. 1998b. *Grassroots Warriors: Activist Mothering, Community Work, and the War on Poverty*. New York: Routledge.

———. 1998c. "Women's Community Activism: Exploring the Dynamics of Politicization and Diversity." Pp. 327–349 in *Community Activism and Feminist Politics: Organizing Across Race, Class, and Gender*, edited by Nancy A. Naples. New York: Routledge.

National Alliance of Women. 2000. *Report of Platform For Action Implementation in India, 1995–2000*. New Delhi.

National Organization for Women. August 2000. *National Organization for Women Home Page*. Online, Internet.

National Organization for Women. August 2000. *New York City NOW Home Page*. Online, Internet.

New York Civil Liberties Union. 1969. "The Burden of Blame: A Report on the Ocean Hill–Brownsville School Controversy." Pp. 338–51 in *The Politics of Urban Education*, edited by Marilyn Gittell and Alan G. Hevesi. New York: Frederick A. Praeger, Publishers.

New York Times. 1997. "Schools' Books on Gay Families Stir Seattle." 147:N20.

O'Donnell, Guillermo. 1989. "Transitions to Democracy: Some Navigation Instruments." Pp. 62–75 in *Democracy in the Americas: Stopping the Pendulum*, edited by R. Pastor. New York: Holms and Meier.

O'Keefe, Michael, and Paul D. Schumaker. 1983. "Protest Effectiveness in Southeast Asia." *American Behavioral Scientist* 26: 375–94.

Oates, Stephen B. 1982. *Let the Trumpet Sound: The Life of Martin Luther King, Jr.* New York: Harper and Row.

Oberschall, Anthony. 1973. *Social Conflict and Social Movements*. Englewood Cliffs, NJ: Prentice-Hall.

Observations on the Ruinous Effects of the Spitalfields Acts to the Silk Manufacture of London: to Which is Added a Reply to Mr. Hale's Appeal to the Public in Defence of the Act. 1822. London: John and Arthur Arch.

Oliver, Pamela E. 1989. "Bringing the Crowd Back In: The Nonorganizational

Elements of Social Movements." *Research in Social Movements, Conflict and Change* 11: 1–30.

Oliver, Pamela E., and Gregory M. Maney. 2001. "Political Processes and Local Newspaper Coverage of Protest Events: From Selection Bias to Triadic Interactions." *American Journal of Sociology* 106 (September) 2: 463–505.

Omvedt, Gail. 1993. *Reinventing Revolution: New Social Movements and the Socialist Tradition in India.* New York: M. E. Sharpe.

Opp, Karl-Dieter, and Christiane Gern. 1993. "Dissident Groups, Personal Networks, and Spontaneous Cooperation: The East German Revolution of 1989." *American Sociological Review* 58: 659–80.

Ornstein, Allan C. 1974. *Metropolitan Schools: Administrative Decentralization vs. Community Control.* Methuchen, NJ: Scarecrow Press.

Out in the Mountains. 1986a. "Dingman defines role." 1 (3): 5.

Out in the Mountains. 1986b. "Liaison interviewed." 1 (3): 8,10.

Out in the Mountains. 1986c. "VT Demos Support ERA/G/L Rights." 1 (9): 3.

Out in the Mountains. 1987a. "VLGR Annual Meeting Planned." 1 (11): 6.

Out in the Mountains. 1987b. "Attorney General's Office Records Discrimination." 2 (7): 9.

Out in the Mountains. 1990. "Hate Crimes Bill Wins in the House." 5 (2): 1.

Pakulski, Jan, and Malcolm Waters. 1996. *The Death of Class.* London: Sage.

Parikh, Kirit. 1999. "Economy." Pp. 39–90 in *India Briefing: A Transformative Fifty Years,* edited by Marshall Bouton and Philip Oldenburg. New York: M. E. Sharpe.

Partington, Charles F. 1825. *A Course of Three Lectures Illustrative of the Rise and Progress of Science, in Mechanics, Pneumatics, and the General History of the Steam Engine Occasioned by the Formation of the Spitalfields Mechanics' Institution.* London: S. Teulon.

Paul, William. 1982. "Minority Status for Gay People: Majority Reaction and Social Context." Pp. 351–70 in *Homosexuality: Social, Psychological, and Bioligical Issues,* edited by William Paul, James D. Weinrich, John C. Gonsiorek, and Mary E. Hotvedt. Beverly Hills, CA: Sage.

Payne, Charles. 1989. "Ella Baker and Models of Social Change." *Signs* 14 (4): 885–99.

———. 1995. *I've Got the Light of Freedom: The Organizing Tradition and the Mississippi Freedom Struggle.* Berkeley: University of California Press.

Petrilli, Susan. 1993. "Dialogism and Interpretation in the Study of Signs." *Semiotica* 97 (1/2): 103–18.

Pfeffer, Jeffrey, and Gerald R. Salancik. 1978. *The External Control of Organizations.* New York: Harper and Row.

Phelan, Shane. 1993. "(Be)Coming Out: Lesbian Identity and Politics." *Signs* 18 (4): 765–790.

Piven, Frances Fox, and Richard A. Cloward. 1971. *Regulating the Poor.* New York: Vintage.

———. 1977. *Poor People's Movements: Why They Succeed, How They Fail.* New York: Vintage Books.

———. 1979. *Poor People's Movements*. New York: Vintage.

———. 1984. "Disruption and Organization: A Reply to Gamson and Schmeidler." *Theory and Society* 13.

———. 1992. "Normalizing Collective Protest." Pp. 301–25 in *Frontiers in Social Movement Theory*, edited by A. Morris and C. Mueller. New Haven, CT: Yale University Press.

———. 1993 (1971). *Regulating the Poor: The Functions of Public Welfare.* Updated edition. New York: Vintage Books.

Plummer, Alfred. 1972. *The London Weavers' Company 1600–1970*. London: Routledge & Kegan Paul.

Polletta, Francesca. 1994. "Strategy and Identity in 1960s Black Protest." *Research in Social Movements, Conflicts and Change* 17: 85–114.

———. 1997. "Culture and its Discontents: Recent Theorizing on the Cultural Dimensions of Protest." *Sociological Inquiry* 67: 431–50.

———. 1998a. "Contending Stories: Narrative in Social Movements." *Qualitative Sociology* 21 (4): 419–46.

———. 1998b. "'It Was Like a Fever': Narrative and Identity in Social Protest." *Social Problems* 45: 137–59.

———. 1999. "'Free Spaces' in Collective Action." *Theory and Society* 28 (1): 1–38.

Pollock, Mary S. 1991. "What Is Left Out: Bakhtin, Feminism, and the Culture of Boundaries." *Critical Studies* 3 (2)/4 (1–2): 229–41.

Ponte, Lowell. 1970. "The Libertarian Link." *Penthouse*, November, 72.

Ponzio, Augusto. 1990. In *Man as Sign: Essays on the Philosophy of Language*, edited and translated by Susan Petrilli. New York: Mouton de Gruyter.

Poonacha, Veena. 1997. "From the Fringes to the Centre: The Changing Context of Feminist Politics in India and Germany." Pp. 1–33 in *Women, Empowerment and Political Participation*, edited by Veena Poonacha. Bombay, India: Research Centre for Women's Studies, S.N.D.T. Women's University.

Porter, G. R. 1831. *Treatise on the Origin, Progressive Improvement, and Present State of the Silk Trade*. London: Longman, Rees, Orme, Brown & Green.

Ports, Suki. 1970. "Racism, Rejection, and Retardation." Pp. 50–92 in *Schools Against Children: The Case for Community Control*, edited by Annette T. Rubinstein. New York: Monthly Review Press.

Post, David. 1992. "Through Joshua Gap: Curricular Control and the Contructed Community." *Teachers College Record* 93 (4): 673–96.

Powell, John. 1824. *A Letter Addressed to Weavers, Shopkeepers, and Publicans, on the Great Value of the Principle of the Spitalfields Acts: In Opposition to the Absurd and Mischievous Doctrines of the Advocates for their Repeal*. London: E. Justins.

PP 1818 (211) IX Second Report of the Committee on Silk Weavers' Petitions.

PP 1818 (134) IX Report of the Committee on Silk Weavers' Petitions.

PP 1832 (678) XIX. Report of the Select Committee on the Silk Trade.

PP 1834 (36) XXXV. Appendices to the Report of the Poor Law Commissioners. Appendix B.2. Answers to Questions Circulated by the Commissioners in Towns.

PP 1834 (44) XXIX. Report from the Assistant Poor Law Commissioners, Pt. III.

PP 1834 (556) X. Report from the Select Committee on Handloom Weavers' Petitions.

Prebble, Peter. 1981. "The Left of the NDP." Pp. 76–82 in *Western Canadian Politics: The Radical Tradition*, edited by Donald C. Kerr. Edmonton, Alberta: NeWest Institute for Canadian Studies.

Purushothaman, Sangeetha. 1998. *The Empowerment of Women in India: Grassroots Women's Networks and the State*. New Delhi: Sage.

Quadagno, Jill. 1994. *The Color of Welfare*. New York: Oxford University Press.

Ramazanoglu, Caroline. 1993. "Introduction." Pp. 1–25 in *Up against Foucault: Explorations of Some Tensions between Foucault and Feminism*, edited by Caroline Ramazanoglu. New York: Routledge.

Ravitch, Diane. 1974. *The Great School Wars: New York City, 1805–1973: A History of the Public Schools as Battlefields of Social Change*. New York: Basic Books.

Ray, Raka. 1998. "Women's Movements and Political Fields: A Comparison of Two Indian Cities." *Social Problems* 45 (1): 21–36.

———. 1999. *Fields of Protests: Women's Movements in India*. Minneapolis: University of Minnesota Press.

Reger, Jo. 1992. "Equality through the Ballot Box: An Examination of Social Movement Community, Identity, and Structure." Unpublished master's thesis, Ohio State University.

Report Adopted at a General Meeting of the Journeymen Broad Silk Weavers, held in Saint John Street Chapel, Brick-lane, Spitalfields, On Wednesday, the 20th of February, 1828, to take into their Consideration the Necessity of Petitioning the Legislature for a Wage Protection Bill and such other purposes as may aries out of the same. To which is Appended, The Petition. 1828. London: W. C. Mantz.

Report of the National Conference. 1980. *Perspectives for the Autonomous Women's Movement in India: 23–26 December, 1980*. Bombay.

Report of the National Conference. 1985. *Perspectives for the Autonomous Women's Movement in India: 23–26 December, 1985*. Bombay.

Rex, J. 1973. "The Compound, Reserve, and Urban Location—Essential Institutions of Southern African Labour Exploitation." *South African Labour Bulletin* 1: 5–20.

Richards, John. 1981. "The Left of the NDP." Pp. 69–75 in *Western Canadian Politics: The Radical Tradition*, edited by Donald C. Kerr. Edmonton, Alberta: NeWest Institute for Canadian Studies.

Riger, Stephanie. 1984. "Vehicles for Empowerment: The Case of Feminist Movement Organizations." *Prevention in Human Services* 3 (2): 99–117.

Ritzer, George. 1996. *Sociological Theory*. 4th ed. New York: McGraw-Hill.

Robnett, Belinda. 1996. "African American Women in the Civil Rights Movement, 1954–1965: Gender, Leadership, and Micromobilization." *American Journal of Sociology* 101: 1661–93.

———. 1997. *How Long, How Long? African American Women in the Struggle for Civil Rights*. New York: Oxford University Press.

Rochon, Thomas R. 1998. *Culture Moves: Ideas, Activism, and Changing Values*. Princeton, NJ: Princeton University Press.

Rochon, Thomas R., and Ikuo Kabashima. 1998. "Movement and Aftermath: Mobilization of the African American Electorate, 1952–1992." In *Politicians and Party Politics*, edited by J. Geer. Baltimore, MD: The Johns Hopkins University Press.

Rochon, Thomas R., and Daniel A. Mazmanian. 1993. "Social Movements and the Policy Process." *Annals of the American Academy of Political and Social Sciences* 528: 75–156.

Rochon, Thomas R., and David S. Meyer, eds. 1997. *Coalitions and Political Movements: The Lessons of the Nuclear Freeze*. Boulder: CO: Lynne Rienner Publishers.

Rose, Sonya O. 1992. *Limited Liverlihoods Gender and Class in Nineteenth-Century England*. Berkeley: University of California Press.

———. 1993. "Gender and Labour History: The Nineteenth-Century Legacy." *International Review of Social History* 38: 145–62.

Rosenberg, Gerald. 1991. *The Hollow Hope: Can Courts Bring About Social Change?* Chicago: University of Chicago Press.

Rosenstone, Steven J., and John Mark Hansen. 1993. *Mobilization, Participation and Democracy in America*. Princeton, NJ: Princeton University Press.

Rothschild-Whitt, Joyce. 1979. "The Collectivist Organization: An Alternative to Rational-Bureaucratic Models." *American Sociological Review* 44: 509–27.

Rothstein, Natalie. 1977. "The Introduction of the Jacquard Loom to Great Britain." Pp. 281–304 in *Studies in Textile History*, edited by Veronica Gervers. Toronto: Royal Ontario Museum.

Rozell, Mark J., and Clyde Wilcox, eds. 1995. *God at the Grassroots: The Christian Right in the 1994 Elections*. Lanham, MD: Rowman and Littlefield.

Rucht, D. 1996. "The Impact of National Contexts on Social Movement Structures: A Cross-Movement and Cross-National Comparison." Pp. 185–204 in *Comparative Perspectives on Social Movements*, edited by D. McAdam, J. D. McCarthy, and M. Zald. New York: Cambridge University Press.

Rucht, Dieter, and Friedhelm Neidhardt. 1998. "Methodological Issues in Collective Protest Event Data: Units of Analysis, Sources and Sampling, Coding Problems." Pp. 65–89 in *Acts of Dissent: New Developments in the Study of Protest*, edited by Rucht, Dieter, Ruud Koopmans, and Friedhelm Neidhardt. Berlin: Edition Sigma.

Rucht, Dieter, Ruud Koopmans, and Friedhelm Neidhardt. 1998. *Acts of Dissent: New Developments in the Study of Protest*. Berlin: Edition Sigma.

Rupp, Leila J., and Verta Taylor. 1987. *Survival in the Doldrums: The American Women's Rights Movement, 1945 to the 1960s*. New York: Oxford University Press.

Sale, Kirkpatrick. 1973. *SDS*. New York: Vintage.

———. 1993. *Celebrating the Self: A Dialogic Account of Human Nature.* Boulder, CO: Westview.

Sandoval, Salvador A. M. 1998. "Social Movements and Democratization: The Case of Brazil and the Latin Countries." Pp. 169–202 in *From Contention to Democracy*, edited by M. Giugni, D. McAdam, and C. Tilly. Lanham, MD: Rowman and Littlefield.

Santoro, Wayne. 1998. "From Protest to Politics." Unpublished manuscript, Department of Sociology, Vanderbilt University.

Santoro, Wayne, and Gail McGuire. 1997. "Social Movement Insiders: The Impact of Institutional Activists on Affirmative Action and Comparable Worth Policies." *Social Problems* 44: 503–19.

Sarkar Tanika, and Urvashi Butalia. 1995. *Women and the Hindu Right: A Collection of Essays*. New Delhi: Kali For Women.

Sassen, Saskia. 1995. *Losing Control? Sovereignty in an Age of Globalization.* New York: Columbia University Press.

Saville, John. 1960. "Trade Unions and Free Labour: The Background to the Taff Vale Decision." Pp. 317–50 in *Essays in Labour History*, edited by Asa Briggs and John Saville. London: Macmillan.

Sawyers, Traci M., and David S. Meyer. 1999. "Missed Opportunities: Social Movement Abeyance and Public Policy." *Social Problems* 46 (2): 187–206.

Schaeffer, Frances. 1984. "A Christian Manifesto." Pp. 127–141 in *American Political Theology*, editedy by C. Dunn. New York: Praeger.

Schmitt, Frederika E., and Patricia Yancey Martin. 1999. "Unobtrusive Mobilization by an Institutionalized Rape Crisis Center: 'All We Can Do Comes from Victims.'" *Gender and Society* 13 (3): 364–84.

Schneider, Beth. 1988. "Political Generations and the Contemporary Women's Movement." *Sociological Inquiry* 58 (Winter): 4–21.

Schneider, Cathy Lisa. 1995. *Shantytown Protest in Pinochet's Chile*. Philadelphia: Temple University Press.

———. 1997. "Framing Puerto Rican Identity: Opportunity Structures and Neighborhood Organizing in New York City." *Mobilization* 2 (2): 227–45.

Schock, Kurt. 1996. "A Conjunctural Model of Political Conflict: The Impact of the Relationship between Economic Inequality and Violent Political Conflict." *Journal of Conflict Resolution* 40 (March) 1: 98–133.

Schurman, Frans, J. 1989. "Urban Social Movements: Between Repressive Utopia and Socialist Panacea." Pp. 9–26 in *Urban Social Movements in the Third World*, edited by F. J. Schurman and A. L. van Naerssen. New York: Routledge.

Schwartz, Michael. 1976. *Radical Protest and Social Structure*. New York: Academic.

Schwartz, Mildred A. 1994. "North American Social Democracy in the 1990s: The NDP in Ontario." *Canadian-American Public Policy* 17: 1–46.

Scott, W. Richard. 1998. *Organizations: Rational, Natural, and Open Systems.* 4th ed. Upper Saddle River, NJ: Prentice Hall.

Segers, Mary, and Ted G. Jelen. 1998. *A Wall of Separation? Debating the Public Role of Religion.* Lanham, MD: Rowman and Littlefield.

Seidman, G. 1994. *Manufacturing Militance.* Berkeley: University of California Press.

Seidman, Steven. 1993. "Identity and Politics in a 'Postmodern' Gay Culture: Some Historical and Conceptual Notes." Pp. 105–142 in *Fear of a Queer Planet: Queer Politics and Social Theory*, edited by Michael Warner. Minneapolis: University of Minnesota Press

Sein Win. 1988. Wire Report from Burma. AP. March 22.

Sellers, Cleve, and Robert Terrell. 1990. *River of No Return: The Autobiography of a Black Militant and the Life and Death of SNCC.* New York: William Morrow.

Shiva, Vandana. 1997. "Democracy in the Age of Globalization." Pp. 34–45 in *Women, Empowerment and Political Participation*, edited by Veena Poonacha. Bombay: Research Centre for Women's Studies, S.N.D.T. Women's University.

Shorter, Edward, and Charles Tilly. 1974. *Strikes in France, 1830 to 1968.* Cambridge: Cambridge University Press.

Shotter, John. 1997. "Dialogical Realities: The Ordinary, Everyday, and Other Strange New Worlds." *Journal for the Theory of Social Behavior* 27 (2/3): 345–57.

Shotter, John, and Michael Billig. 1998. "A Bakhtinian Psychology: From Out of the Heads of Individuals and Into Dialogues Between Them." Pp. 13–29 in *Bakhtin and the Human Sciences: No Last Words*, edited by Michael Mayfield Bell and Michael Gardiner. London: Sage.

Silverstein, Josef, and Julian Wohl. 1964. "University Students and Politics in Burma." *Pacific Affairs* 37 (1): 50–66.

Silverstein, Michael. 1991. "The Uses and Utility of Ideology: Some Reflections." *Pragmatics* 2 (3): 311–23.

Simmel, Georg. 1980. *Essays on Interpretation in Social Science.* Translated by Guiy Oakey. Totowa, NJ: Rowman & Littlefield.

Sinclair, Peter R. 1973. "The Saskatchewan CCF: Ascent to Power and the Decline of Socialism." *Canadian Historical Review* 54 (December): 419–33.

Smelser, Neil J. 1997. *Problematics of Sociology.* Berkeley: University of California Press.

Smith, Barbara. 1998. *The Truth that Never Hurts: Writings on Race, Gender, and Freedom.* New Brunswick, NJ: Rutgers University Press.

Smith, Christian, ed. 1996. *Disruptive Religion: The Force of Faith in Social Movement Activism.* New York: Routledge.

Smith, Christian. 1996. *Resisting Reagan: The U.S. Central America Peace Movement.* Chicago: University of Chicago Press.

Smith, Dorothy E. 1987. *The Everyday World as Problematic.* Toronto: University of Toronto Press.

———. 1989. "Feminist Reflections on Political Economy." *Studies in Political Economy* 30: 37–59.

———. 1999. *Writing the Social: Critique, Theory, and Investigations.* Toronto: University of Toronto Press.

———. 1990. *Conceptual Practices of Power*. Boston: Northeastern University Press.

Snow, David. 2001. "Collective Identity and Expressive Forms." In *International Encyclopedia of the Social and Behavioral Sciences*, edited by Neil Smelser and Paul B. Baltes. London: Elsevier Science.

Snow, David, and Leon Anderson. 1987. "Identity Work among The Homeless: The Verbal Construction and Avowal of Personal Identities." *American Journal of Sociology* 92: 1336–71.

Snow, David A., and Robert D. Benford. 1988. "Ideology, Frame Resonance, and Participant Mobilization." *International Social Movement Research* 1: 197–217.

———. 1992. "Master Frames and Cycles of Protest." Pp. 133–55 in *Frontiers in Social Movement Theory*, edited by A. D. Morris and C. M. Mueller. New Haven, CT: Yale University Press.

Snow, David, and Doug McAdam. 2000. "Identity Work Processes in the Context of Social Movements: Clarifying the Identity/Movement Nexus." In *Self, Identity, and Social Movements*, edited by S. Stryker, T. Owens, and R. White. Minneapolis: University of Minnesota Press.

Snow, David A., E. Burke Rochford, Jr., Steven K. Worden, and Robert D. Benford. 1986. "Frame Alignment Processes, Micromobilization and Movement Participation." *American Sociological Review* 51: 464–81.

Snyder, David, and William R. Kelly. 1979. "Strategies for Investigating Violence and Social Change: Illustrations from Analyses of Racial Disorders and Implications for Mobillization Research." Pp. 212–37 in *The Dynamics of Social Movements*, edited by M. Zald and J. McCarthy. Cambridge, MA: Winthrop.

Spafford, Duff. 1968. "The 'Left Wing' 1921–1931." Pp. 44–58 in *Politics in Saskatchewan*, edited by Norman Ward and Duff Salford. Don Mill: Longmans.

Spitalfields Benevolent Society. 1812. *First Report of the Spitalfields Benevolent Society, Instituted in the Year MDCCCXI for Visiting and Relieving Cases of Great Distress, Chiefly among the Numerous Poor of Spitalfields and its Vicinity*. London: Ellerton & Henderson.

Spretnak, Charlene, ed. 1982. *The Politics of Women's Spirituality: Essays on the Rise of Spiritual Power within the Feminist Movement*. New York: Anchor.

Staggenborg, Suzanne. 1986. "Coalition Work in the Pro-Choice Movement: Organization and Environmental Opportunities and Obstacles." *Social Problems* 33: 374–90.

———. 1988. "The Consequences of Professionalization and Formalization in the Pro-Choice Movement." *American Sociological Review* 53: 585–605.

———. 1989. "Stability and Innovation in the Women's Movement: A Comparison of Two Movement Organizations." *Social Problems* 36: 75–92.

———. 1991. *The Pro-Choice Movement: Organization and Activism in the Abortion Conflict*. New York: Oxford University Press.

————. 1993. "Critical Events and the Mobilization of the Pro-Choice Movement." *Research in Political Sociology* 6: 319–45.

————. 1994. "Can Feminist Organizations Be Effective?" Pp. 339–55 in *Feminist
Organizations: Harvest of the New Women's Movement*, edited by M. M.
Ferree and P. Y. Martin. Philadelphia: Temple University Press.

————. 1996. "The Survival of the Women's Movement: Turnover and Continuity
in Bloomington, Indiana." *Mobilization* 1 (2): 143–58.

————. 1998a. *Gender, Family, and Social Movements.* Thousand Oaks, CA: Pine
Forge Press.

————. 1998b. "Social Movement Communities and Cycles of Protest: The
Emergence and Maintenance of a Local Women's Movement." *Social Problems*
45 (2): 180–204.

Stein, Annie. 1970. "Containment and Control: A Look at the Record." Pp. 21–49
in *Schools Against Children: The Case for Community Control*, edited by
Annette T. Rubinstein. New York: Monthly Review Press.

Steinberg, David. 1981. "Burma Under the Military: Towards a Chronology."
Contemporary Southeast Asia 3 (3): 244–85.

Steinberg, Marc W. 1995. "Repertoires of Discourse: The Case of the Spitalfields
Silk Weavers and the Moral Economy of Conflict." Pp. 57–88 in *Cycles and
Repertoires in Collective Action*, edited by Mark Traugott. Durham, NC: Duke
University Press.

————. 1998. "Tilting the Frame: Considerations on Collective Action Framing
from a Discursive Turn." *Theory and Society* 27 (6): 845–72.

————. 1999a. *Fighting Words: Working-Class Formation, Collective Action and
Discourse in Early Nineteenth-Century England.* Ithaca, NY: Cornell University Press.

————. 1999b. "The Talk and Back Talk of Collective Action: A Dialogic
Analysis of Repertoires of Discourse among Nineteenth-Century English
Cotton Spinners." *American Journal of Sociology* 105 (3): 736–80.

Stern, Susan. 1998. "Conversation, Research, and Struggles over Schooling in an
African-American Community." Pp. 107–28 in *Community Activist and
Feminist Politics: Organizing Across Race, Class, and Gender*, edited by N.
Naples. New York: Routledge.

Stetson, Dorothy, and Amy Mazur, eds. 1995. *Comparative State Feminism.*
Thousand Oaks, CA: Sage.

Stevens, Jacqueline. 1999. *Reproducing the State.* Princeton, NJ: Princeton
University Press.

Stewart, Joseph, and James F. Sheffield. 1987. "Does Interest Group Litigation
Matter? The Case of Black Political Mobilization in Mississippi." *Journal of
Politics* 49.

Stone, Adolph. 1969. "A Criticism of the NY Civil Liberties Union Report on the
Ocean Hill–Brownsville School Controversy." Pp. 352–62 in *The Politics of
Urban Education*, edited by Marilyn Gittell and Alan G. Hevesi. New York:
Frederick A. Praeger.

Stoper, Emily. 1989. *The Student Nonviolent Coordinating Committee: The Growth of Radicalism in a Civil Rights Organization*. Brooklyn: Carlson Publishing.

Student Non-violent Coordinating Committee Papers. Martin Luther King Center, Atlanta.

Swart, William J. 1995. "The League of Nations and the Irish Question: Master Frames, Cycles of Protest, and 'Master Frame Alignment'." *Sociological Quarterly* 36 (3): 465–81.

Swidler, A. 1986. "Culture in Action: Symbols and Strategies." *American Sociological Review* 51: 273–86.

Tarrow, Sidney. 1989a. *Democracy and Disorder: Protest and Politics in Italy 1965–1975*. Oxford: Oxford University Press.

———. 1989b. *Struggle, Politics and Reform: Collective Action, Social Movements, and Cycles of Protest*. Cornell Studies in International Affairs, Western Societies Papers. Ithaca, NY: Cornell University Press.

———. 1992. "Mentalities, Political Cultures and Collectin Action Frames: Constructing Meaning through Action." Pp. 174–202 in *Frontiers in Social Movement Theory*, edited by Aldon Morris and Carol McClurg Mueller. New Haven, CT: Yale University Press.

———. 1993. "Cycles of Collective Action: Between Moments of Madness and the Repertoire of Contention." *Social Science History* 17 (2): 281–307.

———. 1994. *Power in Movement: Social Movements, Collective Action and Politics*. New York: Cambridge University Press.

———. 1995a. "Bridging The Quantitative-Qualitative Divide in Political Science." *American Political Science Review* 89 (2): 471–74.

———. 1995b. "Linking Politics and Collective Action." Paper presented at the Annual Meeting of the American Sociological Association, Washington, DC, August.

———. 1998. *Power in Movement: Social Movements and Contentious Politics*. 2nd ed. New York: Cambridge University Press.

Taylor, Verta. 1989. "Social Movement Continuity: The Women's Movement in Abeyance." *American Sociological Review* 54: 761–75.

———. 1994. "An Elite-Sustained Movement: Women's Rights in the Post–World War II Decades." Pp. 281–305 in *Disasters, Collective Behavior, and Social Organization*, edited by Russell R. Dynes and Kathleen J. Tierney, Newark: University of Delaware Press.

———. 1996. *Rock-a-by Baby: Feminism, Self-Help, and Postpartum Depression*. New York: Routledge.

———. 1999. "Gender and Social Movements: Gender Processes in Women's Self-Help Movements." *Gender & Society* 13 (1): 8–33.

———. 2000. "Emotions and Identity in Women's Self-Help Movements." Pp. 271–99 in *Self, Identity, and Social Movements*, edited by S. Stryker, T. Owens, and R. White. Minneapolis: University of Minnesota Press.

Taylor, Verta, and Nicole Raeburn. 1995. "Identity Politics as High-Risk

Activism: Career Consequences for Lesbian, Gay, and Bisexual Sociologists."
Social Problems 42 (2): 252–73.

Taylor, Verta, and Leila J. Rupp. 1993. "Women's Culture and Lesbian Feminist
Activism: A Reconsideration of Cultural Feminism." *Signs* 19 (1): 32–61.

Taylor, Verta, and Nancy Whittier. 1992. "Collective Identity in Social Movement
Communities: Lesbian Feminist Mobilization." Pp. 104–29 in *Frontiers in
Social Movement Theory*, edited by A. Morris and C. M. Mueller. New Haven,
CT: Yale University Press.

———. 1995. "Analytical Approaches to Social Movement Culture: The Culture
of the Women's Movement." Pp. 163–87 in *Social Movements and Culture*,
edited by Hank Johnston and Bert Klandermans. Minneapolis: University of
Minnesota Press.

Thomas, Clive A., and Ronald J. Hrebenar. 1995. "The Interest Group Political
Party Connection: Fundamentals of the Relationship." Paper presented to the
Annual Meeting of the American Political Science Association, September,
Chicago, IL.

Thomas, Jan. 1999. "Everything About Us Is Feminist: The Significance of
Ideology in Organizational Change." *Gender & Society* 13 (1): 101–19.

Thomas, Owen. 1987. "Freedom of Speech: Schools Are the Center of a Conflict
Over Parents Rights to Restrict What Their Children Hear." *Christian Science
Monitor* (Nov. 24): 16.

Thompson, C. 1994. "Strategy and Opportunism: Trade Unions as Agents for
Change in South Africa." Pp. 349–66 in *The Future of Industrial Relations:
Global Change and Challenges*, edited by John Niland, Russell D. Lansbury,
and Chrissie Verevis. Thousand Oaks, CA: Sage.

———. 1995. "The Changing Face of Labour Law and Industrial Relations."
Pp. 109–32 in *Liber Amicorum for Clyde W. Summers*, edited by R. Blanpain
and M. Weiss. Baden-Baden: Nomos Verlagsgesellschaft.

Thorne, Barrie. 1997. *Gender Play: Girls and Boys in School*. New Brunswick,
NJ: Rutgers University Press.

Tilly, Charles. 1978. *From Mobilization to Revolution*. Reading, MA: Addison-
Wesley.

———. 1993. "Contentious Repertoires in Great Britain, 1758–1834." *Social
Science History* 17 (2): 253–80.

———. 1995a. "Contentious Repertoires in Great Britain, 1758–1834." Pp. 15–
42 in *Repertoires and Cycles of Collective Action*, edited by Mark Traugott.
Durham, NC: Duke University Press.

———. 1995b. *Popular Contention in Great Britain, 1758–1834*. Cambridge:
Harvard University Press.

———. 1997. "From Interactions to Outcomes in Social Movements." Unpublished paper, Columbia University.

———. 1998. "Political Identities." Pp. 3–16 in *Challenging Authority: The
Historical Study of Contentious Politics*, edited by Michael P. Hanagan, Leslie
Page Moch, and Wayne te Brake. Minneapolis: University of Minnesota Press.

————. 1999. "From Interactions to Outcomes in Social Movements." Pp. 253–
270 in *How Social Movements Matter*, edited by M. Giugni, D. McAdam, and
C. Tilly. Minneapolis: University of Minnesota Press.

Timpone, Richard. 1995. "Mass Mobilization or Government Intervention?: The
Growth of Black Registration in the South." *Journal of Politics* 57: 425–43.

Touraine, Alain. 1981. *The Voice and the Eye: An Analysis of Social Movements.*
Cambridge: Cambridge University Press.

Trebitsch, Ed. 1986. "Statewide Network Plots Course." *Out in the Mountains*
1 (6): 5.

Trombley, William. 1992. "Textbook Wars Flaring Up Anew." *Los Angeles Times*
(May 11): A3, A27.

Tuccille, Jerome. 1969. "Report from St. Louis: The Revolution Comes to YAF."
Libertarian Forum 1 (12): 3.

Tucker, Robert C., ed. 1978. *The Marx-Engels Reader.* 2nd ed. New York: W. W.
Norton.

Tyack, David B. 1974. *The One Best System: A History of American Urban
Education.* Cambridge: Harvard University Press.

Vaid, Urvashi. 1995. *Virtual Equality: The Mainstreaming of Gay and Lesbian
Liberation.* New York: Anchor Books.

Valocchi, Steve. 1999. "The Class-Inflected Nature of Gay Identity." *Social
Problems* 46 (2): 207–24.

Venters, Jerry W. 1969. "Young Americans Remain in Traditionalist Grip."
St. Louis Dispatch, September 2.

"Verax." 1822. *Review of the Statements in Hale's Appeal to the Public on the
Spitalfields Acts.* London: J. Hudson.

Vobejda, Barbara. 1987. "Judge Bans 'Humanist' Textbooks; Ruling is Victory for
Fundamentalists." *Washington Post* (March 5): A1, A19.

Volosinov, V. N. 1986 (1929). *Marxism and the Philosophy of Language.*
Cambridge: Harvard University Press.

Voss, Kim. 1996. "The Collapse of a Social Movement: The Interplay of Mobiliz-
ing Structures, Framing, and Political Opportunities in the Knights of
Labor." Pp. 227–58 in *Comparative Perspectives on Social Movements:
Opportunities, Mobilizing Structures and Cultural Framings*, edited by Doug
McAdam, John D. McCarthy, and Mayer Zald. Cambridge: Cambridge
University Press.

Voss, Kim, and Rachel Sherman. 2001. "Breaking the Iron Law of Oligarchy:
Union Revitalization in the American Labor Movement." *American Journal of
Sociology* 106 (September) 2: 303–49.

Walker, Gillian. 1994. "Violence and the Relations of Ruling: Lessons from the
Battered Women's Movement." Pp. 65–79 in *Knowledge, Experience, and
Ruling Relations*, edited by Marie Campbell and Ann Manicom. Toronto:
University of Toronto Press.

Walker, Rebecca. 1995. *To Be Real: Telling the Truth and Changing the Face of
Feminism.* New York: Anchor Books.

Walton Jr., Hanes. 1988. *When the Marching Stopped: The Politics of Civil Rights Regulatory Agencies.* Albany: State University of New York Press.

Walzer, Michael. 1965. *The Revolution of the Saints.* Cambridge: Harvard University Press.

Warren, Jenifer. 1991. "Schools Face Censors' Siege, Group Says." *Los Angeles Times* (August 29): A3, A30.

Watras, Joseph. 1997. *Politics, Race, and Schools: Racial Integration, 1954–1994.* New York: Garland.

Weber, M. 1949. "Critical Studies in the Logic of the Cultural Sciences." Pp. 113–88 in *The Methodology of the Social Sciences*, edited by M. Weber. New York: Free Press.

Webster, E. 1988. "The Rise of Social-Movement Unionism: The Two Faces of the Black Trade Union Movement in South Africa." Pp. 174–96 in *State, Resistance and Change in South Africa*, edited by P. Frankel, N. Pines, and M. Swilling. Johannesburg: Southern Book Publishers.

Whalen, Jack, and Richard Flacks. 1989. *Beyond the Barricades: The Sixties Generation Grows Up.* Philadelphia: Temple University Press.

White, Aaronetta. 1999. "Talking Feminist, Talking Black: Micromobilization Processes in a Collective Protest against Rape." *Gender & Society* 13 (1): 77–100.

White, Gordon. 1994. "Civil Society, Democratization and Development: Clearing the Analytical Ground." *Democratization* 1 (3): 375–90.

Whitehorn, Alan. 1992. *Canadian Socialism: Essays on the CCF-NDP.* Toronto: Oxford University Press.

Whittier, Nancy. 1995. *Feminist Generations: The Persistence of the Radical Women's Movement.* Philadelphia: Temple University Press.

———. 1997. "Political Generations and Social Movement Transformation." *American Sociological Review* 62: 760–78.

———. 2000. "Changing Meaning and Culture: Organizing against Child Sexual Abuse." Paper presented at the Annual Meetings of the American Sociological Association, August 12–15, Washington, DC.

Wilchins, Riki Anne. 1997. *Read My Lips: Sexual Subversion and the End of Gender.* Ithaca, NY: Firebrand Books.

Wilcox, Clyde. 1992. *God Warriors: The Christian Right in Twentieth-Century America.* Baltimore: Johns Hopkins University Press.

Williams, R. 1981. *Marxism and Literature.* Oxford: Oxford University Press.

Williams, Rhys H. 1994. "Movement Dynamics and Social Change: Transforming Fundamentalist Organizations and Ideology." In *Accounting for Fundamentalisms: The Dynamic Character of Movements*, edited by M. E. Marty and R. S. Appleby. Chicago: University of Chicago Press.

———. 1995. "Constructing the Public Good: Social Movements and Cultural Resources." *Social Problems* 42: 124–44.

———. 1999a. "Public Religion and Hegemony: Contesting the Language of the Common Good." Pp. 169–86 in *The Power of Religious Publics: Staking Claims in American Society*, edited by W. Swatos and J. Wellman. Westport, CT: Praeger.

———. 1999b. "Visions of the Good Society and the Religious Roots of American Political Culture." *Sociology of Religion* 60: 1–34.

Williams, Rhys H., ed. Forthcoming. *Promise Keepers and the New Masculinity: Private Lives and Public Morality*. Lanham, MD: Lexington Books.

Williams, Rhys H., and Susan M. Alexander. 1994. "Religious Rhetoric in American Populism: Civil Religion as Movement Ideology." *Journal for the Scientific Study of Religion* 33: 1–15.

Williams, Rhys H., and Robert D. Benford. 2000. "Two Faces of Collective Action Frames: A Theoretical Consideration." *Research in Social Movements, Conflicts, and Change*. Vol. 20.

Williams, Rhys H., and Jeffrey Blackburn. 1996. "Many Are Called but Few Obey: Ideological Commitment and Activism in Operation Rescue." Pp. 167–85 in Disruptive Religion: The Force of Faith in Social Movement Activism, edited by Christian Smith. London: Routledge.

Williams, Rhys H., and N. J. Demerath III. 1991. "Religion and Political Process in an American City." *American Sociological Review* 56: 417–31.

Williams, Rhys H., and Timothy J. Kubal. 1999. "Movement Frames and the Cultural Environment: Resonance, Failure, and the Boundaries of the Legitimate." *Research in Social Movements, Conflicts and Change* 21: 225–248.

Wilson, James Q. 1961. "The Strategy of Protest." *Journal of Conflict Resolution* 5: 291–303.

Wilson, John. 1973. *Introduction to Social Movements*. New York: Basic Books.

Wirt, Frederick. 1997. *'We Ain't What We Was': Civil Rights in the New South*. Durham, NC: Duke University Press.

Wiseman, Nelson. 1979. "The Character and Strategy of the Manitoba CCF, 1943–1959." *Prairie Forum* 27–53.

———. 1985. *Social Democracy in Manitoba: A History of the CCF/NDP*. Winnipeg: University of Manitoba Press.

Wittenberg, Leah. 1986. "A Celebration Is Born." *Out in the Mountains* 1 (5): 4.

Woliver, Laura R. 1993. *From Outrage to Action: The Politics of Grass-Roots Dissent*. Urbana: University of Illinois Press.

Yadav, Yogendra. 1999. "Politics." Pp. 3–38 in *India Briefing: A Transformative Fifty Years*, edited by Marshall Bouton and Philip Oldenburg. New York: M. E. Sharpe.

Yates, Douglas. 1973. *Neighborhood Democracy: The Politics and Impacts of Decentralization*. Lexington, MA: Lexington Books.

Yitri, Moksha. 1989. "The Crisis in Burma: Back from the Heart of Darkness?" *Asian Survey* 29 (6): 543–58.

Young, Walter. 1969. *The Anatomy of a Party: The National CCF 1932–1961*. Toronto: University of Toronto Press.

Zakuta, Leo. 1964. *A Protest Movement Becalmed*. Toronto: University of Toronto Press.

Zald, Mayer. 1988. "The Trajectory of Social Movements in America." Pp. 19–42 in *Social Movement as a Factor of Change in the Modern World: Research in*

Social Movements, Conflicts and Change, edited by L. Kreisberg and B. Misztal. Greenwich, CT: JAI Press.

——. 1992. "Looking Backward to Look Forward: Reflections on the Past and Future of Resource Mobilization Theory." Pp. 326–48 in *Frontiers in Social Movement Theory*, edited by Aldon D. Morris and Carol M. Mueller. New Haven, CT: Yale University Press.

——. 1996. "Culture, Ideology and Strategic Framing." Pp. 261–74 in *Comparative Perspectives on Social Movements*, edited by D. McAdam, J. D. McCarthy, and M. Zald. New York: Cambridge University Press.

——. 2000. "Ideologically Structured Action: An Enlarged Agenda for Social Movement Research." *Mobilization* 5 (1): 1–16.

Zald, Mayer, and Roberta Ash. 1966. "Social Movement Organizations: Growth, Decay and Change." *Social Forces* 44: 327–41.

Zald, Mayer N., and John D. McCarthy. 1987. "Social Movement Industries: Conflict and Cooperation Among SMOs." Pp. 161–180 in *Social Movements in an Organizational Society*, edited by M. Zald and J. McCarthy. New Brunswick, NJ: Transaction.

Zimet, Melvin. 1973. *Decentralization and School Effectiveness: A Case Study of the 1969 Decentralization Law in New York City*. New York: Teachers College Press.

Zuo, Jiping, and Robert D. Benford. 1995. "Mobilization Processes and the 1989 Chinese Democracy Movement." *Sociological Quarterly* 36 (1): 131–56.

Index

abortions, 90, 133, 176, 197, 258
  access to, 173
  funding for, 131
  legal, 131
  policy, 16
  sex-selective, 74
Academic Advisory Committee on
  Decentralization, 229
acceptance, marginal, 273
action
  collective, 105
  radical, 273
  strategic, 210
activism, 9, 14, 20, 90, 135, 136, 173, 176,
  232, 238, 242, 245
  grassroots, 71
  high-risk, 193, 196
  peace, 14
  personalist style of, 130, 135
  political, 132
  two modes of, 37
  women's, 76
ACT-UP, 291
Adams, Jack, 147–48
Advisory Panel on Decentralization, 236
advocacy, 14, 78
  black, 112
affirmative action, 99, 113
AFL-CIOs Organizing Institute, 291
African Americans, 88, 113, 206, 242, 256,
  264, 271
  area of, 234
  leadership of, 231
  religious culture of, 130
African Mine Worker's Union, 58
African National Congress (ANC), 60
Agarwal, Bina, 84

agency, 26, 48, 63, 122, 123, 141, 247,
  249–50, 306
  community action, 227, 234
  historical, 59
  practical, 154
  responsible, 154
agenda, 107
  family values, 258, 265
  movements, 107
  political, 117
  setting, 106, 116
agitation, 272–73
Ahmedabad, India, 70, 72
AIDS, 93, 98
  organizations, 92
Alabama, 282
Alabama District Court, 240
Alberta, Canada, 167
alimony, 75
All-Burma Student Union, 35
alliances, 5, 18, 19, 32, 167–68, 289, 294
  farmer-labor, 160
  mobilizing, 42
  political, 89
  potential, 25, 29
allies, 12, 16, 17, 25, 106, 244, 297
  political, 142, 297, 298
Altshuler, Alan, 229–30
America. *See* United States
American Civil Liberties Union (ACLU), 96
American South, 65
amniocentesis, 67
analysis
  generational, 189
  levels of, 4, 8, 124–25, 205
anarchist, 194, 199
Anderson, Terje, 94–95, 98

Angkatan Bersanjata Republik Indonesia (ARBI), 30, 33, 38, 39, 45
Anglo-American Vaal Reefs mine, 4, 50, 51, 61
Angola, 53
Ansaldua, Gloria, 307
antimjan (the lowest of the low), 68
apartheid, 17, 50
Aquino, Benigno, 40
Arakan, 32
Arizona, 240
army, 36
   volunteer, 198
Atlantic City, 276–77
attorney general, 96, 98
authorities, 14, 27, 43, 107, 115
   authoritarian, 41, 90, 196
   authoritarian practices, 39
   moral, 223
   political, 107
   religious, 251
   state, 96, 103

backlash, 242
   gender/class/race, 283
Baker, Ella, 84, 269–70, 275, 299, 300
Bakhtin, Mikhail, 211
   dialogic theory of, 206
Baldwin, James, 257
Banaszak, Lee Ann, 136–37
Banda, Hastings, 53
Bangaloe, 72
Bano, Shah, 75
Baraka, Imamu Amiri, 282
bar associations, 72
bargaining, 107
Barker, Colin, 121, 292
Basotholand Congress Party (BCP), 60, 61
   networks, 61
   Youth League, 61
BBC radio, 35
Bedford-Stuyvesant, 228
beliefs, 16, 88
Benford, Robert, 51, 125, 209, 249
Bernstein, Mary, 26, 268, 292, 298
Big Brother, 197
Bihar, 68, 76
Birkenstocks, 304
Birmingham, campaign of 1963 in, 111–12
bisexuals, 90, 100–101
   bisexuality, 101
black(s), 206
   Americans, 256
   candidate, 108, 113
   middle-class, 281, 283
   pupils, 232
   registration of, 112
   urban, 282
black consciousness, 281
Black Nationalist, 279, 282

Black Panther Party, 280
black power, 227, 230, 238, 269, 272, 280.
   See also movement(s)
Black Power, 281
   militant, 206
Blakeney, Allan, 160–62
Bloomington, Indiana, 121, 127, 131, 135
Board of Education, 230, 234–37
Bodh Gaya, India, 69
Bombay, 71, 72
Borchorst, Annette, 73
Borderlands, 307
Boudreau, Vincent, 25, 292, 298
boundaries
   class, 282
   collective identity, 284
   construction of, 171
   gender, 281–82
   racial, 281
boycotts, 13, 40, 55, 62, 108, 235
   secondary, 151, 156
Bradley, James, 140–41, 149
Brazil, 49
bridging processes, 125
Bristol, 144
Britain, 4, 16, 73, 127, 144
   seventeenth- and eighteenth-century analysts of English behavior, 58
   struggle against British colonialism, 35
British Columbia, 160, 162, 164, 167
   legislature of, 164
Broadbent, Ed, 137, 162
Bronx Parents United, 235
Brook, Paul, 155
Brooklyn, 237
Brown, Elaine, 282
Brown, Lorne, 169
Brown v. Board of Education, 230
brutality, 196
Buddhist, 69
Buder, Leonard, 237
Buffelsfontein mine, 51
bull dykes, 102
Bundy, McGeorge, 236
bureaucracy, 68, 73, 78, 293
Burke, Kenneth, 262
Burkitt, Ian, 211
Burlage, Dorothy, 189
Burlington, 90–91, 97
Burma, 28–46
   Burmese dissidents, 43
   Burmese regime, 32
   Burmese state, 35–36
   Burmese struggle, 44
   Burmese underground, 44
Burma Socialist Program Party (BSPP), 30
Burmese Communist Party (BCP), 31, 34
Bush, Rosaline, 259

bystander, 264
    support by, 209

Calgary, 158
Calhoun, Craig, 88
Calvinist, 263
campaign, 131–35, 242, 289, 291, 299–
    300
    anti-rape, 72
    lesbian and gay rights, 97
    political, 99
    protest, 111
    voter registration, 116
campuses, 38, 43
    institutions, 37
    linking of, 34
    radicals on, 198
Canada, 19, 158, 160
    Canadian autonomy, 161
    Canadian independence, 162
Canada and Royal Seaforth Docks, 146
Canadian Auto Workers Union, 166
Canadian Labour Congress, 158
Canadian New Democratic Party, 122
Carmichael, Stokely, 276, 281
Carson, Clay, 282
Carty, Kenneth, 170
case work, 72
caste, 70
Catcher in the Rye, 240
Catholic Church, 108, 167, 237
Catholics, 187, 248, 255, 258
    Irish, 187
Central America, U.S. intervention in, 16
Central Park, 174
Century City, 193
changes
    cultural, 122
    implementing, 110
    institutional, 108
    legal, 74, 115
    legislative, 176, 179
    policy, 74, 91, 176, 290, 291
    political, 16, 115, 122
    social, 3, 11, 16, 115
    structural, 48–49, 51, 122
chauvinism, male, 282
Cheadle, Halton, 50
Chhatra Yuva Sagharsh Vahini (CYSV), 68–
    69
Chicago Eight, 185
child
    molesters, 101, 99
    sexual abuse, 297, 305–6
Child Development Group of Mississippi
    (CDGM), 110–11, 116
Chinese student movement of 1989, 125
Chinese women, rape of, 46
Chingari, 72
Chittendon County, Vermont, 96

choices
    strategic, 88, 168
    tactical, 16, 18, 168
Chong, Dennis, 105
Christianity, 261, 304
    anti-Christian, 206
    Christian evangelicalism, 223
    Christian piety, 212, 218, 220
    rhetoric of, 16
Christian Right, 248, 253, 258, 260,
    264
churches, 43
    black, 111, 128
    church groups, 40
citizenship, 213, 217–18, 223
    bourgeois, 223
    training, 111, 116
city hall, 99
civil disobedience, 8, 13, 283
civil laws, 75
civil liberties, 43, 130, 196–97, 236
Civil Rights Act, 117, 206, 230, 267–68,
    270–71, 274
civil society, 82, 289
Civil War, 276
claims, 5–6, 13–14, 18, 25–27, 208, 218,
    224, 250–51, 261–62, 264
    counterclaim, 253
    makers, 32, 46
    moral, 256
    political, 10, 14
    rhetorical, 259, 265
    separatist, 232
Clark, Ana, 212, 223
class, 81, 87, 205–7, 227–28, 266–67, 273,
    293, 295–96, 300
    working-class, 188
clergy, 251
Cloward, Richard, 58, 109, 133, 231, 234
CNN, 243
coalitions, 14, 32, 89–90, 94, 97–98, 102,
    132, 264, 293
    abortion rights, 176
    coalitional politics, 87
    supporting, 29
Coastal Women's Association, 76
Cobb, Charlie, 274
coffee klatches, 99, 101
cognitive liberation, 188
Cohen, 142
COINTELPRO, 193
cold war, 13, 187
collective action, 13, 14, 15, 54, 56, 58,
    123, 125, 129, 131, 133, 135, 137,
    142–43, 145–46, 150, 193, 210, 214,
    224, 290–92, 299
    cycle of, 220
    framing of, 128, 209
    See also frames
collective actors, 206

collective identity, 5, 11, 13, 14, 122, 125,
138, 141, 172–73, 183, 185, 189,
205–10, 223, 264, 266–85, 289–303,
305–6
construction of, 172–73, 179, 206, 283
feminist, 129
narrowing of, 279, 282
nonviolent civil rights, 266
socially constructed, 15
strategic uses of, 268
sustenance of, 266–67, 278
unbounded, 283
collectivist, 296
collectivism, 293
groups, 171–72
structure, 174
Collins, Randall, 125
colonial missionaries, 240
Colorado, 101
Colorado for Family Values, 97
Color Purple, The, 240
Colson, Charles, 259
Columbia University, 195
Combined Action Committee, 236
coming out, 91, 293
Coming Out Day, 102
common sense, 26, 51–57, 63–64, 217,
292
Commonwoman, 91
communism, 34, 42, 187, 196–97
communists, 161, 166
communist revolution, 188
communities, 76, 81, 91, 102, 217, 292,
296
beloved, 190, 247–65
black, 275, 282, 230
building, 172
development, 68
feminist, 127, 131, 137
gay, 93–95, 97, 100–103
gay and lesbian, 26, 92
lesbian, 89–90
lesbian and gay, 89
moral, 257, 263
organization, 231
organizing, 58
policing, 197
religious, 248, 263
white, 275
women's, 181
women's movement, 131
community action programs, 227
community board, 237
community control, 226–45
frame of, 228, 233
heteronormative dimensions of, 241
of schools, 228–29, 232, 238–44
Community Party, 161–62
Community School System, 236
Concerned Women for America, 241, 259

conflict
ideological, 192–93
intergenerational, 121
Congress, 113, 131
Congress party, 69, 75
consciousness, 186, 189, 192
class, 186
generational, 187
individual, 185, 191, 199
political, 185–86, 188, 199
shared, 186
sit-in, 129, 196)
consciousness raising (CR), 19, 70–72, 88–
90, 106, 122, 171, 174–76, 179–82,
193, 297
committee of, 174–75
conservatives, 229, 240–43, 251, 253–58,
260, 263, 298
Consolidated Goldfields, 54
constituencies, 12, 13, 16, 25, 35, 85, 88,
105, 107–8, 127, 135, 192, 199, 227,
233, 243, 257, 273, 294, 303
constituent commitment, 126
constituent preferences, 116
new, 27
shift in, 228
Constitution
constitutional equality, 79
constitutional issues, 241
73rd and 74th amendments to the Indian, 80
constraints, 13
ideological, 37
contention, 208
culture of, 208
patterns of, 33
political, 32
contexts, 27
cultural, 207, 248, 250–51, 265, 277,
284, 290, 292, 299, 306
discursive, 230
external, 206
micro-organizational, 133
contingencies, 48–49, 51, 62–64
continuity, 157, 163, 168–70
Cooperative Commonwealth Federation
(CCF), 158–70
Saskatchewan section of, 160
co-optation, 81, 206, 245, 273, 293
of the political center, 32
Costain, Ann, 16
Council of Supervisory Association of the
Public Schools of New York City,
236
courts, 18, 51, 73, 108
court cases, 69
Cousins, Andrea, 194
creationism, 227
crisis, 42, 108
balance of payment, 39
collective identity, 271–72

economic, 32, 37, 39, 42
  fiscal, 38
critical events, 133, 135, 138
cultural capital, 267–70, 279, 283–84
cultural domination, 210
cultural forces, 123
cultural framing, 48, 57
cultural norms, 86
cultural patterns, 86
cultural transformation, 85
culture, 208, 224
  democratic, 247–65
  dominant, 189, 205–7, 289, 292, 301,
    303, 305–6
  hegemonic, 294
  oppositional, 205
  social movement, 208–25, 249, 291

Davis, Angela, 282
decision making, 4
  collective, 72
  participatory, 72
delegitimation, 200
Delhi, 72
della Porta, Donatella, 125
democracy, 13, 44, 82
  advocates of, 45
  American, 238
  democratic context, 26
  democratic ideas, 37
  democratic participation, 261
  democratic power, 238
  neighborhood, 229
  participatory, 111, 238, 266, 271, 278,
    283
  See also movement(s)
Democratic National Convention, 195,
    267–68, 276, 284
Democratic Party, 93, 95, 137, 272–73
democratization, scholars of, 28
demonstration, 11, 13, 32, 35, 38, 39, 42,
    91, 108, 110, 134, 182, 193, 215,
    298
  anti-war, 192
  demonstrating, 71
  street, 38
  by students, 37
Dempsey, Jack, 146
depoliticization, 254
deradicalization, 245
desegregation, 243
determinism, cultural, 265
development
  international, 67
  sustainable, 67, 76, 78
Development for Women and Children in
    Rural Areas (DWCRA), 77
dialogic, 208–25
  dialogism, 213
  dialogists, 211–12

Diani, Mario, 107
dictator, 33
  dictatorship, 32, 39
Dingman, Beth, 95
direct mail, 133
discourses, 205–20, 225–28, 244, 284, 290–
    94, 297–98, 301–6
  analysis of, 205
  collective action, 222, 224
  cultural, 48
  democratically available, 251
  dominant, 206–7, 233
  feminist, 213
  legitimizing, 289
  political, 262
  public, 73, 254
  radical, 223
  radical political, 221
  religious, 207
  social movement, 210, 264
discrimination, 92, 96, 103
  anti-discrimination bill, 96, 99, 102
  racial, 272
disruption, 108–9
disruptive dissensus, 58
Dobaldson, Ivanhoe, 273
Dobson, James, 248, 258, 260
Dohrn, Bernardine, 190
doldrums, 127, 133, 135, 138
domestic violence programs, 174
Donne, John, 256
Douglas, 161
Downs, Anthony, 231
dowry deaths, 71, 74, 83
draft, 194
  abolition of, 198
  draft card burning, 195, 198
  resistance, 198
drag, 102
Dropkin, Greg, 156
Durban, 49, 50

Eagle Forum, 241
Economic Opportunity Act of 1964, 232, 234
economy
  economic agenda, 80
  economic changes, 16
  economic concerns, 76
  economic conditions, 106
  economic empowerment, 78, 83
  economic forces, 123
  economic inequality, 8, 187
  economic liberalization, 80, 82
  economic life, 13
  Indian, 78
education, 233, 237
  bilingual, 233
  public, 99
  quality, 238
Edwards, Lee, 191

election, 40, 60
  democratic, 43
  electoral campaign, 14, 40
  electoral competition, 114
  electoral participation, 81
  electoral politics, 80–82
  after independence, 79
  presidential, 132
  school board, 237
electioneering, 13
elite(s), 38
  critical, 43
  dissent, 40
  dissidents, 38, 42, 43
  hegemonic, 252
  political, 68, 109
  reform-minded, 43
  South African, 49
  target, 250
  unrest, 38
  See also movement(s)
employment guarantee schemes (EGSs), 68,
  69
empowerment, 178
England. See Britain
English, 55
Enlightenment, 262
Enrile, Juan Ponce, 39, 41, 45
environment
  cultural, 210
  environmentalists, 167
Equal Rights Amendment (ERA), 91, 93–
  96, 103, 127–29, 131, 134, 137,
  173, 258
  anti-ERA campaign, 93–97
  defeat of, 94
  opponents of, 93
  See also movement(s)
Ernsberger, Don, 189
essentialism, 86–87
  essentialist, 88
ethnicity, 54
  ethnic group, 54
ethnic solidarities, union-mobilized, 55
Europe, 263
  Eastern, 13
  Western, 18, 25
Evans, Rowland, 280
evolutionary biology, 240
exclusion, 15
external debt, 32

factionalism, 19, 122, 157, 167, 169, 171,
  175, 183
  diverse, 171
  factionalization, 190, 192, 194
  intensified, 192
factions, 157–70, 289, 294, 296, 305
  continuity, 169
  factional challenges, 166

factional conflicts, 163, 167
factional disputes, 165
  organization, 166
  radical, 168
fairies, 102
Falwell, Jerry, 248, 252, 258
family, traditional, 258–60
family planning, groups, 130
Fantini, Mario, 238
Farmer-Labor Group (FLG), 160
farmers, 122
FBI
  counterintelligence program of, 193
  harassment by, 193
  surveillance by, 193
federal systems, 136
feminism, 129, 171, 174, 176–83, 296
  anti-feminist, 97
  black, 295
  lesbian, 90
  liberal, 176
feminist, 76–77, 84–85, 87–90, 95, 103,
  105, 108, 127, 132, 176, 180–81,
  258, 304–5
  empowerment, 179, 181–82
  feminist epistemology, 226
  groups, 75, 93
  Indian, 74
  lesbian, 131
  liberal, 184
  literature, 71
  Marxist, 73
  materialist, 206, 226–46, 295
  organizations, 74, 174
  political, 176, 179–82
  radical ideology of, 174, 184
  scholars, 77
  state theories, 73
  See also communities; identity or
    identities; movement(s); networks
Feminists, The, 174
femocrats, 74
fields
  discursive, 211–23, 226–27
  multiorganizational, 159, 163
Fighting Peacock Flag, 35
Filipinos, 40, 42
  protestors, 43
  See also Philippines
fire bombing, 13
flag, burning of, 195–96
Focus on the Family, 259
Ford Foundation, 232, 235–36
Forman, Jane, 271
Forum Against Oppression of Women,
  72
Forum Against Rape, 72
Foucault, Michel, 227–28
Fourth World Conference on Women at
  Beijing, 78–79

frames, 154, 192, 205–7, 210–11, 228, 239,
    244, 248–50, 261, 290, 294–95, 301
  adjustment of, 128
  collective action, 228, 249–50
  community control, 227, 295
  construction of, 244
  democratic, 243
  discursive, 227, 230, 244
  dominant, 213
  injustice, 251
  master, 53, 128, 228, 244
  oppositional, 228, 244
  progressive, 226
  strategies of, 122
framing, 65, 121, 123, 141, 185, 208, 210,
    213, 224, 249–50
  literature of, 209
France, 127, 195
  seventeenth- and eighteenth-century
    analysts of French behavior, 58
Fraser, Teresa, 235
freedom rides, 110
Freedom Schools, 111, 277
Freedom Summer Project, 110, 267, 269–
  77
Freeman, Jo, 178, 184
free space, 173
Free World, 187
Freight, Nelson, 144, 146–47
Friedman, Jeanne, 188
fundamentalists, Hindu and Muslim, 75
Fund for a Feminist Majority, 132
fund-raising, 174–75

Gamson, William, 125, 155, 195, 249
Gandhi, Indira, 69
Gandhi, Mahatma, 79, 255
  vision of, 68
  See also movement(s)
Gandhi, Rajiv, 75
Garrow, David, 113
Garvy, Helen, 191
gay, 5, 85, 93, 95, 10–103, 131–33, 135,
    167, 291, 300
  anti-gay activists, 93
  anti-gay campaigns, 97
  anti-gay protests, 241
  attacks against, 241
  bashing, 91, 96, 131–32
  discrimination against, 92, 100
  ethnicity, 85
  gay agenda, 258
  homosexuality, 91, 99–100, 103, 241
  homosexuals, 110
  leadership, 100
  liberation of, 251
  political leaders, 101
  politics, 97, 100–101
  pride rally, 102
  pro-homosexuality, 206

  public recognition of, 91
  rights, 26, 291
  right-wing assaults on, 132
  strategy, 100
  student club, 240
  violence against, 98
  See also communities; movement(s)
Gay, Lesbian, Bisexual (GLB) Coalition,
    131
gay/straight, 87
  Gay-Straight Club, 241
Geertz, Clifford, 252
gemeinschaft, 190
Gencor. See Buffelsfontein mine
gender, 70, 87, 97, 101, 205–7, 226–27,
    266–67, 293, 295–96, 300, 302, 304
generation, 186, 187, 199
  generation-unit, 186–87
Germany, East, 125
Germany, West, 135
Gern, Oppand, 125
Gernhards, Jurgen, 125, 128, 135
Glasgow, 152
Glazer, Nathan, 239–40
globalization, 82, 83
goals, 11, 29, 86, 135, 166–68, 174–76,
    181, 190, 227, 232, 253, 256, 270,
    272, 294–95, 298–99
  cultural, 88
  feminist, 90
  instrumental, 88
  political, 88, 166, 169
  progressive, 226
Goldig, Marcel, 55–56, 61–62
gold mines, South African, 48, 52, 57
gold production, 53
Goldstone, Jack, 49
Goldwater, Barry
  campaign, 189
  plan, 198
good sense, 64
  Marxist, 64–65
  See also Gramsci, Antonio
Goodwyn, Lawrence, 154
Goslant, Keith, 98, 102
gospel, 261
Gould, Roger, 54
government, 71
  corruption, 36
  federal, 188
  funds, 78
  harassment by, 194
  Indian, 75, 77
  infrastructure, 78
  national, 70
  neighborhood, 197, 230
  officials, 36
  personnel, 78
  structure, 77
  student, 188

Governor's Commission on the Status of
    Women, 93
Gramsci, Antonio, 48, 51–52, 64–65
    Gramscian hegemony, 213
grassroots, 99, 103, 122, 133–34, 238, 251,
    272, 282
    local group, 79
    meetings, 82
    mobilization, 269
    women's movements, 76
grave diggers, 35
Great Britain. See Britain
Green Party, 295
Greenville, Miss., 275
Greenwood, 274–75
grievances, 12, 19, 25, 42, 128, 138
guerrillas, 40
Gujarat, India, 70
Gunness, Christopher, 35
Gusfield, Joseph, 258
Guyot, 275
Gyi, Aung, 36

Hackett, David, 232
Hallman, Howard, 227
Hampton, Fred, 195
Hand, Brevard W., 240
Hansons, Bill, 281
Harcourt Brace Jovanovich, 229
Harlem, 227, 232–35
    East Harlem, 234, 238
Harris, Don, 275
hate crimes, 103
    Hate Crimes Act, 96–98
Havel, Vaclav, 17
Head Start, 110–11, 117
Heather Has Two Mommies, 227, 242
Hechinger, Fred, 240
hedonism, 259
hegemony, 48, 64
    counter-hegemonic, 48, 53, 55
heteronormativity, 241
heterosexual, 90
Hill, Anita–Clarence Thomas
    hearings, 177
    incident of, 180
Hindu, 69–70
    Hinduism, 261
    math, 69
    nationalism, 75
Hobsbaum, Eric, 58
Hollingdale, Linda, 100
Htien, Lon. See Ne Win
Hughes and Allen, 265
Hull, 144
human immunodeficiency virus (HIV),
    104
Hunt, Scott, 228
Hurlie, Mary, 98–99
Hyde Amendment, 131

ideational storyline, 29
identity or identities, 5, 10, 13, 25, 26, 28,
    45, 85–103, 121, 123, 142, 155, 171,
    176, 186, 192, 194, 208–9, 211, 224,
    249, 261, 297, 298, 303
    black, 281
    categories of, 87
    Christian, 257
    constructed, 86, 179
    construction of, 87, 142, 182, 290
    deploy, 88
    empowerment feminist, 180
    essentialist notion of, 85, 86
    ethnic, 87
    ethnic-like, 93
    expressions of, 86
    feminist, 93, 176, 178–80
    forging, 85
    as goal, 87
    hegemonic, 292
    individual, 185
    lesbian, 85, 93
    lesbian and gay, 88, 93, 97, 103
    nationalist, 43
    oppositional, 30
    political, 185, 189–92, 199, 244
    political feminist, 178
    politics of, 83, 85–86
    sexual, 92
    shift in, 196
    strategic deployment of, 99
    as strategy, 87
    unique, 164
    See also collective identity; movement(s)
ideologies, 9, 11–13, 18, 48, 51–52, 63, 59–
    63, 166–73, 188–89, 198, 208–13, 48–
    54,   264, 268, 273, 289, 291, 293,
    296, 299
    ideological decisions, 194, 195, 199
    ideological purity, 190, 195
    ideological tendencies, 190
    political, 189–90, 198
imperialist, 75, 79
    anti-imperialists, 194
independent, 79
Independent Labour Party (ILP), 159–60,
    163, 166–67
    autonomy of, 163
India, 4, 6, 26, 66–67, 71, 74, 83
    Indian culture, 75
    Indian reality, 73
    Indian state, 82
    new economic policy in, 79
    Perspectives for the Autonomous
        Women's Movement in, 72
    postcolonial Indian state, 67
    women in, 76
    See also economy
Indiana, 121
Indian National Congress, 79

Indonesia, 28–46
  Indonesian marines, 38
  Indonesian state, 31–32, 43
industrialization, 68
inequality
  class, 233, 238
  gender, 233
  racial, 187, 233, 244
influence, 15, 27–28
institutions, 18, 73, 110, 113
  civic, 32
  cultural, 290
  dominant, 294
  financial, 79
  mainstream, 14
  movement, 293
  parallel, 108
  political, 10, 14, 18, 74, 217, 252, 290
  religious, 32
insularity, of activists, 194–95
integration, 206, 233–34
  integrationist, 260
  rhetoric of, 254
  school, 243
  white resistance to, 231, 244
intellectual, 43
  Burmese, 42
  public, 37, 42
Intermediate School (IS) 201, 234–35
International Monetary Fund (IMF), 38,
  76
International Women's Decade (1975–85),
  67, 74, 77, 83
International Women's Year World
  Conference, 71
intersection of race, class, and gender, 233,
  238, 268, 295, 304
Irvine, Janice, 302
Islam, 261
issues, 12, 25–26, 205
  women's, 67, 71, 75, 77, 80, 212
Italy, 127

Jakarta, 38, 42, 44
Japan, 137
Jasper, James, 129
Jelen, Ted, 262
Jews
  Jewish, 188, 248, 255, 270
  Judaism, 261
  Orthodox, 248, 258
Jharkhand Nari Mukti Samti (Jharkhand
  Women's Liberation Committee), 76
Johanson, Alan, 133
Johnson, Lyndon, 277
Jones, Jim, 272
Jordan, Linda, 242
Joshua Gap, 229
Judeo-Christian content, 257
judiciary committee, 96, 99

justice, 55, 82
  social, 12, 26
Justice Department, 195, 294, 305

kacheries, 69
Kanenga, Ron, 282
Kansas, 188, 241
Kanwar, Roop, 75
Kennedy, John F., 232
Kennedy, Robert, 195
Kerala, India, 76
keterbukaan (openness), 36–37, 43
Kilmartin, Duncan, 99
King, Martin Luther, Jr., 113, 195, 248,
  253–57, 261, 269
  "Letter from a Birmingham Jail," 256
King, Mary, 270, 278
Klandermans, Bert, 125, 129, 190, 193
Klatch, Rebecca, 123, 292, 302
Koopmans, Ruud, 109
Krinsky, Sidney, 155
Ku Klux Klan, 274
Kumin, Madeline, 95–97
Kyan, Maung Maung, 34

labor
  organized, 158, 160
labor law, 50, 59
  South African, 50
Ladner, Joyce, 281
LaHaye, Beverly, 241, 258
Land Ceiling Act, 69
Latino, 206
Lavalette, Michael, 121, 292, 299–300
law, 87–88, 96, 103, 219, 220, 271
  anti-discrimination, 99
  dowry, 67
  lawsuits, 133, 241
  martial, 32, 39, 42, 44
  Muslim, 75
  national, 73
  penal, 75
  rape, 67, 73
leaders, 34, 35, 40, 138–39, 168, 235, 248,
  254, 258, 276, 282, 284
  authoritarian, 25
  female, 282
  local, 55
  professional, 133
  Southern, 277
leadership, 25, 60, 62, 107, 134, 150, 152,
  174, 177, 269, 275, 280
  bridge, 112, 275
  cadre, 59
  charismatic, 112
  community, 269
  group-centered, 270
  political, 18
  Southern, 279
  women's, 177

League for Social Reconstruction, 158, 160, 164
Leatherbarrow, Eric, 149
leather community, 101–2
Lebua, Jonathan, 60–61
Lee, Harper, 241
Left, 11, 168
  leftist, 198
  leftist sympathizers, 196
  parties, 127
Left and Right: A Journal of Libertarian Thought, 198
legislation, 71, 86, 96, 98, 114, 144, 181, 218
  anti-abortion, 131
  anti-pollution, 137
  federal, 114
  hate crimes, 97
  human rights, 88
  legislators, 99–101, 127, 174, 221, 229, 237
  legislature, 93–95, 99, 104, 127, 133, 137, 221
Legislative Advisory Council, 161
legitimacy, 165, 167, 223, 251
  legitimation, 252
  political, 95
  religious, 253
lesbian, 5, 85–103, 131–32, 167, 291
  anti-lesbian discrimination, 92
  credentials, 90
  culture of, 89
  identity, 88
  public recognition of, 91
  radical, 102
  rights, 86, 173–74
  subculture, 89
  violence against, 96, 98
  See also gay
Lesbian and Gay Pride Day, 91
Lesotho, 53–54, 60–61
Lewis, John, 280
liberation, 277
libertarians, 186, 189, 193–98
  Libertarian Forum, 198
  Libertarian Party, 198
Lichterman, Paul, 129, 135
Lindsey, John, 231, 234, 236
Lipset, Seymour Martin, 161, 238
Lipsky, Michael, 109
literacy, 78, 111, 116, 239
Liverpool, 121, 144, 148, 151
  docks, 121, 140, 144, 156
Lloyd, Woodrow, 162
lok shakti (people's power), 68
Lower East Side, 227
Luhrs, Peggy, 100
Lutz, Frank, 238
Lwin, Sein, 35

Macomber, Roger, 97
macro-level, 124–27, 136, 296
Maharashtra, 70, 74, 76–77, 81
mahila mandals (local women's groups), 77
mahila samakhya (Education for Women's Empowerment), 77
Malacañang palace, 41
Malawi, 53
Malcolm X, 195
Mandalay, 32, 35
Manhattan, 227, 230
Manifesto for an Independent Socialist Canada, 162
Manila, 41
Manitoba, 160–68
Mannheim, Karl, 185–87
Maoists, 194
Mapeshoane, Charles, 54–55, 64
marches, 55, 91, 110, 193
  anti-war, 190
  pride, 92, 95, 97
Marcos, Ferdinand, 28–32, 39–44
  anti-Marcos group, 40
Marcos, Imelda, 39, 41
marginality, 43
  marginalization, 192
marijuana, legalization of, 198
marriage, 69, 74, 102
  gay, 258–59
  homosexual, 94
  same-sex, 102
Marx, Karl, 25, 252, 247, 301
  Marxism, 161
  Marxist, 143, 194
  materialism according to, 226
masses, 206
  anger, 43
  appeal, 122
  chaos, 38, 42
  critical, 91, 138
  demonstrators, 38
  mobilization, 70, 111, 113–14
  organizations, 42, 192
  populations, 35
  resources, 42
  society, 36, 41, 43, 197
  unrest, 38, 58
  See also movement(s)
Massive Economic Neighborhood Development (MEND), 234
Match, The, 198
Mathura (rape victim), 72
Mayor's Advisory Panel on Decentralization of the New York City Schools, 230
McAdam, Doug, 16, 133
McCarthy, John, 126, 133
McNamara, Kent, 53
Mead, George Herbert, 59, 63–64

meanings, 296
  construction of, 196
  hegemonic, 213
  moralized, 263
media, 175, 186, 192–93, 196, 199, 208,
    254, 278, 292
  print and television, 72
Melucci, Alberto, 129
Meredith Mississippi Freedom March,
    227
Mersey Docks and Harbor Company
    (MDHC), 140, 145–50
Merz, Carol, 238
meso-level, 121–39, 296
  actors, 134
  analysis, 124
  campaign structure, 134
  connection, 121
  links, 122
  micro-mobilization, 128
  organization, 122, 130, 137
  structure, 127, 129, 134
meso-macro linkages, 128–29, 132
meso-micro linkages, 128–29, 132
metaphors, religious, 251
Mexico City, 71
micro-cohorts, 191, 199
microcredit, 70
micro-level, 121, 124–27, 134, 296
micro-macro bridge, 126
micro-macro gap, 128
migrant, 52
  workers, 47
Mileur, Chelle, 242
militancy, 99, 151–52, 193–94
  escalation of, 194
  increased, 195
  union, 223
militant, 153, 272
  militant dockers' traditions, 145
  working-class, 151
military
  Burmese, 45
  Indonesian, 36, 38
  junta, 41
  officers, 40–41
  professional, 39
Miller, Jim, 277
Milwaukee Parental Choice Program,
    243
mine(s)
  President Brand, 60–61
  mobilization in, 60
  wages, 53
mine workers
  black, 58
  in South Africa, 47, 52, 53, 295, 298,
    304
Minkoff, Debra, 112

Minnis, Jack, 275
Mississippi, 108, 110, 116, 274, 282
Mississippi Freedom Democratic Party
    (MFPD), 206, 267, 269, 276
  Freedom Democratic Party and Freedom
    Vote, 272
Mississippi Project, 272
Mitchell, Don, 162, 168
mob actions, 59
mobilization, 6–8, 14–16, 26, 28, 40–43,
    55, 59, 70, 125, 128, 131–33,
    163–64, 183, 186, 206, 208, 242,
    244, 248, 250–51, 282, 290–91,
    295, 300–301, 303
  black-led, 113
  counter-mobilizing, 143
  extra-institutional, 15–16
  meso-level, 135
  micro-level, 135
  mobilizing, 25, 84, 112, 209
  mobilizing structure, 59, 126, 129, 137–
    38, 141
  political, 187
  potential for, 128
  pro-choice, 177
  unobtrusive, 14
  See also masses
modernization, 68
monologic, 213
Monroe, N.C., 274
Moodie, Dunbar, 26, 68, 292, 295, 298,
    304
Mooney, Patrick, 228
Moore, Barrington, 57
moral, 12, 52, 100, 259, 264
  biblical morality, 219
  crusaders, 215
  moral action, 10
  moral assessments, 263
  moral boundaries, 264
  moral commitment, 13
  moral health, 259, 264
  morality, 223
  moral justification, 252
  moral legitimacy, 264
  moral order, 57, 259
  moral outrage, 57, 62
  moral problem, 259
  moral purpose, 265
  moral society, 260
moratoriums, 196
More, Hanna, 216
Morley, J. T., 166
Morris, Aldon, 105, 111, 248
Morris, Bill, 156
Moses, Donna, 275
mother work, 233
Motlatsi, James, 60–61
Moulmein, Burma, 35

movement(s)
abortion, 130
abortion rights, 132
agrarian, 228
allies, 28
antidictatorship, 42
anti–Gulf War, 131
anti-war, 195
black power, 230, 232, 269, 277, 279, 284
career of, 192
against child sexual abuse, 297
civil rights, 4, 16, 27, 105, 108, 110–13, 115, 128, 131, 187, 206–7, 230, 248, 253, 256, 264–65, 269–70, 276, 278–79, 279, 298
coalition, 26
conservative, 197–98
continuity of, 284
cooperative socialist, 223
countermovement, 108, 131, 133, 173
culture of, 129, 206–7, 250–51
decline in, 133, 138
democracy, 29, 32, 36, 39, 44
elites, 35, 43
emergence of, 3, 127–30, 138
environmental, 12, 135, 290
ERA, 121
as expressive, 86
failure, 44
feminist, 14, 93, 187, 297
Gandhian, 68
identities, 29, 41, 86, 87, 95, 142
as instrumental, 86
labor, 153, 251
language of, 256
lesbian and gay, 86, 88, 91, 94, 98, 290
libertarian, 198
maintenance of, 127, 131–36, 138
mass, 58, 83
Mississippi, 105
movement-movement influences, 17
national social, 138
nationalist, 43, 79
network of, 129
against nuclear peace, 12
opportunism, 141
opposing, 16, 93
organizations, 32, 37, 40, 58, 121
outcomes, 16, 27, 105, 127, 136–38
party, 157, 170, 295
political, 252
prochoice, 133
prodemocracy, 41
radicalized, 29
religiously based, 251
repertories, 29
social democrats, 167
social justice, 71
spillover of, 135, 300
stars of, 192
strategy, 72
student, 60
success, 44, 64
suffrage, 136–37
survival of, 133
symbolizations of, 251
transethnic, 56
tribal, 68, 70
weapons, 26
women's, 6, 10, 12, 16, 19, 26, 65, 66, 68, 71–72, 76–77, 80–84, 93, 103, 130, 132–33, 135–36, 171, 172, 174, 290, 297, 3041
worker's, 151
Mozambique, 53
Mueller, Carol, 129
Mumbai, 80
Muslim, 70. See also law

Napoleonic Wars, 219
National Alliance of Women (NAWO), 79, 82
National Association for the Advancement of Colored People (NAACP), 230–31, 241, 278
National Association of Christian Educators, 241
nationalist, 30, 219
black, 266
black cultural, 281
nationalism, 212, 214–15, 218, 220
National Legal Foundation, 241
National Movement for Free Elections, 41
National Organization for Women (NOW), 19, 134, 173
Bloomington chapter of, 128, 131–32
New York City chapter of, 122, 171–84
National Security Council, 9
National Union of Mineworkers (NUM), 47, 50, 55–57, 59–61
National Women's Musical Festival (NWMF), 131
National Women's Party (NWP), 134
National Women's Political Caucus, 174
Native Americans, 240
Neidhardt, Freidhelm, 109
Neshoba County, 278
networks, 11, 37, 39, 82, 90–91, 99, 116, 125–26, 135–38, 141, 153, 210, 248, 250, 289, 291, 293, 306
of alliances, 187
building, 88
embedded, 9
ethnic, 55
feminist, 131
friendship, 134
informal, 49, 58–59, 73, 77–78, 298
internal, 133
of international, 84

lobbying efforts of the, 77
movement, 135, 293
organizational, 92, 293
personal, 92
recruitment, 59
social, 49, 59
of social and political influence, 107
submerged, 58, 129, 132–33, 154, 291
New Christian Right, 248, 253, 258
"new class," 129–30
New Delhi, 72
New Democratic Party (NDP), 122,
    158–70
New England Quakers, 270
Ne Win, 28–30, 33–35, 44–45
repression by, 34
New Individual Review, 198
New Jerusalem, 257
New Left, 15, 167–68, 191, 193, 196–97,
    301
New Order, 31, 36–38, 45
New Realism, 149, 151–52
New Realist, 153
New Republic, 240
New Right, 15, 248, 265
new social movements (NSMs), 85–86, 289
New Society regime, 30. *See also* Marcos,
    Ferdinand
newspaper, 88
gay and lesbian, 92, 95
New York City, 91, 176, 227–29, 237,
    242
New York State Commissioner of
    Education, 237
New York Times, 237, 242
Nixon, Richard, 240
nongovernmental organizations (NGOs),
    37, 40, 77, 81, 84
nonviolence, 206, 274, 255, 267, 280
norms, 18, 99
Novak, Robert, 280
Nu, U, 36
nuclear
annihilation, 187
arms race, 13
disarmament, 9
freeze, 7–10
test ban, 12
weapons, 7, 10

Ocean Hill–Brownsville, 237
Office for Women's Affairs, 132
officeholding, black, 114
Office of Economic Opportunity, 111, 117
officials
elected, 108, 116
black elected, 112
off loading, 242–43
Of Mice and Men, 240
Ohlin, Lloyd, 231

Ontario, 162
Oo, Tin, 36
Operation Rescue, 11, 173
Opp, Karl-Dieter, 125
opportunities, 11–16, 48, 51, 108, 137,
    141, 143, 154, 157, 163–64, 257,
    298
cultural construction of, 15
missed, 17
perceptions of, 132
potential, 49
structure of, 106
umbrella, 134
order, international, 26
Oregon, 101
organizations, 8, 11, 13, 19, 31, 35, 45, 49,
    55, 57, 59, 71, 107–8, 110, 113, 128
civil rights, 108, 110
divisions in, 197
formal, 58–59, 291
grassroots, 115
organizational capacity, 108
organizational characteristics, 125
organizational form, 18
organizational politics, 4
organizational structure, 141
organizers, 26, 35, 91, 94, 111–12, 132
political, 18, 32, 61
professional, 61, 134, 291
racial-ethnic, 112
religious, 248, 250
secret, 32
suffrage, 136
women's, 66, 70, 82, 84, 112
women's rights, 172
See also masses
Ornstein, Allan, 231
outcomes, 16, 106–7, 112, 114, 122, 130,
    136–39, 299–300
institutional, 132
political, 128
See also movement(s)
Out in the Mountains (OITM), 95
OUTRIGHT, 92

P&O ferry port, 145, 147
pacifist, 142, 167
panchayat (council), 80–81
Panchayati Raj Act, 80
Papuans, West, 46
parades, 35
lesbian and gay pride, 91
Parents and Teachers for Responsible
    Schools, 242
Paris Commune, 54
parliament, 77, 80, 215, 217, 219–21
parliamentarians, 217, 222
parliamentary procedure, 176
parliamentary systems, 295
women members of, 73

participation
  democratic means of, 13
  maximum feasible, 232
  political participation, 13
  rank-and-file, 166
parties, 71
  caste-based regional, 75
  class, 160
  member, 74
  political, 31, 61, 75, 80, 82, 294–95
  politics and, 14, 79
Patai Komunis Indonesia (PKI), 30–31,
    33
patriarchy, 73, 178
  patriarchal privilege, 215
patriotism, 257
  patriotic, 216
Payne, Charles, 84
Payton, Marick, 188
peasants, 67–68, 70
Pegu, Burma, 35
Pentagon, 13
People for the American Way, 241
People for the Ethical Treatment of Animals
    (PETA), 174
People's Board of Education, 235–36
People's Consultative Assembly, 37
Perdue, Holly, 98, 101–2
petition, 215, 217, 220–21
  petitioning, 142
Phelan, Shane, 85
Philippines, 28, 30–31, 39, 41, 43, 45
  state, 32
  transitions, 28
picket, 241
  mass, 151
  picketing, 142, 150, 273
  picket line, 146–48, 152
Pilger, John, 156
Pitso, Qoane, 60–61
Piven, Frances Fox, 58, 109, 133
PlanetOut, 242
Play-Doh, 259
Podlodowski, Tina, 242
polarization, 195
police, 195, 227
  brutality, 71, 193, 195, 197, 199
  harassment by, 233
  reaction of, 193
  suppression on, 193
policies, 6, 7, 10, 13, 15–16, 25–27, 73–74,
    113, 153, 161–62, 289, 302
  changes of, 6, 15–16, 27
  debates of, 168
  demands of, 10
  dimension of, 6
  enactment and implementation of, 106
  influence on, 15
  making of, 16
  policy machinery, 74–75

policy-makers, 77, 110, 174, 227
  preferences on, 109
  process, 109
  public, 6, 13, 19, 26, 292
  reform, 6, 27
  shifting, 28
  social, 105
  structural adjustment, 67, 76, 83–84
political agenda, 95, 103
political alignment, 105
political allies, 39
political arena, 80
political climate, 14
political consciousness, 123
  individual, 185
political context, 88, 127
political culture, 249
political education, 78
political empowerment, 80, 83
political engagement, conventional, 14
political environment, 86
  changing, 11
political inclusion, 16
political institutions, 10, 14, 18, 74. See
    also institutions
political interests, 75, 83
political landscape, 14, 200
political life, 13
political meaning, progressive, 206
political moderates, 43
political opportunities, 6, 26–27, 48–49, 51,
    59, 83, 121, 125, 128, 130, 132, 134,
    136, 138, 139, 205, 268, 290, 292,
    295, 300–301, 306
  issue specific, 135
  perception of, 130, 136–37, 139
  structure of, 8, 14, 48–49, 59, 65, 68,
    128, 134, 137–38, 212, 293
  theories of, 207
political organization, 178, 210
  gay and lesbian, 92
political participation
  black, 113, 114
  women's, 80
political parties, 157, 159
political process, 208, 289–90
political quiescence, 252–53
political reform, 43
political space, 207
political stance, 274
politics, 5, 8, 25–27, 51, 107
  Canadian, 167
  of commonality, 85
  communal, 82
  environmental, 138
  identity, 97, 103
  lesbian, 90
  prefigurative, 297
  radical, 218
  of recognition, 85–86

symbolic, 258
as usual, 88
Polletta, Francesca, 88, 209
Pollock, Mary, 213
population, sex ratio of, 71
pornography, 197, 258
Ports, Sukie, 233
Post, David, 229
postindustrial society, 86
postmodernism, 296
poststructuralists, 85, 87
  poststructuralism, 296
poverty, 13, 26, 67–68, 76, 239
Powell, John, 218
Poyton, John, 218
practices
  cultural, 208–12, 225
  day-to-day, 268
  discursive, 212–13, 226
  monologic, 213
  relational, 211
  social, 211–12, 226
praxis, critical, 238, 345
Prebble, Peter, 168
press
  lesbian and gay, 88
  mainstream, 88
  releases, 88
  women's, 95
prison, 298
procedures, 18
process
  cultural, 210, 225
  interactive, 26
  legislative, 114
  organizational, 112
  participatory, 83
  political, 17, 141
  relational, 143
progressive, 240, 252
Promise Keepers, 260
propaganda, state, 31, 42
prostitution, 91
Protection of Muslim Women's Bill, 75
protest, 6, 12, 14, 16, 27–29, 31–33, 35,
    37–39, 45, 67, 69, 72, 107–9, 111–12,
    115, 138, 154, 229, 241–42, 291, 298
  anti-war, 193–94, 196
  campus, 34, 38
  civil rights, 112
  collective, 53, 57
  cycles of, 125, 130, 137–38, 143–44,
    154–55, 209, 300
  democracy, 28, 44–45
  election, 41
  electoral, 159
  leaders, 33
  leftist, 196
  mass, 68, 113, 115
  method of, 283

peaceful, 29, 35
popular, 28
possibilities of, 14
social, 17, 238
spontaneous, 40
against states, 30
students, 30, 195
university, 38
Vietnam War, 193
Protestant, 188
Protestantism, 248–55, 261–65
  evangelical versions of, 254, 258, 260–61,
    264
  mainline, 253
protestors, 10, 29, 34, 46, 195–96, 198
public hearing, 98–99
public opinion, 105–6, 109
public sphere, 248–49, 254, 258, 260
Puerto Rican, 230, 234, 242
Puritans, 240
Pyinmana, Burma, 32

Quebec, 158, 166
queers, 99, 101
  politics, 87
  strategies, 87
  theorists, 97

race, 87–88, 205, 207, 227, 255–56, 266–
    67, 293, 295–96, 302–3
  racial intolerance, 53
racism, institutional, 232
radicalism, political, 216
radicalization, 186, 194, 196, 198–99
  process of, 194
radicals, 43, 194, 198, 214, 216, 220
Rainbow Curriculum, 242
Rajasthan, 75
Raj Shakti, 68
rakyat (society), 42
rallies, 34, 40, 95, 102, 127
Ramaphosa, Cyril, 47, 59–60
Ramos, Fidel, 39, 41, 45
Rand, Ayn, 189
Randolph, A. Philip, 230
Rangoon, 32, 34, 36
  Rangoon Institute of Technology (RIT), 34
  Rangoon University, 30, 34
  student demonstration, 33
rape, 73, 90
  campaign, 72
  commission on, 73, 83
  rape crisis centers, 90
  See also law
Ravitch, Diane, 231–32, 236
Ray, Raka, 294
reading scores, 236
Reagan, Ronald, 131
Reagon, Bernice Johnson, 270
realms, discursive, 228

recruitment, 138, 164–65, 174–75, 183, 205, 284, 295, 297
  patterns of, 268
redistricting, 234
Reform, 220
  liberal, 230
  social, 232
reform, 38, 45
  institutionalized, 74
  land, 68
  legal, 67, 72, 75, 83
  political, 43
  state, 50
  state-led, 44
  structural, 74
Reform Armed Forces Movement (RAM), 41
reformasi (reform), 37
reformers, radical, 218
regime
  authoritarian, 28
  British colonial, 43
  democratic, 116
  fragmentation of, 28
  of repression, 39
Regina, Canada, 158
Regina Manifesto, 164
religion, 9, 100–101, 212, 239, 248, 251–52, 262
  civil, 252
  moral sphere of, 260
  religious belief, 9
  religious groups, 135, 242, 258
  religious language, 248–53, 262
  religious matters, 75
  religious opposition, 101
  religious systems, 263
  religious traditions, 76
  as a social movement discourse, 250
repertoires, 62, 142
  of collective action, 212, 214
  of contention, 142, 150–51, 154
  cultural, 251, 254
  dialogic, 212
  of discourses, 222, 224
  discursive, 214–15, 220, 223–24
  of genres, 212
  of interpretation, 142, 228, 243
  of organization, 142
  of protest methods, 267
  symbolic, 247, 249, 252, 254, 265
  tactical, 300
repression, 29–30, 33, 40, 106, 109, 186, 192–93, 293, 298–99
  by government, 193–99
  history of, 37
  indiscriminate, 43
  patterns of, 30, 36
  by state, 25–26, 28–29, 32, 34, 37, 41–43, 45, 200
  strategies of, 25

Republicans, 102, 132, 295
Reserve Officer Training Corps (ROTC), 196
resistance
  armed, 272
  discursive, 213
  militant, 149
  working-class, 153
resource(s), 12–13, 77, 83, 98, 107, 128, 132, 136–37, 141, 165–67, 172, 174, 239, 268, 292, 295
  churches', 111
  cultural, 248, 283
  government, 78
  mobilization, 51, 83, 129, 208, 289
  organizational, 40, 128, 248
  state, 69, 71, 76, 83, 108
  See also masses
revolution, 40, 43, 301
  feminist, 258
  homosexual, 258
revolutionary, 30, 32, 40–42, 56, 194, 199, 298, 300
Rex, John, 47
rhetoric, 10, 18, 207, 253, 282
  activist, 250
  changes in, 16
  family values, 260
  Manichean, 260
  public, 248
  religious, 207, 253–54, 257, 264
  rhetorical concessions, 16
  rhetorical packages, 247
  social movement, 147, 154, 164
Rhodesia, 198
Richards, John, 168
rights, 18
  abortion, 131, 133, 135, 295
  citizenship, 86, 103, 212, 218–19
  civil, 11–12, 94, 130, 206, 277, 281
  democratic, 13
  egalitarian, 260
  human, 13, 31, 37, 75
  negative, 217
  parental, 258, 260
  petitioner's, 220
  political, 220
  positive, 219
  religious, 207, 227, 241
  reproductive, 14
  welfare, 233
  women's, 12, 14, 69, 75–76. 79, 83, 175, 183
  See also gay; lesbian
riots, 33, 37–38, 42, 46, 108
  ghetto, 195
  riot police, 34
Ritchie, Bob, 149
rituals, 208
Robben Island, 60
Robertson, Pat, 241, 248, 258–59
Rochon, Thomas, 116

Roe v. Wade, 131
Roosevelt, Franklin D, 188
Rose, Sonya, 218
Rucht, Dieter, 109, 125, 128, 135
Rudé, George, 58
Rupp, Leila, 134
Russell, Howard, 91–92, 94, 98–99
Rustin, Bayard, 231

Saheli, 72
Salae, Puseletso, 50–51, 61
Sands, Paula, 233
San Francisco, 100
Santoro, Wayne, 113
sarvodaya (well-being of all), 68
Saskatchewan, 158, 160–62, 167
Saskatoon, 168
Sassen, Saskia, 83
sati, 74, 75
    anti-sati groups, 75
scabs, 149
Schlafly, Phyllis, 93, 241
school board, 237–39, 242
schools, 34
    charter, 240
    public, 111, 227, 230–31, 242, 258
Schumacher, Dane, 195
Schwartz, Mildred, 122, 292, 295
Seattle, 242
segregation, 112, 253
Seidman, Gay, 49
Self-Employed Women's Association
    (SEWA), 70
self-sufficiency, agrarian, 68
Sellers, Cleave, 276, 279
Selma, 113, 278
Senate, U.S., 98, 271
separatism, 230, 277
separatist, black, 266
services
    provision, 14
    to women, 76
sex, 89
    sex education, 240
    teenage sexual activity, 241
sexism, 179–80
    sexist, 180
sexual behavior, 13, 100
sexual harassment, 180, 226
sexuality, 227, 291, 295–96, 300
sexual orientation, 90, 93, 95–98, 100–101,
    103–4
sexual practices, 100
sexual style, 87
Shanker, Albert, 239–40
Shetkari, Mahilla Aghadi (Farm Women's
    Front), 76
shibirs (camps), 70
Shramik Stree Sangathana (Toiling
    Women's Union), 70

Simmel, Georg, 63
Sin, Cardinal, 41
sit-ins, 110, 235
Smelser, Neil, 125
Smith, Adam, 217, 221–22
Smith, Christian, 16
Smith, Dorothy, 227, 228
Smith, Eve and John, 163
Smith and Nephew, 50
Smithfield, 220
Smith Robinson, Ruby Doris, 272–74,
    282
Snow, David, 51, 249
social capital, 252
social engagement, 14
socialism, 159–62, 1266, 167
Socialist Party of Canada, 158
socialists, 152, 160
social movement community, 12, 126–38,
    173, 195, 199–200, 268, 290–91, 292–
    93, 298
social movement family, 127, 137
social movement organizations (SMOs),
    58–59, 115–16, 172, 189, 192, 199,
    205, 208, 213, 244–45, 249, 266–85,
    290, 292–93, 295–97
    internal balance of power in, 278
    professional, 127
Society for the Promotion of Area Resources
    (SPARC), 76
solidarity, 189, 192, 195, 199, 205
    working-class, 151
South, 111, 256
South Africa, 7, 17–18, 26, 47, 49, 53, 60–
    61, 198
    business, 50
    labor laws of, 49
    mines, 47, 55–59
    police, 57–58
    slums, 65
    state, 26
    workers, 26, 53
Southeast Asia, 25, 28
Southern Christian Leadership Conference
    (SCLC), 261, 278ff
Soviet Union, 14, 187
    Soviet expansionism, 287
spillover. *See* movement(s)
Spitalfields, silk weavers of, 206, 214–25
Spitalfields Acts, 214–20
splinter groups, 168
Staggenborg, Suzanne, 121, 299–300
state(s), 12, 18, 35–36, 42–44, 66, 68, 71,
    74–76, 78–80, 82–83, 86–87, 92, 96,
    99, 103, 108, 115, 149, 173, 178, 197,
    218, 276, 289–94, 298, 300, 305
    actors, 29–30, 43
    authoritarian, 25
    bureaucratic state, 82
    engagement with the, 71

state(s) *(continued)*
  global, 67
  liberal, 77
  patriarchal, 67, 71–73
  policies, 68, 70–71, 76, 83
  postcolonial, 73
  propaganda, 31, 42
  relationship with, 72
  repressive, 45
  state bodies, 73
  state bureaucracy, 69, 74, 83
  state communism, 74
  state defectors, 41
  state feminism, 77, 83
  structure of, 25, 71
  type of, 73
steelworkers, 162
Steinbeck, John, 240
Steinberg, Marc, 206–7, 292, 304
Stell, Bill, 193
stewards, 149–52, 155
  full-time, 145
  shaft, 62
  shop, 144, 147–48
Stokes, Ruth, 101
Stonewall Inn, 91
STOP ERA, 93
Strategic Arms Limitation Talks (SALT), 14
strategies, 6, 14, 26, 40–41, 48, 64, 66, 81,
    90–91, 100–101, 106, 108, 111, 114,
    121, 134, 136–37, 142, 147, 153, 172–
    74, 190, 228, 243, 272–73, 278, 290,
    292, 294, 299, 301, 306
  activists', 18
  expressive, 86
  grassroots, 97
  opposing, 149
  strategic choices, 86
  strategic hinges, 141
strategizing, 140–56, 292, 294, 299
  in collective action, 141
Stree Mukti Sangharsh (SMS; women's
    liberation struggle), 76
street festivals, 127
strikes, 37, 39, 49, 109, 144–46, 153, 215
  illegal, 148, 150
  secondary, 148
  strike committees, 35–36, 45, 147, 150
  violent, 214
structure, 12, 19, 48, 51, 63, 122–23, 141,
    183, 292
  abeyance, 154
  discursive, 211
  mobilizing, 48–49, 62, 65, 121, 133, 172
  political, 88
  social, 57
  structural adjustment, 26
struggles
  democracy, 28, 37
  discursive, 211

labor, 51
mass, 282
violent modes of, 29
working-class, 147
Student and Youth Struggle Vehicle. *See*
    Chhatra Yuva Sagharsh Vahini
Student Non-Violent Coordinating
    Committee (SNCC), 6, 19, 88, 266–
    85
  expulsion of whites from, 284
students, 11, 34, 37–38, 67–69, 131
  masked, 34
  See also movement(s)
Students for a Democratic Society (SDS),
    123, 185–201
  increase in membership of, 192
  survival of, 191
student wages commission, 49
subculture, 90, 213
Subianto, Prabowo, 38, 46
suffrage, 136
Suharto, 28, 29, 31, 37–39
  fall of, 46
Sukarno, 42
Supreme Court, 16, 72, 75, 131, 133
surveillance, 116
  domestic, 195
Sussman, Susan, 96
Suu Kyi, Aung San, 36
Swayam Shikshan Prayog (SSP; Self-
    Education Process), 76, 78
Switzerland, 136
symbolism, 10
symbols
  religious, 247, 251

tactics, 5–6, 10–12, 14–15, 18, 25, 28–29,
    45, 111, 134, 136–38, 172, 196, 278,
    299
  confrontational, 99
  mainstream liberal, 273
  nonviolent, 267
Tanzania, 53
target, 5, 16, 25, 67, 172, 215, 218
Tarrow, Sidney, 59, 63, 65, 154–55
Tatmadaw, 29–30, 32, 35
Taylor, Nikki, 129, 134, 268
teach-ins, 196
textile workers, 50
Thatcher, Margaret, 144
theater, street, 71
theory, 51, 59
  black feminist, 206
  cultural, 207
  democratic, 238
  feminist, 205
  feminist state theories, 73, 83
  new social movement, 86, 289
  political process, 25
  queer, 85, 87

resource mobilization, 57–58, 65
  social movement, 47–49, 65, 205–7, 302, 306
  theoretical generalization, 59
Third World, 73, 77, 83
Thomas, Alan, 110
Thompson, E. P., 58
Thorne, Barrie, 184
threats, 11, 16, 128, 132, 135, 299
Tiffany's, 173
Tillinghast, Muriel, 281
Tilly, Charles, 58, 155, 159, 212
Timor, East, 46
Timpone, Richard, 114
Tocqueville, Alexis de, 252
To Kill a Mockingbird, 241
tokoh dary rakyat (public intellectuals), 37
toolbox conception of culture, 48, 52, 57
tool kits
  cultural, 267, 270
  tactical, 279
Tories, 149
Torside, 140–52
totalitarianism, 187, 197
Towards Equality, 71
Trade Union Council (TUC), 144
traditionalists, 186, 192–93, 195–98
traditions, 75
  cultural, 250
transformations, structural, 48
transitions to democracy, 28
Transkei, 53
Transport and General Workers Union (TGWU), 144–52, 155–56
  legal department of, 149
transvestites, 35
Trisakti University, 46
Trotskyist, 161, 166
Turner, Arthur, 164

underground, 298
  activists, 35
  anti-regime organizations, 39
  cells, 36, 42
  going, 34, 293
unions, 40, 49, 54–57, 59–62, 64, 145–46, 148, 150, 152, 188
  agreements, 140
  anti-union laws, 149, 151
  labor, 37
  leaders, 55, 149
  local, 37, 159
  members, 121
  militancy of, 149
  officials, 56, 61, 150, 153
  organization, 144
  representatives, 56
  social movement, 47, 64
  stewards, 56, 144
  strategies, 62

teacher, 235, 237
  trade, 50, 159, 160, 162, 165–67, 230
  union-busting lockout, 148
  unionism, 149
Unitarian Church, 131
United Auto Workers, 162
United Farmers, 159
United Farmers of Alberta, 158
United Farmers of Canada, Saskatchewan section of, 158
United Federation of Teachers, 236, 239
United Nations (UN), 67, 71, 74, 76, 273
  UN's Draft Platform for Action, 78
United States, 8, 14, 25, 40, 73, 84, 94, 105, 127, 131–32, 136, 162, 166, 173, 187, 197–98, 229, 252–53, 267, 273
universalism, 261–62, 264
universities, 34, 40
Urban League, 230–31

values, 12, 16, 52, 88, 99, 109, 136–38, 196, 240, 262, 273, 298
  dominant cultural, 92
  family, 248, 253, 257–65
  labor theory of, 221–22
  legitimate, 248
Vanguard Press, 93
Vermont, 5, 26, 85–103, 300
  Democratic Party in, 96
Vermonters for Lesbian and Gay Rights (VLGR), 92, 95–96
Vermont Human Rights Commission, 96
Victorian culture, 258
Vietnam, 12, 195
Vietnam War, 187, 195, 199
  resistance to, 198
  withdrawal from, 198
Vimochana, 72
violence, 30, 38, 96, 223
  anti-lesbians and gay men, 95–96, 98, 102
  political, 18, 125
  struggle against, 73
  See also women
Violence Against Women Office, 294
vision, religious, 255
Volosinov, V. N., 224
voluntary associations, 252
vote, 113, 273
voter registration, 117, 272
voters, black, 117
Voting Bill, 276
Voting Rights Act, 6, 19, 114
vouchers, educational, 243

Waffle, The, 162, 165–70
Wagner, Robert, 230–31
Walker, Alice, 240
war, opposition to, 195, 198

War on Poverty, 110–11
Washington, 99, 113, 182
Watkins, Hollis, 274
Weber, Max, 63, 65
Webster, Eddie, 47, 131
welfare, 77, 293
    welfare state, 67, 197
Welfare Reform Act, 173
Western Conference of Labour Political
    Parties, 158
White House, 278
wife battery, 74
Wilcox, Preston R., 234, 248
Williams, Annette, 243
Williams, Raymond, 52, 292
Winnipeg Convention, 162–63
    hard-core, 162
Wisconsin, 243
Wishik, Heather, 98
Witwatersrand, 58
women, 291, 305
    abused, 74
    African American, 282
    battered, 226
    black, 276
    civil rights, 184
    elected, 81
    empowerment of, 83
    enfranchisement of, 79
    equality of, 74, 77, 83
    interests of, 75
    liberation of, 172, 183
    local needs of, 78
    music festivals of, 138
    oppression of, 73
    poor, 76
    reservation of electoral seats for, 81
    shelter for battered women, 90
    spaces of, 90

subordination of, 212
support groups of, 74
violence against, 13, 67, 71, 73–74, 80,
    83, 90
white, 276
women's agenda, 80
women's centers, 73, 90, 128
women's groups, 72–74, 79, 81, 84, 175,
    176
women's status, 75
    See also India; issues; parliament
Women's Action Collective, 177
Women's Manifesto and Charter of
    Demands, 82
Women's Pentagon Action, 13
Women's Student Union, 132
women's studies, 132, 305
womyn's music, 304
workers, 68
    industrial, 122
workplace, 26
World Bank, 26, 76
worldview, 11, 194, 211, 250, 252, 297
Wright, Marian, 110

Xhosa, 52

Ylvisaker, Paul, 232
Young, Jean Wheeler Smith, 280, 282
Young Americans for Freedom (YAF), 123,
    185–201
youths
    lesbian and gay, 92
    mobilizing, 187

Zald, Mayer, 126, 133
Zellner, Dottie, 277
Zimet, Melvin, 230
Zuo, Jiping, 125